What (& how) has Union done
the public (i.e. Public Relations program
for union)

THE IRWIN SERIES IN ECONOMICS

BOOKS IN THE IRWIN SERIES IN ECONOMICS

Collective Bargaining: Principles and Cases *Revised Edition*
JOHN T. DUNLOP AND JAMES J. HEALY
HARVARD UNIVERSITY

International Economics
CHARLES P. KINDLEBERGER   MASSACHUSETTS INSTITUTE
OF TECHNOLOGY

The American Economy: Principles, Practices, and Policies
C. LOWELL HARRISS   COLUMBIA UNIVERSITY

Economic Policy: Readings in Political Economy
WILLIAM D. GRAMPP AND EMANUEL T. WEILER (EDITORS)
UNIVERSITY OF ILLINOIS

Intermediate Economic Analysis *Revised Edition*
JOHN F. DUE   UNIVERSITY OF ILLINOIS

Economics of Labor Relations
FREDERIC MEYERS   UNIVERSITY OF TEXAS

Money, Income, and Monetary Policy
EDWARD S. SHAW   STANFORD UNIVERSITY

Welfare and Competition: The Economics of a
Fully Employed Economy
TIBOR SCITOVSKY   STANFORD UNIVERSITY

COLLECTIVE BARGAINING

Principles and Cases

COLLECTIVE BARGAINING

PRINCIPLES AND CASES

JOHN T. DUNLOP

AND

JAMES J. HEALY

HARVARD UNIVERSITY

REVISED EDITION

1953

RICHARD D. IRWIN, INC.

HOMEWOOD, ILLINOIS

PREFACE TO FIRST EDITION

This book has grown out of the teaching of an undergraduate course, "Trade Unionism and Collective Bargaining," a one-semester introduction to labor economics. As a result of this teaching experience, another introduction to collective bargaining—along less conventional textbook lines is offered. Many aspects of collective bargaining cannot readily be understood in the absence of specific illustration—promotion, layoff, discharge, and discipline problems are illustrative—and few students have had the experience necessary to visualize concretely the issues of the work community. "Collective bargaining" remains an empty phrase, tinged with favorable emotional reactions but devoid of substance or content. Moreover, the operation of collective bargaining cannot be depicted in terms of the day-to-day problems of employees, unions, and managements. The student is likewise frequently unable to make one world of the formal principles of economics and the facts of actual wage fixing. The teacher must constantly struggle against simple generalizations in a field in which students normally bring strong prejudices to the classroom. The discriminating mind cannot be cultivated readily simply by lectures and reading; some other means is required to elicit reaction from students and to challenge them with significant problems and issues.

The cases in this volume constitute an attempt to meet some of these limitations of the conventional introduction to collective bargaining and to supplement the standard readings. They have been built from arbitration awards and proceedings, from umpire decisions, from records of negotiations, and from interviews and field trips. A great many different officials of labor organizations, management representatives, arbitrators and umpires, and state and federal government officials have assisted in the collection of the basic materials from which these cases have been developed. A great deal of sifting, rewriting, and substitution of cases has been necessary in the light of actual teaching experience. The experiment has proceeded far enough, however, to warrant a preliminary judgment. These cases have very materially improved the understanding of my students, and it is hoped that others may have the same experience with them.

The cases may be used in a variety of ways: they may provide assigned reading in a lecture course, the students may be asked to submit a series of short papers in the form of "decisions" on the cases presented; ideally, however, the specific situations provide the basis for discussion in the classroom. Questions at the end of each case have been developed to facilitate the understanding and framing of principles. A discussion section on these cases has been substituted for a third lecture each week in my own course. While sections usually number twenty-five to thirty-five students, it is well to remember that instruction in many law schools follows the same method with classes of several hundred students.

The experience with these cases during the last three years suggests that students have come to have a better understanding of collective bargining and labor economics in the following respects:

1. There are at least two sides, frequently many more, to most issues in this field. It is a healthy discovery to some students to learn that managements can be wrong, and to others that unions make mistakes.

2. The clear statement of contending positions is an education in itself. The student can be lead to identify the premises from which such positions develop.

3. The process of industrial jurisprudence involved in collective bargaining is illustrated in rich detail.

4. A number of different conceptions of labor relations can be illustrated by the various ways in which students will handle a case: there are certain to be legalists and strict constructionists in the interpretation of an agreement; the approach of the social worker or clinician will emerge, concentrating upon the human or personal aspects of the case; and the view will be illustrated that emphasizes the problems of accommodating two organizations.

5. The hard discovery is made that one can never know all the facts about a situation. While cases which hinge narrowly on issues of fact have been excluded, there will be many occasions when ideally more information could be desired. In the world of action and behavior, the decisions of labor leaders, business executives, and arbitrators must be made on partial information.

6. The collective agreement can never cover all contingencies. A great many problems arise which were not envisaged by the parties, and perhaps could not have been. The importance of the spirit or tone of a collective bargaining relationship is recognized in this fashion.

7. The arbitration process is illuminated. Particular attention can be directed to the tactics and policies which lie behind each side in the arbitration of disputes.

8. The union and the company both emerge as organizations whose leaders have internal problems of reconciling conflicting views and interests.

9. The handling of wage cases requires the utilization of economic theory as a tool of analysis rather than as an end in itself. Particular situations cannot be solved by the mouthing of formulas or the duplication of diagrams from textbooks. The richness and complexity of wage issues can lead the student to make economic theory less a formal exercise and more a method of analysis of vexing issues.

10. The process of problem solving is the chief virtue of the method. The compulsion that the student make up his own mind about a particular situation stimulates debate and reflection.

There are no "right" answers to the cases presented, in the sense that there are right answers to typical mathematical problems. No key of correct solutions has been provided in the back of the book. In each case presented, there was a historical answer, in that an arbitrator or a union leader or business executive rendered a decision, or joint negotiations achieved agreement, before or after a work stoppage. In some few instances, those decisions have been presented in the write-up of the cases. The problem has then centered around the wisdom of the decision. In most cases, no answer is provided. The primary emphasis should be placed upon the rationale of an answer, for the understanding of the problem is more important than any answer. The beginning of wisdom in labor relations and collective bargaining is the recognition of problems.

The introductory chapters in Part I are intended to provide for the general reader a survey of the more prominent aspects of collective bargaining. They constitute both a general setting to the cases in Part II and a survey of some of the more significant problems of public policy in the field. If collective bargaining is the accepted national policy, it is imperative that its characteristics and limitations be widely understood.

The author gratefully acknowledges in the preparation of this volume the suggestions and critical comments of colleagues at Harvard University. Professor Sumner H. Slichter reviewed some of the cases in the early phases of this experiment; Professor James J. Healy provided many a complex problem for stimulating discussion from his rich experience as an arbitrator; and Professor Walter Galenson and Mr. Lloyd Ulman have made many helpful suggestions from their experience in teaching the cases in sections.

In the early stages of this endeavor, Mr. Lloyd Ulman and Mr. M. Goodman were helpful in selecting and preparing cases. As research assistant over a two-year period, Miss Esther Ross very materially advanced the project by the effective preparation of additional cases; and the imaginative work of Mr. and Mrs. John Armstrong, as librarians of the Industrial Relations Library, helped to provide much of the basic source materials. Mrs. Lillian Hagg faithfully performed the arduous task of typing the manuscript. In addition, the comments and critical suggestions of numerous students have been indispensable.

This volume is dedicated to D. S., who demonstrated that the handling of individuals is the greatest of the arts and from whom the author learned that an awareness of the real place of men in organizations is the basis for influencing groups.

JOHN T. DUNLOP

HARVARD UNIVERSITY
January, 1949

PREFACE TO SECOND EDITION

      The first edition was prepared for publication in 1949 largely as an experiment in a new method of introducing the study of collective bargaining. This second edition is an extensive revision, particularly in Part Two. The principal changes are as follows:

    1. The introductory material to each group of cases has been substantially expanded and brought up to date to constitute in most cases a brief chapter and a more adequate substantive setting to the particular cases.

    2. The number of sections or groups of cases has been expanded from nine to twelve. The old section on "Employment Rights in Jobs" has been divided into three sections, and new sections have been added on "Health, Welfare, and Pension Benefits" (Section K) and "Special Problems of Contract Interpretation" (Section L). Old sections have been strengthened by expanding the scope of the cases.

    3. There has been very considerable change in the choice of individual cases. Thirty-eight of the 70 cases in the first edition have been discarded; only 32 have been retained. Forty-seven new cases have been added, to make a new total of 79 cases. Thus, 60 per cent of the present cases are entirely new cases.

    4. The introductory chapters in Part One have been revised in minor respects, and a new chapter (Chapter 4) has been added on "The Collective Bargaining Process."

    These revisions have been made in the light of teaching experience with the book, and particularly with the suggestions made in 1950 in reply to a questionnaire sent to most of those using the volume. The excellent co-operation and considered response at that time has materially assisted this revision. We gratefully acknowledge these constructive comments. The revisions have sought to take into account the recent developments in collective bargaining. In each section, cases have been introduced to reflect more current problems. The discussion of seniority rating, programs of corrective discipline, the union-shop issue, and health and welfare plans is illustrative of such revision. These revisions have also been influenced, quite naturally, by a continuing interaction of our teaching and arbitration experience. We have sought on occasion to generalize and to systematize our experience with the parties as they confront stubborn problems.

One of the considerations in mind in making these revisions has been to adapt the volume so that, in addition to being suitable for the normal college course it can be utilized by the growing number of special training programs developed by companies and labor organizations for supervisors and union officers.

It is a pleasure to acknowledge the effective assistance of Mr. Peter Gregory in the preparation of material for this revision and the comments of Dr. Martin Segal and Professor Carl Stevens based upon their experience in teaching the cases in Harvard College. Mrs. Elizabeth Knox effectively performed the tedious task of typing the manuscript.

This edition is a joint product of the authors. We have spent many hours in discussion of the issues presented in collective bargaining, comparing our experience as arbitrators or mediators, and in revising the manuscript.

This volume seeks to expand the area of understanding of collective bargaining. While collective bargaining is the foundation of our national labor policy, it remains too much a cliché. How does it operate? What are its strengths? What costs does it entail? What are its limitations? It is our conviction that an understanding of the issues posed by such questions can best be achieved through the vicarious experience presented in such a volume. Any appraisal of collective bargaining requires a blending of concern with the specific case and general principle.

JOHN T. DUNLOP
JAMES J. HEALY

CAMBRIDGE, MASSACHUSETTS
May, 1953

Table of Contents

1, 5, 33, 37, 51, (54) Not discussed

PART ONE

An Introduction to Collective Bargaining

Chapter

I

THE EMERGENCE OF COLLECTIVE BARGAINING

Labor unions and large-scale business enterprises are both a product of modern industrial society. While each has roots which extend far into the past, they have acquired their distinctive current features during the last hundred years. Both organizations are part of the transformation of an agricultural and commercial community into an industrial society. Both organizations will be decisive, it is widely conceded, in the shaping of the economic destiny—indeed, the total life—of the nation in the next generation.

Collective bargaining has no place in an agricultural society of self-employed farmers. During the past century a predominantly rural society has given way gradually to urban communities. The farm as the principal place of work has been displaced by the factory and the office. The local and regional orientation of affairs has yielded to the dominance of a common national life. The emergence of collective bargaining is one manifestation of this fundamental change in the society, the growth of an industrial nation.

Structural Changes in the American Economy

In 1850 there were 7.4 million men and women in the country who worked for a living. Today the civilian labor force approximates 63 million. In 1850 more than 55 per cent of the community earned its livelihood in agriculture. Today agriculture employs less than 12 per cent of the labor force. While there are more people working in agriculture today than a century ago, its relative share of all workers has steadily declined. The industrial sectors of the economy have rapidly expanded—manufacturing, mining, transportation, communications, and construction.

3

But an industrial community creates other types of employment than factory jobs. The services of wholesale and retail trade, finance, and banking are required. Professional services, clerical occupations, and government employment have been among the most rapidly growing sectors. In 1952 the industrial sectors included 23.5 million, distributed as follows: manufacturing, 15.9 million; construction, 2.6 million; mining, 0.9 million; and transportation and public utilities, 4.1 million. In addition, there were 9.9 million in trade, 4.8 million in service industries, 2.0 million in finance, and 6.6 million in all government service—federal, state, and local. Agriculture had 6.8 million. This diversity of employment is one of the more important structural changes in the economy. The industrialization process has created much more than a "proletariat," to restrict the term to factory employees.

The relative decline of agricultural employment and the expansion in industry, wholesale and retail trade, service trades, and government has created an economy of wage and salary earners. While there may be 6 or 7 million proprietors and self-employed business and professional men and women outside of agriculture, the great majority of our citizens earn their livelihood as wage and salary earners. More than two thirds of the national income is distributed in the form of wages and salaries.

The expansion of other sections of the economy relative to agriculture is related to the rapid increase in the standard of living over the past century. On the average an employee in industry has tended to produce a greater value of output than an employee in agriculture. This statement does not imply that the industrial worker works harder, nor that he is necessarily more skilled. Since his energies and skills are typically combined with more capital equipment and machinery and a high order of management, the product of industry per hour of labor services has typically been greater than in agriculture. The gradual shifting of the work force out of agriculture and into industry has consequently been a means of increasing total output. An employee spared from agriculture typically increased production by a great amount elsewhere when re-employed.

The gradual transposition of the work force from agriculture to industry has had other consequences. Since rural areas have had the larger natural rates of increase in population, a relative increase in industrial employment has required a continuing large movement of workers from farms to cities. The rural and farm origins of the industrial work force, except for those who immigrated from cities abroad, have had important consequences on the ideas, beliefs, and habits of industrial workers. Thus, much of the independence of Detroit workers is to be understood only in terms of the migrations of large numbers from Kentucky, Tennessee, and rural areas of the Middle West. Our industrial work force is not yet composed predominantly of second and third generations of city dwellers. When that day arrives, the industrial worker may be expected to have dropped many of his agricultural antecedents.

In 1850 the national income was almost $5 billion (in 1940 prices). Today national income approximates $150 billion (also in 1940 prices). This enormous expansion in goods and services is partly the consequence of an increase in population and the simple duplication of facilities. However, the national income today would be only $40 billion (in 1940 prices) if the only changes since 1850 had been the extension of existing methods of production with the increase in population. The largest part of the increased income must be ascribed to an increase in the productiveness of the economy.

It has already been noted that a rearrangement of the work force by a transfer of workers from agriculture to industry has tended to increase total output. These reallocations of the man power of the community, it is estimated, account for 40 per cent of the improvement in productiveness of the system.[1] (This factor would account for an increase of $42 billion since 1850.) The most important single factor responsible for the increase in the national income over the century has been the improvement in the productivity of labor within industries and in the growth of new industries. (This factor would account for an increase of $63 billion since 1850.)

Although these figures are necessarily only rough estimates, the accompanying tabular presentation may help to visualize the fundamental forces at work over the past century:

National income in 1850 (1940 prices)	$5 billion
Duplication of facilities with population increases .... $40 billion	
Reallocation of labor force among industries.. 42 "	
Increase in productivity within industries .... 63 "	
National income in 1952 (1940 prices)	$150 billion

[1] Simon Kuznets, *National Income: A Summary of Findings* (New York: National Bureau of Economic Research, 1946), p. 48.

The increase in productivity of a man-hour of work is basically to be attributed to the enormous technical revolution of the period. It is not merely that more capital investment in plant and equipment is combined with labor services. More capital equipment of the 1850 vintage would not have accounted for the expansion in production. The quality of equipment, the technical knowledge of management, the layout and arrangement of industry, and the skill of workers have been so improved that, when combined, they have yielded enormously greater value of output per unit of labor input.

In 1850 a worker typically had the help of only 0.5 horsepower of energy from animals and from minerals. By 1940 the community used 27 horsepower hours for each hour of human effort. In 1850 for each worker in manufacturing, it is estimated there was $557 (in 1850 prices) worth of capital equipment. In 1940 the figure approximated $6,000 (in 1940 prices).[2] These statistics provide some indication of the quantity of capital goods combined with labor services to account for the expansion in productivity. But they do not measure the most significant changes, which were in the technical knowledge and in the quality of the combination of labor services, capital goods, and management. The revolution in technique and the rearrangements in the productive process yielded the striking improvements in the standard of living of the past century.

The gains in productivity were distributed in a variety of forms:

a) The hours of work were gradually reduced. The scheduled hours of work per week approximated 69 hours for non-agricultural employment in 1850. That schedule was slightly less than 6 days of 12 hours each. Today, scheduled hours per week are in the neighborhood of 40, 5 days of 8 hours each.

b) The level of money wages and salaries has increased sharply, even relative to prices. In 1850 the wages of nonagricultural workers probably averaged in the vicinity of 9 cents per hour. In 1940 they averaged somewhat over 60 cents, and today they exceed $1.60 per hour. The level of money wages and salaries has been a rising plane, and, perhaps, even an increasingly rising plane.

c) Since prices have increased over the period, these money

[2] Prices had roughly doubled.

values do not indicate the increase in the real purchasing power of an hour's work. Roughly speaking, living costs doubled in the period 1850–1940; they have since increased another 90 per cent. The real wage per hour today of industrial workers would appear to be over four times that of a century ago. But these figures underestimate the improvement in the real wage rate, since they cannot reflect adequately the improvements in quality and the development of new commodities and gadgets. For any single product, the improvement in productivity typically has been reflected both in an improvement in quality and in at least an initial period of reduction in price.

d) A part of the benefits of increasing productivity has no doubt gone, at least in the first instance, as higher or excess profits to the enterprise introducing the change. Such returns might be designated as the rewards of innovation and are a part of the price the community pays for a dynamic system. In pure competitive theory, these excess profits are removed by competition. They can be restored only by more innovation. In this type of a world, where monopoly elements are not significant, profits are said to be the engine which keeps the system dynamic. One of the central problems of the modern economy—with monopoly elements in business and with unions in the labor markets—is the struggle over the initial division of the gains of increasing productivity.

The basic technological and market changes in the economy, which are at once adaptations to and prime movers of the industrial economy, produced a revolution within the business community. The corporate form of organization became dominant. Ownership and management were separated. Large groups of employees were brought together in a single workplace. An internal management organization suitable to large-scale operations developed. A business bureaucracy of various departments is organized—production, sales, engineering, finances, etc. The personnel or industrial relations department is among the latest additions to the business organization.

These same basic technological and market changes in the structure of the economy have produced a change in the labor market. Factory employment and the growth of cities made the work community the decisive focus of the life of the worker. Not only is he dependent for employment upon the level of industrial activity, but the larger family and the small community cease to be such important instruments of social control and security to the individual. The job determines not only economic destiny but frequently the social and larger aspects of life.

The development of the industrial economy has depersonalized relations in the labor market. The large-scale enterprise must operate by rule and regulation. Consequently, the working boss of the small shop becomes the inanimate corporation, the familiarity of the first name gives way to the badge number, and the attention to individual and unique problems becomes remote.

The dynamic industrial economy involves threats to the skill of the industrial worker. Changes in tastes and methods of production may eliminate a job or drastically change its content. These changes are requisite to the growth of the system; the essence of the increase in productiveness already observed is just such change. It must not be inferred that the net effect of these changes is to produce a less-skilled work force on the whole. The evidence is quite to the contrary. But for individual workers, there must be change with greater or less cost of movement and with greater or less sense of insecurity.

The industrial system, whose spectacular achievements over a century have been noted, has not grown smoothly. The system time and again has been raked with depression. In fact, there were only a few years of full employment in the whole century, and these were mainly wartime periods. These depression periods, particularly when prolonged as in 1873–79 and 1929–33, created great hardship for industrial workers. They raised doubts in the minds of workers, as in the rest of the community, over the basic institutions of the economy. The question could not be escaped at such times whether the notable achievement of the economy had been purchased at too high a price. It is no accident that the periods of greatest labor organization in the century follow these worst depression periods—the upsurgence of the Knights of Labor (1881–86) and the New Deal period (1933–37).

The organization of wage earners into labor unions and the growth of management organization—in a word, the emergence of collective bargaining—is basically a facet of these structural changes in the economy over the past century. Only a broad brush has been used to outline the main contours of the impact of the growth of an industrial economy on the work force and the business organization. The details are written in the history of the growth of each enterprise and the emergence of each local and national union. The emergence of collective bargaining was inherent in the development of an industrial economy, at least in a society in which governmental authority does not make all significant decisions.

Structural Changes in Community Values and Institutions

The ideas and beliefs of an agricultural society are not appropriate to an industrial community. The institutions of the agricultural community—courts and local governments—are likely to be inadequate in an industrial age. The century of rapid technological and market changes, which altered the economic structure, also witnessed a related transformation in the values of the community and in the public institutions of the society.

The American community of 1850 was a testimony to its long apprenticeship to the soil. Emerson observed in 1844 that "the vast majority of the people of this country live by the land, and carry its qualities in their manners and opinions." These qualities included a hostility to the rising industrial world. Thomas Jefferson had extolled the agricultural community: "Generally speaking the proportion which the aggregate of the other classes of citizens bears in any state to that of its husbandmen, is the proportion of the unsound to its healthy parts, and is a good enough barometer whereby to measure its degree of corruption. While we have land to labour then, let us never wish to see our citizens occupied at a workbench . . . ."

The "manners and opinion" which Emerson regarded as derived from the soil might be summarized as follows: Individual advancement was to be achieved solely by hard work; leisure was regarded as a vice; the economic destiny of an individual depended solely upon his ability to work and save; poverty was regarded as the reward for sloth; the poor deserved their fate; and the public care of the impoverished was treated as the encouragement of idleness. These values did not spring from the soil in any literal sense. They had their antecedents in the philosophic preconceptions of the Age of Enlightenment. But the significant point is that these ideas and beliefs were congenial to the agricultural and frontier economy of the first half of the nineteenth century. They were consistent with the objective facts of the society.

The system of values of the American community of 1850 was also congenial to the emerging industrialists. They thrived on the spirit of individualism. The accent on thrift and saving facilitated the requisite accumulation of capital. No strong government was envisaged to curb or direct the great outbursts of industrial energy.

But the community values of 1850 could not persist in a mature industrial society. The technological and market changes, referred to in the last section, were creating an economy incompatible with these values rooted in the soil (and in the philosophy of Enlightenment). Economic prosperity of the individual depended upon the availability of jobs rather than merely upon the willingness to work. The rising productivity made increased leisure possible; it was not necessarily an evil in an economy which permitted an increasing margin over subsistence or which steadily revised upward the content of subsistence. Individuals in the community, particularly wage earners, came to question the costs of the rapid expansion in living standards. The quest for security developed both out of the insecurities of the industrial society and the increasing proportion of older age groups in the population (see Section K, Part Two). Thus, the older order of community values began to change under the impact of the industrial economy. Ideas themselves as advocated by reformers and new social classes played a distinctive role in the creation of a new set of community values. The community has yet to develop a full and complete set of values consistent with the objective facts of the industrial economy.

The labor union was not envisaged in the community values of 1850. A labor union in many ways is the negation of the idea that economic status depends on individual effort. The status of the individual worker depends to a large extent on collective action. The union strives for shorter hours and more leisure. It is an instrument to legislate in the economic or political field the welfare of wage earners. The union stresses higher wages through collective action rather than individual thrift as a means of economic advancement. The intellectual life of the country could envisage little place for a labor union in 1850. The wages-fund doctrine was a "demonstration" that the artificial increase in wage rates, by union action, could not improve the lot of the wage earners of the community. There was no economic rationale for a union. As the industrial community has grown and the values of the community have changed to provide a role for the union, so too has economic analysis developed a place for the labor organization.

The dominant community values of 1850, with their accent on individualism, were to have a decisive impact on the labor movement itself which developed in America with the spread of industrialization. The class-conscious characteristics of many European labor movements did not take deep root. These antecedent community values have created many of the most serious internal problems of the American labor movement. The individual worker was difficult to organize. Union growth was slow. The closed shop and similar forms of union security were developed to hold any ground won. Unions had to contend not only with hostile employers and a hostile community but frequently with hostile wage earners. The unorganized workers would not respect picket lines as would have been the case among European class-conscious wage earners. These community values also help to explain the essential economic or "bread-and-butter" character of American unions.

Despite the dominance of economic objectives in the American unions, it must be recognized that a labor movement always has other activities. The labor organization is broader than collective bargaining. These other activities of a labor movement are primarily beyond the scope of this volume. In some environments the labor union may become, in effect, an instrument of political action. It may become a force in a variety of community activities—public education and health and welfare activities. It is clear that a labor movement cannot become significant in the area of collective bargaining without affecting the whole structure of the community in a variety of other ways.

At no point was the influence of the dominant community values more decisive than in the views of the courts. At the outset the common law, built upon commercial and agricultural antecedents, could find no place for a union. It was a conspiracy against trade. Here, as in all other facets of the life of the community, the impact of industrialization has finally wrought its change. The courts came to tolerate labor organizations if their objectives and purposes were held to be legal. Public policy has since reached the point of declaring it to be in the public interest to encourage the practices and procedures of collective bargaining.[3]

The Extent of Collective Bargaining

The oldest existing international union, the International Typographical Union, is just a hundred years old. It was founded in 1852. By the end of 1952, 17 million workers were estimated to be members of labor organizations in the United States. They were organized into more than 75,000 local unions, which for the most part were constituent parts of 143 international[4] and national unions affiliated with the American Federation of Labor (AFL) and the Congress of Industrial Organizations (CIO). The ten largest unions, each with a membership of over 300,000, comprised 37 per cent of all organized workers. The terms and conditions of employment for these union members were set forth in an estimated 100,000 written agreements negotiated with employers or their associations.

TABLE 1

	Number of Employees (in Millions)	Estimated Percentage under Union Agreement
Manufacturing	15.9	70
Mining	0.9	80–100
Construction	2.6	80–100
Transportation	2.9	80–100
Public utilities	1.2	40–60
Trade	9.9	Below 20
Finance	2.0	Below 20
Service	4.8	20–40
Government	6.6	Below 20
Agriculture	6.8	Below 20

While 46 million workers were employed in nonagricultural pursuits in 1952, collective bargaining was far more significant for setting the terms of labor bargains than a simple comparison with the 17.0 million union members might suggest. The percentage of employees organized in various sectors of the economy were as shown in Table 1. Beyond a certain point in an industry

[3] Chapter II constitutes a discussion of recent public policy toward collective bargaining.

[4] The difference between an international and a national union in practice is that the international union has local unions in Canada and occasionally in Mexico.

or a locality, collective bargaining becomes so significant that it effectively conditions, at least within narrow limits, all labor bargains. The influence of collective bargaining is far greater than the area of union membership.

The industrial community which has emerged in the past century has produced the institution of collective bargaining—labor unions and management organization. It is a fair inference that labor unions will include a larger proportion of the work force in a generation than even at present. Collective bargaining may be expected to become even more extensive. The operation of collective bargaining consequently becomes decisive for the performance of the economy and for the structure of the society.

SUGGESTIONS FOR FURTHER READING

CLARK, JOHN MAURICE. *Alternative to Serfdom,* pp. 61–90. New York: Alfred A. Knopf, 1948.

COMMITTEE FOR ECONOMIC DEVELOPMENT. *How to Raise Real Wages.* New York, 1950.

DEWHURST, J. F., and ASSOCIATES. *America's Needs and Resources,* pp. 17–51. New York: Twentieth Century Fund, 1947.

LESTER, RICHARD A., and SHISTER, JOSEPH (eds.). *Insight into Labor Issues,* pp. 163–93. New York: Macmillan Co., 1948.

SIMONS, HENRY. *Economic Policy for a Free Society,* pp. 121–59. Chicago: University of Chicago Press, 1948.

SLICHTER, SUMNER H. *The Challenge of Industrial Relations,* pp. 1–28. Ithaca: Cornell University Press, 1947.

Chapter	COLLECTIVE BARGAINING:
II	A NATIONAL POLICY

The encouragement of collective bargaining is the announced policy of the country. Section 1 of the Wagner Act (and the same language was carried over into the Taft-Hartley Act) declared it to be the policy of the United States "to eliminate the causes of certain substantial obstructions to the free flow of commerce and to mitigate and eliminate these obstructions when they have occurred by encouraging the practice and procedures of collective bargaining and by protecting the exercise by workers of full freedom of association, self-organization, and designation of representatives of their own choosing, for the purpose of negotiating the terms and conditions of their employment or other mutual aid or protection."

As the cornerstone of our national labor policy, collective bargaining is endorsed by both major political parties. General Eisenhower on September 17, 1952, stated: "An industrial society dedicated to the largest possible measure of economic freedom must keep firm faith in collective bargaining." On Labor Day in the same political campaign, Governor Stevenson referred to collective bargaining as the "keystone of industrial democracy, of free enterprise."

This policy had its antecedents in the Norris–La Guardia Act (1932), the Railway Labor Act (1926), the experience of the War Labor Board in World War I, and in the reports and recommendations of numerous commissions that had investigated prominent strikes and labor unrest over the previous half-century. A distinguished line of special commissions had found that the flagrant denial by employers of the right to organize had been a frequent issue in industrial disputes.

The Wagner Act

The Wagner Act established for the United States the public policy of encouraging collective bargaining as the means of adjusting the relations between managements and their employees. The statute proceeded from explicit premises which may be identified as follows:

1. The inequality in bargaining power between individual employees and large-scale business concerns tends to depress wage rates. The statement of "Findings and Policies" at the outset of the Wagner Act held that this inequality of bargaining power depresses "the purchasing power of wage earners in industry and prevents [sic] the stabilization of competitive wage rates and working conditions within and between industries." The organization of workers results in wage-rate levels which are better, using the test of aggregate national income, for the economy as a whole and which eliminate "unfair competition" between firms based solely on their power to depress wage rates.

2. The denial of the right to organize (the Wagner Act says by "employers" and the Taft-Hartley Act says by "some employers") creates industrial strife. The public protection of the right to organize eliminates this type of dispute. Since interference by management with the rights of organization of workers may take a variety of forms, the Wagner Act designated a series of "unfair practices," including discrimination for union membership or activity, the establishment or support of a company-dominated union, and the refusal to bargain collectively.

3. The Wagner Act was formulated on the assumption that, if the obstructions to organization of workers imposed by managements were eliminated, workers would "naturally" join labor unions. Industrial workers if freed from employer influence could be expected, almost inevitably, to become union members. A union organization would emerge either within the enterprise spontaneously or as a result of the assistance of outside labor unions. The term "self-organization" was applied to both processes. The government would provide election machinery to register the votes of employees in an appropriate unit and certify the collective bargaining representative selected by the majority. The employer was required to recognize and to bargain with this representative.

From the vantage point of almost two decades, these explicit premises of the Wagner Act were substantially influenced by the great depression following 1929. The reference to the effect of inequality of bargaining upon purchasing power reflects the impact of the depression on the economic thinking of the country. The notion that organization of the workers would prevent "unfair wage cutting" and stabilize competitive conditions within and among industries was a result of the experience with creeping wage cuts during the depression. It might even be said that the Wagner Act was a product of the depression. There is much to support such a statement, even beyond the premises and language of the Act. The prolonged failure of the economic system during the depression created distrust in existing institutions and led to interest in labor organizations on the part of millions of workers. But the Wagner Act was not alone a product of the great depression following 1929. It has been noted that labor organizations, and public policies to encourage collective bargaining, were also the result of long-run forces at work in a society gradually adapting itself to industrialization.

The Taft-Hartley Act

The Taft-Hartley Act will be more readily understood if it also is approached both as a product of certain immediately antecedent events and as in part a reflection of basic forces at work in the community. Union membership rose from approximately 5 million in 1935 to 15 million at the end of World War II. The end of hostilities evoked the largest work stoppages in January, 1946, that the country had ever seen. There were nation-wide strikes during the first half of 1946 in the steel, meat packing, railroad, and coal industries. These stoppages alienated large sections of public opinion, some on the grounds that the unavailability of peacetime goods must be due to these strikes, and others through fear that the closing down of vital industries was a threat to society itself which could not be tolerated. These judgments were formed without attention to the merits of the particular stoppages.

The inflationary postwar period with high employment displaced the Wagner Act emphasis on union organization to prevent wage cuts. In the postwar inflation, some individual wage earners had at times considerable bargaining power and did exact wage rates materially above even the union scale. Fixed-income sections of the work force came to believe that the unions were in some way responsible for their plight created by rapidly rising prices. It might be said that just as the Wagner Act was partly a product of the depression, so the Taft-Hartley Act reflects a postwar inflationary period.

Longer-run forces were also at work in bringing about the Taft-Hartley Act. The Wagner Act had never pretended to be a comprehensive labor code. Many problems were not considered, such as emergency disputes, boycotts, and jurisdictional disputes. It would have been surprising, indeed, if ten years of experience on a new policy would not have revealed some modifications at the legislative level. There was reaction to some of the zeal and the administrative procedures used by the National Labor Relations Board (NLRB) which in turn had been vigorously opposed by many managements. The growth of the labor movement to a more influential position in the community created more concern and interest in the internal operations of unions. The view developed that the encouragement of labor organization and collective bargaining by government created a public interest in the processes of bargaining and the internal operation of unions. The isolated cases of abuse of union office or the arbitrary action by a union officer toward a member took on new status in view of the widespread nature of organization. The union could no longer be viewed as a private club without public interest. Many union officers and members were new and had not the discipline, training, and experience of the "old timers."

As a consequence of these longer-run forces and the special postwar inflationary setting and strike record, large sections of public opinion were convinced that "something had to be done" about labor organizations. George Meany, now president of the American Federation of Labor, recognized in a forthright manner this basis of the Taft-Hartley law when he said in October, 1947: "We have built up our organizations and we have raised the wages of the people we represent, but we have failed somewhere, because we haven't got public opinion with labor in this country, and we might just as well admit it. Labor unions are not in good with the public generally, or the N.A.M. [National Association of Manufacturers], and all the reactionary forces couldn't have passed this legislation." The specific provisions of the law are far too technical and detailed to be related to public opinion other than in this general way.

The basic premises which underlay the Taft-Hartley Act may be identified. How accurately these premises reflect the true character of workers, unions, and managements should emerge from an understanding of collective bargaining.

1. The Act reflected the belief that the individual worker should be protected by public policy, not alone in his right to join a labor organization but also in his choice to refrain from being a member if he so elects. To Section 7 of the Wagner Act, which sets forth the "right to self-organization," the Taft-Hartley law added: " . . . and shall also have the right to refrain from any or all of such activity . . . ." It became an unfair practice for a labor union to interfere with this right of the individual employee to refrain from joining a union (except as union membership may be a condition of employment when required in a contract in accordance with union security provisions authorized by the procedures of the Taft-Hartley law). The Taft-Hartley law in effect denied a premise of the Wagner Act noted above, namely, that freed of employer domination industrial workers will "naturally" join labor organizations.

The protection of the right to refrain from union membership qualified the announced policy of encouraging the practices and policies of collective bargaining. Because of the practical possibilities open to an employer to utilize the procedures of the Taft-Hartley law to delay or frustrate labor organization, or because there is an announced neutrality toward labor organization, the basic public policy of encouraging collective bargaining may have been altered. Professor Cox has concluded that "the Taft-Hartley amendments represent an abandonment of the policy of affirmatively encouraging the spread of union organization and collective bargaining."[1]

It is a significant and basic question of public policy whether government can try or pretend to be neutral toward the existence of unions and the operation of collective bargaining. Can it be in an advanced industrial society that it makes no difference

---

[1] Archibald Cox, "Some Aspects of the Labor Management Relations Act, 1947," *Harvard Law Review,* Vol. LXI (November, 1947), p. 44. For another analysis see, Sumner H. Slichter, "The Taft-Hartley Act," *Quarterly Journal of Economics,* February, 1949, pp. 1–31.

whether collective bargaining exists? For the purposes of continued prosperity in a democratic society or for purpose of national defense, can public policy be indifferent on this issue?

2. The interests of labor organizations and their individual members are not to be regarded as identical, according to the Taft-Hartley law. Public policy cannot be restricted to considering labor organizations as an entity; it must push on into the relations between union members and union officers and between members and the union organization. The Act presumed that many union members are captives; they are persistently trying to get out of the union organization. The Act presumed that union leaders do not reflect, in a significant number of cases or in important cases, the true wishes and opinions of the rank and file of members. On these grounds, public policy should go behind the actions of union leaders to determine more directly the members' views or to permit them to escape the organization.

It is this assumption of the Taft-Hartley law, perhaps more than any other, which is responsible for the intensity of the reaction of labor organizations to the law. Labor leaders believe they know and understand their members. They identify themselves and their organizations with the members. They believe their interests are mutual and inseparable. They deeply resent the allegations that they do not really represent their members, or their constitutents, and that the rank and file of union members would in any way be disloyal to the common interests of the union.

3. The activities of labor organizations needed to be regulated in the public interest. Public policy had encouraged the organization of unions without providing restrictions on their conduct—in relation to employers or to their members. There was an imbalance in the Wagner Act which needed to be corrected by regulating union conduct.

On the basis of these assumptions, the Taft-Hartley law developed many detailed regulations of the relations between unions and managements. The law comprises 30 pages of small print. It is easy to get lost in the complexities of this legislation. There are certain fundamental respects, however, in which the Taft-Hartley law sought to introduce major changes in the public policy toward collective bargaining. They will be noted briefly.

1. The Act introduced the principle of the public regulation of the *contents or provisions* of the labor agreement. The Con-

gress had not previously provided any extensive or explicit limitations on the substantive terms of the agreements concluded under free collective bargaining. The Taft-Hartley law provided a series of limitations: (*a*) The closed-shop form of union security is illegal. (*b*) The checkoff clause must provide for the individual member to authorize the deduction of union dues. (*c*) The termination or reopening clauses of the agreement must provide for 60 days' notice to the other party and 30 days' notice to the Federal Mediation and Conciliation Service. (*d*) Welfare funds must conform to specified standards.

The significant point is not so much the merits or the wisdom of the particular regulations of the provisions of labor agreements as it is the innovation in policy itself. Is the public prepared to insist upon a particular contract provision when unions and managements may otherwise agree? What are the mechanics for the enforcement of the public policy when the parties are otherwise agreed? What provisions of the agreement are susceptible to public regulation, and which are to be left exclusively to the parties for collective bargaining? The Congress embarked on a program of regulating the union security provisions of agreements. Should the same policy be extended to seniority provisions, to wage clauses, and to the scope of the grievance procedure? If the Congress is to embark on the policy of regulating the terms of agreements, the question arises as to the method to be used in reaching such decisions and the role which unions and managements are to have in formulating the specific regulations.

2. The Taft-Hartley law also constituted the first attempt to regulate on a national basis the internal processes of labor organizations. In treating the relation between the union and its members, the Act provided that, in order to use the facilities of the National Labor Relations Board, a union must conform to specified standards: (*a*) The union must distribute financial reports or make them available to members. (*b*) The union must file noncommunist affidavits for each officer. (*c*) Initiation fees that are "excessive or discriminatory" constitute the basis for an unfair labor practice. (*d*) The Act made it an unfair labor practice on the part of the *employer* to discriminate against an employee for nonmembership in a labor organization for other grounds than nonpayment of dues. These regulations on the

internal life of the union are indirect and roundabout. They are made a condition to access to the National Labor Relations Board or are imposed indirectly upon the employer.

3. The law specified a number of unfair practices for a labor organization, just as the Wagner Act had first listed unfair practices for an employer. Unions were precluded from interfering with the rights of employees to join or refrain from union membership and from seeking to compel an employer under a union shop to discharge a worker for any other reason than non-payment of periodic dues and initiation fees. It became an unfair labor practice for a union to engage in a secondary boycott, a jurisdictional strike, or to compel an employer to bargain with other than a certified union. The requirement by the union of an excessive or discriminatory initiation fee or the requirement that an employer pay for services not performed (featherbedding) were also designated unfair labor practices. It also became an unfair labor practice for a union to refuse to bargain collectively with an employer.

4. The Taft-Hartley law adopted the principle that some interruptions of work are of such a vital nature to the public interest that special procedures are established to be invoked by the President of the United States. These disputes must involve a substantial part or all of an industry where a stoppage will imperil the national health or safety.

The Taft-Hartley law has been on the statute books six years. How has it operated? What have been its effects on collective bargaining? The law has been so much a matter of general partisan debate that special determination is needed to get to the facts of the record and beyond broad charges and countercharges. Moreover, the law has so many provisions that any generalized judgment would not be applicable to many sections of the statute. It should also be observed that the law has only been in effect during a period of high employment; it would not be appropriate to assume that the law would have identical effects under other circumstances. The following brief observations concern those changes in public policy which most intimately affect the operation of collective bargaining.

1. The unions have been about as successful in winning elections and bargaining rights under the Taft-Hartley law as they were under the Wagner Act. Despite the increased freedom to

employers to advocate nonunionism to their workers, provided there is no "threat of reprisal or force or promise of benefit," and despite the purpose of the Act to protect the right of workers not to join unions, more than three quarters of the votes cast in representation elections have been in favor of unions.

2. The vast majority of unfair labor practice charges, more than 70 per cent, are filed against employers. Less than 30 per cent of these cases are of the type first permitted by the Taft-Hartley law and filed against unions. As under the Wagner Act, only a small proportion (8 per cent) of all unfair labor practice charges originally filed are subject to a final order of the NLRB. The other 92 per cent are settled, withdrawn, or dismissed. The procedures of the NLRB and the courts are so slow that parties may effectively thwart the purposes of the Act by delay.

3. The attempt of the Taft-Hartley law to regulate the substantive provision of agreements, in the form of union security, has no doubt had quite different effects than intended. While closed-shop contracts have generally disappeared, closed-shop arrangements are still very much in effect, particularly in industries with migratory employment patterns. The union shop, somewhat modified in its operation, has become the most common form of union security (see Section C, Part Two).

4. The Act regulated the negotiation process by providing for a 60 days' notice of termination or modification to the other party and a 30 days' notice to the Federal Mediation and Conciliation Service. This section cannot be said to have improved bargaining, and it has a number of complications. The Act imposes penalties on a union for breach of this period, but there are no penalties on an employer for similar conduct.

5. The regulation of the internal government of unions provided in the act has had mixed results. The requirement of the distribution of financial reports is unobjectionable, although it introduces few changes in practice. The attempt to regulate initiation fees has been of no consequence. The noncommunist affidavit has been without effect in eliminating the influence of Communists from the leadership of labor organizations. The affidavits are a nuisance.

6. The section of the law which sought to eliminate "featherbedding" is so written that it can have little or no effect.

7. The prohibitions against secondary boycotts and jurisdic-

tional strikes have had salutary effects, but there are many detailed objections to the scope of the statutory provisions.

8. The emergency disputes procedure is particularly inadequate. It provides an inflexible procedure; there is no provision for recommendations by the fact-finding board on the merits of the dispute; the vote on the "last offer" of the employer is futile. There is grave doubt whether these procedures have contributed to the settlement of disputes which threaten to interrupt production vital to the health or safety of the country.

The temptation must be avoided to make a single capsule evaluation of the law. Each of the great many provisions must be considered separately. The last section of this chapter considers the broader question of the process by which public policy and legislation in this area should be formulated.

The Bargaining Unit and the Scope of Bargaining

There must be a union organization and a management and a defined group of employees represented by the union in order for there to be collective bargaining. The public policy of encouraging collective bargaining practices accordingly requires that a public body be prepared to designate the appropriate unit for bargaining and the organization that represents a majority of the employees.

The National Labor Relations Board holds elections among employees to determine which labor organization, if any, a majority of employees desire to select as its bargaining representative. Before any election can be held, however, it is necessary to determine the election district, that is, the group of eligible voters. The appropriate unit may be a craft, an industrial unit of all employees in a plant or company, or some other grouping of employees. Just as the choice of the election district in the political arena may have decisive effects on the outcome of an election, so also in the collective bargaining field. The introduction of the election process into the organization of unions and the public determination of the bargaining unit—both introduced by the Wagner Act and altered in minor respects only by the Taft-Hartley amendments—have had major consequences for collective bargaining and the labor movement that were not foreseen in 1935.

Prior to the Wagner Act, unions were organized by a variety of informal methods. Perhaps the most general method was for a nucleus of strategic workers to go on strike when an employer had refused to recognize the union. The remainder of the workers were organized on the picket line. Some workers joined unions readily because they had been members of a labor organization in the old country. In other cases, a strong union might approach an employer and secure recognition for his employees on the threat of withdrawal of transportation for supplies or finished goods. In other instances, an employer might be induced to sign an agreement by the threat of refusal of another union, or the same union, to handle the product at the consumer or some intermediate stage. Prior to the Wagner Act, organization was a test of strength. It is not surprising then that labor unions were prominent primarily among groups of strategic workers who were in a position to put considerable pressure upon a company to secure recognition.

Organization by election is quite a different process. The collective bargaining election takes on much of the character of a political election. There are slogans and name calling. The union makes campaign promises. There is resort to means of mass communication and mass appeal. Workers are not asked to go on the picket line, although that may have to come later; they are simply asked to *vote* for the union. Election methods can be applied to large groups of employees to displace or to supplement traditional organizing tactics that are directed to small groups of strategic workers. The election process is especially adapted for the organization of workers who possess little individual bargaining power, that is, the relatively unskilled or semiskilled worker.

The introduction of the election, with the employer required to recognize the victor, has had a major impact on the labor movement. The organization of larger units and less strategic groups of employees is encouraged. The individual union member may be expected to have a different relation to the union when he has simply voted for the organization than when he has joined it via the picket line.

Even more far-reaching effects for the labor movement and collective bargaining have developed from the public determination of the appropriate bargaining unit. Prior to the Wagner Act, the range of employees to be covered by an agreement was left to the bargaining process. Competition between two unions for employees was not supposed to take place. The American Federation of Labor itself was supposed to resolve questions of conflicting claims between unions. The principle of exclusive jurisdiction prescribed for each union an allotted jurisdiction, recognized in a charter. If each union lived within this jurisdiction, serious problems concerning the appropriate unit for collective bargaining could not arise. The public determination of the bargaining unit was made difficult and highly controversial by the split within the labor movement and the emergence of the Congress of Industrial Organizations soon after the Wagner Act was passed. A bargaining-unit determination by the government can vitally affect the survival of a union in competition with rival organizations. An industrial unit may swallow up a craft union, leaving only an unrecognized minority in a larger group; and, conversely, a series of craft-unit determinations may take from an industrial union many of the strategic workers it had relied upon for strength in bargaining.

From the point of view of management, the public determination of the bargaining unit when a number of rival unions are involved may result in highly unsatisfactory bargaining arrangements. A company may find itself in a situation that requires negotiation of separate agreements with a variety of unions. Rivalries among these groups will be reflected in a struggle in bargaining for more favorable contract provisions. The introduction of company-wide policies, an understandable desire on the part of management, may be made impossible in negotiating the diverse demands of a variety of bargaining units.

From the importance of the bargaining unit to unions and managements, it follows that determination of the bargaining unit is one of the most significant responsibilities exercised by the National Labor Relations Board for the future of collective bargaining. But public policy has not alone affected the results of bargaining by the administrative determination of the unit; the Congress in the Taft-Hartley law excluded particular groups of employees, such as foremen, from the law. It also provided that guards could only be represented by a union which admitted no other employees to membership and was unaffiliated with other labor organizations. Public policy has shaped collective bargaining by these determinations of the employees to be included in the bargaining unit.

The public policy of encouraging collective bargaining has

had still another effect on the bargaining process that was not anticipated at the time of the passage of the Wagner Act. That law provided that it was an unfair labor practice for an employer to refuse to bargain collectively. The Taft-Hartley law added a correlate unfair labor practice for labor unions. These requirements appear reasonable enough on their face. But what do they mean? (See Section L, Part Two.)

The requirement to bargain may be interpreted in procedural terms. The parties are required to take certain steps, that is, to confer, to discuss, to consider proposals, to make counteroffers, and so on. To bargain in good faith is at best an elusive concept, and one party may go through the motions without any intention of reaching an agreement. The requirement to bargain, viewed procedurally, injects a government agency into all the intimate details of the bargaining process when a charge of refusal to bargain has been filed.

The requirement to bargain may be interpreted in substantive terms. The government may decide what is, and what is not, an appropriate subject of collective bargaining. The scope of bargaining comes to be defined by public regulation. The following types of questions must be faced: Is a pension plan a subject for bargaining? What about demands or counterdemands regarding the members of the board of directors or union officers? And what about a plan to increase production or improve quality? Until the Wagner Act, the scope of collective bargaining was determined by the bargaining process itself. The policy of encouraging collective bargaining has been extended to determine by public agency the demarcation between subjects that are appropriate for bargaining and those that are not. The future of collective bargaining will be very significantly shaped by the way in which public policy defines the scope of bargaining and the range of topics to be treated in an agreement.

The Functions of Collective Bargaining in the Community

The public policy to encourage collective bargaining requires a scrutiny of the role which collective bargaining plays in the industrial community. What can be expected of it? What does it purport to do? For what purpose is it ill-adapted? Only when these questions have been faced is it possible to appraise the operation of collective bargaining.

Collective bargaining seeks to fulfill three purposes in an industrial community with the traditions of a political democracy: (1) It fixes the price of labor services. (2) It provides a system of industrial jurisprudence, establishing and administering the conditions, other than wages, under which wage earners render their services. (3) Collective bargaining represents the extension of the democratic idea into the work community. These purposes may not be achieved, but such are the claims of collective bargaining. Each of these facets of collective bargaining may be examined briefly.

1. A number of methods could be invoked to determine the price of labor services in a community. Public authorities could fix all wages. A minimum wage is an instance of public wage fixing. During the war period 1942–45 and the Korean stabilization period 1951–53, all wage changes were subject to the approval of the stabilization authorities. Or, wages may be left entirely to the play of market forces. Competition between wage earners for jobs and between firms for employees would govern the price of labor services. Collective bargaining involves the formal organization of buyers and sellers in the labor market. The action of government and the impact of market forces, however, are not without effect on wages under collective bargaining; rather do these various forces affect wage rates through unions and managements. Changes in the competitive positions of firms and industries and in the demand and supply for various types of labor do affect the price of labor under collective bargaining. The chain of effect is through the decision-making processes of unions and managements, and their bargaining, rather than in any automatic or mechanical manner. The market and collective bargaining methods of fixing wages are not to be treated as unrelated. Market forces characteristically influence the collective bargain, although collective bargaining introduces a new element, the union as an organization, into wage fixing.

2. Collective bargaining has the advantage over government wage fixing in that the persons most familiar with the type of work, the special problems of the company and the employees, the surrounding locality and industry influences, make the decision. Collective bargaining permits a flexibility that more centralized wage fixing could not tolerate. This flexibility and adaptability of collective bargaining is superior in many cases to the market

determination of wages. The parties may also experiment with one type of wage payment rather than another. They may develop new forms of compensation, such as vacation payment or health and insurance plans, to meet particular problems. Such individuals also may give fair consideration to many job classifications unique to plants for which no market rate ordinarily would be established.

The determination of wages by collective bargaining may involve problems that other methods of fixing wages in the community would avoid. The parties to the bargain may be able to increase wages and prices at the expense of the rest of the community. Critics of collective bargaining are fearful that strong unions and their employers will act in the labor market like any monopolist in the sale of goods. Wages will be higher in these instances, and employment less. In this way, the wage structure of the community will be distorted and employment distributed among firms and industries in less than an ideal fashion. It is also feared that collective bargaining may push the whole level of wage rates up faster than the long-term gains in productivity. Prices must rise in continual inflation to the detriment of fixed-income groups in the community.

It would be futile to deny that such potential dangers exist in the fixing of the price of labor services by collective bargaining. Every method of wage fixing has its limitations. The crucial question of public policy would be rather to appraise how serious these dangers have been or are likely to be. Can the institutions of collective bargaining be shaped from within or from without to yield a wage structure and a wage level more responsive to the needs of the community as a whole? The issue is a challenge to the unions and managements of the country.

2. Collective bargaining seeks to serve the dual function of, first, creating in a legislative fashion the terms and conditions, in addition to wages, under which wage earners perform services, and, second, administering in a judicial way the agreements which incorporate these terms and conditions of employment. The process of negotiating and administering agreements establishes the common law of the work community. It is difficult for the outsider to appreciate the diversity and complexity of problems which arise in the workplace. One of the purposes of this volume is to introduce the general reader to some of these problems.

As a system of industrial jurisprudence, collective bargaining recognizes certain rights and duties of management and establishes rights and duties *applicable to all workers.* Call-in payment, for instance, is provided for all employees required to report to work. All workers are protected from arbitrary discharge. Then, collective bargaining establishes the *relative rights of particular individual workers in particular jobs.* A contract and its administration will determine the relative rights of two workers in a particular job in the event of a transfer, the possibility of a promotion, a temporary layoff in the work force, or a permanent reduction in the staff. These determinations are among the most important in any contract. They pertain not so much to the rights of management relative to the employees as a whole but rather to the relative rights among different classes of employees or among particular individuals. Finally, as a system of industrial jurisprudence, collective bargaining establishes a *procedure for the redress of grievance.* The grievance procedure, including arbitration as a final step, is in many ways at the heart of the operation of collective bargaining.

As a system of industrial jurisprudence, collective bargaining seeks to settle disputes short of industrial warfare, without resort to strikes and lockouts. It seeks to maintain *industrial peace.* A distinction should be recognized between a work stoppage arising under a contract and one resulting from a dispute over the provisions of a new agreement. While each new collective bargaining relationship frequently tends to be plagued with stoppages under a contract for a limited period, the record of peace under agreements has not ordinarily been criticized if measured by the absence of stoppages. It is stoppages arising over the terms of new agreements that have caused greatest concern. This observation suggests that it is the legislative function of creating new agreements, rather than the administrative and judicial function of interpreting agreements, that requires most attention as a matter of public policy. The creative potentials of collective bargaining have yet to be applied seriously to this problem.

3. Collective bargaining seeks to introduce a measure of democracy into industry. Through their representatives, wage earners have come to have a voice in the decisions which so vitally affect their economic status and the life of their work community from day to day. Collective bargaining is supposed to provide

the individual worker with a sense of participation in the affairs of the immediate department, and the company, and so on into the affairs of the industry, the community, and the nation. It attempts to provide a significant outlet for the energies and creative ideas of workmen, which can be so easily lost in the hierarchies of any organization. It seeks to harness the latent energy and productiveness of workers who tend to produce most when they are secure in their jobs and convinced of the worthwhileness of their endeavor.

These objectives are sometimes lost because of conflict between unions and management organizations. At other times, the goal of a sense of participation in the affairs of the industry is lost within the union itself. The rank and file may have little opportunity, or may choose to exert little influence, on the decisions of the union organization.

These objectives are high standards by which to judge the performance of any social institution. At times, these objectives may be internally inconsistent. Industrial peace may require stronger and more disciplined organizations, reducing in some degree the democratic element of the influence of the individual members. Wage rates that will bring industrial peace may produce unfortunate economic consequences. The parties at bargaining may have to choose between developing details of the system of industrial jurisprudence and wage increases. In any event, collective bargaining is to be viewed in its many facets. Any over-all judgment of the performance of collective bargaining must be shaped by attention to the three aspects of the relations between unions and managements, which have been discussed in this section.

The Formulation of Public Policy

Collective bargaining is a relatively new institution. The term itself is sixty years old. Many of its features are in the experimental stage as labor unions and managements try various policies within their organizations and various means of conducting their relations. Collective bargaining need take no final form as it adapts slowly to the changes in the total environment in which the parties live. Nonetheless, as judged by the history of the experience of unions and managements in western European countries, collective bargaining in the United States is young.

If the experience of other countries and the tendencies inherent in union and management organizations are studied, they suggest that during the next generation particular patterns of growth in collective bargaining are to be expected. A larger proportion of the work force will be organized and covered by agreements. There will be an extension of multiple-firm bargaining as the employers of the country organize themselves into formal and informal associations for purposes of bargaining. The employers of the country have been as difficult to organize effectively for bargaining as were wage earners themselves for many years. The scope of bargaining can be expected to be broadened to include a larger range of problems affecting the security and economic status of wage earners.

An even more significant range of problems for the next generation concerns the relation of collective bargaining to public regulation. The Wagner Act involved some extension of governmental supervision over collective bargaining, as in the bargaining-unit determination, which even the labor movement did not generally foresee. The Taft-Hartley law, passed by a Congress opposed in principle to the extension of governmental regulation, involved a radical expansion of the authority of government in the collective bargaining process. The terms of agreements were made subject to public policy as noted; the internal affairs of labor organizations were prescribed in some detail; special procedures may be involved in emergency disputes. These remarks are not intended to pass judgment on the wisdom of the particular extensions of public regulations. They do suggest the need for reflection on the implications of these policies. To what extent are the terms of agreements to be the subject of public regulation? How far can governmental determination be extended without excluding from collective bargaining the significant problems? What standards should prescribe the limits of public regulation of the internal government of a labor union? To what extent will the determination of key contracts by fact-finding or other emergency procedures in effect determine contract provisions for other management and labor organizations?

The last decade should have clearly indicated to the parties to collective bargaining that they must learn to solve their problems or the public will insist that public agencies do the job. The failure of labor organizations (and managements, too) to develop their own procedures for settling jurisdictional disputes resulted in legislation on the point. The failure of critical industries, coal and basic steel for instance, to develop by collective bargaining machinery to settle disputes over the terms of new agreements led to the emergency disputes and injunction provisions of the Taft-Hartley law. The internal government practices of some unions have led to the beginnings of public regulation of union operations.

A critical range of problems confronts the country in the question of just how much public regulation of collective bargaining there shall be. The free collective bargaining process has many advantages. It has flexibility. It is relatively decentralized. It can operate close to the particular problem. It provides balance of power in a community in which public decision making becomes more and more important. The further extension of public regulation of collective bargaining can only shift to the political arena more and more of the activities and energies of labor organizations and managements.

The most significant point to be noted in appraising the Taft-Hartley law is not the provisions of the law, significant as were the changes in public policy which the statute sought to establish. Greater importance must be attached to the legislative process by which the law was enacted. It was unfortunate, indeed, for the community that believes in self-government to have had the public regulation of collective bargaining shaped hardly at all by the labor and management representatives most familiar with its operations. If collective bargaining is to be the cornerstone of our national labor policy, the legal framework of collective bargaining cannot remain a partisan political matter. Neither industry nor labor can tolerate a world in which the legal status of collective bargaining changes every 2 or 4 years, depending on the latest election returns. Stable and constructive industrial relations cannot be established on such foundations.

The time has arrived to establish the principle that the legal framework of collective bargaining shall represent largely the consensus of labor and management. The time has passed for more "get-even" labor legislation. There will be some issues on which the public interest will require limitations and regulations of collective bargaining. In such instances, it is important that the proposed regulations be filtered through the experience and thinking of the representatives of both sides in collective bargaining.

If the problems of the division of responsibility between collective bargaining and public regulation in the field of industrial relations are to be understood, there is need for widespread knowledge of the processes, procedures, and institutions of collective bargaining. The cases which comprise this volume are intended to contribute to this end.

SUGGESTIONS FOR FURTHER READING

CLARK, JOHN MAURICE. *Alternative to Serfdom,* pp. 118–53. New York: Alfred A. Knopf, 1948.

COX, ARCHIBALD. "Some Aspects of the Labor Management Relations Act, 1947," *Harvard Law Review,* Vol. LXI, pp. 1–49, 274–315.

MILLIS, HARRY A., and BROWN, EMILY CLARK. *From the Wagner Act to Taft-Hartley.* Chicago: The University of Chicago Press, 1950.

SLICHTER, SUMNER H. *Trade Unions in a Free Society.* Cambridge, Mass.: Harvard University Press, 1947.

SLICHTER, SUMNER H. "Revision of the Taft-Hartley Act," *Quarterly Journal of Economics,* May, 1953, pp. 149–80.

TAYLOR, GEORGE W. *Government Regulation of Industrial Relations.* New York: Prentice-Hall, Inc., 1948.

WRIGHT, DAVID McCORD. *Democracy and Progress.* New York: Macmillan Co., 1948.

| Chapter III | UNION AND MANAGE-MENT ORGANIZATION FOR COLLECTIVE BARGAINING |

The parties to collective bargaining are *organizations*. It is a relationship between formally constituted groups. Any study of collective bargaining, consequently, requires insight into the internal structure and operation of unions and managements, as well as into their interrelations. If the group character of collective bargaining is understood at the outset, two pitfalls can be avoided.

First, there are many good people who have treated labor-management issues as problems primarily of personal relations, the rapport between a foreman and an operator, or between a business executive and a labor leader. From this viewpoint the improvement of industrial relations is a feature of "how to win friends and influence people." A pious version contends that industrial peace is to be achieved primarily through personal morality; better industrial relations await more moral individuals.

Second, there are many sophisticated people who envisage problems of collective bargaining primarily as questions of managerial administration, the operation of a plant or a department. The existence of a labor organization is viewed as the result of inefficient management and the poor "handling of men." The improvement of industrial relations, from this perspective, requires the development of more efficient administration. When pieces of paper flow more promptly and "lines of communication" are securely established, industrial peace will have been achieved.

There can be little doubt that a sensitivity to human relations and an understanding of administrative techniques both have much to contribute to collective bargaining. The primary fact must be firmly grasped, however, that collective bargaining involves the relations between two organizations. Representatives of labor and management in the collective bargaining process do not act as autonomous individuals or administrators. They have a role to fulfill within their organizations, and their relations involve the dealings between two complex institutions.

Like any continuing organization, unions and companies point with pride to founding fathers. In the histories of both, there have been periods of crises and difficulty. Frequently, both have grown from humble beginnings in the face of real difficulties. Slogans and principles come to be formulated. An elaborate folklore is developed on the place of the organization in the industry and the community and its contribution to both. There are varying degrees of authority and responsibility among the individuals associated with companies and unions. Some are leaders and others followers. In both organizations there is designation of responsibility for policy decisions and for administration of the affairs of the body. In brief, each organization is a distinct entity with a life of its own. Collective bargaining is the process by which unions and managements accommodate each other at points where the two organizations come into contact.

Both unions and managements normally perform a variety of activities outside of the collective bargaining relationship. Companies require an organization, for instance, to produce and distribute their output, to handle the requisite financial transactions, and to deal with governmental and community agencies. Unions similarly require an organization to handle relations with other unions, to undertake political activity in some cases, to represent the union before the community and government agencies, and to "educate" members. Some management organizations are created solely for purposes of collective bargaining; thus, some associations are restricted to handling virtually all problems of a group of firms pertaining to union relations. Likewise, there are some unions whose activities seldom extend beyond a narrow construction of collective bargaining. Unions and managements, however, usually perform a variety of functions not closely related to collective bargaining; their internal structure and organization must be understood, consequently, in terms of the full range of their activities.

Contrasts between Unions and Managements

While unions and companies share the common features of continuing groups, striking contrasts between them are frequently noted. These contrasts are more the differences between the *ideas* about unions and managements than differences between the ways they actually behave. Companies are primarily economic institutions; unions are said to be characteristically political. The one is supposed to be controlled by stockholders; the other controlled by members voting as individuals rather than in accordance with relative financial interests. Companies are said to maximize profits; it is not clear what is the analogous prime objective of unions. Some unions have been interested in maximizing the income of their members; others have been interested mainly in furthering the power of the union, in some instances even against the economic interest of the members; still some few others have been interested primarily in political power or revolutionary objectives. Thus it is said that, while each union partakes of some elements of a business, every union is a part of a social *movement*. Although the proportions vary, each labor leader is part business executive or administrator, part politician, and part high priest. The business executive in contrast is seldom characterized as a politician or leader of a movement.

The hierarchy of offices in a business is supposedly filled by appointments in which merit and ability are the basis of selection. The company is supposed to be managed efficiently with responsibility centered at the top. The union, in contrast, is expected to meet the test of a democracy. Efficiency is subordinate in principle to the civil rights of the members within the union. Leaders are chosen by ballot in the atmosphere of elections in which demagoguery inevitably finds a place. While administrative responsibility may be centered at the top of the union, approval of many detailed policies may be required by the rank and file. The labor executive or administrator on even routine matters is ever conscious of a constituency and an electorate.

These contrasts between unions and companies are in accordance with idealized pictures of the two organizations; they follow from the way unions and companies are supposed to behave. In actual practice the contrast is not so sharp. A great many unions function as highly integrated organizations primarily concerned with negotiating and administering agreements. Most companies, in turn, have certain political elements in their operation. It would be dangerous indeed to approach a study of collective bargaining with a highly stereotyped model of the operation of unions or companies.

broader than the case is posed for decision. The recognition and formulation of problems is one of the most significant aspects of decision making in any organization.

The discovery of alternative solutions to the problem and the exploration of the consequences of these alternatives may involve many different levels of an organization. In fact, most top-level decision making involves the choice among alternative plans which have been formulated in detail by many sections of the organization. If a single plan is presented, the choice is between approval and disapproval. Many decisions involve the approval of actions proposed by subordinates.

The decisions made by an organization—whether administrative or policy making—will be significantly shaped by the information available to decision makers. This information reflects the procedures and lines of communication that have been established within the organization. Frequently these arrangements restrict a decision maker to the information as presented by immediate subordinates. A subordinate is understandably anxious to appear in the best possible light, and an account of a problem or situation is accordingly colored. Such bias is normally not deliberate.

It is a basic problem of every organization to provide channels of information, an intelligence system, which present to a decision maker an account of situations that has been carefully checked for partiality. It may be possible to get reports from different sources. Written statements may facilitate accurate reporting. The "facts of the case" do not normally pre-exist for the decision maker. A number of different bits of information, each with a tag indicating its source, is the raw material for the decision maker. He must come to some judgment from these as to "the facts" of the situation.

When two organizations deal with each other in collective bargaining, the representative of each must have a degree of confidence in his own internal information-gathering system. A company official handling a grievance will wish to feel that he knows exactly what went on in the department in which the grievance arose. Similarly, the union representative does not care to be shown to be ignorant of the facts. Each may not disclose the full extent of his knowledge, particularly if it appears to be advantageous not to do so; but each will desire confidence in the reliability of his own information system. In order to make decisions in the interest of the organization, the internal channels of information must be orderly and reliable.

The growth of collective bargaining has centered considerable attention on the internal communication system of managements. Where there was no labor organization in a plant, there was little basis for top decision makers to question the information that was filtered up to them through layers of supervision. It made little real difference whether a foreman's report of a discharge, to be filed in the personnel records, was entirely accurate. Similarly, there would be no one to question a report as to the basis for promotion of an employee. When a union enters the picture, however, management representatives require a new confidence in the reliability of information. Not only must they know a great many things that previously did not concern them, but they must be prepared to defend management action before a union representative and frequently before an arbitrator. An extensive and reliable information system is indispensable for these "foreign relations" of an organization.

The Impact of Unions on Management Organization

Among the most prominent consequences of the organization of wage earners is the reorganization and change required in the internal management of companies. The administrative and policy-making machinery of the company must be oriented to confront a labor organization. The change in internal management is no less conspicuous in "well-managed" concerns than in less well-run firms. The task of treating with a union compels these changes. Some of the more prominent features of this management revolution may be noted.

1. The necessity for a reliable information system has already been noted. The top management is compelled not only to ascertain the behavior of its representatives but also to develop intelligence on the conduct of the union in various parts of the bargaining unit.

2. The existence of a union impels management to establish an internal organization to insure uniform standards of administration of policies throughout the departments or plants organized by the union. The union will be quick to call to management's attention that a more favorable practice is followed in one place than in another, contending that the more favorable practice should be extended. In the absence of a union, such

differences may escape the attention of top management. They may be sources of discontent, but these differences ordinarily do not have much leverage. Under union conditions such differences serve as excellent arguments for a concession to the union.

The union is usually organized, either formally or informally, so that small differences in handling wage payments, layoffs, promotions, leaves of absence, or a thousand other matters are quickly noticed. Before the introduction of unions when foremen had extensive responsibilities, such minor differences were certain to develop. Under union conditions, managements develop administrative practices to secure a higher degree of uniformity to escape whipsaw tactics. Among these devices are detailed, written administrative rules; conferences of management representatives; and review of departmental action.

3. The introduction of a union tends to centralize the process of policy making in management organizations on labor relations problems. Management cannot afford to have a variety of policies determined on the same problem when the union maintains a vigilant watch to detect such inconsistencies. Centralization of policy making is intended to prevent undesirable precedents. If management deals with an organization whose policy decisions are centralized, it too must be prepared to act in a highly centralized fashion.

4. The growth of a collective bargaining relationship tends to require management to develop a staff organization concerned with affairs and problems dealing with the union. There is need to compile information on the activities of the same or other unions in similar circumstances. The operating management must be serviced with all relevant information on problems that touch the union. The staff functions of the labor relations department emerge.

The introduction of a union affects the operation of a company in many other ways. Unions tend to provide an incentive for managements to use their work force more efficiently; they may compel attention to human problems otherwise neglected; they have been instrumental in some cases in improving the technical processes of production. But attention has been directed above to ways in which the introduction of a union contributes to the internal reorganization of the decision-making process within management. The administrative and policy-making arrangements are themselves altered. Those changes are among the most far-reaching in the community associated with the introduction of collective bargaining.

Management Organization

No two companies have the same management organization for collective bargaining. Formal arrangements will vary with the size of the concern and its operating units, the geographical range of operations, the general management organization, the number of unions with which the management bargains, the contents of its policies, and the personalities on both sides. A national chain store in the retail field, for example, has different problems than a company with a single manufacturing plant. The general dispersion in operations and the employment of young girls with a high turnover rate in the chain store typically will require unique features of organization. It would be ridiculous to expect a single form of management organization for collective bargaining. Each management hierarchy is likely to be shaped to deal with its distinctive internal and external problems. Each management system is also likely to be changed from time to time as these problems alter.

Despite these differences, there are at least three persistent aspects of management organization related to collective bargaining. In any given situation, the student of collective bargaining, or the practitioner, will seek out these relationships in order to understand the operation of the management side of the table.

a) *Top-Management Organization.* The organization of top management for decision making directly affecting collective bargaining is a salient feature of management organization. What is the status within the management hierarchy of the officer directly responsible for industrial relations? What is his delegation of authority? Does he contribute his viewpoint in the councils of the company on broad questions of policy? Does he know what is "going on" in the company? What are the procedures whereby legal considerations, the financial position of the company, operating and production views, and public relations find their impact on collective bargaining decisions of the company? The final decisions of the company will be significantly affected by the mechanism within top management to balance and to weigh the influence of the legal, production, sales, financial, and industrial relations departments of the company on collective bargaining problems.

In some few companies, the chief spokesman in contract negotiations is the chief executive. In other cases, the company may be represented primarily by an operations man, by the industrial relations officer, or by legal counsel. These differences may reflect simply the accidents of personalities, or they may reflect fundamental views of the management organization toward collective bargaining. The use of the chief executive of the company may symbolize a belief in the critical importance of industrial relations in the company. A production vice-president may reflect the conception of bargaining primarily as a continuing relationship with the main chain of operating authority in the company, from the top down to each foreman. The use of counsel may reflect a legalistic approach to labor relations in the company. The choice of representative will also have been influenced by the practices and policies of the union.

The significant point is that the procedures and division of responsibility within the top-management organization will be a critical factor in most collective bargaining relationships. In small companies with one-man managements, these issues of balance among departments become problems of analyzing the thought processes and emotions of that one man. In larger enterprises the decision process is more institutionalized. The procedures within top management attract the attention of every student of a particular case.

b) Management Hierarchy in the Grievance Procedure. Although no two companies may have the same internal organization, the grievance procedure hierarchy is a feature common to all managements under collective bargaining. A chain of management command is recognized in the steps of the grievance procedure. This chain is one of the innovations in management organization accompanying the introduction of a union. A typical procedure would provide for appeal to the foreman as step one, the superintendent of the department as step two, the plant manager as step three, and the vice-president in charge of operations or the industrial relations officer as step four.

A consequence of the grievance procedure is to identify points of decision making within the company affecting relations with the union. Responsibility which may have been diffused or not clearly defined is concentrated in the grievance chain of command within the company.

The top step in this chain of command within management,

before the arbitration step, has important consequences for the whole organization. The top appeal may be to the head of the industrial relations department or to the vice-president in charge of production, or to the chief executive of the company. In choosing among these alternatives, top management must establish procedures to define the relative responsibilities of the industrial relations department and the main operating departments of the company. Both departments have real interest in the policy implications of the settlement of any grievance. In fact, the administration of the management side of a grievance procedure requires at each step the clearest possible designation of responsibility and the closest co-operation between the operating and industrial relations departments of the company. Even then top management may have to decide differences in views between these two departments.

In the collective bargaining process, the grievance-procedure steps are points in union and management organizations where representatives meet to consider cases in behalf of their whole organizations. Behind the management representatives, foreman to top step, there must be procedures for reconciling or choosing between the views of the operating and industrial relations departments. The industrial relations department may wish to replace a foreman because he handles workers badly; the operating department finds him technically proficient. The industrial relations department may believe that no case has been established for the discipline or discharge of a worker that would stand up before an arbitrator, whereas the operating department may believe the worker is so "objectionable" as to warrant risking a reversal with possible award of back pay by an arbitrator.

The grievance procedure steps are points at which management deals with the union. Necessarily, they are also points at which management must present a single position, and hence procedures must be established to reconcile or resolve internal conflicts within the management organization.

c) *Industrial Relations Administration.* A management organization must have machinery to make many decisions within the framework of its agreement with the union organization. The decisions do not involve top management directly, but they are requisite to the daily operation of a business. Thus, the contract may provide that new employees must join the union, but the company must establish machinery to select particular new employees. The contract may provide for "reasonable leaves of absence," but more administrable standards must be formulated for the instruction of supervisors and for the choice among applicants for leave. The contract may allow a union to question a piece rate on a particular operation, but a whole system of setting rates must be administered by the company. A contract may require that seniority be the basis for promotion where ability is equal. If this clause is to be meaningful, the company will have to establish seniority lists and tests of the performance of each worker. In brief, there is a substantial administrative organization required within a management to direct a labor force under the terms of a labor agreement. The industrial relations department typically co-ordinates this responsibility.

A great many of management's activities that are directly related to employees fall outside the scope of the typical agreement. Organizational arrangements must be provided for these activities. Terms of the agreement usually do not apply to some employees, such as foremen, technicians, and may not be applicable to clerical employees. Policies comparable to those established for employees under an agreement must be made for employees within the management hierarchy or for employees outside the bargaining unit for other reasons. A company may elect to establish many programs not required or covered by contract, such as recreation and medical care. These programs require administrative machinery. In any specific situation, there will be difficulty in distinguishing industrial relations and personnel activities. The same organizational arrangements within the company may handle both. The machinery for the administration of industrial relations and personnel policies must be closely integrated.

Despite the diverse forms of management organization, the student of collective bargaining will in any particular situation concentrate upon the top-management organization, the management machinery related to the grievance procedure, and the administration of personnel and industrial relations policies.

Union Organization

No two unions, just as has been observed in the instance of companies, have identical internal arrangements for reaching decisions in the collective bargaining relationship. The level within the union at which a decision is achieved varies with the type of problem. Such observations may seem to preclude any attempts to generalize about the decision-making process within unions. It is true that far too few facts are known (and even fewer can be documented) to generalize with confidence on the many aspects of the internal life of the labor organization. But the careful observer or the practitioner will concentrate upon three important aspects of union organization for collective bargaining.

a) *The Elected Hierarchy.* In the international union, top policy making may be made at one of three levels: the convention of elected delegates, the executive board frequently composed of vice-presidents and other elected officers, and the chief executive of the organization. The convention is almost always the body of final policy-making authority, short of appeal to the rank and file of members through a referendum (in some few cases) or through the delegates elected to the next convention. The division of authority between council and chief executive differs widely among unions. In some few unions the president and secretary are not even members of the council; they are directed to carry out policies adopted by the council. At the other extreme are unions in which the chief executive alone formulates all major decisions.

Just as title does not infallibly indicate the chief executive of a corporation—it may be the chairman of the board or the president—so likewise in a union. In a few instances in which the influence of the older German trade unionists was strong, the secretary-treasurer is the chief executive. The Amalgamated Butcher Workers and Meat Cutters of North America is an example. In most international unions the president is the chief executive, although old age or sickness may result in the unofficial delegation of active responsibility to another officer, frequently the probable successor.

Over the years, the centralization of top-level decision making in the chief executive of the labor organization no doubt has increased. The council may approve or advise in varying degrees in different unions. The national rather than local character of many problems no doubt has been most significant in creating the centralization tendency. The interdependence of wage rates in one locality upon those in others, the influence of national legislation, and the growth of the large-scale enterprise with activities throughout the country are indicative of the national scope of many decisions in the labor unions.

In the local union, there are levels of policy making roughly analogous to those that have just been indicated for the international union: the local union meeting, the local executive board, and the business agent and the stewards. Here again, the division of the decision-making responsibility at different levels will vary considerably even among local unions that are a part of the same international union.

While local unions elect a president and other officers, the business agent typically is a full-time union employee. In the usual case, he is elected. The steward is the elected or appointed representative of the union in a department or other unit of operation of management. The steward typically is an employee working at his trade or in the shop; he is usually compensated by the union only for such part time as he spends on union business involving a loss of earnings from his regular employment.

b) *The Union Representative.* In order to operate on a national basis, the chief executives of the unions have created, largely in the last twenty-five years, two devices of internal union organization. The first is the national office staff, comparable to staff employees of other organizations, to advise the chief executive and carry on the routine business of the national office. Thus, many unions have established research, legal, financial, contract files, technical and engineering, welfare, and public relations departments. The second, and more important, creation in organization has been the international representative or organizer, to use the most common designation. These officers are normally appointed by the chief executive, although approval of the council may be necessary. In a few unions, they are elected. They supervise and service the local unions in an assigned territory or branch of the industry. They may take part in local negotiations in which their role may be anything from adviser to active chief negotiator. They may direct the conduct of strikes. They may represent the union in arbitration and in relations with government agencies. These positions in the labor union would be called "bureaucracy" by the student of government. The international representative and the organizer constitute the emergence in the labor movement of a professional group. Their livelihood depends upon the union as an organization.

The ordinary local union does not employ comparable full-time representatives; the elected full-time business agent normally is sufficient. In some large local unions, however, there are appointed assistant business agents, full-time employees of the union, who correspond to the international representatives in the national union.

c) *Union Organization in the Grievance Procedure.* The grievance procedure in the union, just as in management organization, represents a chain of command or a hierarchy of decision making extending from the steward at the bottom, through the business agent, to an international representative, and in rare instances to the international chief executive. The steps in the procedure identify in the union organization points of decision making in its relation to a management organization.

The rank and file of union members, the constituency of the elected officers, play a decisive, though variable, role in the decision-making process within labor organizations. Members in mass cannot make "decisions," as the term is ordinarily understood. The individual members of a labor organization, however, do influence the decisions of the organization in a variety of ways—election of officers, votes on proposals submitted for ratification, expression of views and opinions at meetings, withholding of dues payments where no checkoff exists, interest in rival organizations, etc. One of the chief tasks of an elected or appointed union officer is to maintain contact with the pulse of the union membership. The union has many of the features and, consequently, the problems of a political democracy.

The decisions which the hierarchy of a labor organization make frequently involve a choice among the interests of different members or groups of members. One member rather than another is entitled to a promotion or must be laid off. The officers must choose between the long-run and the short-run interests of the members. This choice may take the form of a decision favorable to the organization as against the members as individuals. Such a question may be involved in the decision between a wage increase and improved union security or in discussion of the level of union dues. A decision may be required as to the form of concessions to be sought from managements. Vacations and pensions may be preferred by senior employees, while a particular department or group may prefer larger wage increases. In the process of making these decisions, the officer of the labor organization acts as a politician, in the best sense of the word. He seeks a working compromise among the conflicting interests of the individuals who compose the organization.

It may be contended that this political element of the decision-making process is not absent in management organization. The stockholders are analogous to the rank and file. In some cases the relationship of management to the stockholders may resemble that of union officers to members. Managements have real problems of reconciling conflicting interests of different types of stockholders and bondholders. But, in the ordinary case, the economic destiny of the stockholder is not so completely dependent upon the one management as the employee is upon the single job. The members of the union are more frequently in contact with the union officers than most stockholders with the company. These differences in degree yield a labor hierarchy much more sensitive to the membership than most managements are to stockholders.

The relationships of a union officer to the constituency and to the rest of the union hierarchy is frequently the most important aspect of a decision. It is a commonplace that most political representatives attempt to avoid alienating groups of their constituency. In the same way, union officers may seek to avoid unpopular decisions. In relationships with management, for instance, a union representative may elect not to settle a questionable grievance on account of the internal hostility such a settlement would produce. The decision of the union representative is not to be narrowly interpreted in terms of the technical merits of the particular grievance but rather in terms of the political context of the representative in his relations with the rank and file and with management. To understand decision making within the labor organization is not only to grasp the workings of the union hierarchy but also to be sensitive to the subtle relations between the officers and their representatives and the rank and file of union members.

The Question of Prerogatives

The preceding sketch of decision making in management and labor organizations can help to clarify the discussion of "prerogatives." (See Section L, Part Two.) Managements have frequently regarded unions as an encroachment upon a given territory of management "rights." The union is pictured as continuously engaged in expanding its activities at the expense of these prerogatives of management. From this viewpoint, all decision making within the area of collective bargaining originally "belonged" to management. The unions secured a beachhead which they have been seeking to enlarge. The union is said to be motivated by an irresistible urge to "share" in all the decision-making processes within a management. Collective bargaining is even depicted as a form or method of management. Managements which have approached the collective bargaining relationship with a central emphasis upon prerogatives have devoted great energy to seeking to contain the union and the scope of its activities. The National Labor Relations Board, as was noted in Chapter II, in defining the content of bargaining has been drawn into the prerogatives controversy. Some managements contended that pension plans, for instance, were not a required subject for collective bargaining; they were the exclusive prerogatives of management. The NLRB and the courts held that pensions were a proper subject for collective bargaining within the law.

There is no doubt that labor organizations constitute a challenge to the dominant influence of business in the community over the past century. Unions also provide limitations on the range of possible decisions within a management. But the problems involved in the discussion of prerogatives will be more clearly understood if the collective bargaining process be depicted as that of accommodating two organizations—a union and a management.

a) The two organizations each face certain intimate questions of internal operations. Officers and leaders must be selected. The structure and internal government of each must be established. Lines of authority and a communications and "intelligence" system free from external domination are imperative. Such activities are indispensable to the existence of an independent organization.

b) The collective bargaining contract explicitly defines an area of the respective rights and duties of the union and management. In general terms the management is guaranteed the right of administrative initiative,[1] that is the right to make initial

---

[1] Thomas Kennedy, *Effective Labor Arbitration* (Philadelphia: University of Pennsylvania Press, 1943), pp. 90–127.

decisions and to put these decisions into effect. The union in turn is provided the right of protest and redress from a decision usually with the explicit understanding that, if the management is found to be in error, under the grievance procedure, full restitution (retroactively) will be made to the union. But the management is provided in the right of administrative initiative the authority to proceed to undertake operations to get the job done. The agreement also typically provides that these decisions may be carried out without stoppage of work on the part of the union.

c) The scope of the collective bargaining relationship is never static. The agreement cannot anticipate all problems and contingencies which arise under its provisions. Furthermore, at renewal dates the parties in negotiating a new agreement continually reshape the prescribed rights and obligations of each organization. The quest for prerogatives in the sense of a final definition of these rights and duties is certain to fail in a dynamic world.

d) A great deal of confusion over prerogatives can be eliminated in practice when both organizations recognize the difference between the authority for a decision and the consultative process. There are large areas of the relationship between the organizations where consultation in advance of final decision will be found to be highly useful. Managements will receive many useful suggestions from union representatives and unions in turn will be assisted by comments and information from management representatives. The consultative process in advance of decision need not prejudice the formal authority for decision making. Management may consult the union in advance of many decisions but retain the responsibility for making the decision. In the accommodation of union and management organizations, which is the collective bargaining process, advanced consultation has a significant role to play.

SUGGESTIONS FOR FURTHER READING

BAKKE, E. WIGHT. *Mutual Survival: The Goal of Unions and Management.* New Haven, Conn.: Labor Management Center, Yale University, 1946.

FRIEDRICH, C. J. "Responsible Government Service under the American Constitution," *Problems of the American Public Service*, pp. 3–74. New York: McGraw-Hill Book Co., 1935.

52 · COLLECTIVE BARGAINING

GORDON, R. A. *Business Leadership in the Large Corporation.* Washington, D.C.: The Brookings Institution, 1945.

HARDMAN, J. B. S., and NEUFFELD, MAURICE F. *The House of Labor.* New York: Prentice-Hall, Inc., 1951.

HERBERG, WILL. "Bureaucracy and Democracy in Labor Unions," *Antioch Review,* Fall, 1943, pp. 405–17.

MERTON, ROBERT K. *et al.* (ed.). *Reader in Bureaucracy.* Glencoe, Ill.: The Free Press, 1952.

ROSS, ARTHUR M. *Trade Union Wage Policy,* pp. 21–74. Berkeley: University of California Press, 1948.

Chapter
IV

THE COLLECTIVE
BARGAINING PROCESS

The collective bargaining process has been caricatured in a variety of ways. It is said to be like a poker game. The largest pots go to those who combine deception, bluff, and luck or ability to come up with a strong hand on the occasions they are challenged or "seen" by the other side But the rules of the collective bargaining game are not so well established or determined in advance as poker, and victory is not always so easy to identify.

Collective bargaining is sometimes likened to a debating society. There is the same flow of words, massing of arguments, and name calling. But unions and managements are engaged in no academic affair; there are great issues at stake.

Collective bargaining is also depicted as power politics. The strong impose their terms upon the weak. Take it or leave it. The structure of wages reflects the distribution of power within the economy. But the determinants of power are apparently so complex that little understanding is conveyed by the analogy.

Collective bargaining is described as a rational process in which the parties are persuaded to alter their original positions by the facts and arguments presented by the opposite side. Disagreement is dissolved by careful investigation and appeal to logical argument. The parties have no adamant positions. They may be pictured, in somewhat idyllic terms, as coming to the bargaining table with a fully open mind to the suggestions of the other side. But the depth of feeling displayed in some negotiations and strikes suggests that logical argument is not the only ingredient in collective bargaining.

Each of these four cartoons of what men do at the bargaining table, no doubt, has its counterpart in some actual experience.

There may be no simple prototype of the bargaining process. But analysis must proceed beyond analogy, and the essential character of the collective bargaining process must be probed before one decides what caricature is most descriptive or most useful in understanding the facts of industrial life.

Bargaining Demands

The initial positions of the parties in contract negotiations are typically very far apart. Both the size of the union demand on any single issue and the number of separate demands are likely to be large, much larger than any realistic expectation for settlement on the part of either company or union negotiators. The same disparity in positions characterizes contract counterdemands presented by employees. How is one to explain bargaining demands? Why do union leaders arouse expectations in their members which they know cannot be fulfilled? Why do employers make counterdemands which may create animosity since they typically involve taking away an existing practice or compensation? Is one to join editorial writers who pass judgment at the outset upon the merits and the size of contract demands? Insight into bargaining demands is requisite to any understanding of the bargaining process.

1. Contract demands proposed by unions or managements are ordinarily initiated by many people making suggestions: union members from the floor of a meeting, executive board members, or elected members of a wage policy committee; foremen called into conference with the industrial relations department, heads of operating departments, or staff committees in a company. While some screening takes place before demands are first presented, at the outset the hard choices are not decided by rating these demands and determining the trading value of each in terms of other demands. The relative valuation of demands is typically made by the respective negotiators later in the process. Thus, the large initial demands of the parties reflect the process by which demands are formulated and the fact that to reduce or to withdraw demands it is essential to know something of the position of the other side on these demands.

2. A large number of demands makes it difficult for the other side to ascertain one's "real" position. Many demands cover up the hard core which one might accept as a settlement and mask

the relative importance which the side making the demands ascribes to the various demands. With one's own position shielded, negotiators seek to probe the "real" position of the other side. This includes the willingness of the other side to concede particular points, the relative importance the other side attaches to each demand made upon it, and the significance which the other side attaches to points which one might be willing to concede to it. One side could be said to be in an ideal bargaining position if it knew what demands and combinations of demands the other side would concede under various circumstances without the other side having any comparable knowledge. A large number of demands helps to mask one's own position as he probes to ascertain the position of the other party.

3. A large number of demands may be useful in the actual stages of bargaining. It is possible to drop or reduce a relatively unimportant demand and contend that one has made a concession which should be followed by some concession from the other side. A demand may be included which has been found to be obnoxious to the other side and for which the other party is willing to make some concession. More than one company has "bought" the withdrawal of a union-shop demand for an additional nickel in a series of contract negotiations.

It is possible to shift one's "real" position or settlement offer with a large number of demands. Large demands afford plenty of room in which to maneuver. Some minor demands have a nuisance value; they may be made the condition of final settlements when the principal points have been concluded. These demands may become the "icing on the cake."

Large demands protect the negotiator from substantial changes in conditions which occur during the period of contract negotiations. Many negotiations are protracted, and economic conditions may change or other relevant settlements may be made between the time demands are served and a new agreement finally achieved. While new demands ordinarily can be introduced technically as long as no agreement has been reached, it is probably tactically better to be protected from the contingency of having to increase initial demands by large demands at the outset.

If there results a breakdown of negotiations and there is a strike or lockout, a large number of demands provides issues to be used as talking points and symbols in a serious struggle.

4. Some demands may be introduced to facilitate future bargaining. Neither side can ordinarily be expected to concede a new demand the first time it is presented. A new idea may initially produce only opposition from the other party. The demand will be less novel and appear less outrageous a year later. The other side may have had occasion to think it through and to consider administrative problems which need mutual exploration. Thus, a pension or a health and welfare proposal introduced by the union for the first time will ordinarily receive a cool reception. Management may need several years to consider types of plans, to gather data on the age distribution and health experience of its work force, and to get used to considering this range of issues. New contract demands ordinarily require a period of gestation, and some demands are on the list to be seasoned.

It is apparent that large demands are related to basic features of the collective bargaining process. They are not simply to be dismissed as avarice or as evidence of unreasonableness. The careful observer, just as the skilled negotiator, will seek to get behind the demands to the possibilities of settlement and will recognize that the demands serve a variety of purposes in the collective bargaining process.

There is a relative minority of parties who follow a different bargaining procedure from the "large demand." They seek to develop the bargaining pattern in which their initial demand is virtually their final offer for settlement. There are some advantages if the other party can be persuaded that such is the case. The time required to probe the position of the other side can be saved, and each side has only to decide whether to settle or take a strike or lockout. This bargaining procedure is difficult to develop for it sacrifices maneuverability and must be followed consistently to be effective. It also requires considerable knowledge and experience in dealing with the other party to judge the level of demands to be set on a "take it or leave it" basis. This procedure may be used by unions in dealing with companies who have followed customarily the settlements of other companies. The demand of the traditional pattern removes most of the risk from the resort to this bargaining procedure. Some companies have developed the policy, after hearing the union demands, of stating a settlement position and sticking to it, even though it means a protracted strike. A strong company in a relatively unique or protected competitive position is most likely to adopt such a bargaining procedure. But these instances are exceptions to the normal collective bargaining process.

The Deadline: Threat of Strike or Lockout

Disputes over the terms of collective bargaining agreements are frequently settled only at the last minute. The last-ditch all-night parleys are as familiar to newspaper readers as they are wearing on reporters keeping vigil. Why all this rush at the end? Why could not the dispute have been settled in more calm a week or two earlier? The frequency of these photo-finishes suggests that something may be involved fundamental to the process of collective bargaining.

1. For reasons that have been explored in some detail, the parties are likely to be far apart at the outset of negotiations. Neither side is anxious to improve its offer of settlement, i.e., make further concessions, if its present offer will ultimately be accepted by the other side. Accordingly, each side will be slow to change its position and to make its offer of settlement more attractive. If the dispute can be settled for lesser terms, there is certainly no point in raising the ante. Likewise, there is no point in accepting an offer if an improved one is likely to be forthcoming in the negotiations. But there is no certain way of knowing the best offer which the other side will actually make. In this uncertainty the deadline serves a purpose.

It is customary in this country for agreements to have designated expiration dates and for extensions to be for a specified period. Even where there is no anniversary date, it is common for the union to set a date on which it states it intends to strike if no settlement is reached. Occasionally a company may set a date after which it states it intends to lock out employees if there is no agreement or impose its proposed terms and conditions of employment. As this deadline approaches, each side is faced with the alternative of making its offer of settlement more attractive to the other side or face a work stoppage. As each day of negotiation passes, this alternative is sharpened and becomes more real. Eventually the hour arrives when decisions must be made. There is either an agreement or a work stoppage. The deadline forces decisions on both parties. The deadline is a basic feature of collective bargaining which impels the parties to weigh and to evaluate the choice between agreement and a work stoppage. The gap between the parties is very frequently closed at this time.

2. The imminence of a strike or lockout compels each party to reassess its offers of settlement. A management may decide that it can afford a little more when it is faced with a shutdown of its facilities in the morning. A union negotiating committee may decide to concede a clause or take a lesser increase when it faces the prospect of walking the bricks in a few hours. A work stoppage is a much less effective pressure for settlement when it is weeks off than when it is scheduled for midnight. Looking down the barrel of a strike or lockout causes negotiators on both sides not only to make the best offer they planned in advance but also to reappraise their positions and even to make more acceptable offers to the other side than they had intended. It is this genuine change in position, induced by the immediacy of the shutdown, that frequently produces settlement.

3. The approach of the deadline at which a threat of strike or lockout passes into an actual work stoppage tends to eliminate much of the element of bluff in any negotiations. It exposes for each to see the hard core of the position at that time of the other side. The emergence of the position of each side in greater clarity and the elimination of extraneous demands, which have now served their purpose, enhance the prospects of settlement.

At the deadline, as the parties are poised between agreement and a work stoppage, there is likely to be more room for agreement than has previously emerged in the negotiation. The strike introduces a discontinuity. Up to a strike the union is normally thinking only in terms of gains; the company is thinking of gains in contract clauses or some added costs. The strike ordinarily introduces losses for the first time to the union and its members and reduced revenue ordinarily for the companies.[1] A work stoppage once started is likely to be of uncertain duration. The zone of possible agreement is temporarily enlarged as the parties stand between possible agreement and the uncertainties of a shutdown. If either side gives up a specific small amount, it may save itself a loss of unknown proportions. Each side, comparing the costs of known concessions against the prospects of unknown

[1] There may be cases in which a strike improves the market of a company or industry. This factor will no doubt enter the calculations of the company in determining whether to take a shutdown.

losses, has a greater likelihood than previously in the bargaining to bridge the gap between them.

4. The deadline serves still other, and more mundane, purposes in collective bargaining. Each side must make certain technical and organizational preparations if there is to be a work stoppage. Management must arrange for an orderly cessation of work, particularly in continuous process industries like aluminum, steel, and flat glass. Plans must be made for essential orders. Goods in process and shipments due must be rescheduled. Arrangements must be made for essential maintenance and repair. Supervision must be alerted and scheduled to perform some of these emergency functions. Unions in turn have to organize picket lines; banners and information about the strike must be prepared within the union and the community. If many localities are involved, effective communications must be arranged in the event of any last minute change in plans. It is a major organizational problem for a large company or union to prepare for a work stoppage. A deadline facilitates the planning and timing of these numerous details.

An appreciation of the significance of deadlines and the threat of work stoppages to the operation of collective bargaining has important implications for public policy.

a) A strike vote by members of the union can have little significance other than a vote of confidence in the union negotiating committee. A vote by union members to authorize a strike is a vote to accept the judgment of the negotiating committee and the elected officers as to the wisdom of settling or accepting the employer's best offer. Ordinarily, there can be no time long enough to permit an election between the breakdown of negotiations and the start of a strike. This is apparent from the very function of the deadline.

The Congress of the United States, however, twice in the past decade has sought to rely on the strike vote in part as a way to prevent strikes. In the 1943 Smith-Connally Act (War Labor Disputes Act)[2] a secret ballot was to let workers decide whether or not they "will permit any such interruption of war production." The Taft-Hartley law (Labor Management Relations Act, 1947) provided in its emergency disputes procedures that a secret ballot

[2] See George W. Taylor, *Government Regulation of Industrial Relations* (New York: Prentice-Hall, Inc., 1948., pp. 164–71.

should be taken on the question of whether or not the employees ". . . wish to accept the final offer of settlement made by the employer as stated by him. . . ." Experience has confirmed to all, what analysis of the bargaining process reveals, that these proposals are ineffectual and even comical.

b) There are some sectors of the community where the threat of strike or lockout cannot be effectively used to promote agreement, since a strike or lockout may be unrealistic. Such is the case, for instance, among employees in the executive branch of the government. Where the threat of a work stoppage cannot be effectively used, it is likely to be most difficult to make collective bargaining operate. The deadline cannot be used to serve its normal function to induce agreement. Indeed, under these circumstances the forms of collective bargaining may take on quite different substance. Thus, it is no accident that unions in government service, such as the postal clerks, have become primarily lobbying organizations seeking increases from the appropriate legislative bodies. While the problem requires further attention, it is clearly most difficult to find any substitute for the strike or lockout and yet to preserve the essential character of the collective bargaining process.

c) There is a point in bargaining after which a strike cannot be postponed. The technical and organizational arrangements which the parties must place in effect to conduct a work stoppage, particularly a large one, cannot readily be turned off and turned on. When the time arrives that these steps must be placed into effect if a stoppage is to begin at a designated hour, the organizational wheels cannot readily be reversed. Indeed, further bargaining may be impossible as leaders on both sides will be preoccupied with these administrative matters.

Changing Positions and Reaching Agreement

If the collective bargaining process is to be understood, attention must be directed particularly to the problems involved in changing a position and the process by which these changes are made. Parties starting far apart must change their positions if there is to be any agreement. But changing a position is difficult because it may harden the other side and create the hope, if not the expectation, that the moving party will go all the way and close any gap between the two sides. It is not easy for a negotiator to drop a demand he has been arguing for with great enthusiasm without casting some doubt on positions taken on other issues as well. Changing positions is at the heart of the collective bargaining process, and the way in which a negotiator handles these problems distinguishes a skilled veteran from a novice.

No two agreements are reached in the identical way. But certain common stages and characteristics of the agreement-making process are discernible. The process of bargaining may be described in terms of the following ideal type. These steps and stages overlap, and the actual course of negotiations may backtrack to an earlier phase. Not all negotiations follow any one pattern. The stages of negotiations discussed below purport to be a summary of what actually happens, not an outline of what ought to be.

1. Contract negotiations normally start with the presentation of the formal demands to be made by each side in specific or general terms. These demands will be supported by statements or "speeches" which set forth why the other side should concede the demands and why they are necessary to the moving side. These proceedings normally take place before the full negotiating committees which comprise a relatively large group. The negotiations have been launched; the formal demands are on the table by type of demand if not in exact amount, and the formal distance or gap between the parties is ordinarily now known.

2. There follows, or is interspersed, a stage in which each side explores the demands and arguments presented by the other. This is likely to be a period of questioning, where the objective is to understand the meaning of at least some of the demands presented by the other party. What problems have there been in the past year which prompt, for instance, the requested change in seniority, in the lunch period, or in the management rights section of the agreement? It may become necessary to ascertain certain facts in dispute between the parties. Individuals in the company and union familiar with alleged events or problems will have to be contacted by each side for later report at a future bargaining session. What is the meaning of the proposal of the other side, and how would it actually work? There is probing and debate over the arguments advanced with regard to "money" items. What have other people gotten? What about cost of living and profits? What are the applicable wage stabilization regula-

tions if there are wage controls? Each side is likely to appear very adamant on its own position as it seeks to probe the other side. On which point does the other party appear most reticent, and on which is there most likely prospect of "movement," "give," or "change." Even at this stage, on relatively minor questions a negotiator may indicate on some questions that there is a possibility of change of position by: "that's negotiable," or "some consideration might be given to that," or "if that was all between us we could probably wash it out." The relations between the principal negotiators and the rest of each committee is significant at this stage, and a change on minor issues alone can be expected.

3. There follows, or is interspersed, a stage in which the negotiating committees are "scaled" down to smaller size, to a few on each side. The sessions are much more informal. There is a continued attempt to explore the position of the other side, to seek to ascertain on which issues some concession is possible and on which no change is likely. There is to be expected some change from the initial formal position of each side. These indications are likely to be quite indirect, but they will be very real and meaningful to the skilled negotiator.

At this stage, each side may be expected to indicate some combination of positions on the items in dispute which it would "consider" as a basis for settlement. Each side indicates some "package" on which the dispute might possibly be settled. These "packages" are most significant, even when the parties are far apart. Normally the union will have failed to mention some of the original demands; this is for practical purposes an offer to eliminate them. In presenting its package, a management will indicate something of its evaluation of the demands it has served upon the union and its willingness to concede particular demands of the union. The discussion of these packages affords each side further opportunity to appraise the position of the other side. What items in the package are satisfactory? What ones do not go far enough? What other items may have to be added to secure settlement? These questions may not be directly approached, but discussion of the "package" proposals will permit judgments on such questions. Bargaining at this stage may produce more than one "package" proposal for settlement from a side.

4. In the ordinary collective bargaining negotiation, agreement is not actually reached initially at the bargaining table.

Despite the symbolism of the "bargaining table," a meeting of minds ordinarily occurs first elsewhere. Occasionally, a subcommittee of one member from each side may be formally agreed upon to explore further the package proposals already under discussion. More ordinarily, an informal meeting with one from each side first bridges the gap between the parties. These sessions are "off the record" in every sense of the term. The representative from each side is either the chairman of that side or a most influential person in the union or management organizations. Each such representative usually has no formal authority to settle, even for the negotiating committee; but the person is recognized by the other side to be in a position of leadership or by experience to be able for practical purposes to indicate that a settlement would be forthcoming on particular terms. These meetings may even be held without the knowledge of other members of the negotiation subcommittee, although ordinarily members of both committees would be informed in advance. These sessions between the two may take place at a meal or over a drink, if they are extended. For brief conferences the hall or the men's room is standard procedure.

One party is likely to suggest a further proposal, a greater concession than has so far appeared in the negotiations, provided that it be accepted by the other. The other party may accept or propose a further basis for settlement. Each party will be likely to emphasize that he will have to try to "sell" acceptance to other members of his committee and that may be expected to be difficult. Eventually a "proposition" or "package" is formulated that each believes to be a basis for settlement and is likely to be acceptable to the full negotiating committee of each side. At this stage, there has been a meeting of minds; and an agreement, tentative and preliminary, has been advanced.

5. The settlement is then brought back to the subcommittee and the full negotiating committee for acceptance. This may be done in a variety of ways. The persons who formulated the "proposition" may each first explain it to his committee; and if acceptable, the "package" may then be explained to the committees in joint session and accepted. The persons who first reached agreement may not inform their committees in advance; and the proposals for settlement may be advanced by one side, as an apparent surprise to the committee of the other side. At this

stage, the settlement will have normally been reduced to writing in the form of a "memorandum of agreement" with a listing of agreed upon terms. Contract language will be fully developed only where the details of the language have been a significant issue. This memorandum may be initialed or signed by the negotiation committee or its principal members. This memorandum may require ratification by other bodies to which the negotiating committees are responsible or to which they report.

6. The final stage in the making of an agreement is to reduce the memorandum agreement to contract language and to incorporate the language in a full agreement. The details of the contract language may require the advice and draftmanship of lawyers on both sides.

No such outline of the stages of the agreement-making process can convey the full subtleties of bargaining any more than a diagram of key football plays can fully reflect an understanding of the game. In each the elements of surprise, makeshift, and improvisation are important. But in each case a careful observer can, with the aid of these diagrams or sketches, achieve insight into what is really going on.

At any of the stages in the negotiating process—in formal conferences, subcommittees, or in private sessions of the principal negotiators—the change of a position by either side is an intricate operation. There will be differences of opinion within each side that will have to be resolved. The position that the other side has so far taken may be an important factor in changing the judgment of members of a negotiating team as to the possibilities of settlement in particular directions. Before a position can be changed, accordingly, there will have to be conferences or "caucuses" within each side. In some instances, more authority may be required by the negotiating group.

It is customary for "feelers" to be put out by the side changing its position. A new offer is ordinarily "in the air" before it has been placed on the table. Questions may be asked to determine the relative interest in various possible offers. How big a step to take may in part depend upon possible reactions of the other side. A side, while preparing to make a concession, will try to have created as favorable an atmosphere as possible in which to launch the new proposition. In stating a new "package" or concession, the party will be likely to emphasize the reasonableness of the proposal, the difficulty it has had with its principals in securing this further concession, and the impression will be created by indirection or explicitly that no further concessions can be expected to be forthcoming. The offer ordinarily will be conditioned upon the other side making some concession or withdrawing all other claims for a settlement.

In the negotiation process, it is understood that there can be no agreement until all contract items in dispute have been settled or procedures have been agreed upon to settle them. All settlements must be "package" settlements when there is more than one item in dispute, as is ordinarily the case in contract negotiations. It follows that all offers and acceptances on particular issues are provisional and may be formally withdrawn if there is no settlement of the total dispute. It is customary to add that such withdrawal is without prejudice to the position of either side, permitting each to revert to its original position. In terms of the eventual settlement of the dispute, such withdrawal is ordinarily more of a ritual than a fact. Offers made are seldom effectively withdrawn, except when one side or the other has suffered serious defeat in a strike or a lockout.

In concluding this section, it is also appropriate to note some of the implications of the analysis for public policy.

1. If negotiations break off and a strike takes place, the announced and public positions of the parties are likely to be farther apart than they were during the negotiations. Concessions by either side are formally withdrawn, and the parties are likely to revert to their initial demands or their last public position. The negotiations may actually have failed by only a hair's breadth, although the formal positions may indicate they are miles apart. It is impossible to know the true extent of the dispute without knowledge of the actual negotiations.

2. The agreement-making process does not thrive with constant publicity at each step. Negotiations in a "gold fish bowl" are not likely to be productive of an agreement. Parties who are constantly running to the newspapers with statements seeking to justify their position are not likely to come to a meeting of minds. It is no accident that experienced negotiators almost invariably seek to shield from the press the details and the steps of the negotiations while they are in process. Why this sensitivity to the light of day?

Negotiators themselves want to explain any concession in position to their principals or to their membership rather than to have it come as a surprise through other channels. Union members and company officers have expectations as to the outcome of the negotiations; they are familiar with the formal demands. In order to preserve the position of leadership and integrity of the negotiators with each side, they desire to explain directly the problems they confronted, the reasons for any change in position, and the gains they "purchased" with the concession. Moreover, during the course of negotiations, publicity to concessions made by either side may build up opposition to the action of the negotiators. If a particular demand is dropped or reduced, those who insisted on the demand most strongly in the first place may become vocal and seek to get the negotiators to change their position and withdraw the concession. It would be difficult at best, if not impossible, to negotiate with (or against) the other side and to keep having "to repair fences" within ones own organization at each step. It is the final "package" settlement on which the negotiator is willing to stand or fall before his organization as a whole. The agreement-making process is delicate and intricate. The "light of day" during the course of negotiations inhibits the capacity of the negotiator to change his position and to reply to the other side.

A most difficult problem of public policy arises for the labor reporter and the newspaper. Some negotiations concern collective bargaining contracts which are of considerable public interest. The contract provisions in major agreements affect a great many people and have widespread effects throughout the economy. The failure of the negotiators to reach agreement may shut down facilities vital to the public health and safety, or at least to public convenience. The interest of the newspaper reader in the details of the steps of the negotiations must be weighted against the harm to the agreement-making process. This is not easy to do. What obligation does a newspaper owe the parties to the negotiations? What obligations do the parties have to keep the general newspaper reader informed? These tough problems illustrate the need for specialized and professional reporters in this field. The solution to this difficult problem lies no doubt in the details of the negotiations that are reported while they are in process.

3. An appreciation of the subtleties of the bargaining proc-

ess has significant implications for any attempted governmental regulation of collective bargaining. Fundamentally, you cannot "make" the parties agree. You cannot legislate agreement or a meeting of the minds. Government prescription of collective bargaining procedures cannot produce agreement, nor is it demonstrable that on balance it can increase the prospects of agreement. Today the NLRB and the courts have built from the legislative mandate "to bargain collectively" a vast code of detailed regulations. The NLRB has prescribed in particular cases the information that each side must furnish to the other, the authority of the negotiators, the frequency of meetings, the topics on which the parties must bargain and the issues on which they need not negotiate, in what language they can say "yes" or "no" to the other side, under what circumstances the parties must negotiate on subjects not mentioned in the agreement during the term of a contract, what items or decisions either side may negotiate for exclusive control, and a thousand and one other matters. Despite the legislative intention to foster the growth of collective bargaining, the effect of the NLRB and court cases is to attempt to reconstruct or remold collective bargaining in the image of the ideas of board members and judges who have had, with a few notable exceptions, no collective bargaining experience.

The agreement-making process cannot be enhanced by detailed public negotiation of the procedures and steps which should be followed in collective bargaining. The prescription of process cannot create the will, spirit, or interest to agree. Regulation can only prescribe the form of bargaining; and the motions required can be gone through forever by both sides, without necessarily producing agreement or improving the chance of agreement. Moreover the public determination of bargaining forms must be uniform among all parties. But one of the great advantages of collective bargaining is that each bargaining relationship will tend to develop its own procedures and practices suited to the particular problems.

The present system of regulation of collective bargaining brings the NLRB particularly into various "fights" between parties simply as a maneuver. Neither party desires the Board to be involved, but there seems to be some temporary advantage which one side feels it can enjoy and some added pressure for settlement it can put upon the other party by involving the Board. When an agreement has been reached between the parties, all charges are withdrawn from the Board before any final ruling has been issued. The Board becomes in these cases a mere catspaw in the struggle between the parties. It is simply another instrument of war in these cases. Agreement making can only be inhibited by this type of public intervention in the bargaining process, particularly where mature parties are involved.

SUGGESTIONS FOR FURTHER READING

COOK, ANNE P. (ed.). *Mature Collective Bargaining: Prospects and Problems.* Berkeley, Calif.: Institute of Industrial Relations, 1952.

HARBISON, FREDERICK H., and COLEMAN, JOHN R. *Goals and Strategy in Collective Bargaining.* New York: Harper & Bros., 1951.

JACKSON, ELMOR. *Meeting of Minds: A Way to Peace through Mediation.* New York: McGraw-Hill Book Co., 1952.

KERR, CLARK, and RANDALL, ROGER. *Crown Zellerbach and the Pacific Coast Pulp and Paper Industry.* Case Study 1, Causes of Industrial Peace under Collective Bargaining. Washington, D.C.: National Planning Association, 1948.

SHACKLE, G. L. S. *Expectation in Economics.* Cambridge, England: The University Press, 1952.

Chapter V : THE LABOR AGREEMENT

The terms and conditions of a labor agreement are designated to govern the relations between a union organization and a management. The negotiation of such an agreement is akin to the creation of a constitution. The labor contract, however, is typically limited to a specific period, such as a year, although sections of the agreement may have a longer or shorter or even an indefinite term.

The phrase "collective bargaining" is sometimes restricted to the legislative act of the creation of the charter of the relations between the parties. At other times, the term is used to include the discussions between management and union representatives under an agreement. These discussions may be of a mixed character; they may constitute the administration and interpretation of the agreement or they may consist of the creation of supplemental agreements. The administration of a contract involves judicial elements, interpreting the meaning of particular sections of the agreement. The creation of supplemental agreements is a return to legislative action. In actual practice, it is frequently impossible to separate these elements in discussions between the parties under an agreement. As a consequence, general usage loosely applies the term "collective bargaining" to all discussions between representatives of unions and managements. It is desirable for many purposes, however, to distinguish the general process of creating an agreement or supplemental agreements and the process of interpreting and administering an agreement on a day-to-day basis.

The Total Contractual Relationship

The initial contract between a union and a management is likely to be a very brief document, particularly when neither organization has had extensive collective bargaining experience. As the relationship extends over time, through successive contract negotiations, the agreement typically becomes longer and more complex. The initial contract, for instance, between the Carnegie-Illinois Steel Corporation and the Steelworkers Organizing Committee, negotiated in March, 1937, was confined to a single page. In 15 years the agreement between the United States Steel Company and the United Steelworkers of America, CIO, became a small booklet of over 75 pages of fine type. This agreement even today is a relatively simple contract if account is taken of the number of plants and employees covered.

An examination of labor agreements suggests a twofold classification: (*a*) simple agreements which are confined to a few fundamentals and procedural steps for disposing of problems as they arise, and (*b*) detailed agreements which seek to specify the rights and duties of the parties in a great variety of circumstances. These two types of agreements symbolize different conceptions of the labor-management relation. The first seeks to designate a few fundamental rights and duties and specifies procedures which the parties will employ as problems arise from day to day. This conception of the agreement is derived from the fact that it is really impossible to anticipate all the types of problems which will arise under a contract during a year. The second view may recognize the difficulties of anticipating problems, but it contends that it is better to have as many contingencies as possible reduced to writing. It is felt that this method involves less misunderstanding.

These differences in the conception of the agreement are reflected not only in its length and detail but also in the operation of the grievance procedure. The procedural type of agreement will ordinarily provide for a broader definition of problems which can be taken up as grievances. Virtually any question may be raised in some cases. The more detailed agreement is likely to limit grievances strictly to questions of interpretaton of the contract. In actual practice, it may be difficult to classify particular agreements as examples of these two extreme types.

The choice between these two types of agreements will be a distinctive feature of each labor-management relation. It is doubtful that either type is to be preferred on general grounds. The internal requirements of a union and management, the custom in the industry, and the types of problems that confront collective bargaining in the industry will be among the factors which dictate the choice between the two types. In the railroad and transit industries, for instance, where there are enormously complex questions of scheduling operations, the agreements contain many detailed rules covering this problem. In the construction industry, on the other hand, in which a particular craft performs fairly standard operations, the agreements are usually quite simple.

The total relationship between a union and a management is normally considerably broader in a number of respects than the text of the signed agreement. The contract is to be viewed as the skeleton of the relation. The parties, in a variety of ways, from day to day, build the flesh and blood of a relationship between the two organizations. The total charter of rights and duties, or the constitution, of a labor-management relationship must be broadly conceived to encompass the following items:

a) Many agreements provide for a series of supplemental agreements, or they incorporate by reference existing conditions, practices, and conditions of employment. An agreement may provide, for instance, that each plant establish a seniority agreement specifying appropriate districts and lists. Many agreements append a list of job classifications, specifying the rate for each job. Other contracts provide that the existing wage scales shall be maintained throughout the contract period, including any general wage increase or decrease provided in the agreement. Still other contract provisions may specify that the company will maintain existing benefit plans through the contract period. The actual content of the agreement thus may be very extensive by resort to incorporating existing conditions and practices.

b) The total relation must be conceived to include the interpretations of the contract that the parties have developed in the settlement of grievances or that have been established through arbitration when the parties themselves did not reach agreement on a grievance. In this fashion, the words of a contract come to have specific meaning in a variety of circumstances. In many relationships, careful records are kept of the grievances handled and the understandings achieved in particular cases. These constitute an intricate system of precedents, filling in the necessarily general provisions of a contract. In some instances, only oral understandings are made. One of the real problems of both labor and management organizations is to be certain that oral understandings between lower levels of the hierarchy do not later embarrass the policy-making levels.

c) In some relations, there is a practice to exchange letters setting forth agreement on problems discussed between representatives of the union and management organization during the contract period. These letters frequently concern problems that were not explicitly covered in the contract; they are to be regarded as a series of minor supplemental agreements. The file of these letters constitutes a significant aspect of the total relationship between the parties.

d) In some cases, the constitution and the bylaws of a union may come to have the status of a facet of the total contractual relationship. The agreement may explicitly provide, as has been the case in certain unions in the printing industry, that no union member will be required to perform any act in violation of the union constitution or bylaws. The same result may be achieved by prolonged practice and oral understanding. Under these circumstances the union may seek unilaterally to change the terms of the relationship by altering its constitution or bylaws.

e) Many managements have extensive rules and written policies requisite to their operations. At times, parts of these rules may become formally a part of the written definition of rights and duties between the parties. Thus, the agreement may provide that the company shall establish reasonable rules of discipline. Such written rules which have been unchallenged and accepted for a long period or which have been tested through the grievance procedure can be conceived as a part of the total relationship. A unilateral change by management in these rules may be challenged by the union as an unwarranted change in the relationship.

The relationship between a labor and a management organization thus consists of an agreement which may be the skeleton of the formal definition of rights and duties. There may be a variety of other formal documents comprising the total relationship— supplemental agreements, minutes of negotiations, codified practices, settled grievances, and arbitration awards. In addition, there may be a variety of practices and oral understandings. All of the factors of this relationship between the parties are meshed into the rules, regulations, and bylaws of each organization requisite to its own purely internal operation. Such is the nature of the constitution at any one time defining the total relationship between the two organizations.

Provisions of the Agreement

The provisions of agreements between various unions and managements differ widely. The reasons for these differences deserve brief attention. The effect of the length of time the parties have been dealing with each other on the detail and complexity of the agreement has already been noted. Other influences may be grouped under two headings: first, the internal requirements of the union and management organizations and, second, the objective problems with which collective bargaining must deal.

Illustrative of the first heading is the fact that some unions are impelled to bargain for a checkoff and other unions prefer the individual collection of dues as a result of tradition and policy. The steps in the grievance machinery will be adapted to the internal organization of both parties. Illustrative of the second heading is the fact that the problems of the sequence of layoffs will be different in a seasonal industry, such as clothing, from one with steady employment, such as a public utility. There are many problems unique to a piecework operation. The significance of these environmental factors on the provisions of agreements will be elaborated briefly in the next section.

Although contract terms do vary widely, a listing of the captions of the provisions of a single agreement may help to visualize the relationship of particular clauses to the total agreement. The following headings have been adapted from an agreement in the woolen and worsted industry. The agreement tends to be simple and procedural rather than detailed.

PREAMBLE AND STATEMENT OF PURPOSE

ARTICLE

   I. Bargaining unit, or definition of employees covered by the agreement
       Form of union security and checkoff

  II. Powers and duties of the employer

 III. Wages
       Provisions for a general increase
       Wage reopening during contract period
       Revision of rates on particular jobs when there is a change in method or work load

Reporting time
Shift premiums
Equal pay for women when performing the same work as men
Rates applicable when employees transferred
Waiting time under piece rates

IV. Hours of work
Overtime pay schedules
Holiday pay

V. Vacation pay

VI. Group life, accident, and health insurance

VII. Bulletin boards

VIII. Grievance procedure

IX. Discharge cases

X. Arbitration

XI. Seniority
Seniority districts
Seniority lists
Probationary periods
Layoff and recalls
Promotions
Transfers
Top seniority
Leave of absence
Termination of seniority and employment

XII. Military service

XIII. Term of the agreement

A brief examination of the above captions will indicate that these provisions may be grouped under a more limited number of headings: the bargaining unit (I), the rights of the management and union organizations (I and II), compensation of employees (III, IV, V, VI), the grievance procedure (VIII, IX, X), the relative rights of different employees to particular jobs (XI), and the term of the agreement (XIII). These headings in variant forms appear in the great majority of agreements.

The Influence of Environment on Contract Provisions

It is easy to overemphasize the role of personal and accidental factors in collective bargaining. It is difficult to discern the persistent and underlying forces at work in the bargaining process. Yet the provisions of agreements—the policies agreed upon by

unions and managements—fundamentally reflect the more endur-
ing features of the environment of the collective bargaining
relationship. This fundamental fact must be perceived or collective bargaining will appear capricious.

Some agreements provide for piece rates; in other cases
neither party would accept a piecework system. Some agreements
provide for layoffs by seniority; others require that a reduction in
work be spread evenly among all employees. Some agreements
permit any disagreement or difference between the parties to be
raised as a grievance, while other contracts explicitly limit the
grievance machinery to questions of interpretation. Some agreements provide that the wage rate for a particular job classification
may be re-examined at any time; others provide for a fixed wage
scale during the life of the agreement, except for changes in job
content. If these types of differences are to be understood, the
influence of the environment in which the parties negotiate and
operate must be discerned.

The term "environment" is used in this discussion to signify
a number of influences exterior to the union and the management
which shape and mold the problems with which negotiators must
grapple. These factors characteristically limit the range of discretion of the parties. It is convenient to think of these environmental
factors under three headings.

a) The technological and physical characteristics of the
industry and its operation will decisively affect the problems posed
for collective bargaining and the range of answers that can be
found. The intermittent and casual nature of employment in the
longshore and construction industries helps to account for the
emergence of the closed shop with the union-controlled hiring
hall to allocate the employment opportunities. The physical
necessity for peak loads in the morning and evening rush hours
in the transit industry creates problems that are the subject of
extended rules in the agreement. The fact of increasing speeds
of airplanes created a divergence of views on methods of wage
payment, with the union favoring pay per mile and the companies pay per hour. The method of payment finally accepted
involves a compromise, with the wage rate including both hourly
and mileage elements. The variation in the quality of yarn and
the unevenness in the flow of work in the textile industries create
the necessity for guarantees and other features of piece-rate

systems. These illustrations could be multiplied endlessly, yet they should indicate that the keen observer of collective bargaining will seek out the technological and physical factors that create problems for the parties and fashion the particular labor-management relationship.

b) The market and competitive features of the firm and industry will decisively shape the collective bargaining relationship. The uniformity in timing of wage changes among companies in the basic steel industry is to be attributed to pricing arrangements and practice within the industry. The prevalence of arbitration in the transit industry is largely the result of the practice of setting fares by a public regulatory body. The great world-wide shortage of coal after 1940 is probably basically responsible for the fact that the wage rates in the coal industry in most countries have risen relatively to one of the highest in the structure of wage rates. The large number of small firms in such industries as women's clothing and millinery, combined with their weak competitive position in dealing with buyers of their products, account for the fact that the unions in these fields have used the collective bargaining mechanism to affect competitive conditions in the industries. The competitive relations among a group of firms will account frequently for the timing of expiration dates of contracts.

c) The relations of a union to other unions and a management to other managements are a decisive feature of the environment in which collective bargaining operates. The idea can be generalized to encompass all industrial relations ties. Thus, when Mr. Murray and Mr. Lewis were rival leaders of American labor, the contract developments in the coal industry were of additional significance to the total environment and climate of basic steel negotiations. Or, a machine tool company located in a predominantly textile or steel community may be compelled to follow the wage patterns of these industries by virtue of the overwhelming influence of this feature of its environment. A collective bargaining relationship may have developed into following the leadership of another bargaining relationship. Or, a rival and factional condition within a local union may compel concessions to a particular group of employees, or a larger wage increase, simply to secure a settlement.

The relative importance of these industrial relations dependencies to contract provisions varies considerably. These factors are likely to be most decisive where rival unionism and internal factionalism is most keen. These rivalries and factions are temporary in many cases, although some have persisted for many years. The technological and competitive features of the environment in which collective bargaining takes place are likely to be most decisive in contract provisions where factionalism and rivalries are relatively insignificant.

The recognition of these external or environmental factors in a collective bargaining relation will guard against the fallacy that negotiators have almost limitless discretion and that relative "bargaining power" is the final arbiter in all negotiations. If bargaining power is understood to include a reflection of these environmental factors, there may be little basis for quarrel. But at times the term implies arbitrary and capricious results in the bargaining process. The fundamental point is that both the problems of collective bargaining and the resulting contract provisions are decisively shaped by the total environment, regarded as the technological, competitive, and industrial relations context in which the parties bargain.

One illustration of the necessity of recognizing the influence of these environmental factors is provided by an examination of the action of the Congress in seeking to eliminate the closed shop in the Labor-Management Relations Act (1947). The Congress appeared to find the closed shop in conflict with certain individual rights which it regarded as fundamental. On the level of moral principle, it seemed to contend that no man should have to join a union in order to secure a job, although it would be all right for him to have to join in thirty days' time under an authorized union shop. The Congress appeared to believe that the distinction between a closed shop and a union shop was arbitrary and followed from the greater bargaining power, or abuse of that power, on the part of a union.

The simple fact is, however, that the collective bargaining process over the years had developed closed shops in those sectors of the economy where special problems existed which could not be handled under union-shop provisions. Thus, the fact that unions in the building and construction industry were characteristically used as a source of supply of skilled labor by itinerant contractors, frequently engaged on projects of a short duration, accounts for the existence of the closed shop. The closed shop is thus deeply rooted in the characteristics and environment of the industry. It serves a particular purpose. It is already apparent that the law has not altered such deeply rooted institutions.

The moral of the story is not that the closed shop is above abuse or beyond the scope of legislation. Rather, the point is that the attempt to draw a line between a closed shop and a union shop without regard to the environmental factors which basically produced the closed shop was doomed to failure. The influence of the total environment will claim the attention of the person seeking to explain collective bargaining contract provisions.

The Grievance Procedure

Just as the grievance machinery was found to be one of the principal facets of management and union organization for collective bargaining, so does it constitute one of the major provisions of an agreement. As with all the mechanics of collective bargaining, the parties can mold and fashion the grievance procedure in a variety of ways to their special problems. The grievance procedure may serve many diverse purposes in a collective bargaining relationship, depending upon the language of the agreement and the intention of both parties.

a) The grievance procedure may be used to locate problem situations in the relations between a union and management and to discern difficulties within both organizations. From this vantage point, the explicit grievance is not to be taken at its face value. The real problem may be a foreman or a shop steward. It may be evident that subordinates are not receiving proper instructions. The grievance is seen as a symbol of some maladjustment, and the skillful representative of the union or management will seek out the real and submerged difficulties.

So also in the complaints of single employees there may be little overt basis for the grievance; but the real difficulty may be a health condition, or a family situation, or a long standing personality problem (see Section A, Part Two). In a day when more than 60 per cent of the visits to the doctors' offices of the country are found to have a psychic rather than a purely physical basis, it should not be surprising that a large proportion of grievances of individual employees should also have their roots in psychic difficulties. A careful study of British experience[1] has shown that 30 per cent of factory employees suffer from some form of neurosis. The well-known fact that many grievances are filed by the same persons is a reflection of the problems of individual adjustment that are involved.

The clinical approach to a grievance must be used with care. Such an approach is likely to be inappropriate for most grievances filed by groups of employees or by the union and management as such. The problems of individual personalities must not be allowed so to engross the attention of representatives of both sides that they overlook the task of accommodating the two organizations. There is no question, however, that the grievance procedure can be made to serve the function of discovering problem situations, both of individuals and of parts of the organization, when the grievance is approached as a symbol of some maladjustment.

b) The grievance procedure may be utilized by both organizations as a device by which information is channeled both ways between the top and the bottom of the hierarchy. In language that has become popular, the grievance procedure is a channel of communication. The top-management officers and the union leaders who follow carefully the status of grievances are frequently able to keep in touch with developments at the level of the individual worker. New problems are rapidly reflected in the grievance procedure.

As a channel of information, the grievance procedure is likely to be more reliable than most chains of command in a hierarchy, since both the union and management (steward and foreman or plant manager and business agent) are aware that the grievance may go a step higher or even to arbitration. Any statement they make will be subject to check by the other side before a superior officer. In this way the grievance procedure as a channel of information may be expected to be less subject to self-serving statements of fact than most chains of command within an organization.

In most grievance procedures, when a unique problem is presented, there may be considerable advance consultation with higher levels of authority before action on a case at a lower stage.

[1] Russell Fraser, *The Incidence of Neuroses among Factory Workers*, Great Britain Industrial Health Research Board Report 90 (London, 1947).

This practice may be carried to the detrimental extreme in which all decisions are, in fact, made at the top. The practice of advance consultation, however, is indicative of the way in which the grievance procedure is used as a channel of information and policy making within an organization.

c) The explicit purpose of the grievance procedure is to interpret the provisions of the agreement, to apply the contract to the new and changing aspects of everyday relations between a union and a management. This procedure must translate the necessarily general language of a contract into particular decisions in specific cases. It will also be used to achieve uniformity of interpretation in various units of management and divisions of the union.

The grievance procedure is related to the periodic negotiations of a new agreement in at least three ways. First, the general policies and language agreed upon in contract negotiations, as has been noted, are applied through this procedure. In this sense the grievance procedure is sometimes referred to as "collective bargaining." Second, the contract negotiations may re-examine and alter interpretations established by the grievance procedure. One side or the other may request a reconsideration of the whole problem in the light of experience. Third, the grievance procedure discovers and records many problems which one side or the other may wish to raise at the next contract negotiations period.

d) The contract language of some grievance procedures is so broad as to permit the raising of any problem or difficulty that may arise. The procedure may not be limited to contract interpretation. Under these circumstances the whole relationship of the parties may be shaped through the grievance procedure. Each side is committed to discuss and settle any question that may be raised during the contract period. The grievance machinery in these circumstances serves the purpose of providing an orderly and systematic way in which problems may be studied and decided.

It is apparent that a grievance procedure may serve a variety of purposes. In a single union-management relation, the two organizations may not necessarily regard the grievance procedure in the same light or expect from it the same results. Thus, any particular grievance may have many facets, and there will be a variety of types of grievances.

There are undoubtedly a great many ways of classifying the types of grievances that arise. It may be helpful to consider grievances in their relation to the contract and to the two organizations as follows: (1) Some grievances involve a conflict between two or more sections of the agreement. The union will point to one clause, and the company will refer to another. The problem may involve a reconciliation or clarification of conflicting sections of the agreement. (2) The contract may be silent on the specific problem. The issue may clearly involve a subject treated in the agreement; in this sense the grievance is within the scope of the agreement. The problem in such a grievance is to fill in the gap in the agreement. (3) The grievance may raise the question of the applicability of a general rule to a particular case. (4) Some grievances present exceptional circumstances, the type of situation no general rule or regulation can be formulated to handle. (5) At times a grievance presents no contract problems but arises as a device to "save face" for one side or the other. A union or management representative may find it expedient to pass along a grievance rather than to make an obvious settlement. These various types of grievances are represented in the cases that have been selected for this volume.

The Arbitration Step

Arbitration is the final step in the grievance procedure. Just as with other aspects of the grievance procedure, the parties may mold and shape this step to their special problems and predilections. There are a variety of ways in which the last step may be arranged. These various systems will influence the results of arbitration and the confidence which each organization will have in its operation.

The parties may select a number of different arrangements regarding the neutral person in arbitration. Some contracts provide for a single *impartial umpire*. A continuing relationship has the advantage that the neutral becomes familiar with the technical operations of the industry, with the special problems of internal organization of both parties, and with the personalities on each side. Where the parties intend to present a great many cases to a neutral, the continuing umpire eliminates the time and energy required to select an arbitrator for each case. A variant of the impartial umpire arrangement provides for a panel of three or five names from which a single name may be selected when a case reaches the final step. Other contracts provide for a succession of *ad hoc* arbitrators selected for a single case or a group of grievances. In this way the parties may select a neutral whose background qualifies him to solve the special problems of a particular case. The parties may also have in mind the fact that an arbitrator may become too familiar with a relationship; they would prefer to take a chance on a new man.

The parties may shape the arbitration process in another way by electing to associate with a neutral a representative from each side. The result is a *tripartite arbitration board.* This board may in turn be a continuing-umpire arrangement or a case-by-case appointment. The addition of a representative from each side has the advantage of giving the parties a method of directing and channeling the mind of the neutral. When problems are complex and technically peculiar to an industry, the arrangement has advantages. It permits the neutral to establish through these representatives on the board particularly close relations with both sides.

In some tripartite boards the chairman alone has a vote, while in others the parties provide that a majority vote shall decide the case. The difference between these forms of arbitration can be substantial. When the chairman alone has a vote, he may decide the case as he sees it. When a majority vote is required for a decision, he may have to compromise his position in order to secure the vote of one representative or the other. In cases in which the parties are quite far apart and the neutral finds neither position acceptable, the requirement of a majority vote may introduce a three-way bargaining process into arbitration or may even deadlock the arbitration board.

The parties may further influence the arbitration process by the arrangements agreed upon for the selection of the neutral. The role of the parties is greatest when they agree in advance upon a simple umpire or upon a panel of names. Their role is less prominent when they simply agree upon an agency to appoint the neutral. The agencies most commonly designated in contracts are the Federal Mediation and Conciliation Service and the American Arbitration Association, the latter a private organization. Both of these agencies have attempted to restore to the parties some participation and responsibility for the selection of the arbitrator by furnishing a list of names from which the parties may agree upon the neutral. The role of the parties in the selection is ordinarily least when they merely designate a person, such as a governor or a judge, to name the neutral.

The precise language of the issue presented in arbitration is shaped by the parties. The definition of the issue is decisive to the results of arbitration. On many occasions when the parties may not be able to agree on a grievance, they can agree on the formulation of the issue to be arbitrated. The decisive nature of the definition of the issue in dispute is illustrated in the cases presented in this volume.

The arbitration process in the relationship between a particular union and management will be shaped by the internal policies of each toward arbitration. For instance, either side may follow a policy of carefully screening cases that go to arbitration. The objective may be to present only "good cases" so that the record before the arbitrator of cases won will be as nearly perfect as possible. This record may be intended to create the impression in negotiations with the other side over a grievance that, whenever arbitration is threatened, the other side ought to concede the case. The policy may be effective in doubtful cases and may be instrumental in reducing the number of grievances. The policy may be derived from a desire to avoid the creation of precedents that may be unfortunate. If an issue is to be tested in arbitration, a careful selection of cases may be made to secure the most favorable case on which to contest the issue.

Another possible policy in arbitration may be designated as the "percentage theory." Either side may elect to present any doubtful case to arbitration on the theory that arbitrators will tend to compromise as among cases. On this basis, the party following this policy may expect to win certain points that it might otherwise have conceded.

In a given union-management relationship, the parties may adopt opposite policies; one side may elect to screen cases carefully and the other may adopt the percentage theory. It is basically for this reason that the "box score" of cases won or lost in arbitration decisions is meaningless. One side may be carefully selecting cases, and the other side may be permitting any case to go through to arbitration.

Two statements are made about the arbitration process, both

of which have a measure of truth. Neither is a complete description by itself. It is said that "arbitration is an extension of collective bargaining." It is also held that "arbitration is a judicial process." The simple fact is that the arbitration process is flexible. While both elements are involved in most cases, the parties are in a position to alter the proportions of collective bargaining and judicial content within very wide limits. The careful specification of the issues in dispute, the designation of a single arbitrator, and a contract which provides only for the arbitration of questions of interpretation of the agreement—all tend to increase the judicial element. The absence of a clearly defined issue, a three-man board with a majority vote, and the possibility of arbitrating "any difficulty or problem" arising during the contract period tend to enhance the collective bargaining feature of an arbitration. If one examines the arbitration arrangements between a great many unions and managements, it will be evident that actual experience runs the full range of these extremes.

SUGGESTIONS FOR FURTHER READING

DIVISION OF LABOR STANDARDS, DEPARTMENT OF LABOR. *Settling Plant Grievances.* Bulletin 60. Washington, D.C., 1943.

GARDINER, GLENN. *When Foreman and Steward Bargain.* New York: McGraw-Hill Book Co., 1945.

KENNEDY, THOMAS. *Effective Labor Arbitration, The Impartial Chairmanship of the Full-Fashioned Hosiery Industry.* Philadelphia: University of Pennsylvania Press, 1948.

ROETHLISBERGER, F. S. *Management and Morale.* Cambridge, Mass.: Harvard University Press, 1946.

SELEKMAN, BENJAMIN M. *Labor Relations and Human Relations.* New York: McGraw-Hill Book Co., 1947.

SLICHTER, SUMNER H. *Union Policies and Industrial Management.* Washington, D.C.: The Brookings Institution, 1941.

| Chapter | STANDARDS FOR WAGE |
| VI | DETERMINATION[1] |

The debate over wage rates in the public press and in proceedings between management and labor organizations has popularized economic analysis of wage setting. A limited number of cliches or standard arguments have come into use, which are employed by the side that regards them as most effective at the time in negotiation or in arbitration proceedings. Illustrative of these phrases are "comparable wages," "productivity," "cost of living," and "ability to pay." These slogans are not the distinctive trade-mark of any one side. Either party may use one of these arguments today and repudiate it tomorrow as a factor in wage determination under a different set of circumstances.

The interest in arguments and slogans in wage negotiations has increased spectacularly in recent years with the growth of private arbitration, the participation of government in wage setting through the machinery of the Railway Labor Act, the wartime experience under the National War Labor Board, the postwar vogue of fact-finding boards and boards of inquiry, and the wage stabilization program of the Korean crisis. The employment by management and labor organizations of technicians, such as lawyers, economists, statisticians, accountants, actuaries, industrial engineers, and publicists, who produce voluminous briefs and statistical appendices, has given wide currency to such wage-determining principles or slogans.

The purpose of this chapter is to appraise some of the more prominent arguments and slogans used in wage negotiations. Much of the discussion will be devoted to exploring problems that

[1] The chapter is adapted from an article by John T. Dunlop, "The Economics of Wage Dispute Settlement," *Law and Contemporary Problems,* Spring, 1947, pp. 281–96. In connection with this chapter, see the cases in Section H of Part Two, below.

arise in giving meaning to these standards and in translating them into definitely measurable guides to decisions in particular situations. The problems will be found to be stubborn and not always tractable. This emphasis is not, however, fundamentally defeatist with respect to the contribution of economics to wage-dispute settlement. The identification of problems is the beginning of economic wisdom.

Comparable Wage Rates

No argument is employed more frequently in wage discussions than that wage rates in one bargaining unit should be equalized with, or related by a particular differential to, wage rates in other "comparable" bargaining units. While other arguments are more decisive in the "key" wage bargains affecting the general level of wage rates, the appeal to comparable rates is frequently employed in transmitting the impact of these critical decisions through the rest of the wage structure. Resort to this standard is also frequently the basis for the numerous changes in differentials that are made among occupations, plants, and industries each year.

The principle that wage rates in one bargaining unit should be adjusted to the level of wage rates in comparable plants has an alluring simplicity. The economist indicates that in equilibrium the same wage rate will be paid in a "market" for a specified type of labor service. The slogan "equal pay for equal work" commands wide support. However, for reasons which will now be surveyed, the illusion of simplicity vanishes in the attempt to give meaning to the concept of "comparable" wage rates in any particular situation.

1. The content of job classifications designated by the same job title varies widely among different employers. The range of duties assigned to a single worker has not been as standardized among plants as is widely assumed. The varying ages and types of equipment, the differing scales of operation between large and small plants, the variations in plant layout and work flows, and the different techniques of various managers are factors making for different job contents among firms producing roughly similar goods. Various arrangements may be made, for instance, in machine operations for the cleaning, oiling, and greasing of equipment. The flow of materials to a machine and the handling

of processed parts and waste products permit different plans of organization. The extent of supervision and inspection in a job may also vary widely from one plant to another.

For instance, a study of the distribution of spinning-room duties in forty-seven cotton textile firms divided the work of five customary job classifications—spinner, cleaner, oiler, sweeper, and doffer—into twenty-five separate operations.[2] No two of the mills divided these operations in the same way among the job classifications. Except for the operation of "creeling" and "piecing up," performed by the spinner in all cases, no operation was assigned to the same job classification in all mills. The total duties of the spinner varied from these two operations in one mill to as many as ten in another. The comparison of the wage rates by job classification among these various cotton textile mills under these circumstances requires a certain amount of temerity.

2. Comparability in wage rates is impaired by variations in the method of wage payment. Some workers and job classifications are remunerated on an hourly-rate basis, others are on individual piece rates or incentive rates, while still others are paid on group incentive plans. The content of job classifications may be identical, but the amount of services performed and purchased will ordinarily vary with the method of wage payment. Commission methods of wage payment add the further complexity of variations in the price structures of the products being sold. Among incentive systems there are substantial differences in the definitions of the "standard performance" and the extent of "incentive pull" for additional output. The provisions regarding minimum guarantees, including rates for machine breakdowns, poor materials, etc., and the method of calculating these guarantees—by day, by week, or other period—affect the meaning of interplant comparisons of wages.

3. The influence of regularity of employment upon wage rates must be assessed in defining comparable wages. The level of rates for maintenance occupations with steady employment is frequently, although not always, below the level of rates for the same crafts engaged in seasonal construction work. While there are some important differences in job content, the regularity of employment is usually indicated as the principal reason for

[2] Presented as an exhibit before the National War Labor Board in the cotton textile cases decided February 20, 1945, *War Labor Report*, Vol. XXI, p. 793.

this difference. The difference between wages of mechanics in the repair shops of taxicabs and truck companies and those of their fellow-craftsmen in commercial garages also reflects the factor of regularity of employment, although job content and methods of wage payment again differ. In fact, wage rates in "captive" departments of a company with relatively steady work opportunities are typically below those of the "outside" or "contract" firm with greater fluctuations in available work. Comparison of two groups of employees for wage-setting purposes will be complicated by the task of assessing the extent to which wage rates reflect differences in the regularity of employment.

4. The terms and conditions of employment typically include not only the occupational rate but also other "money" conditions, such as shift premiums, vacations and holidays with pay, sick leave, pensions, social and health insurance, paid lunch periods, Christmas bonuses, etc., to mention the more prominent terms. The total contract of employment involves many other items that are less immediately "money" terms, such as union recognition, seniority, management rights and grievance machinery, and arbitration. In the bargaining process, there is frequently give-and-take among the "money" terms. Substitution is likely among basic rate adjustments and shift premiums, vacations, and health insurance plans. There may even be important trades between the "money" items and other provisions of a contract. Comparison of wage rates under these circumstances may become particularly tenuous.

5. The geographical implications of "comparable wages" can be most perplexing. The concept of a "labor market" has no unique correspondence in geopraphy. Specifying the labor market in accordance with the cost of transportation or the knowledge of job and wage opportunities does not yield precise results. The inclusion of suburbs and satellite communities in a grouping has definite effects. The War Labor Board for the Boston Region was plagued throughout the war with the question whether to include Torrington (16 miles away) in the Waterbury, Connecticut, labor market for metal-trades occupations. The areas of uniformity of wage rates may vary widely among occupations even in the same industry. In the construction industry the rate for ironworkers typically extends over many counties or even a state, while the rate for laborers is usually confined to each com-

munity. The areas of uniformity have been extended in recent years, although uniformity appears to be greater in periods of high employment than in loose labor markets. If the standard of comparable wages is to be employed, we cannot escape the difficult task of defining the geographical limits of the appropriate labor market.

6. The complications of "comparable" wage determination developed so far in this section relate to labor-market difficulties. They derive from comparing the exact work performed by the wage earners in different bargaining units or from what are essentially labor-market influences on wage rates. However, another group of problems must be faced in giving meaning to "comparable wage rates." These have their roots in the product market or, more precisely, in the divergent competitive positions of the firms employing the wage earners.

Business enterprises are ordinarily regarded as clustering into industries, segments, or smaller groups among which product competition is relatively closer than with firms outside the group. But every business, except for a few cases of perfectly competitive markets, has its specialized market and clientele. The grouping of firms according to similarity of product-market conditions is a convention always subject to further subdivision. The definition of these clusters of "comparable" firms is probably as difficult as any issue in applying the wage standard discussed in this section. Moreover, a large number of firms appear to have relatively unique product markets where any comparison with other firms is most difficult.

The local transit industry includes primary and feeder-line companies; hotels are divided into first-line and several other classes; bakeries may be classified as large-scale businesses and specialty shops. Are the larger or smaller units appropriate for comparison? The trucking firms in an area may be subdivided into over-the-road and local trucking enterprises. The latter may be classified in turn into product groups—oil, coal, grocery, department store, contract, express, etc. Any one of these groups, such as oil, in turn could be further subdivided into: national distributors, local companies, home delivery, industrial uses, etc. While many of these groupings are associated with important differences in job content (type of equipment) and method of wage payment, competitive conditions among these various groups of firms no doubt vary widely. The important question is to determine when these differences in competitive conditions are so significant as to warrant a separate wage determination regardless of labor-market influences.

The problem may be posed even more sharply by an instance in which labor-market influences are relatively more uniform than in the trucking case. An engine-lathe operator may work for companies ordinarily classified in such groups as electrical machinery, textile machinery, machine tools, and shoe machinery. In determining the "comparable" wage rates, what grouping of firms should be selected?

There can be little doubt that wage rates do, in fact, vary by virtue of the influence of divergent product-market conditions. Maintenance workers, for instance, have rates that vary substantially through the range of industries, even where job content is quite similar. The choice of groupings among firms presents the most difficult of problems.

The foregoing discussion of six groups of problems is adequate to divest the slogan or standard of "comparable wages" of any alluring simplicity. It is doubtful that there are any royal answers to these problems in principle or in measurement. The difficulties arising from the product market can be mitigated, however, if agreement is secured from the parties as to a list of comparable firms. This device has been used frequently by mediators.

Many of these problems involved in giving meaning to the standard of "comparable wages" are more difficult in the abstract than in their actual application to a particular case. In many cases conventions develop over time, and the wage rates in a particular firm are related to changes in wage rates in a particular grouping of firms. However, difficulties may arise when one party or the other desires to change such a traditional relationship. In such a case the argument over the appropriate grouping of firms with which to make comparisons starts all over again.

Productivity

No argument is used with more conviction or sophistication than that wages should vary with changes in productivity. In the mid-twenties, the American Federal of Labor adopted the policy that wage earners should share in rising productivity in the form of wage-rate increases. In recent days management, editorial writers, economists, and some labor leaders have been preaching that increased productivity alone provides the basis for wage increases. These views have normally been associated with the conviction that wage rates have already outstripped productivity. The General Motors—UAW contract in 1950 for a five-year term with an annual improvement factor has helped to popularize productivity as a factor in wage setting. (See Case 50.) As part of the mores or folklore of an industrial community, there may be little objection to the contention that productivity is a basis for increases in the general level of wage rates in the long run. As a guide or a rule of thumb in any particular negotiation, the principle has grave difficulties which may be briefly summarized.

1. The rate of change in productivity in our economic system varies widely among the component segments. Within an industry the rate is normally quite different among firms. Even within a firm or plant the rate varies among departments, machines, and operations. The wage structure of a particular plant or department, if it were geared absolutely to changes in productivity, would soon become intolerable. Employees in continuous strip mills and on tin-plate operations in the steel industry, for instance, would have had enormous wage increases in the last twenty years in comparison with employees in other sectors of the industry. Under such circumstances the wage structure would bear very little relationship to skill, experience, or other factors typically taken into account in settling rate structures. Nor would the wage structure bear any relationship to wages paid for comparable operations in other industries in steel centers. The exclusive adoption of the principle of adjustment according to changes in productivity would result within a very short time in an utterly chaotic wage structure within a single plant or industry.

In the same way, the adjustment of wage levels among industries exclusively in proportion to productivity would distort the wage structure of the country. Industries in which productivity increased rapidly would experience large wage increases; while in others in which productivity did not increase or actually declined (especially in extractive industries), wage rates would remain relatively unchanged. Either as a matter of allocation of resources or as a means to the maintenance of industrial peace, the absolute adoption of such a principle for determining the structure of wages among industries would be a catastrophe.

The movement of productivity, as best we can measure it, is not steady from year to year. If wage rates were precisely geared to productivity, on a year-to-year basis, wage movements would be quite erratic and would not accommodate to other necessities for wage changes.[3]

All this is not to say that changes in productivity do not have effects upon the structure of wages within plants or among industries. It can be established, for instance, that wages in the last twenty-five years have increased more rapidly than the average in those industries in which employment and productivity have increased more rapidly than the average. Similarly, the wages have increased less rapidly than the average in those industries in which employment and productivity have either increased less rapidly than the average or actually declined. A substantial part of the increase in productivity, where productivity is increasing fastest, is translated into price declines, increases in profits, and improvements in quality.[4]

2. The term "productivity" seems to have a fascination that impels many devotees to regard it as a formula for wage adjustments. The measurement of productivity presents, however, one of the most difficult problems of economic analysis, econometrics, and statistical measurement. The customary measure of productivity is "output per man-hour," a measure secured by dividing a measure of product in physical units by a measure of man-hour inputs.

In many industries the task of constructing an index of physical production is formidable, if not impossible. There may be many different products, and their proportions in total output, or the "product-mix," may change frequently. While changes in quality and specifications will be particularly important in a job-order business, these factors are present to some extent in almost every case.[5]

3. Between any two periods, output per man-hour may vary

[3] Clark Kerr, "The Short-Run Behavior of Physical Productivity and Average Hourly Earnings," *Review of Economics and Statistics,* November, 1949, pp. 299–309.

[4] See John T. Dunlop, "Productivity and the Wage Structure" in *Income, Employment and Public Policy: Essays in Honor of Alvin H. Hansen* (New York: W. W. Norton & Co., Inc., 1948), pp. 341–62.

[5] See Solomon Fabricant, *Labor Savings in American Industry, 1899–1939,* National Bureau of Economic Research Occasional Paper 23 (New York, 1945).

as a result of a great many different factors, among which are the following: a change in the level of output, a change in the composition of production, changes in the average effectiveness of plant and equipment (as a result of scrapping obsolete facilities and bringing in new ones), increased effort and application on the part of the work force, a change in the composition of the work force, improvements in earlier stages of production (as in the concerns which supply materials and parts), and the substitution of other factors for labor as a result of a wage-rate increase. These circumstances are hardly equally valid bases for an increase in wage rates in a particular plant or company.[6]

In negotiations and public discussion, little effort has been made to separate the effects of these factors influencing "productivity" in the sense of output per man-hour. The union may argue, on the basis of general knowledge of the industry, that productivity increases which have taken place provide a basis for wage increases.

Evidence of changes in productivity is not readily transformed into cents-per-hour wage adjustments. In a number of industries, such as local transit and utilities, wage costs are to some extent a fixed cost, so that changes in output substantially influence output per man-hour. A higher wage rate in some industries may induce more careful inspection or use of higher-quality materials. Such a change would be reflected in output per man-hour. As has been indicated, these various types of factors affecting output per man-hour are not equally valid grounds for a wage-rate adjustment. Not only is the measurement of changes in productivity difficult, but their interpretation for relevant wage negotiations is even more ambiguous.

4. Depending upon the precise meaning given to the productivity argument, the problem of the relation of wage changes to declines in productivity may have to be faced. In the normal case, changes in productivity may be regarded as typically in one direction. There are instances, however, in which performance per average-unit-of-labor input may decline as a result of the exhaustion of a resource, the use of a less-skilled labor force on the average, or as the result of less-intensive application. Under these circumstances is there an argument for a wage decrease?

[6] See *Cost Behavior and Price Policy* (New York: National Bureau of Economic Research, 1943), pp. 142–69.

Cost of Living

The change in the Consumers' Price Index[7] has been used, at least during some periods, as a standard to determine changes in wage rates. The relative emphasis on the cost of living by management and labor organizations depends on whether living costs are rising or falling. The attention given to this influence in wage discussions is greatest during periods of pronounced changes in living costs. In a number of collective bargaining situations, sliding scales or escalator arrangements have been established to adjust wage rates automatically to changes in the cost-of-living index. The more typical case involves using the cost-of-living argument as one factor among many in negotiations or in other forms of wage fixing.

As an absolute principle of wage determination, the cost of living has severe limitations:

1. The cost-of-living index typically contains important components, such as food and rent, whose price movements are not necessarily good barometers of the change in other wage-determining factors. For reasons peculiar to agriculture and housing, these prices may be out of line relative to the general level of prices. If this were the case, there would be serious question as to the propriety of altering the general level of wage rates, or any rate, by the application of the cost-of-living standard. There have been periods, such as the twenties, in which industrial prosperity has been associated with agricultural depression. To contend that this fact should be binding in industrial wage-rate determination is dubious, just as a temporary rise in the cost of living arising from a disappointing harvest would hardly be regarded as a conclusive basis for an upward revision in industrial wage-rate levels.

The absolute application of the cost-of-living standard would force practically uniform wage-rate adjustments in all cases. (Admittedly, there are minor geographical variations in rates of change in the cost-of-living index.) But there may be occasion for important variations in the rates of change in wages among firms and industries.

[7] In 1945 the Bureau of Labor Statistics changed the name of its index to "Consumers' Price Index for Moderate-Income Families in Large Cities." This index "measures average changes in retail prices of goods, rents, and services purchased by wage earners and lower-salaried workers in large cities." For a description and appraisals of the Revised Consumers' Price Index, see *Monthly Labor Review*, February, 1953, pp. 161–75.

2. Labor organizations have frequently indicated that application of the cost-of-living principle over any considerable period would result in a stationary real standard of living for wage earners. The gains of productivity in our system have normally been translated in part into increases in wages and salaries. The rigid application of the slogan of cost of living would result in a stationary real wage rate.

3. Mention may be made briefly of the difficulties of measuring changes in the cost of living. These problems received widespread attention during World War II.[8] It is not always clear whether the proponents of the principle in collective bargaining are interested in measuring the price of a constant bundle of goods and services, or whether they are attempting to measure the change in average expenditures. The latter concept includes the effect of changes in income levels, the effects of administering price structures so as to make available particular price lines of commodities and "forced" substitutions of the type necessitated by wartime conditions.

4. The application of any cost-of-living principle to wage determination must surmount the difficult problem of an appropriate base period. If wages are to be adjusted to the changes in the cost of living, there must be some starting point. The unions normally would select the period of the last wage change, in cases of increasing cost of living, while employers would emphasize the point that some more representative period of real earnings should be selected.

5. Automatic adjustment of the general level of wage rates to the cost-of-living index is not always appropriate policy. There may be times of high employment and output in which such a policy would result in cumulative wage and price increases. High employment is always loaded with inflationary dangers, and wage-rate adjustments at such periods must be approached with care in order to avoid unstabilizing consequences.

Ability to Pay

The slogan, "ability to pay," has received particular attention in the course of postwar wage discussions in the public press and

---

[8] *Report of the President's Committee on the Cost of Living* (Washington, D.C.: Office of Economic Stabilization, 1945). The various reports by labor and management representatives and by technical experts are appended.

before fact-finding bodies. The argument is not new; probably it is as old as collective bargaining. In its simplest form the argument should be looked upon as a mere reflex of a wage demand. A union would not normally make a wage demand without at the same time stating that the demand could be met. There are, no doubt, some exceptions to this view, as in cases involving marginal concerns; but a union cannot make a demand with conviction unless it also implies that the company or industry can afford the wage increase. In much the same way, in the initial stages of bargaining, the employer in rejecting the demand almost has to imply as a stratagem that it cannot be afforded. There are situations in which a company rejects a demand, admitting that it can afford the requested adjustment; but these are not typical circumstances. On the most elemental plane, consequently, statements regarding ability to pay have been necessary adjuncts to the demand or to the rejection of the demand.

Any discussion of ability to pay in more serious terms in wage negotiations necessarily raises a host of conceptual and statistical problems regarding the meaning of the phrase in any particular case. Among the more prominent of these problems are the following:

1. What is the period over which one is concerned with ability to pay? A firm may be able to pay a specific increase for a short period but not for a longer one. A large part of the difficulties in the postwar period arose from the fact that the unions demanded immediate wage adjustments, while the view of many companies in the reconversion industries was that wage adjustments should be postponed until output had been raised to more nearly normal conditions. Here was a conflict concerning the period of time to be considered in decisions concerning ability to pay.

2. How shall one estimate the effect of wage-rate changes on costs? This question involves the problem of labor productivity, which is dependent not alone on the efforts of wage earners but also on the flow of materials and supplies and the effectiveness of management organization. In estimating the effect of wage-rate changes on costs, a decision must also be made on the allowance, if any, to be made for the indirect effects of the wage adjustment on materials, prices, purchased parts, and equipment.

3. The volume of production will no doubt materially affect

ability of an enterprise to pay wages. This difficulty concerns not merely the level of production but also the way in which production may be distributed among different types of goods (broadly, the product-mix), particularly among high- and low-profit items.

4. The character of competition in the markets in which the products must be sold will substantially affect the ability to pay wage increases. These circumstances will influence the extent to which wage adjustments may be translated into price increases and the effect of such adjustments upon volume of output.

5. The rate of return on investment to which the company is regarded as entitled will create a problem in determining the ability to pay wages. The familiar complications that have arisen in the regulation of public utilities indicate that this is not a problem to be treated lightly. Differing views on rates of return and valuation will significantly influence the content of the ability-to-pay slogan.

6. The ability to pay wage increases before and after income taxes will vary substantially. Which measure is appropriate?

Several attempts have been made to apply the ordinary multiple-correlation technique to the problem of determining the capacity of enterprises to pay wage increases.[9] The analysis of the General Motors Corporation, for instance, determined the level of profits by these variables: the level of output, average hourly earnings, cost of materials, prices of the finished products sold by the company, and a productivity time trend. By solving for the values of these relationships to profits on the basis of average relationships for the period 1929–41, it is possible to estimate the level of profits with specified values for output, wage levels, prices, material costs, and productivity (a function of time). The effects of wage-rate changes on profits may be estimated under designated conditions regarding prices, material costs, and output.

This type of analysis no doubt warrants further examination. At least it should contribute to a better understanding of the quantitative relations among production, prices, and costs. The

---

[9] *Purchasing Power for Prosperity, the Case of the General Motors Workers for Maintaining Take-Home Pay,* presented by International Union, UAW-CIO G.M. Department, Walter P. Reuther, director (1945), pp. 55–74. Also see Harold M. Wein, "Wages and Prices—A Case Study," *Review of Economic Statistics,* May, 1947.

method cannot, however, provide any automatic formula for measuring ability to pay. Its proponents have never claimed that it does. The problems summarized and enumerated above are not suddenly dissolved. The level of output for the future contract period remains dubious. There may be grounds to question whether productivity will be above or below levels predicted from any time trend.[10] The statistical technique does not eliminate these problems; it may present them in different form.

The correlation technique may present its results in the better-known form of a "break-even chart," showing the level of output or the percentage of capacity operations at which the enterprise "breaks even." This point will vary with changes in the prices of the products of the firm, the wage rates, and the productivity of the enterprise. This simple device may provide a helpful basis for discussion in collective bargaining over the economic position of the enterprise. What level of output should an enterprise regard as normal for wage-setting purposes? The analysis may help to suggest that temporarily high or low levels of output are not satisfactory standards by which to fix wage rates expected to be maintained over relatively long periods.

As an absolute principle of wage determination, the ability-to-pay principle is widely recognized as having several limitations. The general adoption of the principle of determining wage rates absolutely in accordance with ability to pay would result in very unequal wage levels among different firms. It would be incompatible with many union programs for equalization of wage rates among firms in the same industry or locality. The principle would appropriate to wage earners the incentives that lead the more profitable firms to expand production and employment.

Just as unions have stressed that employers have the ability to pay wage increases in good times, so managements have emphasized inability to pay on other occasions (Case 47). For instance, one of the major headings in the brief of a company resisting a demand for a wage-rate increase stated: "The financial condition of the company with revenues of practically the lowest point in twenty years makes it impossible to increase wages already adequate and at the same time maintain the present standard of transportation service, retain the present number of employees,

[10] See *General Motors Reply to UAW-CIO, Brief Submitted in Support of Wage Demand for 52 Hours Pay for 40 Hours Work* (1945) pp. 14–19.

and continue to render unified service."[11] The ability-to-pay argument has been employed frequently by companies attempting to make a case for a lower wage scale than other companies in an industry or locality. By virtue of location, machinery, size, or temporary financial embarrassment, an enterprise may seek to secure special wage treatment on grounds of inability to pay.

There will be wide differences of judgment in any particular situation concerning the net effect of the factors defining and measuring ability to pay wages—differences not only between parties but also within any group of relatively disinterested observers.

Fundamental Problems

The analysis of the slogans and principles of wage determination summarized in the four preceding sections indicates that there are fundamental limitations to the application of these principles to particular situations. These limitations must be faced with candor.

First, the range of possible wage rates which would follow from the various possible applications of each of the principles would generally be wider than normal variance between the parties in collective bargaining. The alternative meanings and measurements of each one of these standards are so diverse that the principle frequently can provide little help as an authoritative determination of wages. The same point may be made in alternative language: the differences between the parties are simply translated into alternative meanings and measurements of a particular wage slogan or standard. The range of disputed application of any of these principles is likely to be much wider than the normal range of disagreement between the parties.

Second, since all wage determination must be considered with reference to a prospective period, conflicting expectations as to the future are certain to result in divergent applications of any set of wage principles. The point is not merely that the future in general is uncertain but that uncertainty exists in respect to the magnitude of specific factors—such as output, price, and productivity—vital to *present* wage determination.

Third, the application of wage slogans or principles is com-

---

[11] "Brief on Behalf of Pittsburgh R. Co., Arbitration between Pittsburgh R. Co. and Div. No. 85, Amalgamated Ass'n. of Street and Electric R. Employees of America" (hearing held from July 16 to August 18, 1934).

plicated by the fact that the parties frequently have conflicting and divergent basic objectives. These are particularly contentious when the "time horizons" of the parties are markedly different. The company may be interested in remaining in business over the long run; whereas, a union may be interested in its position during the next year. Or the union may be interested in maximizing the position of union members during their lifetime without regard to new and younger employees. A further illustration of this basic conflict exists in a situation in which the management of a particular company may be interested in the continuation of its own position over a period of time, while the union may be concerned with the industry more broadly. Such conflicts in basic objectives are certain to yield divergent wage levels.

Fourth, even if any one of these standards could be applied in an unambiguous way, the problem would remain of choosing among these alternative standards or weighting the results they yield. No two of the principles would result in the identical wage-rate change in a specific situation. The successive application of these four standards, however, may serve to delimit the range of controversy. In arbitration proceedings the limits indicated by the various standards help to identify the practical range of judgment of the arbitrator (Case 49).

These basic difficulties may seem to suggest a pessimistic conclusion as to the contribution that economics can make to the solution of wage disputes. There is no royal road to the application of economics to wage determination. There is no simple formula that may be simply applied to particular cases. The rigor of the classroom diagram blurs in the face of the complexities of collective bargaining when the rigid assumptions of the formal economic analysis have been removed. In fact, there are no "economic" problems in the real world. There may be economic aspects of problems, but the real problems which require decision must be faced as entities. The more frankly and explicitly technical economists admit this fact, the greater the assistance they may eventually give in the solution of practical problems of wage determination in particular cases.

Criteria for the General Level of Wage Rates

The slogans and cliches used in discussions of the general level of wage rates would require another major chapter. Only some of the more prominent issues can be indicated. There is fairly general agreement among economists that the average increase in productivity constitutes the appropriate norm for the *long-term* movement of the general level of wage rates. As average productivity increases, the level of money wage rates and salaries should rise. The price level as a whole should remain relatively stable. These norms would roughly continue the actual relationships of the past century.

In order for the price level to remain constant, however, industries with greater-than-average increases in productivity must decrease prices. In a day of extensively administered prices, these decreases may not be forthcoming. The pricing mechanism may not have the flexibility requisite to this standard of wage setting. Moreover, the internal requirements of the labor movement may necessitate larger wage-rate increases than are possible under the productivity standard. Intense leadership rivalries may produce greater wage-rate increases, with a consequent rise in the price level.[12]

Purchasing power is a slogan that has received as much attention as any other in discussions of the general level of wage rates. While the cliche is used in particular cases, a separate section has not been devoted to it in the preceding discussion since no single wage bargain is so extensive as to permit a particular wage change to affect directly and appreciably the purchasing power expended on the products of the firms in negotiation. The standard of purchasing power must refer to the general level of wage rates.

The crudest form of the argument identifies wage-rate and purchasing-power changes. There is no need here to expand on the fact that the relation between changes in wage rates and the aggregate expenditures for consumption and investment in any period is not simple nor direct.

A more sophisticated form of the purchasing-power standard relates to the balance between wage rates and prices. The Nathan Report was cast in these terms.[13] The level of wage rates was

[12] See John T. Dunlop, "American Wage Determination: The Trend and Its Significance" in *Wage Determination and The Economics of Liberalism* (Washington, D.C.: Chamber of Commerce of the United States, 1947), pp. 34–48.

[13] Robert R. Nathan and Oscar Goss, *A National Wage Policy for 1947* (Washington, D.C., December, 1946).

regarded as too low at the existing level of prices to sustain high levels of employment. Decreases in the price level were regarded as unlikely. "Businessmen show no signs of exercising such self-restraint in their natural search for profits as would bring about a decline in prices except in the face of a sharp reduction in demand."[14] The Nathan Report concluded that a substantial increase in the level of wage rates without corresponding price increases was required to sustain purchasing power and high-level employment.

The fundamental question arises concerning the standards to be applied in appraising whether the levels of wages and prices are in balance. If a lack of balance is determined, the issue must be faced whether wages or prices should be corrected. These questions cannot be answered by rote. Judgment as to appropriate policy must be based not only on the level of profits but also on the structure of wage rates and prices.[15] Judgment as to appropriate wage-price policy must also be influenced by monetary policies.

An annual appraisal of the economic outlook, such as is provided by the Council of Economic Advisors to the President, can promote a widespread understanding of the problems to be confronted in particular wage negotiations. A greater economic literacy among the rank and file of union members and business executives can improve the atmosphere in which specific wage conferences take place.

The Contribution of Economic Analysis

The restraint of the previous sections follows not so much from modesty as from candor. It must not be concluded, however, that the economist has nothing relevant to say in the process of wage determination, whether it be collective bargaining, arbitration, or governmental wage fixing. Economic analysis can make at least these distinctive contributions to the settlement of wage disputes:

1. The parties or other wage fixers need to be reminded of the longer-run consequences of any decision. While no simple

[14] *Ibid.,* p. 3.
[15] See John M. Clark, *Guideposts in Time of Change* (New York: Harper & Bros., 1949), pp. 147–77; David McCord Wright (ed.), *The Impact of the Labor Union* (New York: Harcourt, Brace & Co., Inc., 1951).

formula or standard may be available to fix a wage, the possible effects of any decision on the employer and the union involved need to be explored. Regardless of the standards used in setting wage rates or the objectives of the parties, economic analysis calls attention to the channels of effect of any wage decision on output, prices, and employment. It can serve as the conscience of the parties as to many of the less immediate effects of a wage-rate decision.

2. Economic analysis points to the impacts of wage rates in sectors of the economy outside the immediate decision. It is particularly concerned with the effects of wage changes on the total national income and the aggregate level of output and employment. "What is true of a firm or of a particular industry or of a set of industries need not be true of the economy as a whole. To draw attention continually to such relationships between the parts and the whole is probably the most distinctive function of the economist."[16]

The processes of wage-dispute settlement need to develop, as they are developing, specialized personnel within unions, employers' organizations, and public bodies who are skilled in the exercise of judgment in the intricate and complex business of wage determination. A person so skilled may profitably utilize the technical services provided by statisticians, lawyers, economists, actuaries, accountants, publicists, industrial engineers, and others; but the primary need is for the mature practitioner to exercise judgment.

Economic analysis purports to deal with one aspect of human behavior. Wage setting must involve the totality of behavior. Any practitioner must develop the art of applying the tools of the technicians in the light of all of the complexities, and frequently the perversities, of human behavior.

---

[16] A. P. Lerner, "The Relation of Wage Policies and Price Policies," *American Economic Review Proceedings,* 1939, p. 158.

PART TWO

Collective Bargaining Cases

DISCIPLINE AND
DISCHARGE

Problems of discipline and discharge go to the heart of the collective bargaining relationship. Many seemingly trivial situations conceal issues fundamental to each party. Few questions are charged with more emotion and are more explosive in day-to-day relations. The volatile character of these cases is not surprising since the right of management to direct the operations and personnel of an enterprise efficiently and the desire of employees to seek protection from arbitrary and discriminatory discipline are vital to both. These basic objectives may be in conflict.

The extreme form of employee punishment—discharge—is of vital importance to an employee since his job is ordinarily his only means of livelihood. A job entails more than wages. The discharge of an employee means the loss of the increasing number of rights which have become attached to the job: pensions, holiday pay, sick leave, vacations, seniority. Moreover, the body of rights is ordinarily greater in the case of long-term employees; not only do they lose more, but their opportunities for re-employment in the labor market are considerably less. It is for these reasons that unions frequently speak of discharge as "capital punishment." The union seeks to protect employees against the risk of arbitrary discharge and the loss of economic and social status.

Most managements recognize that a disciplinary program is designed primarily for those few persons who find it difficult to conform with reasonable standards of behavior. They recognize that the use of penalties for infraction of rules is oftentimes less effective than the social pressure brought to bear on the recalcitrant employee by his fellow employees. Two approaches of management to disciplinary problems can be summarized as follows:

The *clinical approach* is based upon the underlying philosophy that the emphasis should be less on punishment than on constructive education. It is reflected in the statement: "Discipline is that type of training which makes punishment unnecessary." Normally in administering such a program, company rules are not applied inflexibly; there is an attempt in each case of infraction to study the mental and emotional factors which may have given rise to the misconduct. Although a company rule calls for discipline of an employee with a production record below standard, the clinical approach would try to ascertain the personal circumstances which might explain the low output; and if serious illness in the family, for instance, was found to be the explanation, the company would not apply the rule. This approach, where carried to an extreme, gives rise to a serious dilemma in hardship cases, such as alcoholism or nonconformist behavior in the plant which has its roots in an apparently insoluble domestic problem. To what extent can a company devote its energies to the necessary clinical correction of the personal problems of its employees? Most companies which have adopted the clinical approach have not resolved this question, but are firm in their belief that attitudes of supervision and employees as well as the union-management relationship have improved.

The *legal approach* is based on two premises. First, in a large enterprise, it is impossible to entertain a flexible disciplinary program because the resultant lack of uniformity will undermine management's ability to defend its action in a given case. Second, management cannot interest itself in the nonworking life of its employees to the extent required by the clinical approach. The legal approach results in a management codification of rules, the infraction of which is accompanied by a set list of penalties, from formal warning to discharge. Personal circumstances seldom mitigate the punishment prescribed for a given offense. While this approach to discipline may appear to be harsh, its proponents argue that in the long run it is likely to be more equitable than the clinical approach. They say, for example, that there is a lesser tendency to be "soft" when it is to the company's own advantage, as in times of a tight labor market or when the imposition of penalties to a whole department would interfere with production operations. They also argue that a firm, but reasonable application of rules and penalties places all employees on an equal footing and indirectly may hasten the maturing process of a union.

Many companies have never attempted to formulate an explicit policy concerning discipline, nor have they consciously or consistently adopted either the clinical or legal approach. However, with unionization of a plant and the right to challenge company action, there is a growing awareness in management that haphazard action in discipline cases can destroy any effective discipline.

In the great majority of labor-management agreements, the employer retains the right to administer discipline. The following clause is representative:

"The Company retains the exclusive rights to manage the business and plants and to direct the working forces. The Company in the exercise of its rights, shall observe the provisions of this Agreement. The right to manage the business and plants and to direct the working forces include the right to hire, suspend or discharge for proper cause, or transfer, and the right to relieve employees from duty because of lack of work or for other legitimate reasons."[1]

Unions are normally content with this arrangement, since it gives them freedom to challenge company action on two fronts: the reasonableness of the rule and the question of "proper cause" in a given case. It is for this reason that unions are reluctant to agree in collective bargaining contracts with management on detailed disciplinary rules and on the penalties to apply for infraction of the rules.

Under some agreements the union has a more active role in the administration of the disciplinary program. Whenever action is taken by management which is to appear on the personnel record of an employee (written warning or disciplinary layoff), the union is to be notified in advance. A few agreements provide that before outright discharge may be effected the employee is to be suspended and is to be given a hearing if the union feels that recommended discharge action is unwarranted. Union officials are

[1] Agreement between United States Steel Company and United Steelworkers of America, CIO, August 15, 1952.

to be present as such a hearing.[2] Another clause of this nature provides as follows:

"Before any penalty is imposed upon any employee following warning notices, except for discharge for obvious cause, such employee shall be notified one week in advance during which time he may refer the matter to the Local representative and, if the Local so desires, the matter may be negotiated with the management. If no satisfactory agreement is worked out during the period of such notice, the management shall retain the right to impose such penalty pending final settlement of the case."[2]

The penalties in any disciplinary program vary from oral warning to outright discharge, depending upon the nature of the infraction of the rules. A number of lesser infractions, no one of which may justify discharge, in their cumulative effect may result nonetheless in discharge. Most companies, however, establish a forgiveness period which wipes out the record of minor violations which are older than 1 year. Within recent years, more companies are questioning the use of the disciplinary layoff as an effective penalty. Too frequently the employee suspended for 2 or 3 days actually enjoys the forced layoff, while the company suffers from his absence. In a tight labor market the company may have difficulty in replacing the suspended worker. In any event, employees who have been previously laid off are likely to be reluctant to serve as temporary replacements and thereby lose unemployment compensation. These companies have adopted the policy of a more liberal use of written warnings; and in the event the infractions continue, they resort to discharge. An increasing number of companies have found it desirable to prevent the "on-the-spot" discharge of an employee by a foreman; instead, flagrant violations result in immediate suspension of the employee by the foreman. The employee is required to leave the premises immediately, and he is notified of final disposition of his case within 24 or 48 hours. This procedure is based on the belief

[2] Agreement between United States Rubber Company and United Rubber, Cork, Linoleum and Plastic Workers of America, CIO, November 20, 1951.

[3] Agreement between General Electric Company and United Electrical, Radio and Machine Workers of America, April 1, 1946, as modified June 11, 1948.

that too often the anger of the moment, the flow of adrenalin, interferes with sound judgment and careful investigation of the facts. When the facts are known and when the initial flare of tempers has passed, the decision to discharge can be made more calmly by the foreman after review of the case with higher management.

The following are among the more difficult problems which confront managements and unions in the handling of disciplinary cases:

1. Should the factor of seniority affect the degree of penalty to be imposed? Should a long service employee be treated more leniently than a new employee for the same violation of a company rule?

2. Should all employees in a department be disciplined for infraction of rules, such as in the case of a deliberate slowdown when new standards are introduced? Mass discipline is likely to create a hardship on the company. To single out only the worst offenders for discipline, however, jeopardizes the company's defense of its action, since all the employees have violated the rule.

3. Does the behavior of an employee off the premises of the company and outside working hours come within the purview of the disciplinary program? This question arises in the case of individual employees who have been found guilty of certain violations of local law, such as assault and battery. Some off-premise conduct of employees may be regarded as damaging to the company. A bank, for example, may wish to discharge a teller who frequents the race track. Conduct during a strike frequently raises questions under this heading. Most arbitrators have held that the exercise of disciplinary action in such cases is valid if it can be shown that the employer-employee relationship has been adversely affected.

4. Under what circumstances should the individual member's case for redress against discharge be overruled by the union organization? Should the local union steward ever take this responsibility? Can he ever afford to do so politically, in view of the fact that he must normally face an election in the department? Is the international union the level at which cases should be settled by the union against the individual employee when the member seems to have no case? Or, should union policy be to take all

discipline cases, regardless of their merits, to arbitration?

5. What type of records should be maintained by the foreman, personnel office, shop steward, or local union office in disciplinary matters? The legal approach requires the maintenance of complete records of all verbal and written warnings. Given the propensity to arbitrate discharge cases, both parties recognize the importance of good records.

The discharge by management of an employee may be subject to review in a variety of proceedings. (a) The union may protest the action under the collective bargaining agreement through the grievance machinery and to review by an arbitrator. (b) The union or employee may protest a discharge under the Labor-Management Relations Act as discriminatory and as an unfair labor practice. The National Labor Relations Board and the courts may review the discharge to determine whether there has been a violation of law by the company. (c) The union may protest the disqualification of an employee from unemployment compensation benefits who has been discharged by a company. The union will seek to have the state unemployment commission and the state courts rule that the separation from employment should not bar the employee from drawing unemployment compensation. While these proceedings are distinct, a single discharge may involve any one or all of them. In all cases the company may incur additional costs if its decision is overruled by these outside bodies. In the first two types of cases the employee may be ordered reinstated with back pay.

These potential reviews of decisions on discipline and discharge have tended to make most managements more deliberate and more careful. Employees will normally be warned in advance. Management will seek to build a strong case so that it can defend its action before a government or arbitration tribunal. It will want to be certain that its rules are widely known and consistently and fairly applied. Management may be expected normally to bear the burden of showing that the rule under which discipline or discharge was applied was proper and that the facts of the particular case are as asserted by the company. The cases which follow illustrate that it is not always easy to establish the facts and the propriety of a rule.

The net effect of these proceedings which challenge the discipline of management has been to reduce the relative number of discharges in American industry. The high levels of employment in recent years and the fact that some workers are more difficult to replace have contributed to the same result. It is an open question whether standards of conduct are less satisfactory by virtue of this decline in the relative number of discharges.

Case 1

DISCHARGE OF A LONG-SERVICE EMPLOYEE FOR CHRONIC ABSENTEEISM

UNION: United Automobile Workers of America, CIO

COMPANY: Scovill Manufacturing Company, Oakville Division

The following case concerns the discharge of Joseph Kuharick, a long-service employee, for excessive absenteeism which the Company attributed to drinking. The Company defends its action by referring to the contract which states:

"The right of the Company to hire, suspend, or discharge for proper cause, or to transfer to new duties, or its right to relieve employees from duty because of lack of work or for other legitimate reasons, or to extend, limit or curtail its operations when in its sole discretion it may deem it advisable to do so, shall not be limited except as specifically set forth in this Agreement."

POSITION OF THE COMPANY

Joseph Kuharick worked as a service man in the Common Pin Department. His work was to supply 6 women operators with pins and to label the cartons in which the pins were to be packed. The foreman of the department complained that frequent absences by Kuharick caused difficulty in the department. It was necessary to replace him by taking another man off his work, a procedure which was highly unsatisfactory since 4 to 6 weeks' training are needed to become an accomplished service man. In 1951 the records show that Kuharick was absent 96 hours for personal reasons and 85.5 hours for sickness, although the Company suspects that his "sickness" was the result of drinking. In addition, 1 week of alleged sickness was treated as part of his vacation at his own request.

The following episodes were described as part of the background of the discharge action:

1. Late in 1950 the aggrieved had been out sick, but he came to the office in the middle of the week to collect his pay. He showed definite signs of having been drinking and talked in a loud voice about his domestic difficulties and other subjects. The department foreman spoke with him and urged him to go home, sleep it off, and get back on the job as soon as he could. Kuharick returned the following Monday.

2. In May, 1951, Kuharick came to the foreman on a Monday and asked if he could go home to attend to some personal business. He was granted permission; but the next day when he called in to request a longer absence, the foreman thought he sounded peculiar on the telephone. Accordingly, after conferring with the plant superintendent, the foreman and an Employment Office supervisor visited Kuharick's home. His wife said he was in bed. When asked what the trouble was, she said, " . . . the same trouble. It is drink." The company representatives did not see Kuharick.

When Kuharick returned the following Monday, he was called into the conference room. The superintendent asked him if his absenteeism had been caused by drinking and received an affirmative answer. Kuharick was warned that the drinking habit and the absenteeism would have to be stopped or more drastic action would be necessary. He promised he would try to improve.

3. Late in 1951, Mrs. Kuharick called the company and said her husband wouldn't be in because he was going to Boston. When questioned further, she said it was "the same old trouble." The next day when he did not show up for work the foreman and superintendent went to his home. Kuharick came into the front room, and the following conversation took place:

J. K.: "What are you up here for, to check up on me?"

SUPT.: "No, Joe, we just came down to see if we could get you back on the job."

J. K.: "I'm celebrating. I'm drunk. Why don't you fire me? Go ahead, fire me."

SUPT.: "We don't want to fire you. We want to do something to help you. We came down here to try to get you back on the job again."

J.K.: "Well, I don't know when I'll be back." (He then offered the two visitors a drink which they declined.)

When Kuharick returned the following Monday, it was decided to give him a week to calm down before talking to him. Then the foreman and superintendent met with Kuharick in the conference room. They prefaced their remarks with assurances that they did not want to do anything drastic but that his drinking and the resultant absenteeism would have to stop or discharge might be necessary. It was suggested that he work with the Connecticut Alcoholics Association or Alcoholics Anonymous. Kuharick replied that these organizations would be of no help to him. When asked to promise that there would be no recurrence, he said he could not. Whereupon the superintendent told him that, since he would do nothing to help himself, another such incident would result in his discharge.

4. The final episode occurred soon afterward. At 7:10 A.M., on December 26, 1951, Kuharick went to the foreman and asked for a pass, saying that he was not feeling well. When asked if he had been drinking, he admitted that he had had a couple but insisted he was too ill to work. Each time Kuharick repeated his request, the foreman "talked him out of the pass." The foreman had to leave the plant at noon, but he left instructions that no pass was to be issued to Kuharick unless he went to see the superintendent. At 12:15 P.M., Kuharick again sought a pass and was told to see the superintendent who was then at lunch. However, he refused to wait and walked out of the plant. He did not report for work on the following day.

As a result of these repeated offenses, Kuharick was discharged for absenteeism on the following day. Although "absenteeism" was the specific cause stated on the slip, the Company stressed that the problem of drinking cannot be divorced from the absenteeism.

Since 1943 the Company has not used disciplinary layoffs. Instead, it exercises a high degree of tolerance and then utilizes discharge as a last resort. It has not been a regular policy of the Company to give written warnings prior to discharge, nor to discuss proposed discipline with the Union. Nothing in the contract requires these steps. Kuharick was warned orally on many occasions, and the Company exercised great forbearance before reaching its final decision. It desired to help, just as others had been helped by the rehabilitating efforts of outside agencies. However, Joseph Kuharick showed no desire to be helped or to help himself. The Company cited seven cases of other employees who had been discharged for similar reasons in a similar manner. These discharges took place under the same contract language and were not protested by the Union.

POSITION OF THE UNION

The Union offers the following observations with respect to the Company's complaints against Kuharick:

1. The Company constantly assumes that the aggrieved was a chronic alcoholic. There is no evidence whatsoever to support this bland assumption. In fact, the discharge slip did not even mention alcoholism or excessive drinking as a cause of the discharge.

2. It should be noted that the Company relies heavily on the comments of Mrs. Kuharick. Her statements are of questionable accuracy when one considers that a separation and divorce action is pending.

3. The Company implies that on his last day at work Kuharick left the plant without securing a pass. It neglected to add that from 12:00 Noon to 12:30 P.M. no pass is needed to leave the plant, and therefore the aggrieved was entirely within his rights.

Kuharick is an employee with 24 years of service, and by the Company's own admission his work has been entirely satisfactory up to a year and a half prior to his discharge. Given this long service the action is an unusually harsh penalty, since it deprives him of his vacation benefits and pension rights. The potential loss, therefore, is more than just the loss of his job. The Company's action is contrary to a proper concept of discipline: to correct rather than to be vindicative. In the seven cases of comparable discharge cited by the Company, the longest service record was only 4 years compared with 24 years in the case of Kuharick.

The Company at the very least should have tried a degree of discipline short of discharge. There have been a few cases of excessive absenteeism in past years in which the Company used disciplinary layoffs and written warnings with favorable results.

In this case the aggrieved was never given the benefit of a written warning, nor was the Union consulted about Kuharick's problem. Since the Company has been inconsistent in its application of the rules, the discharge should be rescinded.

QUESTIONS

1. What is the rationale behind discipline administered by a company? What is its purpose? Do you think the Company's practice of issuing oral warnings is adequate? Is the purpose of a disciplinary layoff to punish an offense, or does it play some constructive role? Would a suspension of a few days be fruitful in a case such as this?

2. May the arbitrator rule on the appropriateness of the Company's warning procedure? The Union suggested that the Company's resort to written warnings and disciplinary layoffs in the past in some cases established a precedent which should have been followed in the present instance. Do you agree?

3. What obligations does a company have toward long-service employees? Do you think the Company fulfilled its obligations to Kuharick adequately? Would transfer to a less responsible job have been a better or fairer solution?

4. Can separate standards of behavior for long-service employees be justified in terms of maximum shop efficiency and discipline?

5. If you were the business agent of the Union, what would you have suggested in this case if the Company had consulted the Union in advance?

6. What is to happen to Kuharick if he remains discharged? In the work force of the country there are many such employees. How is the community to treat such employees? Is it any concern to the Company and the Union?

Case 2

COMPANY RULES

UNION: United Automobile Workers of America, CIO

COMPANY: General Motors Corporation

James O. Wiltone has been employed in the Buick Flint plant since December, 1935. On July 1, 1940, he was discharged for getting signatures in the plant to a petition to place the Communist party on the official ballot of the state of Michigan. The petition had been circulated in May, but it came to the attention of management only at the end of June when the names and addresses of signers were published in a Flint newspaper. Hence, discharge occurred weeks after the violation of a plant rule reading: "Soliciting or selling or distribution of literature for any cause, and by any person, without the permission of the Management is forbidden in the factory or on company property at any time. Employees violating this rule are subject to dismissal."

Wiltone disclaims any knowledge of such a rule, which management states had been printed, along with many others, in April, 1934, and posted on bulletin boards until sometime in 1939, when it was necessary to revise some of the rules because they had come to be in conflict with the provisions of the current agreement with the Union. Wiltone disclaims ever having seen such a set of rules posted, as does the Chairman of the Bargaining Committee. Both of these men claim that numerous petitions, political and otherwise, frequently had been circulated for signatures, with or without the permission of management. At times, these petitions had been signed by supervisory officials.

No one had been discharged for circulating a petition. In one case, the chairman and another employee had sought to have a worker discharged for circulating a petition offensive to the Union. Local top management disclaimed all knowledge of the matter. It declined to discharge this worker but stated that he would be spoken to. The worker was placed on another shift, but it is claimed that "every time he was brought [back] on the second shift he has circulated petitions."

When Wiltone was discharged, a request was made by the Union that he be reinstated and that notices then be posted stating the penalty for any future unauthorized circulation of petitions, penalties to be equally enforced against offenders. The request was not granted. The Union claims that this was due to a feeling that, in the language of one management represenative, Wiltone's case was one of a "different sort."

In an appeal from an adverse decision on a claim for unemployment compensation, a referee for the Michigan Unemployment Compensation Commission ruled that Wiltone had not been guilty of misconduct because the rule had not been publicized.

Management emphasizes that Wiltone admits circulating the petition. The rule had been on the bulletin board during Wiltone's period of employment. While it was frequently violated during the hectic days of 1937, and now and then violated more recently, violations were not generally overlooked when they came to the attention of management. The case cited by the Union was one in point. The worker was admonished, and the two union representatives had been personally given notice that "anyone caught passing petitions would be released." The rule, said the Company, was not a "dead letter."

The umpire's power under the agreement is different from that of an arbitrator under many agreements. Paragraph 20, reads in part: "In disciplinary lay-off and discharge cases the Umpire shall have the power only to adjudge the guilt or innocence of the employee involved."

QUESTIONS

1. Can management invoke a rule that has not been consistently enforced?
2. Does it make any difference whether Wiltone personally had knowledge of the rule?
3. The rule stated that employees violating the ban on soliciting *"are subject to dismissal."* Does this language grant management the right to use its discretion as to when to invoke the rule? From this viewpoint, management may not have chosen to use the penalty previously. What do you think of this argument?
4. Is the decision of the referee for the Unemployment Compensation Commission relevant to the problem posed to the umpire under the contract? Explain the issue confronting each.
5. What is the status of company rules under a collective bargaining contract? Has the Union agreed to this rule?

Case 3

COMPANY DEMERIT SYSTEM

UNION: Industrial Union of Marine and Shipbuilding Workers of America, CIO

COMPANY: Cramp Shipbuilding Company

James Westfield, a truck helper, had been out on a job during the afternoon of July 17, 1945, and arrived back at the yard approximately 12 minutes prior to his quitting time of 4:00 P.M. He reported to his leadman and then proceeded to the washroom. At about 3:55 P.M., while he was at his locker with his shirt off, he was approached by a representative of supervision who asked him his number and requested that he show his badge. Westfield resented the manner in which he had been approached and replied that he had no number. Upon further questioning, he stated that his number could be found at the office; he did not show his badge. At this point the whistle blew, ending the shift. On the following day, Westfield was discharged for violation of company rules. The Union is protesting this discharge.

POSITION OF THE COMPANY

The Company holds that Westfield was guilty of infraction of four company rules by loafing in the men's room, leaving his job before the allowed quitting time, failing to wear his identification badge where it could be seen, and refusing to show his badge when requested to do so by a supervisor.

Further, the Company argues that discharge is justified under its announced and established demerit system. The Company relies on its general memorandum No. 228 entitled "Demerits for Given Offenses." This memorandum provides: "Any employee who commits three offenses in any one year, each of which carry 30 or more demerits, will be subject to discharge, decision in such cases to be made by the Foreman and the Foreman's Committee." It also provides that an employee is subject to discharge when demerits total 100 or more after credits have been given for merits of 10 points for each calendar month of "good behavior." The company demerit system allowed the point values as shown in the accompanying table for the infractions in question.

Item No.	Item	Demerits
3	Loafing in toilets	40
7	Leaving job before allowed quitting time	40
12	Failure to wear identification badge where it can be seen	40
13	Refusal to show badge when requested to do so by a supervisor	40

The Company did not cumulate Items 3 and 7, but rather gave 40 demerits for both offenses. However, Items 12 and 13 were judged as two separate offenses with total demerits of 80. The sum of Items 3 (and 7), 12, and 13 yield 120 demerits and makes discharge the appropriate disciplinary action. Finally, the Company argues that it has discharged other employees under its demerit system, and the Union has in the past acquiesced in these decisions.

POSITION OF THE UNION

The Union argues that Westfield's offenses did not warrant discharge either on their own merits or under the company demerit system. It is admitted that Westfield was in the washroom before the whistle blew. However, it is felt that there was little if any productive work for Westfield to do in the few minutes of the shift which remained after he had come in with the truck. In this sense he was not really loafing, and the offense was minor as a practical matter.

Further, inasmuch as Westfield had his shirt off when the supervisor addressed him, he could not be expected to be wearing his badge at the moment. And his failure to show his badge upon request was due to the manner in which the supervisor had approached him by grabbing Westfield's arm and saying, "Hey, boy, where's your button?" These offenses are not considered sufficient to merit a discharge.

If analyzed purely on the basis of the company demerit system, the Union argues that the Company still does not have grounds for discharge. The demerits against Westfield would not reach the total of 100, if correctly assessed. The Union maintains that in order to build up more than 100 demerits, the Company penalized Westfield twice for a single offense.

The Union considers the Company to have been unduly technical in charging Westfield 40 demerits for failure to wear a badge as well as refusal to show a badge. As is pointed out by the Union: "He (Westfield) could not be expected to pin it on his skin." Thus, if scored properly, 40 demerits for Items 12 and 13 combined and 40 demerits for Items 3 and 7 combined would yield a total of 80 demerits and would not warrant discharge.

QUESTIONS

1. Does the company demerit system have any status under the agreement? Why did the Company develop such a plan? What purpose does it serve? Does the Company have to justify its discharge under the demerit point system?
2. Would the alleged conduct of the supervisor make any difference?
3. If quitting early were a common complaint of management, would management be within its rights in singling out Westfield as an example?

Case 4

REFUSAL TO ACCEPT WORK ASSIGNMENT

UNION: American Federation of Hosiery Workers, AFL

COMPANY: Full-Fashioned Hosiery Industry

Mrs. Belsky was a worker in the parachute department of Company X, covered by the master agreement in this industry. She usually performed her operation as one member of a two-worker team, but on the evening of June 7 her partner was absent from work. The Company desired to put a learner on the job with Mrs. Belsky and offered to guarantee Mrs. Belsky her average earnings. The usual method of wage payment was piece-work. Mrs. Belsky requested that she be permitted to work alone, claiming that she could make higher earnings that way. The Company insisted, however, that she instruct the new girl. Mrs. Belsky refused, whereupon she was discharged.

The Union contends that the Company had no justification for the drastic action it took and asks that Mrs. Belsky be reinstated with retroactive pay for the time she lost as a result of the discharge.

POSITION OF THE UNION

The Union argues that Mrs. Belsky is a very efficient worker and has co-operated fully with union and company officials in their attempt to increase production in her department. At the time of her discharge, she was not an instructor and therefore had a just complaint when the Company asked her to take on a new girl as a partner. The Union maintains that the Company had an instructor in the department on the night in question and that this instructor, not Mrs. Belsky, should have been asked to do the teaching. Moreover, since Mrs. Belsky was the committee-woman in her department, it is felt that the Company had no right to place her in a capacity which interfered with her union activity.

As to the offer of the Company to pay Mrs. Belsky her average earnings, the Union contends that the Company was actually offering her considerably less than she could have earned by herself on the night in question. It appears that Mrs. Belsky's regular partner was a very slow worker and pulled down the total production. The relatively slow pace of Mrs. Belsky's partner is evidenced by the fact that the Company later removed her from this operation. Working alone, Mrs. Belsky was able to earn considerably more than any "average earnings" figure. Thus, the performance of the instruction job requested by management would have involved a substantial monetary loss for which the Company offered no adequate compensation.

POSITION OF THE COMPANY

The Company argues that it was completely justified in discharging Mrs. Belsky for her refusal to perform an assigned job. The regular instructor was busy on other tasks on the night in question. The Company feels that it did not make an unreasonable request of Mrs. Belsky when it asked that she take on the learner for one night only. The Company offered to pay her average earnings, and thus she would suffer no loss of earnings. The Company contends it acted equitably and in good faith.

But when Mrs. Belsky refused to do the task assigned to her, management argues that it had no other choice but to discharge her. It could not permit one girl to decide what she would or would not do in the plant. The Company holds if one girl were permitted to make such decisions, it would only be fair to give other girls the same privilege. The result would be a complete lack of discipline.

QUESTIONS

1. If the Company has the right to assign work, are there any limitations on this right?
2. Is the Company under any obligation in this case to allow Mrs. Belsky to make the maximum earnings she could by working alone?
3. Is the refusal of a work assignment grounds for discharge in this case?
4. Does this case represent a problem that should be clarified in a contract?

Case 5

DISCHARGE FOR INSUBORDINATION

UNION: United Automobile Workers of America, CIO, Local 1604

COMPANY: Scovill Manufacturing Company, Main Plant

Since 1948 Claude Jennings has been regularly employed as an annealer on roller hearth furnaces on the second shift, 3:00

to 11:00 P.M. Annealing is a process of treating metals by heating and cooling so as to remove hardness and brittleness. Several types of furnaces are employed in the process, and annealers in this plant are trained to handle various types of annealing equipment. When Jennings reported to work on Monday, August 13, 1951, he was temporarily assigned to open end muffle annealing furnaces from his regular position on a roller hearth muffle as a replacement for an employee on vacation.

The events leading to Jennings' discharge transpired during the evening of Thursday, August 16. Shortly before 8:00 P.M. Harold Jones, the immediate supervisor, approached Jennings regarding some silver coils which were to be annealed. Jones later stated to the industrial relations director that he received the "impression" from Jennings that he would not deliver the loads of silver coils from the rod roll area, a distance of approximately 500 feet, and would not place the material on the pans for annealing. Jones accordingly reported to Sullivan, the foreman.

Sullivan then approached Jennings, following a conversation with Jones, the immediate supervisor. Sullivan asked (ordered) Jennings to unload the silver alloy. There is some doubt as to the precise order given by Sullivan to Jennings. In any event, Jennings stated that he could not or would not unload the alloy. Jennings states he was asked to unload the alloy immediately, while Sullivan and Jones say he was asked to unload the silver alloy any time before the end of the shift at 11:00 P.M.

Jennings then called Bartholomew Shea, the shop steward of the Union. Shea sought to discover the cause of the argument from both Jennings and Sullivan. When Sullivan stated that he had asked Jennings to perform the work any time before the end of the shift, Jennings stated to Shea that Sullivan was lying. Jennings then called his foreman an "Irish son-of-a-bitch" and started to take a swing at Sullivan. Shea stepped between the two. Sullivan immediately discharged Jennings who checked out of the plant at 8:17 P.M. A grievance was promptly filed protesting this discharge.

When the grievance reached the level of the director of industrial relations of the Company, he undertook an investigation of his own to determine all of the facts bearing on the case. His records show that Jennings was one of the best employees of the Company and that no disciplinary action had ever been taken against him. In fact, the only complaint ever raised was by workers on the first shift who complained because Jennings produced considerably more than anyone else. Further inquiry disclosed the following information.

Jennings appeared to have been irritated earlier in the evening by Sullivan's inquiries about the progress of his work. He had also suffered a minor mishap in the course of taking a load of metal out of the furnace when the metal fell forward, half on the floor and half hanging from the muffle. Moreover, the men are generally expected to eat their lunch between 6:00 and 7:00 P.M. Jennings had not yet eaten at 8:00 P.M., nor had he been able to eat his lunch at all on the first two evenings of the week on the new assignment because he had been busy.

The industrial relations director also discovered that when Jennings was approached by Jones shortly before 8:00 P.M., the muffles were occupied. He had seven pans in advance filled for later placing into the muffles, and these pans would not be out of the furnace before approximately 9:30 P.M., nor cool enough to use for the silver alloy until approximately 10:00 P.M. This alloy could not be placed into the muffles until the third shift which started at 11:00 P.M. It would then require 3 hours of processing. The annealed silver could not be used until the start of the first shift the next morning at 7:00 A.M.

The relevant section of the agreement, aside from the management clause, reads as follows:

"Article XI—Discipline
"1. Discipline for infraction of Company rules and regulations or inefficiency on the job will vary, depending upon how serious the case is, and upon the past record of the individual. Among others, disciplinary measures may be warnings, time off without pay, discharge, transfer to less desirable department or job, demotion, loss of other benefits, etc.
"2. A discharge will be for cause. It will be final 24 hours after the hour designated for the discharged person to leave the plant."

The Company Manual, *Scovill You and Your Job,* which sets forth rules and regulations of the Company, reads as follows:

"The employee's record may determine the degree of discipline in each case. The record of an employee who breaks a rule is reviewed for the previous six months and is given consideration and weight . . . .

"The following is not permitted on Company property and will result in discharge except in those cases in which the Company orders a lesser penalty because of mitigating circumstances.

"Willful disregard of, or refusal to comply with, Company rules or instructions of your superiors: as for example, walking off of or refusing to do an assigned job if within your physical capability . . . .

"Disorganizing conduct such as fighting, use of abusive or threatening language, or immoral acts or indecencies . . . ."

QUESTIONS

Assume you are in the position of the director of industrial relations and that you must decide what to do with this grievance.

1. Which alternative course of action would you take?
   a) Reversal. Can you reverse your foreman without damaging his status and authority in the shop? Would reversal tend to encourage future laxity in the foreman's enforcement of discipline? If you were going to reverse the foreman, how would you actually do it?
   b) Modification. On what basis might you modify the foreman's decision?
   c) Arbitration. Under what conditions would you allow the case to go to arbitration? Would you advise arbitration even though you were reasonably certain of what the arbitrator's decision would be? If you decide that the foreman was wrong, would you still prefer to let the question go to arbitration rather than reverse the foreman yourself?
   d) Support. The employee has broken a company rule and accordingly should be discharged in accordance with the rule. Is not support of the foreman necessary to prevent others from engaging in violent language, misconduct, and insubordination?
2. Was there sufficient cause for discipline?
   a) Should Jennings be charged with insubordination and be discharged at 8:00 P.M. for failure to perform a task which could not possibly have been done before 10:00 P.M.?
   b) Could Jennings have reasonably expected a fuller explanation of the order before tempers had flared and had gotten out of control?

Does an employee technically have a right to explanations of orders? Would it be wise for purposes of labor-management relations?

Case 6

DISCHARGE FOR MISCONDUCT ON PREMISES

UNION: Federation of Glass, Ceramic and Silica Sand Workers of America, CIO

COMPANY: Rohm and Haas Company

Hans Jaeger and Paul Pertucci were discharged for fighting during working hours in violation of a posted company rule. The Union does not deny that the fight occurred. In the opinion of the Union, however, the attendant circumstances in this case do not justify the extreme penalty.

The contract provision on discipline reads as follows:

"The Company has the right to discipline employees for cause, provided that in the exercise of this right it will not act wrongfully or unjustly or in violation of the terms of this Agreement. Complaints that the Company has violated this paragraph may be taken up through the grievance procedure provided in this Agreement."

The Union does not challenge the right of management to maintain discipline among its employees; it only questions the discipline management chose to use under the facts of this case.

The Company justifies the discharges on the grounds that both men struck blows in the fight, and they were accordingly equally responsible. Since the fight occurred during working hours, just cause for discharge is established.

FACTS OF THE CASE

About a year before the fight, Jaeger was charged by the local police with an alleged morals offense. He was cleared of the charge, and on his return to work the Company sought to help him by sending him to a psychiatrist. About a month before the fight, offensive writings appeared on the lavatory walls which made reference to the badge numbers of both men, Jaeger and Pertucci. On the day of the fight, new writings referring to

Jaeger appeared on the walls. Jaeger decided that something must be done to put an end to his harassment. He testified he considered going to the personnel department or to Dr. Morrison, who had sent him to a psychiatrist earlier. Instead, he decided to seek out Pertucci and to speak to him directly. Failing to find an opportunity to talk to Pertucci in private, he approached Pertucci at his workbench. He attributed the writings to Pertucci and was convinced that he was being "ridden" because of the alleged morals offense of the previous year.

Pertucci's story follows: "Well, I was talking to another fellow at the table, and Jaeger came up to me and he says, 'When are you going to stop writing about me on the wall?' . . . I told him, 'I didn't write nothing about you; when are you going to stop writing about me?' He stated he didn't write nothing about me. We had a few words, different things, and we started to get a little hot under the collar, I guess. He said, 'You dirty Dago ————' . . . I said, 'You're nothing but a ————' . . . . When I called him a ————, he struck me, then I lashed back to defend myself . . . . It did sting me. I fell back and then swung back." Under cross-examination Pertucci denied writing on the wall but did admit that, whenever there were references to his badge number, he would change the number to Jaeger's in the belief that Jaeger was the author of the insults directed at him.

While circumstances might point to Pertucci as the author, no evidence could be offered to support such a conjecture. Cahall, a company representative, testified that Jaeger had told him he had suffered considerable hostility in the plant following his difficulties with the police the previous year. However, Jaeger felt that although the general hostile attitude had diminished, Pertucci was still riding him about the incident. Cross-examination of company representatives, who interviewed Jaeger immediately after the altercation, revealed that the notion of continuous harassment by Pertucci emerged only after the writings began to appear on the walls. No one in the shop had ever observed Pertucci picking on Jaeger.

Mr. Judge, the local union president at the Industrial Relation Committee meeting stated, "I think the culprits are not either one of the people that you have chosen to discharge but the person or persons who have deliberately agitated by writing these obscene things on the wall and signing these persons' numbers to those sayings . . . . It is unfortunate that we can't find those people out. We'd like to find them out as well as you. They're the people that keep an upset condition in a department . . . . They're no good for you, and they're no good for us."

POSITION OF THE COMPANY

The fact that both men participated in a fight is sufficient reason for their discharge. As Cahall testified, "As far as I was concerned, both men had been fighting. Whatever incited the incident, both men had gone into this thing as a fight . . . . I think a man should consider his position. He knows the rules of the Company. He knows what will happen. If he has a family, he knows whether he should do those things or not. Personally, if I was struck I would not strike to protect myself. I know if I did strike back it would be my job, just as anybody else's. I wouldn't strike back . . . with a slap you could control yourself."

POSITION OF THE UNION

The Union emphasizes that there is a difference in the degree of guilt between the two men. "As far as Pertucci is concerned, we don't feel as though the Company is justified in firing a man for defending himself. We're going to rest on that. As far as Jaeger is concerned, we take this position: Under the ridicule that is given by the employees either inside or outside of the plant, the guy was certainly suffering a tremendous mental strain; and under these conditions we think that what happened was inevitable, and we think the Company should realize it. We think they were not justified in discharging this man because, if they put themselves in this man's place, they certainly would not come up with anything but an effort to correct a situation that Jaeger was free from all blame in starting the fight." There were mitigating circumstances in his case calling for the imposition of a lesser penalty than discharge.

QUESTIONS

1. The union asked the arbitrator in rendering his decision to consider the "pathetic conditions" which formed Jaeger's background. A plea for mercy was in effect entered on Jaeger's behalf. May an arbitrator heed such an appeal, or would he have to stretch the proper boundaries of his jurisdiction to do so?

2. If there is disagreement between the parties on important points of fact, to whom should benefit of the doubt be given? Should the arbitrator rely on circumstantial evidence?

3. Emphasis was placed in this dispute on the matter of physical violence. May not a situation arise which never results in violence that does more to sap morale and efficiency? In this case, would the situation have been more satisfactory if it had never come to a head?

4. May the Company be considered partly to blame for the altercation because it took no steps to halt the practice of writing obscenities? Does not a tolerance of such a condition invite violence?

5. What is the jurisdiction of an arbitrator in this case? Does he rule on whether the Company had sufficient evidence to support its discipline, or does he make an independent judgement of the appropriate discipline?

Case 7

UNAUTHORIZED WORK STOPPAGE

UNION: United Steelworkers of America, CIO

COMPANY: Jones and Laughlin Steel Corporation

Seven crews, consisting of one engineer and one brakeman per shift, operate the narrow-gauge trains that service the open hearth department at the Aliquippa works of the Jones and Laughlin Steel Corporation. These small locomotives bring raw materials to the furnace and carry away molds filled with hot steel.

On Friday, January 31, 1947, the 4-to-12 shift reported 15 minutes before the regular starting time but did not go to work immediately. Instead, they huddled together with the men of the 8-to-4 shift. After some moments of milling around, Lechman made the following statement to assistant foreman L'Grady:

"Somebody has to tell you what this is all about, so I might as well do so, if no one else will. We've complained about the hazards here for more than three months. Yet little has been done about it. We won't work under such unsafe conditions and are giving you notice now that we will stay on the job only long enough to protect the equipment from damage."

The crews then went to work under the direction of their supervisors who ordered a general conditioning of the department preparatory for a shutdown. The operation was gradually shut down, as fast as technologically possible. At a hurriedly called meeting in the mill at 8:00 P.M. on Friday, Ray Dye, management's representative, told the local union offiers that, if Lechman and Cooke, two of the rebellious crew members, went out that night, he was going to fire them. At that moment Lechman and Cooke were working, as were all the other crew members; and they continued working until sent home by Foreman Albaugh at 9:00 P.M. Friday. On Saturday, February 1, Ray Dye told the union officials that instead of the two he had planned to discharge, it would be four, and that the other two would be Belsky and Mezmar, none of whom would be allowed to return to work.

Operations were resumed Monday, February 3, at 8:00 P.M. when the Union finally succeeded in prevailing upon its membership to return to their jobs, leaving the four discharges to be resolved by arbitration or negotiation. Lechman, Cooke, Mezmar, and Belsky received their suspension notices at home by mail on February 6, 1947. The Union holds that these four employees were discriminately discharged and asks for their reinstatement with back pay.

POSITION OF THE UNION

The Union, at the outset, explains that it has no intention of defending an unauthorized walkout. It views a wildcat strike not only as a violation of a solemn assurance given to management but also as a challenge to union responsibility and as an act destructive of democratic principles. However, the Union contends that, while it is charged with the responsibility of keeping employees at work, management has an equal responsibility, negatively at least, not to establish such conditions as will make continuous operations onerous or impossible. Work stoppages presuppose a cause. The cause must be of sufficient magnitude to persuade men to stop their own income, injure their fellow-workmen, and undermine the principles of collective bargaining.

In the present case, the Union contends that it is inaccurate to term the events of January 31, 1947, as a "work stoppage." The Union holds that, in its most extreme expression, the events constituted merely a refusal of certain employees to work under conditions that they felt to be unreasonably hazardous. It holds that the conditions of work are pertinent to an understanding of the causes of the walkout. It would be unjust to judge the relative guilt of the employees without an appraisal of the circumstances that led to the refusal to work. The Union insists that, although the employees were unwise in their choice of the walkout weapon, it was an understandable response to a series of unsuccessful frustrating efforts to remedy a dangerously unsafe condition. Had the Company been alert to its responsibilities of maintaining safe and healthy conditions of employment, the walkout would never have occurred.

The Union further maintains that the Company is especially unjust in selecting four out of a total of fifty-four offending employees and offering them as a sacrifice, presumably to "establish discipline." This is held to be contrary to Section 9 of the contract which reads: ". . . the right to . . . discharge for proper cause . . . is vested exclusively in the Corporation, provided that this will not be used for purpose of discrimination against any member of the Union . . . ." The Union insists that the discharge of the four employees is a gross example of unwarranted discrimination. They are not more guilty than any other of the fifty; yet they are discharged while no penalty whatsoever is attached to the rest. When the Company chooses to apply a penalty to some and not to others, such action is discriminatory, unjust, and consequently contrary to the plain content of the contract. The four employees should be reinstated to their former jobs and compensated for their lost time.

POSITION OF THE COMPANY

The Company considers the events that occurred on January 31, 1947, as constituting a "strike" or "work stoppage." Work stopped during the turn (shift) in question and continued at a standstill for several days. Eventually all the departments of the works were affected, thus showing no temporary or transient interruption but a serious cessation of operations. The Company argues that the aggrieved men were discharged "for their participation in that stoppage" and that it is basing its action on Section 2 of the February 18, 1946, supplemental agreement, which reads as follows:

"The Union agrees that during the term of the April 6, 1945 agreement, as amended and supplemented by this supplemental agreement neither the Union nor its agents, nor its members, will authorize, instigate, aid, condone, or engage in a work stoppage or strike. The Corporation agrees that during the same period there shall be no lockouts."

The Company also cites Sections 8 and 9 of the basic agreements, which read in part as follows:

"The Management of the Works and the direction of the working forces, including the right to hire, suspend, or discharge for proper cause, or transfer, and the right to relieve employees from duty because of lack of work, and for other legitimate reasons, is vested exclusively in the Corporation; provided that this will not be used for purposes of discrimination against any member of the Union . . . ."

While the Company acknowledges that the "work stoppage" was not, at the time, "authorize(d), instigate(d), aid(ed), condone(d), or engage(d) in" by the Union, it insists that some, if not all, of these forbidden acts were committed by "its members." It argues that discussion of the cause of the work stoppage or of any condition precedent to the discharge is out of order. The Company holds that if the aggrieved employees had a valid complaint, if they considered their conditions of employment hazardous and unsafe, then the agreement between the Company and Union outlines in a detailed fashion the responsibility of the parties to deal with complaints brought in the specified form of a grievance. Under the terms of the agreement, either party can be held to prompt and full response on specified matters which the other party desires to have determined. The Company insists that the employees had no justifiable excuse for taking matters into their own hands, especially since they had not yet exhausted their remedies under the bargaining agreement. Complaints had been made by the employees and had received the courtesy of a response by letter from the Company. If this was not considered adequate, means were available to require further response; yet a formal grievance was never filed by these employees.

Finally, the Company argues that although fifty-four employees were involved in the work stoppage and, although all of these were in some degree guilty, its choice of four employees does not constitute a discriminatory discharge. These four employees were discharged "for proper cause," and the Company did not use its authority "for purposes of discriminating against any member of the Union." The Company, contends that, so far as its own knowledge is concerned, these four employees are alone indicated to be near enough to the center of the concerned events to be surely responsible for them. It argues that if the Union desires to produce other employees who are equally guilty, the Company will deal them equal punishment. If the four discharged employees are not to suffer arbitrary penalties beyond their fellows, the only remedy would be that others be brought up to their level of pain. The Company argues that in selecting the four employees who appear most responsible, it is being lenient rather than discriminatory in its handling of the problem.

QUESTIONS

1. Does the discipline of the four workers out of a total of fifty-four constitute discrimination? Discrimination against the Union? May the Company discipline some workers as an "example" to others?
2. If the workers believed that continuing at work constituted a threat to their health, would such a cessation of work be a work stoppage? Would it violate the agreement?
3. Why did the stoppage take place? How would you assess responsibility? What steps would you advocate by the management and the Union to avoid the recurrence of similar cases?

Case 8

CONDUCT OFF THE COMPANY PREMISES

UNION: United Automobile Workers of America, CIO, Local 6

COMPANY: General Motors Corporation, Buick Motor Melrose Park Division

Two Negro employees became involved in a dispute with a white employee and a member of his family outside the plant. After the white employee had brought the situation to the attention of management, the Negro employees were discharged. The Union protested their discharge.

The Union based its protest on the grounds that, since the

entire situation occurred outside of the plant, the Company lacked authority to impose discipline. It therefore requested that the two men be reinstated with reimbursement for all time lost.

Management's position was that, although the incident occurred outside the plant, it gave rise to a latently extreme racial issue, which had already evidenced itself in several ways within the premises of the plant. Management claims that it is within its rights in discharging the complainants whose actions outside of the property of the Company resulted in the existence of dangerous tensions among the employees of the Company while they are actually working on the job.

QUESTIONS

1. Do you agree with the position of management? What limitations, if any, would you place on the principle advocated?
2. On what basis would discipline be applied to some employees and others excused? In this case, should not all employees involved in the dispute be disciplined, if any are to be subject to company action?
3. Can an employee be disciplined for getting into trouble outside the plant? Would the Company have a right to discipline a worker who had served a short term in prison for an offense occurring outside the company premises?
4. Do you think it possible to establish a clear relationship between events outside the plant and a real threat of trouble within the plant? What kind of evidence would be required?
5. Do you accept the principle that anything that happens outside of working hours is of no concern to the management? If not, under what circumstances would you hold otherwise?

Case 9

DISCHARGE FOR INABILITY TO PERFORM WORK SATISFACTORILY

UNION: Rubber Workers' Union, Federal Local No. 21914, AFL

COMPANY: The Hood Rubber Company

Miss Helen Wood was hired in January, 1946, in the Making Room of the Company where she worked on the cementing and rolling operation. At that time she did only the counter and toe cap on one shoe of a pair. She continued on this work until 1950, when extensive layoffs resulted in her transfer to the Prep Department where she was trained on the conveyor belt. After approximately 6 weeks on this new work, the Company concluded that she was unable to keep up with the other operators and she was reassigned to the stripping job. She was warned several times that her incentive point hour would have to improve or it would be necessary to drop her from the payroll. The union steward protested these warnings and urged that Miss Wood be allowed to return to the Making Room, her resident department, where work had become more active. On September 9, 1950, her transfer to the Making Room was effected; and she began rolling vamps and counters on the conveyor, a job unlike the one she had from 1946 to 1950. Her former job no longer existed in its original form. During the first 2 weeks in her old department, an instructor was assigned to work closely with Miss Wood. However, the record shows that the following warnings were issued for poor quality work: (*a*) October 9, 1950, loose shoes; (*b*) October 11, 1950, loose vamps; (*c*) October 16, 1950, 32 pairs of wrinkled vamps. As of this latter date, a warning was given to the operator in the presence of the union steward and the chief instructor. An instructor was again assigned to her for several days; (*d*) October 27, 1950, many bad pairs. The Company discharged the employee on this date for poor quality work, specifically allowing blisters, wrinkled vamps, and looseness of cement.

POSITION OF THE UNION

During the 4½ years of work in the Making Department prior to her transfer to the Prep Department, there were no complaints whatsoever about Miss Wood's work. The trouble started when she was transferred and found it difficult to make an 80-point hour. When the Union urged that she be returned to her resident department to which she was entitled by virtue of her seniority, it was very clear that Mr. Conroy of the Making Room did not want her back. He told a Grievance Committeeman in the Prep Department that she should stay where she was; at another time he told a union steward when Miss Wood was transferred that "she won't last long." The background suggests that supervision was out to "get" Helen Wood for some reason. When work increased in her resident department, Mr. Conroy never made a move to call her back, although he had been quick to recall other transferred employees. It is also significant that the girl who replaced Miss Wood in the Prep Department had a much lower point hour, but she has received no warning. This is further evidence of discriminatory behavior.

As for the specific cause of discharge, poor performance on the rolling job in the Making Room, the aggrieved does not believe she was at fault. She testified that either too much or too little cement was put on by the girl who cements. It is true that Miss Wood did not give this reason when she was warned, but she recalls having spoken to the other girl about it on several occasions. The Union also points out that blisters can show up even if the shoes are rolled properly.

However, even if it is proved that her work on rolling was unsatisfactory, the Union contends she should be given another chance on different work in the Making Room rather than be discharged. It is customary to try to adjust the girl to the work for which she is best suited. The hasty resort to discharge in this case is proof that the supervisors of the Company were anxious to rid themselves of Miss Wood.

POSITION OF THE COMPANY

The Company emphasizes that the discharge action did not stem in any way from the poor work of Miss Wood in the Prep Department; in fact, the Company questioned the admissibility of union evidence on this phase of Miss Wood's work history. The discharge action was taken only because of her inability and unwillingness to do satisfactory work after her return to the Making Room. The Company did not behave arbitrarily nor discriminatorily. The aggrieved was warned many times, and she was given ample instruction. Although her work improved for a few days after each warning (suggesting that she *could* do the work), a relapse to inferior workmanship recurred beyond the tolerance point. On October 27, following at least four warnings in a 3 weeks' period, there were no less than 66 pairs which showed poor rolling and had to be classified as seconds. The Technical Department checked the cause for the high number of rejects on both October 16 and October 27, and it concluded that the explanation of too little or too much cement was invalid; the cause was nothing more than an inferior rolling job. It is significant that since her discharge, there has been no trouble with blisters and wrinkled vamps on this type of shoe.

Mr. Conroy did admit making a passing remark to a union representative to "keep her where she is," but he was certainly not out to "get her" when she returned to his department. It was her own record of poor quality work which brought about her discharge.

QUESTIONS

1. Is it proper to discharge an employee when there is no evidence of deliberate misconduct? What distinction should be made in a disciplinary program between poor quality work which stems from inability to perform a particular task and that which stems from indifference to quality standards?
2. Assume that the contract between these parties contained a 60-day probationary period after the date of initial employment during which time the Company could discharge an employee for any reason. Would that fact affect your judgment in the case of Miss Wood?
3. Assume the Company offered to give Miss Wood one more chance on another job with the understanding that the first proof of poor quality work after a 2 weeks' trial period would result in her immediate dismissal without challenge rights in the grievance machinery. If you were the Union Business Agent would you accept such an offer?

Case 10

CONDUCT OF EMPLOYEE DURING ECONOMIC STRIKE

UNION: United Packinghouse Workers of America, CIO

COMPANY: Swift & Company

On March 16, 1948, the employees represented by the United Packinghouse Workers Union in a number of Swift & Company plants throughout the United States engaged in an economic strike. It was resolved officially with the signing of a strike settlement agreement on June 8, 1948. There was no question concerning the legitimacy of the strike, since it was called by the Union as result of a failure to agree on a wage issue raised pursuant to the wage reopening provisions of the master agreement. In most cities, tension on the picket line reached a critical peak shortly after May 1, 1948. In part, the mere length of the conflict heightened the desperation of the strikers. A greater contributing factor was a letter sent by the Company to the production and maintenance employees on April 29, 1948, which, after a brief statement of the efforts to settle the dispute, stated:

> "Therefore, effective May 3, 1948, the wage rates of all employes in the bargaining units of the UPWA master agreement and the supplements thereto are increased 9 cents per hour.[1]
>
> "Employes who do not report for work by May 10, 1948, will be subject to replacement by new employes and employes who are replaced will lose all rights to be reinstated in the Company's employ . . . ."

The tightening of picket lines and the preparation for action were timed for the deadline date, May 10, 1948. In many cities, mass picketing had been used; and the Company had turned to the courts for injunctive relief. More than 100 employees were discharged for alleged improper actions during the strike. The case described below involves the discharge of an employee at the St. Paul, Minnesota plant. It was referred to arbitration following the strike settlement.

DISCHARGE OF HAROLD TORGENSON

On May 19, 1948, Torgenson was advised that "because of unlawful acts committed by you and particularly because of unlawful acts committed by you on May 12, 1948, you are hereby discharged." In the arbitration hearing the Company cited three specific offenses:

a) Mass picketing from March 16 to April 2 and again on May 13 and 14.

b) An assault against a timekeeper by the name of Weston on May 12.

c) Assault on officers of the law making arrests on May 13.

a) Mass Picketing

From the morning of March 16, 1948, when the strike began up to and including Saturday, April 3, the pickets gathered *en masse* from the north to the south side of Grand Avenue. The Company states that employees were not able to enter the plant

---

[1] The 9 cents adjustment had been offered by the Company prior to the strike and was already in effect at those plants organized by the rival AFL Union.

during this period and that attempts to drive down Grand Avenue were repulsed by failure of the pickets to move aside and open up the line. The Company, however, did admit that employees were invited to get passes from the Union before they would be permitted to proceed through the line. On March 20, the Company applied for a temporary restraining order in the District Court of Dakota County, Minnesota, basing its claims on Section 13 of the Minnesota Labor Relations Law. The hearing which followed was ex parte; and a temporary order was issued the same day, naming officers of the Union and all other members. In spite of the order the mass picketing continued until April 3, and the Company undertook the prosecution of contempt of court proceedings. Throughout April hearings were held on the application of the Company for a temporary injunction; but since the lines were open and access to the plant free from April 3 to May 13, the judge on April 30, 1948, not only denied the motion for temporary injunction but also dissolved the restraining order.

Again, during the week of May 3, 1948, the Company moved the District Court to set aside its order of April 30 and grant a temporary injunction. No decision was made until May 12, 1948, when the Court finally issued a temporary writ of injunction. The writ was the result of a personal inspection of the strike scene by the judge.

The Union is willing to admit that Torgenson and many other employees did participate in mass picketing, but it denies that this is a proper basis for discharge. Mass picketing was not designed to undermine the employer-employee relationship. Since many who were known to have been on the mass picket line returned to work after the strike, the Union argues that the Company has no case for showing any harm to that relationship from mass picketing. The power to discipline does not carry with it the power to discipline in a discriminatory manner. Finally, the Union states that any illegal conduct is redressed adequately through the civil authorities; "punishment for such conduct, when proven, is to vindicate the public interest, not to serve a private interest or to wreak a private vengeance."

b) Assault against Timekeeper Weston

Early in the day on May 12, 1948, William Weston, a timekeeper of Swift & Company, became involved in a fight near

Aller's Cafe on Grand Avenue. Although Torgenson was in the crowd which surrounded Weston, the latter makes no claim that Torgenson hit him at this time. The incident referred to in the charge occurred later that day.

Torgenson stated that he left the picket line about 2:30 or 3:00 P.M. He crossed Concord and continued down Grand Avenue when Weston grabbed his arm and said, "You are the cause of all my troubles." Since Weston had his fist doubled and looked as if he were going to swing, Torgenson pushed him off. Torgenson claims he struck no blows but that Weston kept swinging at him until Officer Waldhauser, Deputy Sheriff of the County, arrived and took Torgenson to the police station. Weston also went to the station. It was also pointed out that Torgenson had a cast on his left arm which was put on by Dr. Johnson at the Swift Plant on April 18, 1948.

The account of the company witnesses is quite different. Weston says he was walking up Grand Avenue and saw Torgenson going up the street. Weston admits saying, "Why point me out in the crowd?" Whereupon Torgenson put up his guard and said, "I'm going to punch you in the nose" and started to dance around "like a would-be fighter." Then the officer arrived and took both men to the station charging Torgenson with disturbing the peace. Weston quotes Waldhauser as saying to Torgenson, "Why defend yourself, the other man did not even swing on you." Weston admits that Torgenson did not hit him.

It is established that Torgenson tried to file a charge against Weston, but it was not accepted by the District Court; that Weston had been drinking on the day in question, and while at the police station Torgenson asked that Weston be given a liquor test but was denied. Torgenson was released on $25.00 bail.

Assault on Police Officers

On May 12 more intensive activity was started on the picket line. Early in the morning of May 13, 23 officers of the law attempted to open the picket line on East Grand Avenue. Officer Waldhauser, who had testified in the Weston incident, was one of the officers on the scene. He describes the crowd as belligerent and determined to let no officer through the line. Orders were issued to start arresting men for refusing to obey the District Court order of May 12. He testified further that Torgenson, the aggrieved, was in the front line and was collared by two other officers (Tomek and Lehman) but broke away from them. "He took a swing and hit one officer on the shoulder." Later he was picked up on a warrant.

The Union sought to establish, by cross-examination of Waldhauser, that all of the people were considered by the witness to be in the same category as Torgenson, i.e., they had refused to break ranks and therefore were resisting arrest. Torgenson denied he resisted arrest; he remembers only that in the confusion he was knocked to his knees. In any event, the Union concluded that there was no evidence of "assault" as charged by the Company.

After the arbitration hearing but prior to the issuance of an award, the arbitrator received the following telegram from the Company:

"Re St. Paul discharge involving Harold Torgenson. Saturday, November 6 this aggrieved pleaded guilty in District Court of North Dakota County, Minnesota to the charge of resisting the execution of lawful process in connecting events of May 13, 1948 when Sheriff Dieter and force of deputies and South St. Paul police attempted to enforce temporary injunction by opening mass picket line on East Grand Avenue. Court sentenced aggrieved to six months in county jail or fine of $500. $500 fine was immediately paid. By his plea of guilty this aggrieved admits the commission of unlawful acts which plainly constitute cause for discharge . . . . Company accordingly requests arbitrator to take judicial notice of District Court proceedings."

In reply to this statement, the Union sent the following telegram to the arbitrator:

"Re company telegram Harold Torgenson case. Offense charged was riot, a felony. Offense pleaded to is gross misdemeanor. Torgenson did nothing more on picket line than hundreds of other pickets known to Company did. Company charge as basis for discharge was very specific assault on police officers on May 13. Torgenson denies such assault. He did not plead guilty to assault on officers. Plea of guilty to general statutory charge of resisting execution of process does not constitute admission of assault on officers. Company's wire claims plea constitutes admission of unlawful acts which constitute cause for discharge. This amounts to change of basis for discharge from asault on officers to commission unlawful acts after record in case was closed."

QUESTIONS

1. "Acts which constitute a deliberate interference with the rights of fellow employees and the Company's lawful effort to conduct its business and protect its property may lead to discharge. The Agreement in no way deprives the Company of its inherent authority to discipline employees who commit unlawful acts against its interests wherever and whenever they may be committed. Neither the contract nor law gives employees immunity to supplement their right to strike with lawlessness." Are these acceptable tenets in judging the Torgenson case? To what extent may their observance result in management's utilization of its disciplinary powers to destroy the basic right to strike?

2. Is it proper to use disciplinary action when the alleged offenses are also subject to criminal action in the courts?

3. Strike action involves a great number of persons. Is a company foreclosed from disciplining specific individuals for improper acts on the picket line if (*a*) it recognized other employees who committed the same or similar offense but failed to discharge them, or (*b*) it tolerated actions on one date and made the same actions the basis of discharge at a later date?

4. If you were the arbitrator, would you accept and consider the evidence concerning Torgenson's plea of guilty which was filed after the hearings were concluded?

5. The strike ended on June 8, 1948, and the submission of all evidence on Torgenson's case was not made until many months later. If he were reinstated, would you allow him back pay in the absence of proof that he had tried to secure other employment in the interim?

Case 11

A MEDICAL REPORT AS A BASIS FOR DISCHARGE

UNION: International Association of Machinists, AFL

COMPANY: Boeing Aircraft Company

Wallace was employed at Renton as a tool repairman B at $1.20 per hour. He was assigned to the repairing of electric motors. On July 1, a medical restriction was placed on Wallace prohibiting him from employment at work involving the danger of electrical shock. Sometime prior to July 1, Wallace had filed a grievance with the Company in which he charged misassignment and requested the rate of $1.29½ with retroactive pay. Upon the issuance of a medical restriction, Wallace was asked to transfer to another department at a lower rate of pay. He refused to transfer and was subsequently terminated on July 28. The Union holds this termination to have been unjust and requests reinstatement with back pay.

POSITION OF THE UNION

The Union contends that Wallace had been employed as a tool repairman for almost a year prior to his termination. During this period the Company had ample time to judge his work and determine whether or not he was physically able to be assigned to his particular job. However, shortly after Wallace had filed a grievance, the Company ordered him to stand a medical examination. The medical department issued a medical recommendation (not a restriction) advising: "Our examination shows that this employee should not be exposed to the possibility of electrical shock." This recommendation was allegedly based upon the condition of Wallace's heart. Upon receiving this report, the Company took the view that Wallace should not continue his work in repairing motors; it placed a medical restriction on him.

The Union explains that it chose to verify the medical report of the Company and had Wallace submit to a medical examination by an outside doctor. The second examination revealed that Wallace was in "perfect health." The Union insists that an employee has a right to consult a disinterested doctor regarding a medical restriction. Such a procedure would prevent the Company from using the medical department to punish or reprimand workers.

In the present case, the Union is concerned with the reasons which prompted the Company to place a medical restriction on Wallace. The Union holds that Wallace was discharged because he had asked for upgrading on the basis of a misassignment. The timing of the restriction is held to be significant since it came only after Wallace had filed a grievance for upgrading and retroactive pay. The Union further states that it refused to permit Wallace to transfer to another department at a lower rate of pay because it felt that the request of the company arose from the fact that Wallace had filed a grievance.

POSITION OF THE COMPANY

The Company denies that there is any connection between Wallace's filing a grievance and the subsequent medical restriction. The timing is said to be purely coincidental, and the restriction is in no sense a retaliation for Wallace's actions. According to the Company, the Safety Supervisor, in a routine tour, suggested to the foreman in shop No. 603 that is was poor policy to have a man of Wallace's age—71 years—doing repair work which involved the danger of electrical shocks. The foreman thereupon sent Wallace to the medical department for examination. The medical report recommended that the "employee should not be exposed to the possibility of electrical shocks." The Company feels that the actual degree of risk of shock in the classification of tool repairmen is sufficiently great to preclude Wallace's continuing on the job. Consequently, a medical restriction was issued. The Company expresses its faith in the ability of its own doctors and argues that the introduction of an outside physician is unwarranted.

It is the view of the Company that, since the Union refused to permit Wallace to transfer to a lower-paid job, and, since the Company could no longer employ him as a tool repairman B, its only alternative was to issue an order of termination. The Company states that it stands ready to re-employ Wallace at any job for which he may be eligible.

QUESTIONS

1. Who should be the judge of the physical qualities of a worker to continue in a particular job classification? Is the testimony of an outside physician relevant? How should such a physician be selected? Who should pay his fees?
2. May the Company establish standards of risk for employees not subject to review or grievance? In this connection may the Company appeal to potential accidents and its rates for workmen's compensation?

THE STATUS OF UNION AND MANAGEMENT REPRESENTATIVES

Few issues are more fundamental to collective bargaining than the status of the representatives of each side. Union stewards and local union officers are frequently full-time employees of a company. They have a dual role as employees of the company and as representatives of the union. In an analogous way, many foremen are members of a union. Some foremen are working foremen in that they perform some work operations in addition to supervisory duties. Foremen also have a dual role to fulfill. They are both employees and representatives of management. Even when foremen are not union members, the union may be concerned in defining and restricting the activities of foremen as employees and as representatives of management. These interests of each side in the status of representatives of the other side present many basic problems.

It is not always easy to distinguish when the union representative who is also an employee acts as an employee and when he acts as a union official. This distinction is most difficult to draw in discipline cases when the union may contend that management is seeking to discipline for the exercise of union functions, and management may insist that it is treating the union officer simply as an employee. It may be contended that the union steward should be held to higher standards of discipline by virtue of the responsibilities of union office. On the other hand, it may be held that the union officer should be permitted more freedom of action. Consider a steward who talks back to a foreman in language that might otherwise warrant discipline. Is such conduct to be immune by virtue of the union office? Are the standards that are applicable to all other employees to be used? Is a different standard to be used in the case of a steward? Is an attempt to be made to dis-

146

tinguish between discussions of union business and discussions of problems of the steward as an individual employee?

The attempt to bifurcate the union representative is certain to meet practical obstacles. The steward is the personalized symbol of the union; almost invariably members will treat discipline of the steward as an attack by management upon the union. It is most difficult for management to convey to the rank and file that discipline is directed to the steward as an employee rather than as a union officer. Their total experience will have been to regard him as their leader and champion.

The union typically seeks to give its stewards or other representatives who are also employees a preferred employment status. Many collective bargaining contracts provide for superseniority, an arrangement where a limited number of stewards or union officers, regardless of length of service as employees, are put at the top of the seniority roster in the applicable seniority unit so that they would be the last to be laid off. The union wants a continuing organization where its representatives are not changed or where their effectiveness is not lost through layoff. Stewards are normally elected each year; and in the typical industrial plant, considerable turnover among stewards takes place each election. Management has commonly agreed to superseniority since it provides a measure of continuity among experienced stewards. Frequent changes in foremen and stewards may inhibit the handling of grievances and other collective bargaining matters.

The question arises as to how stewards and other officers of the union, who are also employees of a company, are to be compensated for time spent in handling grievances and in negotiations. Some unions insist that they alone compensate its representatives for time spent in dealing with management. In industrial plants, it is more customary for the company to compensate shop stewards and committeemen for some time spent in handling grievances. The parties develop under collective bargaining a variety of arrangements to suit their particular problems. Thus, an over-all limit or pool of hours may be agreed upon. Pay may be confined to regular scheduled working hours so that an employee receives no additional weekly pay for serving on a union committee. Pay may relate to grievance handling and only to some contract negotiation sessions. A specific contract clause will help to illustrate the types of accommodation the parties may make on this subject:

"Shop stewards shall be paid for regularly scheduled working time spent in the performance of their duties . . ., and for such other time as may be spent by them at the specific request of concerned supervision.

"Grievance Committeemen will be paid for regularly scheduled working time lost, and for other time spent at the specific request of the Company limited to the following:

"A. Handling grievances as provided in . . . Grievance Procedure, but not including any time spent in connection with arbitration.

"B. Meeting with company representatives for purposes of negotiations but not including any time spent in conciliation, arbitration, or as a result of referral to any Government agency."[1]

While managements are normally anxious to facilitate the settlement of grievances, they seek to put limitations on compensation to union stewards and committeemen to prevent financial abuse and to discourage the development of unnecessary grievances.

The union may also be interested in defining the rights of its elected officers and representatives, who are also employees of a company, to take time off to attend to union business. Contracts frequently provide for such leaves of absence without compensation. The following contract provision is illustrative:

"Accredited union officers shall be granted a reasonable number of leaves of absence without pay, not exceeding fifteen (15) calendar days consecutively to attend conventions or other pertinent business of the Union provided such leaves will not interfere with operations. It is agreed that ten (10) days' notice of such leaves of absence will be given except in emergencies, and that not more than five (5) employees shall be absent at any one time for such purpose, except by special request of the Union; and if conditions will permit, this number may be increased by permission of the Company.

"Such leaves of absence shall not affect the seniority of employees.

---

[1] Agreement between International Chemical Workers' Union, AFL, Local 57 and the Monsanto Chemical Company (Everett Plant), and the Nealco-Monsanto Company, June 16, 1952.

"Any employee whose continued absence over a longer period is necessary because of his duties as an elected officer of the Union will be given a leave of absence not to exceed one (1) year, without pay, for such purpose. Annual leaves of absence shall not be granted for consecutive years unless mutually agreeable to the Company and the Union . . . .

"The Group Insurance of such an employee shall be continued in force during such authorized leave of absence in case and in such a manner as the provisions of the Company Group Insurance contract permit, provided he pays his share of the Group Insurance Premiums at least monthly in advance."[2]

Collective bargaining agreements frequently regulate the activity permitted by a union steward or committeeman during working hours. The union is anxious that a steward be permitted freedom to perform his function for the members and for the labor organization; the company is concerned to avoid any abuse which may lead to disruption of production. The following contract provision is illustrative:

"Local officers and stewards will not conduct any form of union business during working hours except after they have been granted permission to do so as provided below. Before leaving work to conduct union business, the Local officer or steward will report to his foreman or supervisor and request permission to leave his job, which will be granted unless his departure would cause serious interference with operations. In such cases the foreman or supervisor will make arrangements for the Local officer or steward to leave his job as promptly as possible.

"For the purposes of this section union business is defined to mean: (*a*) investigation of a problem concerning rates of pay, wages, hours of employment, or other conditions of employment; (*b*) attendance at a meeting with one or more representatives of Management for handling or adjustment of grievances or for the purpose of collective bargaining; and

---

[2] Contract between Carbide and Carbon Chemicals Division, Union Carbide and Carbon Corporation, Oak Ridge National Laboratory and Atomic Trades and Labor Council, AFL, August 24, 1950.

(*c*) absence from the plant to conduct union business off Company property."[3]

A different range of problems may arise with regard to union officers who are full-time employees of the union rather than employees of a company. May they have access to the plant during working hours? Under what circumstances? May they participate in the discussion of grievances with stewards and management representatives at lower steps in the grievance procedure? The answers to these questions will be influential in shaping the relationship between the parties. The union desires access to the plant and participation by its officers in order effectively to administer the contract for its members.

The following contract provision is illustrative:

"The International President of the Union or his representative and the President or Vice-President of the Local Union shall have access to the plants in order to contact foremen, employes or members of the Industrial Relations Committee on matters pertaining to this Agreement. Such visits to the plant must be prearranged with the Superintendent and conducted so as to avoid interference with the operation of any departments. The Company may designate someone to accompany these representatives on such visits. The Company, through plant officials, will provide plant passes in such a manner that no representative of the Union shall be inconvenienced when he wishes to make such a visit. Such visits need not be confined to any certain part of the plant and may be extended to other departments, except Experimental and Research Departments."[4]

As in other matters, this contract provision seeks to accommodate the different interests of the union and the management; the clause provides rights which the union regards as essential and yet also provides protection to management on matters it regards most vital.

[3] Agreement between Westinghouse Electric Corporation and International Union of Electrical, Radio and Machine Workers, CIO, October 1, 1950.
[4] Agreement between Libbey-Owens-Ford Glass Company and Federation of Glass, Ceramic and Silica Sand Workers of America, CIO, May 18, 1949.

Managements likewise seek to protect and fortify the status of foremen and other of its representatives in the collective bargaining process. An increasing number of companies have adopted personnel practices which seek to draw a sharp distinction between supervisory employees who are regarded as a "part of management" and those who are not. Numerous steps have been taken in these companies to achieve this separation, including foreman training courses, newsletters to foremen, advanced information and briefing on collective bargaining developments, grievance handling, and salary differentials over all employees supervised.

Foremen are free under the law to join unions; and in a few industries, such as the printing and building trades, they traditionally have been union members. The Taft-Hartley law defines an "employee" so as to exclude supervisory employees from the rights which other employees have under the law. Supervisory employees are those ". . . having authority in the interest of the employer, to hire, transfer, suspend, lay off, recall, promote, discharge, assign, reward, or discipline other employees, or responsibility to direct them, or to adjust grievances, or effectively to recommend such action, if in connection with the foregoing the exercise of such authority is not of a merely routine or clerical nature, but requires the use of independent judgment."

Despite the attempts of company practice and the statute to draw an absolutely clear line between management representatives and other employees, a number of collective bargaining problems persist. In some cases there may be a question whether a particular employee, with minor supervisory duties, should be included in the bargaining unit. There may be doubt under particular contracts whether a foreman is permitted to perform other than supervisory work; the union seeks to deny to foremen the right to do any work ordinarily performed by workers in the bargaining unit. Questions arise as to the seniority rights of workers promoted to managerial positions. Comparable problems arise for workers who take full-time jobs with the union. Do they lose all rights to come back to work? Do they retain the seniority they had when they left, or do they accumulate seniority while working with management or the union?

The union and the management each has a reciprocal interest in the competence and responsibility of officers of the other organization. Managements have a real interest in the quality of union leadership, just as unions have in the character of supervision. Where collective bargaining relations are advanced, there may even be frank discussions of the problem spots in the personnel of each organization's hierarchy.

The cases in this section illustrate some of the problems that arise by virtue of one party's interest in, and concern for, the organization and operation of the other.

Case 12

DISCHARGE OF A LOCAL UNION PRESIDENT

UNION: United Steelworkers of America, CIO

COMPANY: G. F. Wright Steel and Wire Company

BACKGROUND

Ralph Sanders has been employed by the Company as a wire drawer for 20 years. In 1944, he was elected president of the newly formed local Union. At the time of the case, Sanders had been re-elected each year.

In January, 1947, Sanders approached Mr. Cabot, Personnel Director of the Company, and told him of the Union's desire to co-operate in the forthcoming March-of-Dimes campaign by soliciting money at the plant. In the course of their conversations, Mr. Cabot instructed Sanders to hang up a collection box near the time clock. Sanders questioned the effectiveness of this method and proposed that someone be sent around the plant soliciting individual workers. He offered to have the Union pay for the time lost of such a man. Mr. Cabot was unconvinced in spite of a recital of the possible disadvantages of posting a box. He insisted that the box be used for the time being; if it proved inadequate, other methods could be tried later. Sanders was dissatisfied with this conclusion and did not hang up a box.

On Sunday, February 2, the regular monthly meeting of the Local was held at which Sanders made a report on his conversations with Mr. Cabot concerning the March-of-Dimes collection. Although the testimony concerning this report was conflicting, it appears he left the impression that the Company would not co-operate in the solicitation. The report prompted someone to make a motion, which was adopted, that a letter be sent to the March-of-Dimes expressing regret that management's failure to co-operate prevented solicitation of funds.

The letter, dated February 4 and signed by Sanders, stated that "the President of Local 3190 regrets deeply that the members of the Union cannot contribute to the Worcester Infantile Paralysis Fund. The Management of G. F. Wright Steel and Wire Company refuses to let the shop stewards of our local solicit in their departments for this very worthy cause . . . ."

On Wednesday, February 5, Sanders was called to Mr. Cabot's office. Mr. Cabot said he had been advised by several of the grievance committeemen and union members that Sanders had made misstatements to the union meeting and had implied that the Company refused any solicitation of funds for the March-of-Dimes. He asked Sanders to "retract" or "clarify" the statements. The discussion became heated. Sanders suggested that what went on at a union meeting was none of Mr. Cabot's business, and he demanded the names of the "squealers." Sanders then returned to his machine.

An hour later he was again called to Mr. Cabot's office. Mr. Cabot and Rowman, Plant Superintendent, urged Sanders to "retract" or to "clarify" his statements. They asked Sanders to join the Company in a notice which would set forth the true facts. Sanders refused, and he was immediately suspended by the Company and told he would be advised within a day if the suspension action was to be converted to a discharge after a full review of the case. The following day the Company sent Sanders a registered letter which converted his suspension into a discharge. The cause of the discharge was set forth as follows in the letter:

"Your discharge is due to the fact that you have made misstatements about and concerning the Company and its officers and agents, that you have consistently violated rules of the Company, and your production record indicates that you are not performing your duties as a wire drawer in accordance with your ability. These various matters have from time to time been called to your attention and you have refused to co-operate with the officers and agents of this company in either remedying or attempting to produce better results."

On February 10 Sanders filed a grievance on the discharge which was later submitted to arbitration.

POSITION OF THE COMPANY

In the formal hearings before the arbitrator, the Company presented four charges against Sanders:

1. *Repeated violation of rules.* Sanders' record revealed four instances of violation of the rules governing starting time, rest periods, lunch time, and quitting time. The only penalty was a 2-day suspension, later reduced to 1-day, for being in the locker room before quitting time. Sanders failed to attend a safety meeting which is held periodically on company time; instead he stayed in the mill talking to an employee. Another violation was charged for failure to obtain a pass to leave the mill. Finally two violations of the rule on absenteeism were noted. No disciplinary action was ever taken in these cases other than the suspension already noted. All of the violations occurred during the period between late 1944 and the date of discharge in February, 1947.

2. *Inadequate production.* The Company introduced data showing the average straight-time hourly earnings of Sanders and other employees in the same job classification. The job is paid on an incentive basis. The data showed that Sanders' earnings were generally lower than the average of the other employees.

The Company not only criticized the volume of production by Sanders but also argued that the quality of his work was inferior. Wire-drawing reports covering 19 different days during a $2\frac{1}{2}$-year period were introduced. On each of these days, Sanders was at fault on one or more counts; the most frequent fault was oversized wire. Finally, on July 16, 1946, a demerit for faulty production was given to Sanders. Two of the nineteen reports followed the demerit date. The Company pointed out that such faults are extremely costly, since it sells wire by the lineal foot rather than by the pound. Poor quality wire results in extra costs for reprocessing and may result in damage to wire weaving equipment.

3. *Misstatements concerning the Company, its officers, and agents.* The Company disclaimed any desire to interfere with the conduct of union meetings. However, the report made by Sanders at the February 2 union meeting left the impression with the workers that the Company had refused Sanders the right to solicit

for the March-of-Dimes by any method. No indication was given of the Company's willingness to permit the posting of a box for a trial period. The misstatement by Sanders at the union meeting is of direct concern to the Company, since it destroyed employee morale and damaged public relations.

In addition to this episode, other statements were attributed to Sanders by company witnesses. In the main, they were derogatory and defaming comments about officers and agents of the Company.

The Company sought to establish that Sanders on many occasions used abusive language, threatened physical harm to a supervisor, was insubordinate, and disrupted plant efficiency.

In summary, the Company expressed a belief that the goal of good labor relations had been blocked by Sanders' "very unreasonable and unco-operative attitude." For a man with 20 years' service, his production records were deplorably low. He had been given many opportunities to improve. "It has been our practice not to discharge men without warning, and we feel we have gone further in his case because of his position here as president of the local than we have with the few other discharges made in this Company."

POSITION OF THE UNION

The Union elicited from Mr. Cabot the admission that the initial suspension of Sanders by the Company was a result of his failure to go along with the Company in advising the employees that certain misstatements had been made to them concerning the collection for the March-of-Dimes. Mr. Cabot later expressed doubt whether Sanders would have been discharged had he been willing to "clarify" or to "retract" his misstatements.

Given this initial contention, the Union confined most of its argument to the March-of-Dimes episode. First, it was stated by union witnesses that Sanders had given a full account of his conversation with Mr. Cabot, including the alternate proposals of individual solicitation versus box collection and the disadvantages of the latter. Second, regardless of the statements made by Sanders, the Company has no right to discipline an employee for any statements made at a union meeting. The Union treated this as the basic issue in the Sanders' case: Whether a company has a right to interest itself in what transpires at a union meeting or in any union activities except an overt act of the Union, which may result in violation of a contract provision or in a stoppage, slow-down, or cessation of work.

Not only did the Company take an unhealthy interest in intra-union matters, but it had the "brazen affrontery" to seek retraction of statements made by the union president. Failing to secure re-traction, the Company discharged the employee. To uphold the discharge would be to sanction a dangerous and improper action by the Company.

If no disciplinary action is justified by Sanders' statements at a union meeting and if these statements were the prime motivation for discharge, then reinstatement with back pay and unimpaired seniority rights is clearly in order. But the Company has intro-duced an elaborate record on Sanders. This record the Union dismisses as "an accumulation of trivia to get a man" and as a futile attempt to support the weak props of the discharge. For example, the use of abusive language and the alleged misstate-ments concerning officers of the Company were never deemed im-portant enough to be recorded, although the system of records of the Company is unusually detailed. The low-production record might conceivably be attributable to more frequent absence from the machine because of official union business. Sanders was gen-erally considered an exemplary employee prior to being elected local union president.

It is interesting that an employee who has worked for the Company since 1927 becomes less desirable when he assumes the presidency of the local Union. The record of "trivia" dates from 1944, and the Union has reason to believe that Sanders was under close and special surveillance since he began to work zealously and conscientiously for his constituents. His every move was watched, and the slightest infraction was recorded.

In summary, the Union urges the arbitrator to resolve the issue by answering two fundamental questions: (1) Can a presi-dent of a local union speak freely before a union meeting without molestation by the company? (2) Can a company build up an accumulation of trivia to support an unjustified disciplinary action?

QUESTIONS

1. What do you think is the real issue in this case? How would you resolve it? What is the cause of discharge? Is it a sufficient cause?

2. Is there any basis for questioning the legality of this discharge under the Labor-Management Relations Act?
3. May an employee be disciplined for actions committed as a union member off the company premises, or must discipline be confined to violations of on-the-job rules of employment?
4. Does the Company have the right to concern itself with statements made at a union meeting? What redress does a Company have for damage to its reputation arising from statements made by a union?
5. What standards of conduct would you recommend for Sanders in his relations with the Company as a union officer and as an employee? Does he have any responsibilities to the Company, or are all his responsibilities directed toward his constituents?
6. May a review and reweighting of past offenses be used as a legitimate basis for discharge where the immediate cause of discharge is insufficient to justify or sustain it?

Case 13

DISCIPLINE OF UNION OFFICERS FOR ILLEGAL STRIKE

UNION: United Automobile Workers of America, CIO

COMPANY: General Motors Corporation

The Union is protesting a 30-day disciplinary layoff of two local union officers: Shop Committee Chairman, Frank Alter, and Shop Committeeman, Paul Bayliff, for engaging in a work stoppage.

BACKGROUND

At the beginning of the lunch hour at 11:30 A.M., the employees of the Trim Department went to the nearby union hall to attend a union meeting for the purpose of discussing three grievances, two of which had been filed in writing. Eighty-five employees failed to return to the plant at the end of the lunch period, resulting in the layoff of all production employees by management at 1:00 P.M.

Union witnesses testified that Alter chaired the meeting, in accordance with the rules of the Union, but he was voted out of the chair when he refused to entertain a motion from the floor calling for a work stoppage. Both Alter and Bayliff spoke from the floor several times and urged the men not to strike in violation of the agreement. This version of the meeting and the officers' role in it was buttressed by signed statements of 32 employees present at the meeting, including some who returned to the plant at the end of the lunch hour in response to the committeemen's efforts. Management was unable to contradict this testimony, though it had interviewed the employees in order to find out whether Alter and Bayliff had attempted to prevent the strike at the union meeting.

About half of the employees in the department returned to work at the end of the lunch hour. The rest voted to engage in a "protest" and to instruct the committeemen to present management with three demands which, if granted, would have settled the pending grievances to the Union's satisfaction.

At about 12:13 P.M. Alter and Bayliff entered the plant. Instead of proceeding to their work stations, they went to the office of the superintendent of the Trim Department. They encountered Lauder and Hackett, supervisors of the department. Lauder asked where the men were. Committeeman Alter stated that the men were at the union hall and had voted to return to work provided the three pending grievances were settled in accordance with the terms voted at the meeting. Superintendent Aiken was summoned from the Personnel Director's office. When he arrived he asked the committeemen to repeat their demands. When they remained silent, Aiken repeated the demands as they had been related to him by Lauder and stated that the answer to each of them was "No." He said further, "You might as well let the men know that this is it. They are in bad shape." The committeemen left the building without further response.

Alter and Bayliff returned to the union hall and told the assembled employees of management's answer. They were successful in persuading the men to return to work and to handle the grievances in accordance with the agreement. About 2:00 P.M. Alter notified Superintendent Aiken that the employees had voted to return to work the following morning. The 85 employees were subsequently given penalties ranging from 2 to 5 days for participation in a work stoppage in violation of the national agreement.

POSITION OF THE COMPANY

Management assessed 30-day layoff penalties against the two committeemen for giving leadership to the work stoppage in violation of Paragraph 117 of the national agreement which states that "The Union (will) not cause or permit its members to cause nor will any member of the Union take part in any strike or stoppage . . . ." The Company charge is based on the fact that the committeemen sought out management after the shift had begun for the sole purpose of presenting the men's demands; that Alter and Bayliff made no effort to advise management representatives that the employees were in error in striking and that they were trying to persuade them to return to work; and that they acted as spokesmen for the strikers by presenting demands backed up with the force of a strike, thereby aiding the continuation of a contract violation. These actions, in the Company's opinion, constituted leadership of an illegal work stoppage to a degree sufficient to warrant the penalty imposed.

POSITION OF THE UNION

The Union denies that Alter and Bayliff either led or participated in an illegal work stoppage. They were away from their jobs after 12 Noon because they were fulfilling their obligations as committeemen in an attempt to end the illegal work stoppage. They presented the men's demands to management, knowing that the answer would be in the negative; they felt a statement of management's firm position would provide them with an additional weapon to end the stoppage. No arguments on the merits of the grievances were presented, nor was there any attempt to negotiate them. Regardless of their failure to disassociate themselves from the illegal strike in the presence of management, they did, in fact, state their disapproval of it to the employees; and they exerted every effort to prevent and end the stoppage.

ARBITRATION AWARD

The failure of the committeemen either to be on the job or to advise management of their role in the strike had the effect of suggesting outward tolerance and even support of a strike. Instead of disassociating themselves from a show of force, they effectively contributed to it by presenting the men's demands without stating their own position. Thus they ran the risk of being considered participants. Even though they spoke against the strike in their own councils, they became reluctant instruments of a group engaged in violation of Paragraph 117 by their subsequent behavior. An officer must make his position clear to management;

otherwise his action has the effect of adding to the sum total of pressures on management to yield. The position of the committeemen in this case was not one of leadership, although they tried to dissuade the men from striking and were instrumental in terminating the stoppage. Rather they acted as participants by presenting the men's demands.

Alter and Bayliff did not live up to the highest standards of their jobs as committeemen. They should not only do everything in their power to prevent violation of Paragraph 117 but also should make their efforts evident to management. The obligations of a committeeman are to represent his constituents to the fullest extent within the framework of the national agreement and to preserve the integrity of that agreement. In this case, they sought to preserve the integrity of the agreement but were reluctant to reveal that fact to management. Reluctance springs from the mistaken concept that a committeeman who reveals to management his conviction that his constituents are wrong is disloyal to the rank and file. Nothing can be further from the truth. For such a revelation is in furtherance of his obligation to preserve the integrity of the agreement. In so doing, he protects the fruits of collective bargaining and performs an act of service to the rank and file.

While there is no basis for the charge that Alter and Bayliff gave leadership to the strike, their participation was established and some penalty is appropriate. The other participants received penalties of 2 to 5 days, according to their prior disciplinary record. Alter and Bayliff have clean records. On the other hand, as committeemen, they should have been aware of an obligation to avoid involvement in the stoppage. The 30-day layoff is reduced to 5 days.

QUESTIONS

1. Be prepared to discuss the obligations and responsibilities of a union officer during a wildcat strike and the means by which his responsibilities are discharged.

2. If the committeemen had returned to work on time having taken no action whatsoever, would they then not have been subject to discipline by the Company? Does the position of union leadership involve an obligation to take positive action against contract violations as well as to offer violators no support?

3. How is leadership or participation in an unauthorized walkout to be established?

4. Were not the committeemen, as representatives of their membership, obliged to follow the instructions of the members democratically arrived at, even though they had argued against the wisdom and appropriateness of the action?

5. Are the primary loyalties of a local officer to his immediate constituents or to the national agreement? Consider the question from both a legal and political standpoint.

6. This Company for a number of years has developed a consistent policy of firm discipline in cases of wildcat stoppages, and as a result such violations of the agreement have been very substantially reduced. What difference does it make in appraising disciplinary action if the discipline is part of a long-term consistent program or if it is taken as an isolated case? Would you apply the same standards in the two types of situations?

Case 14

DISCIPLINE OF UNION OFFICERS FOR ALLEGED CONTRACT VIOLATION

UNION: Optical and Instrument Workers' Organizing Committee, CIO, Local 30.

COMPANY: Bay State Optical Company

BACKGROUND

The question before the arbitrator is whether or not the Company was justified under the terms of the agreement in discharging Donald Ryan, Henry Duvall, George Cheevers, and Robert Leonne.

Prior to June 9 the plant was operating on a 5-day week. On that day the Company and the Union conferred about a possible reduction in the workweek necessitated by a curtailment of orders. This conference was in accordance with the provisions of Article VI, Section 2. (See below.) Some of the union representatives took the position that it would be better to lay off junior employees, thus affording the older men a full workweek. The Company, on the other hand, opposed layoffs as a detrimental alternative since the period of curtailment was to be brief; it suggested that a 4-day week be instituted. Ryan, the local union president, then asked to confer alone with his group. This was done; and when both parties reconvened, it was clear to the plant superintendent, Donald Gilson, that an intra-union conflict existed, for one of the union men said: "Don Ryan says if we don't work 4 days, we'll have to get out of the Union," whereupon Ryan turned to him and said, "Did you have to open your mouth?"

Following this meeting, the Company posted a notice signed by Gilson stating: "Effective this week, the workweek for the balance of June will be 4 days, Monday through Thursday, for all departments . . . ."

On Thursday, June 16, the production engineer, H. Loeffler, decided that it would be necessary for some men to work on Friday in order to complete an order which had a Monday deadline. He told the foremen of the Zyl and Metal Departments, LaRoque and Lyons respectively, to ask men to work on Friday.

Lyons approached a group of truers about working Friday, and they all agreed to come in. Of the six polishers asked, four were undecided and promised to tell him later, one said he'd do what the rest did, and one (Thayer) said that Cheevers, the Steward, had told him not to come in on Friday. Lyons later talked to Cheevers who said that Thayer's statement was correct and that there was to be "no work on Friday on the orders of the Union President, Don Ryan." This was denied by Cheevers in his testimony.

None of the men in the Zyl Department indicated a willingness to work Friday. Ryan, who worked in this department, said he had another job for Friday and couldn't come in. Other excuses offered by the men were appointments, planned absences from town, and an unwillingness to work unless others worked. All of the men approached in the Shipping Department agreed to work while the maintenance men were mostly noncommittal, indicating that they would have to wait until after a union meeting that afternoon.

As a result of the reports of these foremen, higher management authorities began to interest themselves in the apparent reluctance of employees to work on Friday. Loeffler, for example, called in Ryan who again explained that he had taken outside work for Friday as a result of the short workweek and therefore couldn't come in. Loeffler testified that he told Ryan he would have to get someone else in his place, and Ryan replied: "Don't think you'll get anyone else." He cautioned Ryan against making a comment like that, saying, "You're threatening a work stoppage." Ryan corroborated part of this story but insisted that Loeffler exaggerated. He states he told Loeffler that the employees had a right to refuse to come in. Loeffler reported this conversation to Gilson, the superintendent, who then prepared a statement to be read over the public address system. He showed it to Ryan and "offered Ryan a chance to go on the P.A. system," but he refused. Ryan testified that he had been asked to urge everyone to come in and to tell them that he was planning to be in. This Ryan refused to do because it would be prevarication. He insisted in his testimony that the statement was not shown to him prior to this request and that at no time did either Gilson or Loeffler mention "strike," "stoppage," or "slowdown." Nor was he reprimanded or warned by the two men for having done anything wrong.

At 11:45 A.M. on Thursday, Gilson read his statement over the P.A. system as follows:

"Certain individuals, named by management to work on Friday of this week, have rejected the additional work. The management has been informed that the instruction for this rejection has come from the union officials. At this time, it should be pointed out that there is work available tomorrow, only in a few spots where deadlines must be met.

"It is not the wish of the Company to operate a four-day week, but economic considerations dictated some action. After considerable deliberation, it was decided that rather than make further layoffs, it would be more advisable to provide a four-day week for as many as possible. We would like to point out to you the following provision in your contract:

(*Article V, Sections 1 and 2, were read here.*)

"We all should remember that if an effort is made to prevent the Company to meet certain shipping deadlines, and loss of business results, it affects the job security of each one of us. In other words, the security of our own job is only as strong as the business security of the company for which we work."

Other episodes were recounted by company witnesses. One Martin Modeste said he talked with Henry Duvall, one of the four discharged on Thursday, who said the Union didn't want the men to work on Friday. Later he saw Duvall going around the plant talking to others. He also heard Robert Leonne, another of the employees discharged, tell people to "stick by Don Ryan." However he did agree that he didn't hear Leonne tell anyone *not* to come in.

A union meeting was held in the late afternoon of Thursday, June 16. Ryan testified that he advised the members of their contract rights and that he called the meeting because of the P.A. system announcement. He felt that they should be told that they didn't have to come in. Ryan insisted that he had not ordered anyone to stay away on Friday nor, to his knowledge, had other union officials. He had merely told the committee members that under the June 9 schedule no one *had* to work on the fifth day of the workweek.

On Friday, June 17, it appeared that the efforts of the foremen to persuade people to come in had yielded varying results. In the Metal Division, none of the polishers came in; but all of the truers reported for work. None of the 16 men approached in the Zyl Division came in, and no maintenance workers appeared. All but one of the men in the Shipping Department worked Friday. The foremen made checks on Monday to find out what excuses the men had. The reasons offered were many and, to the Company, very unconvincing.

Gilson, on the June 17, prepared letters of suspension for 6 employees. On the following Monday morning, he gathered all the information he could. In addition to the reports already mentioned, he learned that there was a "general feeling in the Union not to work," that "the fellows ought to stick together," that "you have your rules, we have ours." After the investigation Gilson, Loeffler, and M. M. Brown, a Vice-President of the Company, agreed that the suspensions of 4 of the 6 men should be converted to discharge because of their activity in fomenting an illegal work stoppage. It was this action which gave rise to a grievance and the arbitration proceedings.

The provisions of the contract which are relevant in this case are as follows:

"Article IV—Management Responsibility.

"The Union recognizes and agrees that the management of the company's business, including the hiring of employees, the direction of the working forces and the maintenance of order and efficiency in its plant and operations are sole responsibilities of the Company. In recognition of these principles, the following provisions are agreed to:

"*a*) The Company retains the sole right to hire, lay off, assign, transfer and promote employees and to determine the starting and quitting times and the number of hours to be worked, provided, however, that these rights will not be used to discriminate against any member of the Union. However, before exercising its right to transfer or layoff any employee, the Company will inform the Union thereof.

"*b*) The Company retains the sole right to discipline and discharge employees for cause. Probationary employees may be discharged without assigning any reason. Complaints that the Company has violated this paragraph may be taken up through the grievance procedure provided in this agreement. When any employee has been discharged or disciplined for cause, the Company will inform the Union thereof and the cause therefor . . . .

"*Article V—Strikes and Stoppages*

"1. The Union agrees that there shall be no strikes, walkouts, stoppage or slowdown of work, boycotts, secondary boycotts, refusal to handle any merchandise, sit-down strikes of any kind, sympathetic or general strikes, or any other interference with any of the operations of the Company during the term of this agreement.

"2. Any employee guilty of participating in, instigating, fomenting or actively supporting or giving leadership to illegal work stoppages is subject to discharge.

"*Article VI—Hours of Work*

"1. The regular work week shall consist of 40 hours commencing on Monday and ending on Friday. All work in excess of eight hours in any one day or 40 hours in any one week shall be paid for at the rate of time and one-half . . . .

"2. Any proposed changes in the scheduled hours of work or the starting and quitting time will be discussed in advance with the Union Committee, after which they may be put into effect by the Company . . . ."

POSITION OF THE COMPANY

The issue is whether or not the discharged employees, all officials of the Union, violated the no-strike provision of the agreement and were guilty of "participating in, instigating, fomenting or actively supporting or giving leadership to illegal work stoppages." The Company submits that the part played by each one has been amply demonstrated by the evidence. The 4 men not only participated in the work stoppage but were the ones who instigated and gave leadership to it. They not only failed to live up to their responsibilities as union officials but took affirmative action in violating the contract. Company representatives appealed to them and, through the P.A. system announcement, pointed out specific provisions of the agreement which they were violating. Nevertheless, these men pursued the course of advising people not to report for work on Friday.

The record shows that in the past when the plant was on a scheduled 5-day week, employees willingly worked a sixth day when production schedules required additional work. Although on a shortened workweek, the Company requested certain employees to work on Friday on essential production; the 4 discharged men usurped the rights of management and countermanded the Company's "orders."

Under cross-examination Gilson, the superintendent, was asked whether the employees had fulfilled their obligation under the contract by working Monday through Thursday, the scheduled workweek. His reply was in the affirmative, and he went on to say that there was no contractual obligation on the part of the employees to work on Friday of that week. In response to the arbitrator's questions, Gilson made the following statements:

"The 4 employees were not reprimanded on Thursday.
"Employees are expected to work overtime as a matter of co-operation.
"The employees satisfied the contractual obligation by working Monday through Thursday."

When Mr. M. Brown, Vice-President and General Manager, was on the stand, he corroborated Gilson's testimony, adding that the "work-stoppage" under Article V, Section 2, in this case was the refusal of people to come in "when requested." These two company representatives were the negotiators, signers, and administrators of the contract.

QUESTIONS

On the basis of the contract provisions and the information presented above, prepare the union rebuttal arguments to be offered before the arbitrator. On the basis of the evidence, at least three alternative courses would appear open to the Union: (1) Admit violation of the contract but contend that the penalty was too severe, (2) deny violation and any grounds for discipline, and (3) deny violation and state that, while conduct of officers was not exemplary, no discipline is justified. Consider the following questions in the preparation of the rebuttal argument.

1. Was the June 9 notice a change in the work schedule under the agreement?
2. Was the failure of the men to work on Friday a work stoppage in violation of the contract's no-strike clause? Is there an obligation under the contract to work outside the regularly scheduled hours of work?
3. What was the role of the union leadership in this case? Can it be justified? Can it be said that the officers instigated, led, or encouraged a work stoppage?
4. Can anything be said about the nature (reliability) of the Company's evidence? On what sources of information must a Company rely in such a case?
5. Would you concede that perhaps the leaders acted in violation of the spirit of the agreement? Can such a violation be considered as justifiable grounds for discipline?
6. What difference does it make that some of the employees did report to work on Friday?

Case 15

SENIORITY RIGHTS OF EMPLOYEES PROMOTED OUT OF THE BARGAINING UNIT

UNION: Lennox Workers Industrial Council

COMPANY: Lennox Machine Tool Company

Four members of the union contract negotiation committee are meeting to discuss and formulate demands on several issues in preparation for the forthcoming negotiations with the Company. The conversation on one of the issues follows:

ALEX: "Let's move on now to the problem of seniority of those men who have been promoted to supervisory positions and then, at some future date, demoted back into the shop. How is the accumulation of seniority to be affected by promotion?"

NED: "I've got the answer for that. Just strike them off the seniority list."

CLARK: "What do you mean by that?"

NED: "Like I said, their names should be dropped from the list. That would mean that they would lose their seniority status in the shop."

FRANK: "You mean a guy with 20 years' seniority that gets promoted and then is demoted into the shop would have to go back down on the bottom of the roster? Hey, now, that's kind of rough!"

NED: "What do you mean rough? When a guy gets promoted into a supervisory position, he's no longer one of us. He doesn't have to belong to the Union, so why should we worry about what happens to him? A supervisor is a part of management, so let the Company worry about him."

ALEX: "Hold on, Ned. That's a pretty drastic way to handle this. Just think how it will affect the long-service men in the shop. To them, promotion would involve taking a big risk. You know how long we've been plugging for promotion from within the plant. We don't like it when the Company fills all the good production jobs and supervisory jobs by hiring new people. Well, we would be pushing them right back to hiring from the outside if we follow your suggestion. No guy in his right mind would risk promotion if he's piled up a few years' seniority."

FRANK: "Yeah, the only guys that would take the promotions would be some of these young squirts that don't know from nothing. And they can be a terrible pain in the neck to work under."

CLARK: "You're right, Frank. It makes a big difference whether or not the foreman has come up through the shop. If they've been around the shop a long time, they're a lot better foremen because they know and understand all the operations and the problems connected with them. That way, they know what can be expected of each man in the shop."

ALEX: "And don't forget that a foreman who is always faced with the possibility of being transferred back into the shop will treat the union a lot better if the Union looks out for his job protection and his seniority rights."

NED: "Where do you get this union protection of a foreman's seniority rights? What obligation do we have to a supervisor? Can we bargain for him? No! What you'll have is a seniority roster packed with names of guys you can't even bargain for. The Company never asks us who to promote. Why should we be responsible for taking care of the supervisors they demote? I say, when a guy takes a supervisor's job, he quits his production work and loses all the rights that went with that job. When he becomes a part of management, then he's the Company's responsibility."

FRANK: "What if the Company argues that way about our full-time union officers? Under the contract, they all continue to accumulate seniority, even though they're working for the Union. Would we like it if our officers had to quit to take their official positions? Who would run for office?"

NED: "That's different though. Union offices aren't permanent. The guys may not get elected again, so you got to take care of them. Besides they don't quit the Union like company supervisors do."

ALEX: "Isn't there really a little more similarity in the two cases than you've admitted so far, Ned? Look. The Union always encourages advancement through the ranks both in the Union and in the shop. We can't encourage guys to advance if we leave them hanging on a limb. Sure the union office may be considered temporary, but so may a supervisory position turn out to be temporary. Maybe the guy doesn't work out well, or maybe things slack off. You can't turn a guy out completely when he's worked with you all his life."

NED: "You just made a good point on my side of the argument. When things are rosy and the work force is increasing all the time, your idea would be fine. But what about slack times when they begin to lay off guys? If foremen continue to accumulate their seniority, they'll be bumping our guys right out of a job. In a situation like that, we've got to protect our own members."

CLARK: That does raise a problem, but we can't have our cake and eat it too. Either we encourage promotion from within and we offer some protection, or we don't give a damn how the upper grade jobs are filled and we refuse to accept any responsibility."

FRANK: "Well, I'm for letting a man accumulate seniority in his supervisory job like the union officers do."

NED: "Hey, are you crazy? You can't load the top of the seniority list that way. You've got to give the guys who stay in the shop some breaks. The most I would be willing to concede is retention of accumulated seniority at the time of promotion with no continued accumulation. That would be fairest to the guys in the shop and would still give the promoted man a lot of protection."

ALEX: "I agree with Ned on this accumulation of seniority problem for the most part. But I was thinking of the case of the man who is promoted and doesn't work out well, doesn't like it, or for some other reason is returned to the production unit a short time after he is promoted. Shouldn't he be allowed to continue to accumulate seniority on the supervisory job for awhile at least, say for a year? Then, if it looks like a permanent thing, he stops accumulating any more seniority."

CLARK: "That sounds like a fair possibility. The only thing that worries me is the rules for bumping back into the unit. Does he bump into his old job or does he bump anybody with less seniority?"

NED: "I wouldn't go for any deal that lets a man bump into the unit. After all, the guys who are on the jobs deserve some protection too. I suggest that a demoted man wait till there is a vacancy in his department. Then he steps into that vacancy, and no one gets bumped out of a job or out of the department."

FRANK: "That doesn't sound too practical to me, Ned. What if there is no vacancy opening up at the time? What happens then? Besides, your method of re-entering the unit could mean a terrific cut in pay if the job that opens up carries a low rate."

NED: "But that cut would only be temporary. With his seniority he should be able to move up to his former job within a short time as vacancies open up."

CLARK: "Don't we accept the principle of bumping in other circumstances, like in cases of layoff? Well, why shouldn't some bumping be proper here? I think a man should be able to exercise his seniority to take any job in the department for which he can qualify. This would probably mean some bumping, with the man at the bottom of the departmental seniority list being dropped."

NED: "There's something else you fellows are forgetting in this business. Once you let the Company get a foot in the door and let them shove demoted foremen back into the unit, they'll want permission to shove everybody and his uncle back into the department. What about the man that takes a guard's job, or one that transfers over to the Jasonville plant where they have that Commie Union, or like Butch Beazley goes into the time-study department? You gonna let all those birds back in, too? Cripes, if things get slack they could clean out the whole department!"

ALEX: "Easy, Ned, don't get excited. Can't you give us

credit for having just a little sense? Sure, we have to draw the line somewhere, and I think we can do it. My own suggestion is that seniority rights be protected only for shop foremen."

NED: "I can't say I go for your suggestion. My heart just doesn't bleed that much for the guy who gets a fat promotion into management and then wants to come back on the job."

ALEX: "I think we have kicked this around enough for now. Let's see if we can't reduce our ideas to writing in contract form for presentation to management."

QUESTIONS

1. Prepare a proposed contract provision governing the seniority rights of employees in the bargaining unit who have been promoted to positions outside the bargaining unit.
2. What are the principal reasons to support the particular contract provision you have drafted?
3. What are the major circumstances which would determine the type of clause you propose?

Case 16

EMPLOYEE WORKING PART TIME AS FOREMAN

UNION: United Steelworkers of America, CIO

COMPANY: Mann Steel Company

The following grievance, having been duly processed through the grievance procedure of the contract, was submitted to the arbitrator for final decision: "We request that when Class A Millwrights fill in on turns [shifts] as turn foreman that they be paid the new rate of the turn foreman and that this rate be retroactive to date new rate was put in effect."

The employee involved in this grievance spends part of his time in a supervisory position known as "turn foreman." The rest of his time is spent as a millwright. The Company feels that he is not a member of the collective bargaining unit represented by the Union; while the Union, on the other hand, considers him to be within the bargaining unit even when he may temporarily work in a supervisory position.

POSITION OF THE UNION

The Union contends that the employee involved in this particular dispute is entitled to whatever differential exists between his rate and that of the turn foreman whose job he takes over temporarily. The Union also states that it is up to the arbitrator to decide whether the Company, under the terms of the contract, has to answer a grievance or accept a grievance for this particular man or any man who is working part time in the collective bargaining unit as an hourly and production worker and part of his time as a supervisor. The Union feels that this is a very vital issue because it involves not only this employee but other men who are filling the same kind of job. The Union also contends that the worker has been a member of the collective bargaining unit since an election conducted by the National Labor Relations Board and that his union dues have been checked off by the Company. The Union contends that by checking off his dues the Company has recognized that the worker is within the collective bargaining unit.

POSITION OF THE COMPANY

The Company, at the time the grievance came up, took a position that the employee was not a member of the bargaining unit. The Company argues that this employee was excluded from the list of employees who were eligible to vote at the NLRB election. The Company also argues that the Union is attempting to bring through the grievance machinery a case involving an issue in which the Union has no interest and over which the arbitrator has no jurisdiction. The case involves compensation for work as foreman. Foremen, however, are not members of the collective bargaining unit which the Union is authorized to represent and for which the Company deals with the Union. In this case the worker's name should not have been listed by the Union on the checkoff list.

CONTRACT PROVISIONS

Section 1 of Article III of the agreement between the parties provides as follows:

"Subject to the provisions of the National Labor Relations Act, the Company recognizes the Union as the exclusive representative of all the employees for the purpose of collective bargaining in respect to rates of pay, wages, hours of employment, or other conditions of employment."

"Employee" is defined in Article I:

"The term 'Employee' means an employee of the Company who is included in a unit, and the term 'Employees' means two or three or all of such employees."

"Unit" is defined in Section 2 of Article II:

"The Unit at each of such Plant and Works shall include all production and maintenance employees of the Company there, except all executives, office and salaried employees, foremen, assistant foremen, supervisors who do not work with tools, draftsmen, timekeepers, watchmen and guards, and full-time first aid and safety employees, and except also die sinkers in the Die Sinking Division at the Mann Plant and pattern makers at the Sarrows Paint Plant."

The arbitrator concluded from the testimony that the employees worked more than half his time as turn foreman.

QUESTIONS

1. If the Company intends to classify a part-time supervisor as a foreman, should it continue to check off his dues to the Union? By checking off the worker's dues, does the Company recognize that the worker is still in the collective bargaining unit?
2. Does the checkoff list determine who is in the bargaining unit?
3. Could the worker in this case be represented by the Union in a matter involving his status as a millwright?
4. Was the worker eligible under these above circumstances to belong to the Union?
5. Would the decision in the case be different if the "employee" worked less than half the time as a turn foreman? If he worked a negligible proportion of his time as a turn foreman?
6. Is there any barrier to this employee being a *member* of the Union?

Case 17

LAYOFFS BY FOREMEN WHO ARE UNION MEMBERS

UNION: International Union of Operating Engineers, AFL, Local 181.

COMPANY: F. H. McGraw and Company

The Company is engaged in the construction of a large atomic energy plant in Paducah, Kentucky. The peak employment of operating engineers has been reached, and it is now necessary to lay off 160 of the more than 1,200 operating engineers employed. These men perform the work of operating steam shovels, bulldozers, scrapers, tractors, and other similar equipment.

There is no contract provision on layoffs in the national agreement between the Company and the International Union which provides essentially that in each locality in which the Company builds a project it will follow the conditions of the local agreement between the local contractors and the local union. Nor is there any provision on layoff procedure in the local agreement.

POSITION OF THE UNION

The Union holds that these men should be selected for layoff by the foreman in accordance with the general practice in the construction industry and the past practice of this Company on other jobs. The foreman should select the individuals primarily on the basis of ability so that the contractor will retain the most able men the longest on the project, thus reducing costs and rewarding the ablest men. These are the men who can operate more than one piece of equipment, who keep their machinery in best repair with least damage, and those who get the largest production out of equipment.

The Union states that it has had considerable difficulty in dealing with the Company at this site and suggests that any layoff procedure and standards be reduced to writing. It urges the following language:

"In the event the Company is desirous of reducing the force of Operating Engineers it shall:

"1. Notify the Master Mechanic of required number to be terminated in each classification.

"2. Master Mechanic will notify each general foreman of required number to be terminated in his department.

"3. General Foreman will in turn notify their Foreman as to required number of men to be terminated.

"4. Foreman will terminate men with regard to ability, special qualifications, attendance and job attitude."

PROBLEM

Consider this case from the position of the project manager of the Company and decide how you would handle this situation:

1. In the construction industry, it is customary for the foremen and general foreman to be members of the union. They are on this project. Indeed in the early stages of the project the Company needed foremen, and the Union recruited the foremen for the Company. The master mechanic, in charge of all general foremen supervising operating engineers, is also a union member. The master mechanic, who is on an annual salary, reports to an assistant superintendent, who is not known to be a union member but may have been when he worked at the trade.

2. There has been a disgruntled group of operating engineers who have quarreled with the leadership of Local 181 and who have hired a lawyer to represent them in order to secure a separate local union charter.

3. You have been advised by your lawyer that it may be an unfair labor practice to permit foremen, who are members of Local 181, to lay off men since they may discriminate against members of the disgruntled group. The lawyer for this faction is standing by waiting to file unfair labor charges with the NLRB.

4. You are confronted by the practical fact that probably no one other than the foremen or the general foremen are in any position to know and to evaluate the ability and work of some 1,200 men. The personnel records would not be very helpful.

5. The Company now permits the foremen and general foremen to discharge men for cause, for misconduct, or for poor work.

6. Your lawyer suggests that the only sure way around the problem is to institute job seniority, that is, to lay off men in accordance with the reverse order in which men were hired onto

the job. Not only would this be an innovation in the industry and company, but not all men can operate all types of equipment. To keep lists by 60 or 70 types of equipment would be almost impossible. Moreover, the Company is concerned to retain the best men as long as possible.

7. The Company has long had a "termination report" which foremen have filled out when workers separate from the payroll. The form provides for rating each man on the following qualities: production performance, quality of work, dependability, co-operativeness, versatility, and general knowledge.

QUESTIONS

1. What type of layoff procedures and layoff standards do you propose? How would you solve the present problem? Draft a proposed memorandum of agreement to submit to the Union that you would be willing to sign.
2. Who should have the burden of proof that a layoff is discriminatory: the man laid off to prove discrimination or the Company to prove no discrimination? In either case, what weight would you give to the fact that the foremen, general foremen, and master mechanic were union members?
3. Would it make any difference in actual operation, and before the NLRB, to have an appeal procedure available in the event that an individual has been discriminatorily laid off?
4. Aside from the question of NLRB proceedings, what are the possible consequences of making layoffs by foremen who are also union members?
5. Why do you suppose these foremen are union members? Do you suppose the absence of any contract provision on layoff procedure is related to the union membership of foremen?
6. Is the Company free in this situation simply to institute any layoff procedure it desires since the agreements are silent? Would such unilateral action be a refusal to bargain collectively and be a violation of Section 8 (*a*) 5 of the Labor-Management Relations Act?

Case 18

UNION INTEREST IN DISCIPLINE OF FOREMAN

UNION: United Automobile Workers of America, CIO

COMPANY: General Motors Corporation

At the Pontiac plant discipline was imposed by management upon a foreman for alleged improper remarks of a personal nature about a committeeman. The Union insisted that the foreman be discharged. In any event, the Union claims it should be informed by management of the discipline that was imposed upon the foreman, since such information would be necessary for a proper answer to the grievance filed by the Union.

The supervisor referred to by the Union had been a foreman over two departments for 5 years. His record was good, and he worked well with the employees. Union representatives charged this foreman with having made derogatory remarks of a personal nature about a committeeman. The Union insisted on his discharge.

POSITION OF THE PARTIES

Management states that it thoroughly investigated the case. The foreman vigorously denied making the statement attributed to him. Management thought him guilty, however, and reported that "proper action has been taken." The foreman was not discharged but was disciplined in some other way, according to management.

The Union then requested a written answer to its grievance, which answer would detail the discipline that was imposed upon the foreman. The case should not be closed, contends the Union, merely by a general report from management that "proper action has been taken." It is held by the Union that a proper answer to its grievance under the terms of the agreement[1] requires information concerning the exact nature of the discipline imposed upon the foreman.

Management refused to comply with this demand on the ground that "foremen are a part of Management" and that any discipline imposed upon them is a matter not covered by the national agreement and one that is the sole function and responsibility of management.

Management claims that the request of the Union in this case is really that the discipline imposed by management upon its foremen, at least in certain kinds of cases, should be considered by collective bargaining procedure. This, it says, would mean a reversal of the traditional rules of the two parties.

The issue, says management, comes down to this: Does the

---

[1] The grievance procedure reads in part: "Written answers will be given by the Management to all written grievances presented by the Shop Committee."

Union have a right to be informed of the discipline imposed by management on the foreman in this case? It should not be overlooked, says the management, that the provision of such information would most likely lead to an appraisal by the Union of the adequacy or inadequacy of the penalty and possibly to an effort to discuss its findings in collective bargaining procedure.

After a discussion of the matter, the Union recognized that the disciplining of foremen was the sole responsibility of management and that the terms of any such disciplinary action were not subject to collective bargaining. The Union insisted, however, that "as an equal" under the agreement it is entitled to information concerning the discipline that was imposed on the foreman. Management resists giving such information in the belief that, once given, the Union might then proceed to pass judgment on the decision and to strive to encompass such penalties within collective bargaining.

Nothing in the agreement gives the Union the specific right to receive information on discipline meted out to foremen in such cases. Management's argument closes with the statement:

> "When a foreman violates the Agreement, he subjects the Corporation to possible penalty. Management has the sole responsibility for taking steps to prevent a further violation of the Agreement by the foreman and must be accorded latitude of action in this direction so as to enable it to balance the necessities of efficient operation of its business with the need for avoiding exposure to penalties for Agreement violations by the foreman."

QUESTIONS

1. What is the issue before the umpire? State it precisely.
2. What intent has the Union in requesting the information? What purpose would the information serve the Union?
3. What is the meaning of "equal partners to the contract?" Would the Company have a right under the contract to demand information concerning the discipline of union members by the Union?
4. If you accept the position of the Union, how far up the hierarchy of the Company would you carry the principle?
5. What does this case indicate concerning the relationship of the parties?

Section C

UNION SECURITY

Union security provisions of agreements, as the name implies, are intended to maintain and to enhance the union as an *organization*. While there is great variety in these contract clauses, in general they specify that all or certain individual employees be members or remain members of the union in good standing and maintain the financial obligations of regular dues and assessments to the union.[1] Union security clauses thus concern primarily the relation between a union and the individual employee or member. It may appear strange that *management* should assume any contractual obligation for the relation between the union and its members. Indeed, that intimate area might be held to be the sole concern and responsibility of the union. A little background is required to explain this apparent anomaly.

Union security contract provisions are relatively unique to the labor movement in the United States.[2] The American wage earner has been less class conscious and more difficult to organize, and to keep organized, than the industrial work force of most other countries. The individualism and agrarian background of the work force were serious obstacles to the growth of strong unions. Workmen frequently would strike and join a union to seek support in redress of some grievance or injustice, but it was difficult to build these men into stable and continuing organizations. Moreover, American employers historically opposed the growth of unions more vigorously than the employers of other countries. Many industrial employers sought to have individual employees sign the "yellow dog contract" in which they were

[1] See Case 19 for actual contract language.
[2] Jean A. Flexner, "Union-Security Safeguards in Foreign Countries," *Monthly Labor Review,* August, 1952, pp. 134–39.

required to agree as a condition of employment not to join a union. These employers sought a closed no-union shop. Faced with this type of opposition of employers and a lack of continuing cohesiveness among the workers, the unions developed union security clauses to strengthen the union organization.

These clauses were traditionally designed to protect against at least four threats to the stability of the union. (*a*) A fluctuating union membership rendered the union financially insecure. Employees who joined the union in times of crises, for instance to secure a wage increase or to prevent a wage cut, and then who floated out of the union, secured benefits from the union without bearing their share of the continuing costs of the union organization. (*b*) Normal turnover or expansion in employment would tend to dilute the union. A union must find some way to attract new employees if it is to retain its strength. In some industries where jobs are of short duration, the unions found the only way they could maintain their position was to require that all hiring take place through the union. (*c*) The union sought to protect itself from rival unions which might seek to attract members. These raids or attacks might be expected at a time of internal dissension and weakness. (*d*) An employer might seek to establish a company dominated union or institute a complete no-union shop. Union security clauses were developed to protect the union organization from the risks of these contingencies.

In a social milieu in which employees "naturally" join and support their unions, where union rivalries are not intense or where a strong central labor organization is effective to curb raids, and where there is little tradition of open hostility by employers to the *existence* of unions, union security contract provisions would not be expected to be prominent. These factors substantially account for the absence or relative unimportance of union security provisions in agreements in western European countries. They likewise account for the pivotal attention given to such clauses in collective bargaining in the United States.

There are a variety of contract provisions relating to union security. The most important provisions can be grouped under the two headings: the checkoff and union membership as a condition of employment. Checkoff provisions require that union dues and initiation fees, and sometimes union assessments and fines, be deducted from the pay of each employee and be forwarded by the management directly to the union. A checkoff may be *voluntary* in the sense that the personal authorization of an employee (member) is required before deduction. The authorization ordinarily is valid only for the contract period, although in some agreements an authorization may run indefinitely. A checkoff provision is said to be *automatic* when it applies without individual authorization to all employees under the scope of the agreement. The Labor-Management Relations Act permits the voluntary checkoff but precludes the automatic checkoff. A checkoff provision may on occasion be the only form of union security provision in a contract.

There is a rich diversity of contract provisions requiring union membership as a condition of employment. The most common shop types are: the *closed shop* under which union membership is required before employment; the *union shop* under which union membership is required after an initial period of employment, usually 30 days; the *maintenance of membership* provision according to which any employee who is a union member or who joins the union must maintain membership as a condition of employment during the term of the agreement; the *modified union shop* under which some employees, such as new hires, are required to join the union after an initial period of employment but other employees, such as long-service employees, join only if they so desire and only then must they remain members in good standing; the *preferential shop* in which union members have first claim on employment opportunities. The *exclusive bargaining rights* under the statute provide a union a measure of protection from rival unions and from management, although exclusive representation is not ordinarily regarded as a form of union security. There is great variety possible within each of these types, and there are numerous combinations of the several shop types with the forms of the checkoff. As with other contract provisions, the collective bargaining process typically has "tailor-made" the union security provisions to the special problems of the industry and to the traditions of the two bargaining organizations. Thus, the intermittent nature of employment in the longshore industry has produced the union hiring hall. Some unions are not interested in the checkoff; their traditions lead them to prefer to collect dues directly from members on the grounds that the process of personal collection is significant to the union member and to the union officer.

The relative importance of these various forms of union security, and their changes in recent years, is indicated by the percentage of all employees covered by union agreements under each type for 1946 and 1951. The Bureau of Labor Statistics reported for 1946 that 33 per cent were covered by the closed shop, 17 per cent by the union shop, 25 per cent by maintenance of membership, an additional 3 per cent by preferential hiring arrangements, and the remaining 22 per cent simply by checkoffs or by no explicit form of union security other than exclusive bargaining rights as required by law.[3] The same investigation revealed that 24 per cent of all employees under union agreements were covered by automatic checkoff provisions, 17 per cent by the voluntary checkoff, and the remaining 59 per cent by no checkoff. The report for 1951 revealed that 61 per cent of all employees covered by agreements were under union-shop provisions, 13 per cent were under maintenance of membership clauses, and 26 per cent had no form of union security other than exclusive bargaining rights. Checkoff provisions applied to 78 per cent of employees under union contract in 1951. This total is comprised of 26 per cent who checked off dues alone, 17 per cent who included dues and initiation fees, 4 per cent who provided for dues and assessments, and 31 per cent who checked off dues, initiation fees, and assessments. The remaining 22 per cent of the employees under agreements were covered by no checkoff provision. Financial obligations of members, when collected, were presumably paid directly to the union steward, agent, or office.

A number of changes are reflected in a comparison of the figures for 1946 and 1951. In this 5-year period the closed shop has apparently disappeared; the maintenance of membership which was adopted as a wartime compromise by the War Labor Board has declined in importance; the voluntary checkoff has been greatly extended; and the union shop has become the dominant

3 "Extent of Collective Bargaining and Union Recognition, 1946," *Monthly Labor Review*, May, 1947, pp. 765–69; and "Union Status Under Collective Agreements, 1950–51," *Monthly Labor Review*, November, 1951, pp. 552–56.

form of union security, covering more than 60 per cent of all employees under agreements. These changes reflect the impact of the Taft-Hartley law.

The Wagner Act placed no limitation on the form of union security which an employer and a duly recognized or certified union could write into a contract. Indeed, a closed-shop provision was explicitly permitted. The Taft-Hartly law prohibited the closed shop. The statistics reflect that closed-shop *provisions* have disappeared from contracts. The figures, however, do not purport to reflect what actually happens in practice. The closed shop still remains very much in actual effect, despite the law, in industries such as longshoring, printing trades, and construction. The union is used in these situations as a source of supply for labor. The only practical source of workers, particularly in any numbers, is the union. The union supplies men only if it supplies all men required under union contract conditions. While occasional cases may result in an NLRB cease and desist order, the closed shop, in fact, generally continues in these situations.

The Taft-Hartley law, as originally enacted, introduced two changes in the traditional union shop.

a) A union-shop provision could be made effective only after a majority of eligible employees in the bargaining unit had voted to authorize a union-shop agreement. This authorization permitted, but did not require, the adoption of a union-shop contract provision. The Congress apparently believed that if employees were given the opportunity to vote on the union security question, a majority would frequently oppose the union shop. The record of these elections, however, discloses that employees voted overwhelmingly in favor of the union shop. In the 46,119 union-shop elections conducted by the NLRB in 4 years and 2 months, more than 6.5 millions of workers were eligible to vote. Negotiation of union-shop provisions were authorized in 97.1 per cent of the elections. Almost 85 per cent of the workers eligible to vote actually cast ballots, and 91.4 per cent of those voting were in favor of the union shop.[4] In the face of these results, and the delay and considerable expense involved in these union-shop elections, the Congress in 1951 amended the law (approved by the President October 22, 1951) to remove

[4] *Sixteenth Annual Report of the National Labor Relations Board* (Washington, D.C., 1952), p. 54.

the special election requirement. Any recognized or certified union which complies with other provisions of the Act and which negotiates a union-shop provision with an employer can now effectuate a union-shop contract without further authorization from the NLRB. The unions had used the union-shop election results as an added argument with management, contending that the vast majority of all employees were in favor of the union shop. This episode is another illustration of the difficulties Congress has had in understanding labor organizations and collective bargaining.

b) The Taft-Hartley law provides in Section 8 (*a*) 3 that it shall be an unfair labor practice for an employer to discharge a person as a consequence of a union-shop provision for any other reason than nonpayment of periodic dues and initiation fees. This provision creates a form of union shop which is substantially different from that previously in effect. Under the traditional union shop a union could insist that an employee be discharged for virtually any reason the union regarded as sufficient. Thus a union member may have been disciplined by the union and discharged by the employer for a variety of "crimes": fomenting a rival union, communist membership, poor standards of workmanship, "conduct unbecoming a union member," running for office against the incumbents, etc. The Taft-Hartley law provides that the employer can only recognize a union request for discharge under a union-shop provision if the reason for the failure to be in good standing is a failure to pay periodic dues and initiation fees. This limitation places a very great restriction on the old form of union shop. The new form of union shop, permissible under the Taft-Hartley law, requires no more than financial obligations to the union. The new form of the union shop is so different from the old that a new term had better been used: the "dues shop" would be more descriptive.

There has frequently been deep feeling and a considerable show of emotion regarding the union security provisions of collective bargaining agreements. The railroad and basic steel cases of 1952 are illustrative. Strong convictions are expressed not alone by management and union representatives but also by editorial writers, pamphleteers, and politicians. Why all the show of emotion and fireworks? Any explanation must include the unique historical significance, already noted above, of union security to the parties in collective bargaining in the United States. Further, both sides ordinarily contend that there are great issues of principle involved. The process of placing opposing principles against each other is not likely to lead to practical compromise but rather to further argument. The explanation of the feelings on this issue should also include the fact that union security clauses are widely thought to strengthen the position of the union in its future bargaining.

This introductory section to union security cases will not attempt to summarize the contending principles that have been advanced for and against all or particular union security provisions. The main arguments will be presented later in the context of a particular situation, the basic steel case of 1952; and each reader may make his own appraisal of the contending positions. (See Case 20.) One general comment, however, may be in order. It is the experience of the authors that the union security issue is never resolved in a particular contract as long as the parties debate general issues of principles. Only when this level of discussion is abandoned and the parties seek practical solutions to the questions raised by union security is agreement possible. Which group of employees should be included and which excluded? What redress is there for employees who feel they have been discriminated against within the union? How are new employees to be notified about the union and the agreement? What about religious objections to taking an oath of membership? When these questions are considered, there are almost limitless possibilities in the variety of union security provisions and related administrative arrangements.

In addition to the central questions concerning the terms of union security clauses of agreements, some problems arise in collective bargaining over the adminstration of these clauses. (*a*) May an individual employee (member) use the provisions of the contract to seek redress against any action of the union? May the grievance and arbitration provisions of an agreement be used to establish the facts as to payment of dues and other requirements of good standing membership? Or, is the conclusion of the union on such matters final for the employer? (*b*) What is the range of activity open to a union under an agreement in dealing with employees who are not required to join the union? What are the limits of activity in treating employees who may have been expelled from the union but who may still remain employees?

Case 19

UNION SECURITY CONTRACT PROVISIONS

There follow a number of contract provisions, including the language of one arbitration award, to illustrate the principal forms of union security. A comparison of these provisions will indicate in detail the differences among these principal types of union security and will also outline some of the administrative arrangements developed by the parties to implement union security.

1. *Closed Shop:*

"Employer agrees to hire all workmen it may require hereunder, in the classifications contained in Schedule 'A' hereto attached, through and from the unions and to continue in its employ in said classifications only workmen who are members in good standing of the respective unions signatory hereto and affiliated with and in good standing in the [parent body]. All workmen employed hereunder shall be required to present a clearance card from the appropriate union before being employed.

"The unions agree, on requisition of the employer, to furnish competent workmen in the classifications contained in Schedule 'A' for the prosecution of work covered by this agreement. The employer may refuse to employ and may discharge any employee for any just and sufficient cause . . . ."

"In the event that the union is unable to furnish workers in the numbers and with the qualifications required, it shall so notify the company within 48 hours after receipt of written request, and the company shall then be free to secure such employees from any source, provided that such right shall be restricted to the immediate needs of the company and shall not be extended to cover any future needs, which same shall be met in the manner provided above. Provided, further, that new employees not hired through the office of the union shall be directed by the company to report to said office for clearance within 48 hours of hiring, and, in any case before commencing work. The union shall not unreasonably withhold the issuance of such clearance when proper application is made."[1]

2. Union Shop:

A union-shop agreement was negotiated by the Eastern Railroads and seventeen operating railway labor organizations during 1952. This agreement was in part the outgrowth of a recommendation of an Emergency Board appointed under the Railway Labor Act. In order to facilitate an understanding of the contract language, excerpts from the Emergency Board Report are included which clarify the problems peculiar to the industry. One of the important points at issue was the "scope" of any security clause. To which employees shall any union-shop provisions apply? Some provisions of the agreements in the railroad industry have applied to some employees and not to other employees.

"It is well established by the Railway Labor Act that each labor organization upon being duly chosen by the majority, becomes the representative of the craft or class, and that thereupon it assumes the right and the duty of representing all the employes (defined to include subordinate officials) within the craft or class. [Formerly] many of the positions which the Carriers would now exclude from a union-shop requirement were classified as subordinate officials, and to a very large degree such employes have been included in the coverage of agreements since. Nevertheless, the Organizations have been persuaded to agree that they do not represent some positions at all, that some should be fully excepted from the provisions of their agreements, and that some should be partly excepted. The degree to which the last group are excepted has variations. Some are covered only in a most nominal way, some are covered by all rules except those designated as P.A.D.—promotion, assignment, and displacement. Those excepted only from P.A.D. are generally so-called personal office positions. Management is given free choice in selecting them, transferring them, and in demoting them to their original positions, without regard to normal seniority rights. If they are discharged, however, the union

[1] U.S. Department of Labor, *Union-Security Provisions in Collective Bargaining,* Bulletin 908 (Washington, D.C., 1947), pp. 7–8.

may represent them at hearings and throughout the grievance steps that may be taken." (*Report to The President by the Emergency Board* N.M.B. Case No. A3744, Feb. 14, 1952. pp. 39–40.)

". . . the Organizations now urge that they be granted the right to . . . have all those for whom they substantially bargain be compelled to join and share the expense and responsibility of their activities." (*Ibid.* p. 43.)

"The only definite exceptions from union-shop agreements which we can recommend . . . include the positions not represented by the labor organizations, those fully excepted by the scope rules, and those which have only nominal or token coverage. In the last category are those for whom the union does not bargain for wages, hours, or working conditions in the periodic agreements negotiated between the Organizations and the Carriers on the properties. Thus, positions excepted by the scope rule from all parts of the agreement other than the retention of seniority rights, the right to a hearing or trial before being discharged by the carrier, and/or the right to have handled any question arising out of the transfer from one seniority district to another, would be deemed to be positions with only token coverage and would not be subject to compulsory membership under a union-shop agreement." (*Ibid.* p. 44.)

"Contract Provisions

"*Section 1.* In accordance with and subject to the terms and conditions hereinafter set forth, all employes of the carriers now or hereafter subject to the Rules and Working Conditions Agreements between the parties hereto, except as hereinafter provided, shall, as a condition of their continued employment subject to such agreements, become members of the organization party to this agreement representing their craft or class within sixty calendar day of the date they first perform compensated service as such employes after the effective date of this agreement, and thereafter shall maintain membership in such organization.

"*Section 2.* This agreement shall not apply to employees while occupying positions which are excepted from the bulletining and displacement rules of the individual agreements, but this provision shall not include employes who are subordinate to and report to other employes who are covered by this agreement. However, such excepted employes are free to be members of the organization at their option.

"*Section 3. (a)*. Employes who retain seniority under the Rules and Working Conditions Agreements governing their class or craft and who are regularly assigned or transferred to full time employment not covered by such agreements, . . . will not be required to maintain membership as provided in Section 1 of this agreement so long as they remain in such other employment . . . .

(c). Employes who retain seniority under the Rules and Working Conditions Agreements governing their class or craft and who . . . are not in service covered by such agreements, or leave such service, will not be required to maintain membership . . . so long as they are not in service covered by such agreements . . . .

"*Section 4.* Nothing in this agreement shall require an employe to become or to remain a member of the organization if such membership is not available to such employe upon the same terms and conditions as are generally applicable to any other member, or if the membership of such employe is denied or terminated for any reason other than failure of the employe to tender the periodic dues, initiation fees, and assessments (not including fines and penalties) uniformly required as a condition of acquiring or retaining membership. For purposes of this agreement, dues, fees, and assessments, shall be deemed to be "uniformly required" if they are required of all employes in the same status at the same time in the same organizational unit."

3. *Modified Union Shop:*

A modified union shop differs from the union shop in that it provides specific exemption of certain groups of employees from the membership requirement. These exemptions normally apply to present (nonunion) employees or to long-service employees, and provision may be made for various escape periods. Contract provisions may differ in the particular category of employees who are exempted from the requirement to join the Union. Two contract provisions are illustrative.

1. The 1950 General Motors–UAW agreement provides as follows:

"Any employe who is a member of the Union in good standing on the effective date of this agreement shall, as a condition of employment, maintain his membership in the Union to the extent of paying membership dues and International and local union general assessments uniformly levied against all union members. Such employe may have his membership dues and such assessments deducted from his earnings by signing the form for 'Authorization for Checkoff of Dues,' or if no such authorization is in effect, he must pay his membership dues and such assessments directly to the Union.

"Any employe who on the effective date of this agreement is not a member of the Union shall not be required to become a member of the Union as a condition of continued employment. Any such employe, however, who during the life of this agreement joins the Union must maintain his membership thereafter as provided in [the preceding paragraph].

"Any employe hired on or after the effective date of this agreement shall become a member of the Union upon acquiring seniority, and he shall, as a condition of employment, maintain his union membership for one year to the extent of paying membership dues and International and local Union general assessments uniformly levied against all members, subject to the following:

"(1) If not more than twenty days and not less than ten days immediately preceding the first anniversary date of his acquisition of seniority such employe notifies the Company and the Union in writing that he has resigned from union membership, such action shall automatically cancel his 'Authorization for Checkoff of Dues,' and such employe shall not be obligated thereafter to maintain his membership in the Union, nor to pay any dues or assessments as a condition of employment during the remaining life of this agreement.

"(2) In case no such notice is given, such employe shall maintain his membership in the Union as a condition of employment during the life of this agreement to the extent of paying membership dues and International and local Union general assessments uniformly levied against all members.

"The Local Union will furnish Local Management, within 15 days from the effective date of this agreement, the names of all members paying dues direct to the Local Union.

"Any dispute arising as to the employes' membership in the Union shall be reviewed by a representative of Local Management and the Chairman of the Local Shop Committee, and if not resolved, may be decided by the Impartial Umpire.

" 'Member of the Union' where used herein means any employe who is a member of the Union and is not more than sixty days in arrears in the payment of the union dues and assessments specified herein.

"Initiation fees for membership in the Union shall not exceed the minimum prescribed by the Constitution of the International Union at the time the employe becomes a member.

"During the life of this Agreement, the Corporation agrees to deduct union membership dues levied by the International Union or Local Union in accordance with the Constitution and By-Laws of the Union, from the pay of each employe who executes or has executed the 'Authorization for Check-off of Dues' form . . . . ."

2. The United States Steel Company 1952 contract with the United Steelworkers of America, CIO, provides as follows:

"1. Each employee who, on July 24, 1952, is a member of the Union in good standing in accordance with its Constitution and By-laws and each employee who becomes a member after that date shall, as a condition of employment, maintain his membership in the Union in good standing for the duration of this Agreement; provided, however, that this provision shall not apply to any employee who, within the 15 days next preceding the end of this Agreement, shall withdraw from membership in the Union.

"2. Each new employee shall sign and furnish to the Company at the time of his employment an application card, in duplicate, for membership in the Union, in a form agreed to in writing by the Company and the Union. A copy of such card shall be furnished to the employee. Such application card shall provide that it shall not become effective until the expiration of 30 days after the date of his employment and that it shall not thereafter become effective if such employee shall mail to the Company a written notice of his election not to become a member of the Union, which notice shall be postmarked not less than 15 days and not more than 30 days after the date of his employment. The Company shall promptly furnish to the Union a copy of each such notice received by it. If such application shall become effective at the expiration of 30 days, one signed copy of it shall then be turned over to the Union. The Union shall be given reasonable opportunity to inspect all such notices which shall be received by the Company.

"3. On or before the last day of each month the Union shall submit to the Company a notarized list showing separately for each Plant the name, department symbol and check or badge number of each employee who shall have become a member of the Union in good standing other than through the procedures as provided in Section 2 above since the last previous list of such members was furnished to the Company. The Company shall continue to rely upon the membership lists which have been certified to it by the Union as of December 31, 1951, subject to revision by the addition of new members certified to it by the Union between such date and the date of this agreement and to the deletion of the names of employees who have withdrawn from membership during such period."

4. *Maintenance of Membership:*

Maintenance of membership provisions came into widespread use under the wartime orders of the War Labor Board which sought to compromise employers' objections to compulsory union membership and union demands for the union shop. The prevalence of this type of clause reached its peak in 1946. Since then it has steadily decreased in popularity.

"All employees, who, on January 1, 1952, are members of the Union in good standing in accordance with its constitution and by-laws, and all employees who become members after that date shall, as a condition of employment, maintain their membership in the Union in good standing for the duration of the collective bargaining agreement in which this provision is incorporated.

"The Union shall, immediately after the aforesaid date, furnish the Company with a notarized list of its members in good standing as of that date.

"It is agreed that at the expiration of this agreement before there will be any renewal of the above provisions there will be a 15-day escape period allowed during which any employee may withdraw from membership without such withdrawal affecting his employment.

"The Union, its officers and members, shall not intimidate or coerce employees into joining the Union or continuing their membership therein."

5. *Compulsory Checkoff of Dues:*

Following a 3½-month strike at the Ford plants in Windsor, Ontario, Justice I. C. Rand was appointed to arbitrate the points which could not be settled by collective bargaining. The principal issue before Justice Rand was the union's demand for a union shop.

In analyzing the merits of the union's request, Justice Rand stated that the following premises should be accepted: (1) the social desirability of the organization of workers and of collective bargaining where employees seek them; (2) labour unions must be strong in order to carry on the functions for which they are intended; (3) the power of organized labour, the necessary co-partner of capital, must be available to redress the balance of what is called social justice; and (4) the power of organized labour, in turn, must be accompanied by balancing controls in relation to individual members or workers over whom such power may be exersised, as well as to industry and the public.

"Union security," he stated, "is simply security in the maintenance of the strength and integrity of the union. Disruptive forces may come from the Company or from other competing labour organizations or simply from the lack of centripetal force within the employee body. But the first is now forbidden by law and the second is not in fact present." Therefore, in his judgment, the only threat to security to be found in the case was the indifference of some employees to the value of the union.

In spite of the fact that the Ford Motor Company had accepted the union shop and check off in union agreements affecting 100,000 employees in the United States and although the union-shop principle had been accepted voluntarily by employers in many Canadian industries, Justice Rand concluded that he could not award a union shop in the case before him. First, he felt it would deny the individual Canadian the right to seek work and to work independently of personal association with an organized group. Second, it would subject an employee to the danger of arbitrary action by the union and thereby place his economic life at the mercy of an uncontrolled—and in this case—an immature group.

On the other hand, it is acknowledged that employees as a whole become beneficiaries of union action. It is doubtful if anything provokes more resentment in a plant than this sharing of the fruits of unionist work and courage by the nonmember. Justice Rand advanced the general proposition and that it would not be inequitable to require all employees to contribute toward the expense of maintaining the organization which has struggled for these benefits enjoyed by all employees.

Unlike the employees in craft industries, where skills and long apprenticeship are involved, these employees represent a concentration of manpower in a framework of machines. The initiative and artistry of the individual is nonexistent or becomes stereotyped. Thus one cannot find among these employees "that generalized individuality in understanding and appreciation of the necessity for employee organization which craftsmen have tended to evolve." The objectives of the employees at the Ford Motor Company plant and their conception of union functions were much too simplified in Justice Rand's opinion to provide a natural security for the union. With an annual layoff for retooling, the union is subject to periodic disorganizing tendencies. Further, the union does not have the opportunity to appeal to individuals through social activities in this type of plant.

For these reasons, he concludes that it is "essential to the larger concern of the industry that there be mass treatment in the relation of employees to that organization which is necessary to the primary protection of their interests." It is appropriate that all employees should be required to shoulder their portion of the burden of expense for administering the union contract. "They must take the burden along with the benefit." The obligation to pay dues should tend to induce membership. This, in turn, should promote "wider interest and control within the union which is the condition of progressive responsibility."

Is it unjust to compel employees who do not choose to join the union to pay dues to that organization, particularly when, as nonmembers, they will have nothing to say about the expenditure of union moneys? In Justice Rand's opinion, it is not. First, the dues are only those which members of the union are satisfied to pay for receipt of the same benefits. Second, any employee is free to join the union and still retain his independence in employment. Justice Rand agrees, however, that in one respect even the dues-paying nonmember should have a voice in union decisions: the decision to strike.

On the basis of these conclusions, Justice Rand denied the union shop which would require employees to join the union within a stated time. Instead he awarded a compulsory checkoff of dues and assessments for general union purposes upon all employees who came within the unit to which the agreement applied. The checkoff was not to include assessments for special purposes, such as insurance, in which the nonmember employees could not participate; nor did it include the usual entrance fee. His award provided further that no strike, either general or partial, could be called by the union unless such action was authorized by a majority of *all* employees—members and nonmembers of the union—in a secret ballot supervised by the Department of Labour for Ontario.

Finally, his award imposed certain requirements on the union, designed to develop union responsibility and to insure a fair administration of this formula: (*a*) any employee had the right to become a member of the union by paying the entrance fee and complying with the constitution and bylaws of the union; (*b*) if a strike is called by the union without the required authorization or if the union fails to repudiate any strike action in the manner prescribed by the award, the checkoff provision may be suspended for not less than two and not more than six monthly deductions.

Justice Rand made this appraisal of what is now referred to as the "Rand Formula":

"This mechanism, from the orthodox standpoint, preserves the basic liberties of Company and employee . . . . The assessment affects only the employees; the employer is concerned only in the expense of the check-off and the strength which it may give to the union. But the expense can properly be taken as the employer's contribution toward making the union through its greater independence more effective in its disciplinary pressure even upon employees who are not members, an end which the Company admits to be desirable. I should perhaps add that I do not for a moment suggest that this is a device of general applicability. Its object is primarily to enable the union to function properly. In other cases it might defeat that object by lessening the necessity for self-development. In dealing with each labour situation we must pay regard to its special features and circumstances."

Case 20

UNION SHOP IN THE BASIC STEEL INDUSTRY

UNION: United Steelworkers of America, CIO

COMPANIES: Companies Comprising the Basic Steel Industry

The individual contracts between the Union and the United States Steel Company, Bethlehem Steel Corporation, Republic Steel Corporation, Jones and Laughlin Steel Corporation, Youngstown Sheet and Tube Company, Inland Steel Company, and most other producers of basic steel expired on December 31, 1951. The union security clauses of these contracts provided for the maintenance of membership. This clause was first included in 1942 in those contracts, over the objections of the Companies, as a result of a directive order of the War Labor Board.

The Union presented a large number of demands (originally 22) to the Companies for the contracts to replace those which expired on December 31, 1951. One of these demands provided that the maintenance of membership clauses be replaced by the "maximum union security permissible under the Taft-Hartley Act or applicable state statutes."

On December 22, 1951, the President of the United States referred these disputes between the Union and the various basic steel companies to the tripartite Wage Stabilization Board. The duty of the Board, pursuant to Executive Order 10233, was to "investigate and to inquire into the issues in dispute and promptly report to the President thereon with recommendations to the parties as to fair and equitable terms of settlement." The Board requested, and the parties agreed, to maintain normal work and production schedules while the Board heard the case. The Board then established a tripartite panel to which the parties presented their case extensively. The panel issued a report on March 13, 1952, outlining the issues in dispute and summarizing the positions of the parties. On the union-shop demand of the Union, the panel made no report but simply presented to the Board the briefs and the transcript of the oral statements made by the parties. On March 20, 1952, the Board issued its recommendations on the issues in dispute including the union security demand of the Union.

POSITION OF THE UNION[1]

The Union proposed that all employees be required, as a condition of employment, to become members of the Union 30 days after the beginning of employment or after the effective date of the new agreement, whichever is later, and thereafter to retain their membership by payment of dues.

At this late date in labor-management relations, there should be no need for lengthy justification of a union-shop provision. Employers who are sincerely interested in dealing with a responsible union must realize that security for the union is a prerequisite of union responsibility. When a recognized union does not have full security, it must dissipate its energies in organizing nonmembers in the bargaining unit and in warding off raids of rival groups which concentrate on employees who have failed to join the recognized union. Under such conditions, it is exceedingly difficult for a union to exercise the internal control and direction which is essential to full responsibility in dealing with management.

Moreover, unions and union members have every right to require that "free riders," who work alongside union members and who benefit from the advances won by the union for all

[1] *In the matter of United Steelworkers of America, CIO, and Various Steel and Iron Ore Companies, Case No. D-18-C, Un. Exh. 6, pp. 31–38.*

workers, shall contribute their fair and just share toward the support of the union. Even the antilabor authors of the Taft-Hartley Act recognized the propriety of requiring free riders to pay their share, although the limited form of union shop permitted by that Act is virtually restricted to compelling free riders to pay dues and initiation fees.

Until recently, the Taft-Hartley Act required unions to win union security elections. This requirement was devised on the theory that workers did not want the union shop and would vote against it. Under the actual operation of this provision, however, workers recorded their overwhelming approval of the union shop.

In the steel industry, as in other industries, the union security authorization elections held under the Taft-Hartley Act disclosed an overwhelming preference on the part of the workers for the union shop. Out of nearly half a million workers eligible to vote in these elections, 70 per cent voted in favor of the union shop; while only 13.5 per cent voted against the union-shop authorization. Slightly less than 20 per cent failed to vote at all.

Maintenance of membership has never been a satisfactory form of union security from the standpoint of the union and its members. It does not give the union the security it needs to administer a contract. It does not compel free riders to bear their share of the costs of winning improved wages and working conditions.

Because they are not adequate even to provide minimum union security, the use of maintenance of membership clauses has steadily diminished since the end of World War II, while the use of union-shop clauses has steadily increased. A recent study by the Bureau of Labor Statistics (*Monthly Labor Review*, November, 1951, p. 554) declared:

> "This type of union status (maintenance of membership) has declined in importance since the end of World War II hostilities, and was provided by only 13 percent of the 1950–51 agreements studied. It is most prevalent in the primary metal industries, in which four-fifths of the employees were covered by such provisions."

This study was based on a survey of 2,651 collective bargaining agreements, covering 5,581,000 workers, in effect in late 1950 and 1951. Of the 26 major industry groups covered in this survey, the "primary metal industries" group, of which basic steel is the largest component, was the only one in which maintenance of membership was found still to predominate. In that group 38 per cent of the agreements covering 80 per cent of the workers were found to have maintenance of membership clauses, while 45 per cent of the agreements covering 14 per cent of the workers had union-shop provisions. Maintenance of membership is an atavistic relic of World War II, which has survived until now almost solely in the basic steel industry.

In contrast with the continued decline in maintenance of membership clauses since World War II, the study found:

"Union-shop clauses in collective-bargaining agreements increased in prevalence during 1950–51, compared with 1949–50, while those providing for maintenance of membership or merely sole-bargaining recognition decreased."

The Union's Research Department, during November, 1951, made a study of 143 outstanding agreements covering 5,000 or more workers each in industries outside of basic steel and iron ore mining. These agreements, covering 3,196,100 workers in almost every major industry group outside of basic steel and iron ore mining, were obtained from the BLS and other sources.

Two thirds of these contracts, covering three fourths of the workers, provided either for a regular union shop or for a modified union shop, exempting old employees. The percentage of modified union shops is presumably about the same as found by the BLS study, i.e., 14 per cent of the total number of union shops. Of the 143 contracts examined by the Union, 10.6 per cent provided for maintenance of membership. About one fourth of the contracts contained no union security provision.

A further study, also during November, 1951, made by the Union's Contract Department of contracts in the steel industry, both basic steel and fabricating, shows that out of a total of 1,964 such contracts covering production and maintenance units, 1,017, or about 52 per cent, have union-shop provisions. Only a few are of the modified type. While the majority of these contracts thus provide for the union shop, they cover considerably less than one half of the employees. It is the prevalence of maintenance of membership in the huge basic steel plants which produces this disparity.

Even in basic steel there are, however, a number of union-shop agreements. Of the 66 Companies having ingot or pig iron capacity, i.e. basic steel plants, with which the Union had contracts in October, 1951, the Union had agreements containing union-shop provisions with 27 Companies. Some of these provisions establish full union shops, while others do not require that old employees join.

It is high time for the entire steel industry, and particularly for the huge basic steel Companies, to get into line with the rest of American industry as respects union security. There is no conceivable reason why the Union, which deals with this country's most powerful corporations, should enjoy less favorable provisions as regards its security than unions which deal with corporations of more moderate size and power.

No doubt, since pious hypocrisy seems to be endemic to this industry, some of the steel companies will argue that they are opposed in principle to the union shop. Perhaps they will say that they are worried about the freedom of their workers, despite the fact that the overwhelming mass of their workers have shown that they do not want to work with nonunion men. It should be sufficient answer to these antique and never genuine protestations that each and every one of the major basic steel corporations has for many years had a union shop or a closed shop in all of the coal mines which it owns and operates. Bethlehem Steel, the second largest producer in the industry, has a union shop in its Pacific Coast shipyards.

The United Steelworkers of America cannot and will not any longer tolerate that their Union should be treated less favorably in this vital respect than any other unions. This discrimination is now going to be ended once and for all.

POSITION OF THE COMPANIES[2]

The position of these Companies with regard to the Union's demand for compulsory membership is as follows:

1. The United Steelworkers of America has made no showing whatever of present *need* for a governmentally imposed union shop.

The 600,000 members of this Union in 1942 has grown to 1,045,000 members in 1951.

[2] *Should the Government Force Employees to Join a Union?* A discussion by John C. Gall, also see *Co. Exh.* 17–20.

The Union collected dues and initiation fees of over $12,-000,000 in the first 6 months of 1951.

Since 1935, various statutes have made legally secure the position of the Union and the right of steel company employees to join the Union and carry on its activities.

Court decisions have reinforced these rights and have protected unions and their members against any possible threats of undercutting or undermining.

We are not dealing with a state of union insecurity. We are dealing with a union state of mind.

2. We reject the Union's idea that the right of an individual to refrain from joining a union is less entitled to protection than is the right to join a union. The Norris–LaGuardia Act treats the rights as equal in nature and extent. So does the Labor-Management Relations Act. That these rights are not equally protected by the Constitution was the basic argument of the American Federation of Labor in the Right-to-Work Cases.

3. We reject the argument of the Union that the only choice of an individual workman in the steel industry is between domination by the employer and domination by the Union. Employers in this industry have no desire to dominate their employees. We assert that the alternative to domination is not domination; it is freedom.

4. We reject the argument that because others have made union-shop agreements with this Union and with other unions *through collective bargaining,* we should be required to do so *by government intervention.* The Union makes this purely statistical approach to a problem of human rights, human feelings, and human emotions. If others have entered into the large number of collective agreements with this Union which the Union alleges, it proves only that the Union has been highly successful in achieving its objective through voluntary processes. It tends strongly to disprove the need for governmental aid to the Union in its campaign.

5. We reject any argument that the union shop necessarily insures peace and harmony in industrial relations. Experience in the completely unionized bituminous coal industry completely refutes this notion.

The Union refers to the fact that some of the steel Companies having coal mines have made union-shop agreements with the United Mine Workers of America.

Leaving aside for the moment the circumstances under which that result came about, the fact is that those are still *agreements* and are not *governmentally-imposed conditions.* The Union continues to talk as if the issue in the present case were merely whether some individual employer should or should not enter into a union-shop agreement with the United Steelworkers of America. But that is not the issue in this case. The issue is whether a governmental board should put the influence of the Government of the United States back of the Union's efforts and thus, in effect compel union membership.

Furthermore, we do not believe the United Steelworkers of America or the Wage Stabilization Board would wish to go before the American public with the contention that the union shop has been a guaranty of peace and harmony in bituminous coal mines in recent years.

From April, 1941, through November, 1949, there were 18 strikes affecting all or a substantial part of the bituminous coal mines; the total number of work days lost during that period was 281, or approximately one entire working year; the total production lost by these strikes was approximately 390 million tons; and the wage loss to employees due to these strikes was 753 million dollars. (BLS data.)

It may be argued by the Steelworkers Union that the difference is in the kind of leadership the two unions have. But we are now talking about permanent government policies. No one but a child could believe that a policy of the kind advocated would endure for only a single contract. Yet the leadership of unions can and does change. The Wage Stabilization Board will surely act on some basis more secure than a prophecy as to the tenure of individuals.

6. There is no basis for the union argument that complete unionization is necessary to the effective observance or enforcement of collective contracts. There is no claim here by the employers that the Union has failed because of inadequate strength to observe the obligation of its contracts. There is not a shred of evidence by the Union that it has lacked strength or security to fulfill its contractual obligations.

7. There is no merit in the "free rider" argument. As Mr. Justice Brandeis said:

"The union attains success when it reaches the ideal condition, and the *ideal condition of a union is to be strong and stable, and yet to have in the trade outside its own ranks an appreciable number of men who are non-unionist.* In any free community the diversity of character, of beliefs, of taste—indeed mere selfishness—will insure such a supply, *if the enjoyment of this privilege of individualism is protected by law.* Such a nucleus of unorganized labor will check oppression by the union as the union checks oppression by the employer."

The unions would make it appear that Congress and the Courts, in writing and sustaining the "majority rule" of the Wagner Act, have imposed upon them a new and onerous duty of representing those in the unit who are not members, and that the Union should be paid for this function. The obvious answer is that the unions asked for this role, fought for it in Congress and the Courts, and we venture to say would be exceedingly loath to part with it.

The Union is really asking for the right to levy a tax on those who do not wish to support it. The very form of the demand here so proves. Mr. Justice Frankfurter said: "Unions are powers within the State." We say, what the Union apparently wants is to be state within the state.

Some people simply do not wish to join and pay dues to a labor union. Up to this time, government has said they have a right to remain out if they wish. The Union wants this Board to say they have a right to join but no right *not to join.* It asks you to reverse the policy laid down by Congress and reaffirmed by the Supreme Court of the United States. In essence, then, the controversy is not over "free riders"—it is over "free choice."

The Steelworkers Union has declared before this Panel that the Union will not bargain over the demand for the union shop. The Union said:

"We have told the companies that there can be *no agreement* with this Union unless the union shop is granted to the Steelworkers Union."

In the face of this flat pronouncement, which is as much a challenge to the Wage Stabilization Board as to the Companies, it appears that a reference back to collective bargaining might well be an idle gesture.

We think the Board should respond to this challenge, and at the same time perform a great public service, by saying to the Union:

"This Board will not recommend that any person be required to join or remain a member of a labor organization as the price of working in the steel industry. We recommend instead that the Union withdraw its demand."

RECOMMENDATION OF THE WAGE STABILIZATION BOARD:

A majority of the Board, industry dissenting, recommends that the parties include a union-shop provision in their new contracts, the exact form and condition thereof to be determined by them in their forthcoming negotiations.

The Public Members would have preferred a different recommendation, one which would have returned the matter to the parties for collective bargaining, with the Board to be prepared to consider further recommendations in the event the parties failed to resolve the issue. But a majority of the Board could not be obtained to support this position. When the Labor Members moved for a recommendation of the union shop, the Public Members voted in the negative, stating that they did so because they believed that the parties should be given another chance to bargain on the issue, since their prior bargaining had been so unsatisfactory. The Public Members then moved their proposal, and this was rejected by both the Labor and Industry Members. The latter took the position that retention of jurisdiction would imply that, if the parties failed to agree, the Board might then make the recommendation, whereas the Board should not recommend the union shop in any case. The Public Members were thus left with only the alternative of recommending the union shop or agreeing that the Board would not do so in any case. Under the necessity of choosing between these alternatives, the Public Members concluded that reason, fairness, and equity required the former.

UNION SECURITY

The Union is vested by law with the right and the duty to bargain on behalf of *all* employees in the various units covered by collective bargaining contracts on wages, hours, terms, and conditions of employment, including union security.

There are a number of alternatives other than the full union shop available to the parties. In considering the particular form and conditions of a union-shop clause as recommended by the Board, the parties will have a wealth of experience and examples to aid them; for employers and unions in this country have, with practical ingenuity, devised and agreed upon various modifications of the basic union-shop formula.

Without attempting to limit the area of discussion between the parties, or expressing a preference, we wish merely to call attention to some of these variations, in addition to the full union shop as authorized by Congress. There is, for example, the modified form of union shop agreed upon by the General Motors Corporation and the United Automobile Workers Union, CIO. This union security arrangement between one of the largest unions and one of the largest and most efficient corporations in the country is an integral part of a collective agreement which secured to each party certain of its basic objectives. One feature of this type of arrangement is that it reserves to old employees who had not previously joined the Union the option to determine whether or not to join, and it limits the obligation to present members or new employees.

Crucible Steel Company of America and the Steelworkers Union have a somewhat similar union-shop clause in their contract. Old employees who are not union members are not required to join, but new employees must become members of the Union. Unlike the provision in the General Motors contract, the Crucible contract provides no "escape" for members once they join.

Another type of union security clause which has received considerable attention is the so-called maintenance of dues or "Rand formula." (See Case 19.)

The heated discussion of the union shop has, we think, tended to confuse the issue. We think it might be helpful to make the following observations.

The development of bargaining relations in mass production industries since the early 1930's is well known. Unions were normally first recognized as bargaining agents for their members only. The principles of majority rule and exclusive representation were accepted as national policy and were embodied in the National Labor Relations (Wagner) Act and continued in the Taft-Hartley Act. Under these laws the union selected by the majority of employees has the legal right and obligation to represent all employees in the bargaining unit, whether members of the union or not. The 1940's saw the extension of maintenance of membership arrangements; and thus to the "sole bargaining agent" clauses were added provisions requiring employees who were union members as of a given date to remain members for the duration of a contract. More recently, the union-shop clause has become most prevalent in collective agreements, with maintenance of membership clauses frequently being replaced by arrangements voluntarily agreed to by employers, under which all employees covered by an agreement must become union members.

These developments have not occurred without extensive debate at each stage, and Congress itself has played a major role in shaping the course of events. In 1935, 1947, and 1951, Congress heard and rejected virtually the same arguments which the steel companies have submitted in the present case. The majority-rule provision which Congress wrote into the Wagner Act in 1935 was attacked as undemocratic, on the ground that it deprived individuals of their right to speak for themselves and subjected an unwilling minority to rule by the majority. Twelve years later, however, when Congress enacted the Taft-Hartley Act and drastically revised federal labor policy, there was little if any opposition to the majority-rule provision. The opposition to the union-shop provision is to some extent a reflection of the original opposition to the principle of majority rule in labor-management relations.

The controversy over union security in World War II was similar in many ways to that occasioned by the present dispute. The arguments then against maintenance of membership were approximately the same as those now employed in opposition to the union shop. Then, as now, it was contended that while the law permits an employer voluntarily to enter into an agreement providing for a union shop in one form or another, it is quite another thing for an administrative agency of government to suggest such a provision in an effort to settle a dispute. Notwithstanding this contention, the maintenance of membership clauses incorporated into the steel industry contracts pursuant to War Labor Board directives have largely been continued by voluntary agreement in successive contracts in this industry and elsewhere. The Companies have stated their willingness to renew such clauses. It seems relevant to inquire, therefore, whether the evils which some employers first saw in the maintenance of membership clauses existed only because such clauses were proposed by a government agency. The effect upon the individual employee resulting from a contract signed pursuant to a government proposal is no different when identical contracts are signed as the result of collective bargaining.

It is now contended, however, that while maintenance of membership is essentially voluntary in character, protecting an employee's "freedom to join or not to join, to stay in or get out," the union shop is wholly compulsory, and therefore undemocratic. We are reminded that the War Labor Board refused to order the union shop, and we are warned that such a recommendation from the Wage Stabilization Board would constitute an intolerable invasion by government into the realm of individual liberty.

In fact, the War Labor Board did order the union shop in a number of cases for a variety of reasons. In some cases, for example, the employer had offered the union shop during negotiations; in others, the employer had agreed to the union shop with another union; and in others, the previous contract contained a union-shop clause.

The War Labor Board declined to order the union shop in many more cases. It is apparent, however, that the basic reasons for that Board's reluctance no longer exist. The type of union shop then sought by organized labor contained none of the statutory restrictions now in effect, which are designed to prevent unions from enforcing union-shop agreements against employees who are arbitrarily denied admission or expelled. The lack of these statutory protections appears to have weighed heavily with the industry members of the War Labor Board. In their dissenting opinion in the *Federal Shipbuilding and Drydock Case,* they said in part:

". . . acting in our capacity as members of a Government agency, we cannot subscribe to any national labor policy which compels an unwilling employer to force an unwilling employee either to join or to remain a member of a labor union in order to play his part in winning this war. *If this*

*position is taken by a Government agency and a national
labor policy is thus established, then Government must of necessity accept the responsibility of supervision of that labor
organization to which it forces an employee to pay dues, fines
and assessments . . . ."* (Italics added.)

Evidently, Congress had the same thought in mind when in
1947 it enacted the Taft-Hartley amendments to the National
Labor Relations Act. After considerable debate, it rejected attempts to outlaw the union shop; instead it prescribed arrangements under which no employee can be prevented from getting or
holding a job because of nonmembership in a union so long as
he tenders his initiation fee and periodic dues. Moreover, these
charges cannot be excessive or discriminatory.

The considerations which led Congress to adopt this course
of action were summarized by the principal sponsor of the legislation, during the debates, stating in part, as follows: (*Congres-
sional Record April 23, 1947, p. 3953*):

". . . We have proposed a proviso in the case where a
man is refused admittance to a union, when an employer
employs a non-union man, and during the first 30 days of his
employment he goes to the union and says, 'I want to join the
union,' but the union refused to take him. It is provided that
in such case the employer shall not be compelled to discharge
the man simply because the union will not let him join the
union on the same terms and conditions as any other member.
In effect, we say, 'If you are going to have a union shop, then
you must have an open union.' You cannot say to people, 'we
have a closed union shop, and we are not going to let you in
under any circumstances.'

"The bill further provides that if the man is admitted to
the union, and subsequently is fired from the union for any
reason other than non-payment of dues, then the employer
shall not be required to fire that man. *In other words, what
we do, in effect, is to say that no one can get a free ride in
such a shop.* The employee has to pay the union dues. But on
the other hand, if the union discriminates against him and
fires him from the union, the employer shall not be required
to fire him from the job . . . .

"I think the justice of such an arrangement should be clear. As I have said, either we should have an open shop or we should have an open union. I do not believe we should permit the complete exclusion from any industry of a man who wants to work in that industry, and whom the employer wants to employ, and who is perfectly competent to work there, simply because the union says 'We do not want you and we will not let you in' or 'We are going to fire you from the union because we do not like the way you act.' " (Italics added.)

We think it unnecessary to analyze at greater length the provisions of the Taft-Hartley Act which bear upon this issue. Congress has sought to eliminate from union-shop agreements those conditions which it considers unfair or contrary to public policy. Congress has, in fact, dealt with this problem of union security on three separate occasions since the matter was before the War Labor Board: in the Taft-Hartley Act in 1947; in the Railway Labor Act amendments in 1951; and in the Taft-Hartley amendments in 1951.

The changes in existing labor laws enacted by Congress in 1951 are significant. After some 17 years of experience under the amended Railway Labor Act of 1934, which prohibited all types of union-security agreements in the railroad and air transport industries, Congress amended the act so as to permit substantially the same type of union security agreements authorized by the Taft-Hartley Act. And Congress went still further. After 4 years of experience under the Taft-Hartley Act, during which time unions had won by substantial majorities almost every union-shop authorization election conducted by the National Labor Relations Board, Congress concluded that it was both extravagant and useless to continue this procedure. Accordingly, it adopted the Taft-Humphrey amendments to the law which, among other things, eliminated the requirement of a union-shop authorization vote as a prerequisite for a union-shop agreement.

The legislation passed the Senate by unanimous voice vote and was approved by the House by a vote of 307 to 18. It is apparent, therefore, that Congress now regards the type of union-shop agreement permitted by law to be consistent with American concepts of equity and fair play.

Thus the fundamental issue concerning individual rights in relation to the privileges of the majority was decided by Congress in 1935; affirmed by the Supreme Court in 1937; and was left unaffected by Congress in 1947, when it passed the Taft-Hartley Act. On these occasions, Congress and the Supreme Court decided that the bargaining agent selected by the majority of employees should and does have the exclusive right to represent *all* employees in dealing with management concerning wages, hours, and working conditions. In turn, the bargaining agent has the obligation fairly to represent all employees, whether members of the union or not. If, in the interests of a group of workers, it is not an unwarranted infringement of individual liberty to deprive a person of the right to make his own labor contract, it cannot be an infringement to ask him to lend financial and other support to the organization which bargains for benefits to all employees in the group. The granting of a union shop thus has relatively minor effect, if any, on individual rights under existing law.

It is alleged by others than the parties to these proceedings that the Wage Stabilization Board lacks authority to make recommendations on the union security and other so-called noneconomic issues. This represents a misunderstanding of the source and nature of the Board's disputes authority.

Unlike the Board's stabilization authority, which rests squarely on the provisions of the Defense Production Act, the Board's dispute functions stem from Executive Order 10233, issued on April 24, 1951. The order contains both general and specific limitations. Only those disputes may come before the Board which "have not been resolved by collective bargaining or by the prior full use of conciliation and mediation facilities and which threaten an interruption of work affecting the national defense." Even such disputes may not be heard by the Board unless the parties in a particular case voluntarily agree to submit their dispute to the Board and the Board agrees to accept it, or unless the dispute is referred to the Board by the President because in his opinion it "substantially threatens the progress of national defense."

The developments which led to the adoption of Executive Order 10233 are well known. About a year ago, when the Wage Stabilization Board was reconstituted in its present form, the most debated issue was whether jurisdiction should extend to noneconomic issues as well as to economic issues. With industry members dissenting, the National Advisory Board on Mobilization Policy recommended to the President that he reconstitute the Board with authority to make recommendations in disputes which threaten an interruption of work affecting the national defense.

The President adopted that recommendation and issued Executive Order 10233. From that point on, it was generally understood that the Wage Stabilization Board had jurisdiction in dispute cases over both economic and noneconomic issues and that among the noneconomic issues would be the union shop. Indeed, that knowledge explains one of the reasons why some people a year ago opposed the National Advisory Board's recommendation to the President. It has thus been clear since the issuance of Executive Order 10233 that the Board would be called upon to make a recommendation on the union-shop issue if the parties were unable to settle it and if their dispute threatened an interruption of work affecting the national defense.

Section 4 of Executive Order 10233 declares that the Board shall take no action inconsistent with the provisions of the Labor Management Relations (Taft-Hartley) Act. The same restriction appears in Title V of the Defense Production Act and would govern any Board established thereunder. In assigning to this Board the limited disputes function described above, therefore, the President imposed upon it the same prohibitions, in this regard, as Congress directed should be applied to a board created under the Defense Production Act.

This means that in making recommendations in disputes cases properly before it, the Board may not recommend terms of settlement which call upon either side to do anything, or to agree to anything, not permitted under the Taft-Hartley Act or any other applicable law.

Once the precise nature of the Board's disputes authority is understood, it becomes apparent that the issue of union security— which is only one of many nonwage issues in this case—is properly a subject for recommendation by this Board, as are all the other issues. In this case, as in many other disputes, the disagreement over purely economic matters is only part of the total dispute. This Board is charged with the duty to recommend fair and equitable terms of settlement on all the issues in this case. It necessarily follows that the scope of our authority to recommend as to those issues must be as broad as the parties' power to agree.

The parties have the power to agree on some solution of the union-shop issue. The authority of the Board is coextensive.

CONTRACT CLAUSE AGREED UPON

After a protracted strike the parties agreed upon the modified union-shop clause which appears in Case 19 above.

QUESTIONS

1. What considerations in your judgment would be different in this case if it were before a private arbitrator for "final and binding determination" rather than before a government agency for a "recommendation" to the parties.

2. Does the recommendation for some form of a union shop in this case mean that a similar recommendation would have to be made in every case? What standards could you establish to distinguish among cases? Would you consider the length of the collective bargaining relationship? The proportion of the bargaining unit who are members of the Union?

3. Does the recommendation of a government agency for some form of the union shop tend to create additional disputes in other plants where the Union may desire to get to a board to secure a similar recommendation? Can this problem be avoided? Is it inherent in any dispute settling machinery? Would *ad hoc* emergency boards be subject to comparable difficulties?

4. Should a disputes settling government agency rule on all questions presented to it? What is the difference between "denial" of a demand and referral back to the parties?

5. How do you appraise the argument that this Union is strong and powerful and has shown no present need for some form of the union shop? Does this amount to the position that strong unions do not need the union shop and weak ones cannot secure one? How significant is the point that the union's interest in the union shop derives not only from concern with the present but even more with the uncertainties of the future?

6. State very carefully the arrangements which would represent the "maximum union security permissible under the Taft-Hartley law." Is it sufficient that an employee tender periodic dues and the initiation fee to the Union? What is the status of employees dropped from the Union for other reasons than nonpayment of dues and the initiation fee?

7. Why should an employer be interested in the union-shop issue? Is there any evidence that employees who refuse to join the Union are more productive employees? What do you suppose would have been the position of the companies if the Union had offered to waive its

demand of a wage increase of 18½ cents per hour (16 cents was eventually agreed upon) in return for some form of union shop? What is an issue of "principle" in collective bargaining?

8. How do you appraise the argument that a large majority of workers desired the union shop in this case? It is contended by the companies that so long as one man elects not to join a Union, his right to refrain from joining deserves the same consideration as that of each man who does join.

9. Write an opinion in this case to support the conclusion you would have come to had you been a member of the Wage Stabilization Board on March 20, 1952.

Case 21

PERIODIC DUES AND INITIATION FEE

UNION: Grain Processors' Independent Union

COMPANY: Union Starch and Refining Company

The Union threatened a work stoppage unless the employer discharged certain employees for "failure to pay dues and assessments" under a union-shop agreement. Since several of the employees named in the request were known to have supported a rival union prior to the representation election, the employer undertook to investigate the circumstances surrounding the Union's demand. Specifically, he wished to know whether or not membership had been available to these employees on the same terms and conditions which were applicable to other nonmembers.

The employer learned that all of the workers named had offered to pay the required dues and initiation fees, but that these were refused by the business agent on the grounds that payment could not be accepted until the employees had become members by the usual procedure. In order to become members the workers were informed that they must (1) attend the next regular union meeting at which the applicants would be voted upon and accepted, (2) take the obligation (oath) to the Union, and (3) then pay the initiation fee and prepay 2 months' dues.

After the Company had completed its inquiry, it was presented with another request from the Union to discharge certain employees for nonmembership. Thereupon the designated employees were given about 20 hours to indicate their willingness to comply with the three conditions imposed by the Union. All but three of the employees agreed to comply with the union conditions for membership; the three who declined were then discharged.

One of the employees discharged, John Ralph, then filed a complaint with the National Labor Relations Board charging the Union and the Company with an unfair labor practice. The relevant sections of the Act are as follows:

> "*Section* 7. Employees shall have the right to self-organization, to form, join, or assist labor organizations, to bargain collectively through representatives of their own choosing, and to engage in other concerted activities for the purpose of collective bargaining or other mutual aid or protection, and shall also have the right to refrain from any or all of such activities except to the extent that such right may be affected by an agreement requiring membership in a labor organization as a condition of employment as authorized in section 8(a) (3).
>
> "*Section* 8(*a*). It shall be an unfair labor practice for an employer—(1) to interfere with, restrain, or coerce employees in the exercise of the rights guaranteed in section 7; . . . (3) by discrimination in regard to hire or tenure of employment or any term or condition of employment to encourage or discourage membership in any labor organization: . . . *Provided further,* that no employer shall justify any discrimination against an employee for nonmembership in a labor organization (A) if he has reasonable grounds for believing that such membership was not available to the employee on the same terms and conditions generally applicable to other members, or (B) if he has reasonable grounds for believing that membership was denied or terminated for reasons other than the failure of the employee to tender the periodic dues and the initiation fees uniformly required as a condition of acquiring or retaining membership;
>
> "(*b*). It shall be an unfair labor practice for a labor organization or its agents—(1) to cause or attempt to cause an employer to discriminate against an employee in violation of subsection (a) (3) or to discriminate against an employee with respect to whom membership in such organization has been denied or terminated on some ground other than his failure to tender the periodic dues and the initiation fees uni-

formly required as a condition of acquiring or retaining membership; . . . ."

QUESTIONS

1. The NLRB found that the complaint was justified and that a violation of the Act had occurred. On what grounds could the Board make such a finding?

2. What is the status of the employee who is willing to pay dues and the initiation fee but refuses to join the Union? Is he subject to discharge?

3. If the three who refused to take the obligation to the Union but paid the required dues continue to agitate on behalf of a rival union, would the union have any recourse for protection from their activities? Should the Union have a recourse?

4. In your judgment does the Act limit too narrowly the grounds on which a union may request discharge of an employee under a union-shop contract provision? Would you expand the basis for discharge beyond nonpayment of dues and initiation fees to include membership in the Communist party? Organizing a rival union? "Conduct unbecoming a union member?"

5. What is the difference between the right of a union to expel a member and its right to request the employer to discharge the employee? Is it practicable in the work community to make this distinction?

Case 22

DUES AND ASSESSMENTS

UNION: United Automobile Workers of America, CIO

COMPANY: Electric Auto-Lite Company

The Union has a maintenance of membership agreement with the Company. On December 1, 1948, Melvin Eck was discharged at the request of the Union for delinquency in the payment of certain union charges which had accrued as a result of his failure to attend membership meetings. The discharge was challenged by Eck on grounds that he was not delinquent in his dues which constitutes the only legal justification for discharging a worker under a union security clause who is not in good standing with his union. The Labor-Management Relations Act states in Section 8 (*a*) (3):

". . . no employer shall justify any discrimination against an employee for nonmembership in a labor organization . . . if he has reasonable grounds for believing that membership was denied or terminated for reasons other than the failure of the employee to tender the periodic dues and the initiation fees uniformly required as a condition of acquiring or retaining membership . . . ."

Section 8 (*b*) (2) forbids a union from causing an employer to discriminate against an employee in violation of the quoted provision.

In September, 1946, the Union passed a motion increasing the regular monthly dues from $1.50 to $2.00 with the added provision that attendance at meetings could exonerate members from the payment of the extra 50 cents. In practice, the 50 cents did not become due until after a member failed to appear at a meeting. Those present at a meeting received cards indicating that a "50-cent assessment" would be levied against those absent from the meeting.

The constitution of the International Union contains several provisions which permit the local Union to act as it did. It provides that dues shall be $1.50 a month without indicating further whether or not locals may increase this amount. However, the constitution defines dues as "special fees levied by the International Union or any of its subordinate bodies." It also specifically authorizes the levying of fines for nonattendance at membership meetings.

Under union procedure, the checked-off monies were applied first to pay delinquent charges other than the monthly dues. Then the delinquent member would be notified by postal card that such action was being taken and that he should report to the union dues office to "correct his record." This procedure appears to be consistent with the International Constitution which provides in part:

". . . where a member has failed to pay an assessment within the time required, but has paid dues in advance, the financial secretary of the Local Union shall apply to the payment of the assessment the dues for the last month or months covered by the advance dues payment in which event the dues payment for such month or months shall be automatically cancelled . . . ."

Eck had executed a checkoff authorization on September 1, 1947, instructing the employer to deduct and pay to the Union

$1.50 a month and not more than two assessments a year. During 1948 Eck failed to pay the 50-cent nonattendance charge on several occasions. Three times the Union sent Eck a postcard notification that his checkoff funds were being applied to pay delinquent charges against him. In May and August of that year, Eck appeared at the union office and adjusted his dues record. But he failed to appear to make an adjustment following the Union's November notice of its application of his checked-off funds. Thereupon the Union suspended him from membership on December 1, 1948, and his discharge followed.

The Union defended the discharge on the grounds that, since the Union applied the checked-off monies first to the outstanding indebtedness to the Union for failure to attend meetings, at the time of his suspension Eck was delinquent only in his dues. It contended that the charges were a proper part of dues and that dues, not fines, were owing at the suspension time. The provision of the constitution quoted above was offered to support the action of the local Union. It was also pointed out that the checkoff authorization did not specify the purpose to which the monies were to be put.

The Union further contended that the Act does not prohibit the Union from increasing its regular dues. Nor does it restrict the common practice of exonerating members from the payment of financial charges for particular reasons, and in this case the Union Constitution specifically permits locals to exonerate members:

> "Where Local Unions deem it necessary they may exonerate certain members from the payment of dues to the Local Union. However, such members . . . shall be considered as dues-paying members and per-capita tax shall be paid on such members."

QUESTIONS

1. How do you appraise the Union's argument that only dues were outstanding at the time of Eck's suspension? Is this definition of dues within the meaning of "periodic dues" of Section 8 (*a*) (3) and 8 (*b*) (2)?
2. Do the provisions of the Union constitution have any bearing on the decision of the NLRB? Do those provisions appear to circumvent the purposes of the Act?
3. Does the Act preclude discharge for nonpayment of fines?

4. Is there any requirement in the Act that all employees pay the same dues? Can the Union charge some employees higher dues? Can dues be made a percentage of earnings? Can a dues schedule be based on length of service? On attendance?

Case 23

DISCHARGE UPON EXPULSION FROM THE UNION

UNION: United Automobile Workers of America, CIO

COMPANY: Ford Motor Company

Twelve to fifteen test-drivers were employed at the Ford plant in Edgewater, New Jersey, whose job was to take trucks from the final assembly and subject them to a prescribed run and inspection. Two of these drivers were John Elvin and Neil Smith.

On January 16, 1944, the local Union notified local management that Smith and Elvin had been expelled from the Union and requested that they be discharged by the Company, pursuant to Section 2 of the parties' agreement which reads:

"It is a continuing condition of employment with the Company that employees covered by this agreement, both present employees and new employees, shall be and remain good standing members of the Union. Persons losing their membership in the Union shall not be retained in the employ of the Company."

The Company refused to discharge the two men. It claimed that they were expelled from the Union only because they did their work quickly without soldiering and thus "spoiled" an easy job for the other drivers who, it was asserted, were accustomed to doing the work more slowly and with considerable loafing. The Company charged that, in expelling the men and asking for their discharge, the Union was abusing and perverting the union-shop provision of the agreement in order to deprive the Company of its rights, particularly those provided by Sections 11, 12, 13, and 62. Section 11 pronounces management's right to hire and maintain order and efficiency; Section 12, the right to promote, discipline, and discharge; Section 13 is a general statement of management's functions and prerogatives; Section 62 is the no-strike, no-slowdown, no-lockout clause which reserves the right to management of disciplining violators of this section.

The situation thus created attracted wide public attention. The Company charged that this case was but an instance of a general condition, that its costs had greatly increased, and its production had been impaired by concerted slowdowns which pervaded its plants. The Union made public answers and countercharges. Accusations concerning lack of patriotism were hurled. There was widespread comment in the press. After the matter was discussed by top officers of the Company and the Union, it was submitted to the impartial umpire on the Union's claim that Elvin and Smith must be discharged, and on the Company's defense and counterclaim that the expulsions should be set aside.

The detailed provisions of the International Constitution with respect to appeals from sentence of expulsion or other disciplinary penalties imposed by subordinate bodies show that the danger of unjust expulsion exists as well as that precautions have been taken against it. The records of the International Executive Board and of the Convention, in reversing the sentences of subordinate bodies, indicate not only that the safeguards are operative but also that the danger of injustice is real and that subordinate bodies do occasionally take unjustifiable action.

The Company concedes readily that the protection of union members against unjust expulsion in general is not the function, privilege, or duty of the employer. His interest in the general justice of an expulsion is no different from or greater than that of any outsider. His special interest, says management, is in the maintenance of a proper level of efficiency in the business.

The Union recognizes its responsibility for guarding against injustice. It has by constitution prescribed the procedure for trial of members on charges. It has provided a number of opportunities for appeals, including appeal to the International Convention. And it submits that it has administered the machinery seriously and with vigilance against injustice, as evidenced by the instances of reversal or modification of penalties with compensation for loss to the member when deemed justified. The Union is proud of the fact that since the beginning of the union shop at Ford Motor Company, there have been relatively few trials on charges and not more than a half-dozen expulsions of Ford employees.

The Company concedes that the justice or injustice of an expulsion, as an issue between the member and his union, is none of its business. But it insists that management of its operations and efficient production are its business; that an expulsion for the purpose of slowing down production is an attack on it and not merely on the expelled member; that the expulsion of a member for doing his work faithfully and refusing to engage in an illegal slowdown is an infringement of its rights under the contract and a violation of the Union's duties thereunder; that expulsion for such a reason is an abuse of the union-shop provision not warranted by the contract; and that it cannot be bound to co-operate in an illegal attack upon itself by effectuating such an expulsion. The Company claims that the expulsions in this case were of this character.

The Union denies that the expulsions were of this nature. It contends that the evidence presented by the Company as proof is highly complex and controversial and that it is not essential to an understanding of the more general issues involved here. More important than the specific facts in this case is the Union's contention that, in any event, neither the Company nor the umpire have any power to go behind the fact of expulsion and inquire into its causes or purposes. Its position is:

". . . the question of whether a worker is a good-standing member of the Union is one which is for the sole determination of the Union, arrived at through the procedure established by the constitution of the Union, the worker having all the benefits which the procedure affords for the protection of members who may be dissatisfied with the decision of any Union tribunals at any stage in the trial and appelate proceedings."

It also states that "decisions of the Union respecting the standing of its members are not and cannot under any circumstances be the concern or responsibility of the employer"; that the umpire "has no jurisdiction over such questions"; and that they "are not arbitrable under the contract."

Interpreting the contract, the umpire comments:

"There can be little doubt that the Umpire does not have the power to order the reinstatement of an expelled worker into good standing in the Union. The Umpire's office is a step in the grievance procedure. That procedure is prescribed for grievances between employer and employees. It does not apply to grievances between the Union and its members. Disciplinary penalties imposed by the Union on its members are, as such, not subject to the grievance procedure and the Umpire's jurisdiction. But this case does not come to me on complaint of the expelled workers against the Union. It comes on the Union's demand of the Company that Smith and Elvin be discharged. And the issue is whether the Company has any defense to such a demand in any circumstances. I must decide not whether the Union should reinstate the men but whether the Company should discharge them."

In answer to a direct inquiry the Union deliberately and unequivocally stated its opinion as follows: Assuming, if you can, that an employee is admittedly expelled only because he refuses to slow down production and for the purposes of impairing the Company's right to a fair day's work for a fair day's pay, the union-shop provision would nevertheless obligate the Company to discharge him upon notice of the expulsion; and the remedy for such action would be elsewhere than in a refusal to discharge.

Commenting on the Union's assumption as to the cause of the expulsion, whether or not true in the case of Elvin and Smith, the Company asserts that this assumption is one of a real possibility and not of a wholly imaginary situation. The Company says:

"It can be fairly granted that the International Executive Board and the International Union would not sanction expulsion for such a cause. The danger that some of its many locals may employ the threat of expulsion to gain adherents to an interference with production is real . . . . To protect the interest in the proper performance of a worker's duties as employee, safeguards against the improper use of the threat of expulsion are much more important than those against improper expulsions themselves."

As further argument the Company states that the provision for a union shop at Ford is not the whole agreement of the parties. The agreement sets down many other rights, obligations, and procedures. It sets down, for example, the Union's "adherence to the principle 'a fair day's work for a fair day's pay,' " and its agreement to "use its best efforts in behalf of the Company both as to work and as to conduct in its performance." The contract states the agreement of the Union and of its members not to cause or to take part in any "slowdown, curtailment of work, restriction of production, interference with work" and the like; and it recognizes the right of the Company to discipline any employee "taking part in any violation of" this provision (Sections 29, 17*a*). And implicit in the right to discipline "for cause" (Section 12) is the right to discipline an employee for failure to maintain production in accordance with fair production standards properly set or for sleeping or loafing on the job.

QUESTIONS

1. Write an opinion in this case.
2. Do you agree that the issue is that formulated by the umpire?
3. Has the management any right under a union shop to inquire into the reasons for expulsion or suspension from membership?
4. Would management have any interest in the problem presented by this case if the Union had fined rather than expelled the two employees?
5. Does the principle proposed by management permit the Company to review every expulsion decided by the Union? What happens to the principle of the union shop under such circumstances?
6. What is the effect of the Taft-Hartley law on this situation?
7. How would you define the relative jurisdictions of the National Labor Relations Board and the arbitrator in this type of situation? What would be the status of the decision of the arbitrator in any proceeding before the National Labor Relations Board?

Case 24

INTERNAL UNION DISCIPLINE

CASE A. DUALISM

Three members of Millinery, Blockers Union, Local 42, were suspended by their local union for acts of misconduct and violations of the International Constitution. They were charged with breaking up a local union meeting, forming an organization outside the Union "for the purposes of influencing or shaping the policies of the Union and the election of its officers," holding separate meetings, publishing and distributing circulars, and other acts "the effect and purpose of which was to bring the organization into contempt."

The constitutional provision held to be violated reads:

"A member may be fined, suspended or expelled for the following reasons:
"i. For holding membership in a dual, opposition or seceding union or in any other organization or combination not constituted or functioning within the framework of this Constitution and attempting to shape the policies and/or determine the choice of officers of the [parent body] or any of its subordinate bodies . . . ."

The accused appealed their suspension to the General Executive Board, and from there to the Committee on Appeals and Grievances at the 1944 Convention. They did not deny the charges but held that the Union Constitution prohibiting "these activities as inimical to the Union and detrimental to its welfare was in conflict with their rights as American citizens, guaranteeing them freedom of speech and the press."

The Grievance Committee upheld the suspension and ruled that when the appellants became members of the Union they took a membership oath solemnly promising to abide by the laws, rules, and decisions of the International Union. The Committee affirmed that nothing in the Union Constitution was in derogation of any rights of American citizens. The decision was sustained by vote of the convention.

QUESTIONS

1. What is dualism? Why is dualism considered the most serious of offenses by trade unionists? Why and how does it arise? How does it affect intra-union relationship? How does it affect the union-management relationship?

2. How is dualism to be distinguished from a legitimate and desirable challenge by any part of the membership to the present leadership of a union? Is dualism to be considered as purely a manifestation of internal union democratic activity involving freedom of speech? Can or should limits be set defining legitimate forms of opposition?

3. The Labor-Management Relations Act, 1947, provides that only a single union, designated by majority vote of the employees, shall serve

as bargaining agent within any bargaining unit. Would an attempt to establish a rival organization within the unit contradict this purpose? Should employees have the right to change their bargaining representative if they so desire? If so, by what procedure, when, and how often?

4. Is the public interest ever affected by dualistic activities? Should they ever be restrained in the public interest? By what means?

5. Does the public have an interest in the internal processes of a trade union, church, university, or other private organization? Is a union a private organization? Is expulsion by a union different from excommunication by a church? Should an aggrieved individual or group have recourse to a public body for redress?

6. If the public does have an interest in the disciplinary processes of unions, is this interest in the procedural or substantive aspects of these processes, or in both?

CASE B. DISCIPLINE FOR POLITICAL AFFILIATION

Article XXIV, Section 1, of the Constitution adopted in 1946 by the International Association of Machinists provides:

"Any member or members of any district or local lodge circulating or causing in any manner to be circulated any false or malicious statement reflecting upon the private or public conduct, or falsely or maliciously attacking the character, impugning the motives, or questioning the integrity of any officer of the Grand Lodge, or officer or member of any local lodge, shall be deemed of conduct unbecoming a member and subject to fine or expulsion, or both."

In 1948 charges of "conduct unbecoming a union member" were filed by a member of Lodge 122 against Hector Duff. The local trial committee found him guilty as charged; but by vote of the membership meeting, the report of the trial committee was set aside, and Duff was ruled not guilty. The complainant then appealed the decision of the Lodge to the International Executive Council.

International President Brown reviewed the evidence as presented in the transcript of the trial. The evidence implied that Duff was a communist. This implication was based on a newsclipping of the *Toronto Globe and Mail* captioned "T.L.C. Turns Down Move to Bar Communists from Union Positions." The clipping went on to report that "Machinist Duff told the delegate he has 'been a communist for fifteen years, and I am proud of it.' "

Since President Brown considered the possibility that Duff may have been misquoted, he wrote him to give him an opportunity to deny or admit the newspaper quotation. Duff replied, "In reference to your letter . . . and the quotation from the *Toronto Globe and Mail,* I want to say, I did say what I am quoted as having said. I am convinced that communists make very good trade unionists. Having sailed the North Atlantic Convoy routes for close to three years, I think I have earned a right to have a democratic opinion in a democratic country." On the basis of this reply, President Brown reversed the decision of the Lodge, whereupon Duff appealed to the Committee on Appeals and Grievances of the 1948 Convention.

The Committee convened to consider the appeal, but Duff neither appeared to defend himself nor did he submit a brief on his behalf. Since Duff failed to produce any evidence that he was not a communist, the Committee recommended to the Convention that the decision of the Executive Council be sustained. By vote of the Convention the report of the Committee was accepted, and Duff's expulsion was ordered.[1]

QUESTIONS

1. Should political beliefs of an individual be grounds for disqualification from union membership? Is the excercise of the civil rights of an individual being denied by such disqualification?
2. Does the public have an interest in the admission or membership requirements of unions? Should this interest go beyond a desire that these be applied without discrimination to all applicants and members?
3. Should failure to qualify for membership constitute sufficient grounds for discharge in a union shop?
4. In this case, discipline was imposed under the broad charge of "conduct unbecoming a member" which, as defined in the 1946 Constitution, does not explicitly include adherence to communism. Is such a broad interpretation of this provision warranted? Is it desirable?

[1] At the 1948 Convention the Constitution was amended by the addition of this clause: "Any member . . . who advocates or encourages Communism, Fascism, Naziism or any other totalitarian philosophy, or who, by other actions gives support to these 'philosophies' or 'isms,' shall, upon conviction thereof, be deemed guilty of conduct unbecoming a member and subject to fine or expulsion, or both" (Art. XXV, Sec. 2).

5. Should an individual have recourse to a public authority in cases of discipline which limit the exercise of his civil liberties?

6. Present law provides that unions with communist leadership shall be denied the protection of the law and the use of its review and enforcement agencies. Should this provision be extended to include union members also, or does the present law already go too far?

7. Should a communist employed in a piano factory receive different consideration from the employer and union than a communist employed in a plant with vital government defense orders?

8. Should a distinction be made between an intellectual Marxist and a member of the Communist party? As long as the latter is a legal party, is discrimination in union membership and employment because of one's political beliefs justified?

9. In this case, discipline was imposed for an offense which was related neither to the defendant's responsibilities to the Union as a member nor to his responsibilities as an employee under the contract. Are acts which lie outside these areas of responsibility within the justifiable province of union regulation?

CASE C. DISCIPLINE FOR CONTRACT VIOLATION

Albro Seaton, President of Local 190, was suspended by the International President of the Glass Bottle Blowers Association for violation of the National Wage Agreement and for violation of a lawful order of the International President. According to the terms of the agreement, to which Local 190 had been a party, the Union agreed to allow machine operators and maintenance men to work on Sundays so that they might ready the machines for the coming week. The Sunday-work provision had been entered into the contract in recognition of the seriousness of the defense effort and as a means of ensuring peak production in the industry. Seaton was accused of ignoring the contract and of refusing to allow the members of his Local to perform the Sunday work, even after he had been ordered to do so by the International President. Suspension from the Union resulted in discharge under the union security provision then in effect.

Prior to exhausting his legal remedies within the Union, Seaton filed suit in court against the Union for loss of his job. The court criticized the procedural aspects of the case arguing that Seaton had not been given adequate notice and hearing, and it ruled that he be remunerated by the Union for his loss of work. However, the court upheld the legality of the suspension under the Union's Constitution and made no ruling to reinstate him.

Seaton then appealed his suspension to the Grievance Committee of the Union at the Convention. The suspension was upheld by the Committee and by vote of the Convention. The opinion was expressed that Seaton had violated the Union Constitution on two counts: (1) by his refusal to obey the order of the International President, and (2) by his appeal to the courts prior to exhaustion of his intra-union remedies.

QUESTIONS

1. Whose responsibility is it to enforce the agreement? Would it be practicable to delegate the whole responsibility of enforcement to only one of the parties? Could the interest of all parties be protected by such an arrangement?

2. Management relies on disciplinary layoffs and discharge as the means for enforcing the agreement. If the Union is to share the responsibility of enforcing the agreement, while at the same time safeguarding its own interests, must not its disciplinary procedure also provide the possibility of discharge? Should the law be amended to permit unions to request the discharge of members suspended or expelled for violating the contract?

3. Should the courts entertain appeals from union disciplinary action before the intra-union appeals procedures have been exhausted? Should they interfere only if final appeal within the union takes an unreasonably long period of time (e.g., in cases where unions hold quadrennial conventions and yet provide for appeal to the convention as the last step of the appeals procedure)?

4. With which aspect of discipline should the courts concern themselves: the substantive issue involved, the adequacy or fairness of the trial and appeals procedure, both, or neither?

5. Should union members be subject to further union discipline for resorting to the public courts before exhausting the internal union appeal procedures?

THE SENIORITY PRINCIPLE

IN LABOR RELATIONS

A large part of the collective bargaining agreement defines the relative rights of individual employees in particular jobs. These "property rights" in a job are specified in terms of contingencies which reoccur in the work community—an increase in the work force, temporary layoffs, transfers, promotion, a permanent reduction in the work force. Who shall be laid off when work is slack? When men are to be rehired following a temporary shutdown, in what order shall they be returned to work? When vacancies arise, should they be filled by promotion from within or by hiring from outside? If promotion is to be from within, which individuals shall be promoted? These questions are not only vital to individual employees whose personal lives are immediately affected, but they concern both the union and management organizations as well.

The principle which has received the greatest recognition in determining these relative rights of employees is seniority, normally defined as length of continuous service. Section D will discuss the meaning of seniority and its use in American industry. The manner in which seniority is used in layoffs will be discussed in Section E, and Section F will consider seniority in promotions.

The extent to which an employee's length of service with a company insures him of certain benefits varies from industry to industry and with the type of benefits involved. For many years, seniority was emphasized in collective bargaining in the railroad and typographical industries; but it is only since the depression of the thirties and the growth of unionization in the mass production industries that seniority has become formalized in industry generally as one of the principal measurements of relative rights among employees. Some companies and unions use it sparingly, because they feel that it is not suitable under the circumstances prevailing in their industries. For example, the building construction and needle trades industries, characterized by seasonal employment, for the most part do not use seniority to govern layoffs. Laying off employees on the basis of length of service in seasonal industries would result in relatively steady employment for older employees and very intermittent employment for the junior employees. Such industries have tended to rely on equal division of work rather than layoffs based on seniority in time of work curtailment.

Even in those industries which have found length of service to be a practical criterion, other factors are usually considered in conjunction with seniority. In prescribing layoff, transfer, and promotion procedures, most labor agreements require that relative ability or the ability to meet the basic requirements of the job must be considered. Sometimes factors other than length of service are included in the definition of seniority itself. For example, the "seniority rating sheet" in Case 26 includes a rating of attendance, quantity, quality, versatility, and co-operation along with service to produce the total "seniority" rating of an employee. Similarly, the clause discussed in Case 36 under Section F provides:

> "For the purpose of this contract, seniority wherever used hereafter, shall be defined as consisting of (1) continuous length of service with the Company and its predecessors, and (2) skill, ability, and experience necessary to adequately perform the available work in line with the job requirements."

In most labor agreements, however, the term seniority is synonymous with length of service.

Length of service is also used to determine some elements of compensation. Among these are sick leave, vacations, pensions, automatic wage progression within rate-ranges, severance pay, and a weekly or annual guarantee of wages or work. Long-service employees receive greater compensation in these forms.

There are several reasons for the extensive use of seniority. First, it is a tangible measurement as opposed to such other criteria as ability, physical fitness, and skill which are often determined subjectively. Second, unions have concluded that the seniority principle is the most effective way to eliminate discrimination and favoritism in selecting employees for layoff, transfer, or promotion. For example, years ago at the time of a layoff employees hired from distant places might be kept on the payroll, while those who lived in the community would be laid off. The employer felt that he could always depend on his stay-at-home employees to assure him of an adequate labor supply when business activity revived. Third, it is commonly recognized by unions and managements alike that the investment of years of service creates an equity in the job which should afford an employee greater protection and greater benefits. Many unorganized companies observe the principle of seniority almost as closely as companies which are parties to a collective bargaining agreement.

There is little disagreement between managements and unions over the acceptance of seniority as one of the criteria for measuring relative rights of employees. But there is conflict concerning the manner in which it is to be used. The unit in which seniority is to be exercised for layoff or promotion purposes is often a subject of disagreement. The company may wish to have seniority applied on a department or a job occupation basis so that employees exercise their seniority rights only within the confines of these units. The union, on the other hand, may argue for the larger division-wide or plant-wide seniority unit. The problem of the seniority unit will be discussed more fully in Section E. Another point of disagreement is the weight to be assigned to ability, physical fitness, and skill as compared to length of service. Management normally wants to assign more emphasis to these non-service factors in the interest of plant efficiency than the union is willing to accept. Even when agreement is reached, many grievances arise on the application of the ability test to particular individuals or on the meaning of the terms "ability" or "qualified to do the job."

In nearly every definition of seniority, it is specified that the length of service shall be continuous. Since this word "continuous" may be ambiguous, parties frequently list those reasons which result in the loss of all seniority credit. The most frequent listings include the following:

1. If the employee voluntarily quits;
2. If the employee is discharged;
3. If the employee has been laid off for lack of work for

a specified period. Most agreements specify 12 or 24 consecutive months of layoff; others relate the length of the layoff to the service of an individual employee. In the latter case, an employee with 10 years' of service might retain seniority for 48 consecutive months of layoff, while a 5-year employee might lose all seniority after 24 months of layoff;

4. If the employee is absent for a specified number of consecutive working days without notification to the employer;

5. If the employee on layoff status fails to return to work within a given period after receiving notification to return.

Even these clarifications, however, do not resolve all of the questions relating to the word "continuous." For example, an agreement might provide that the employees with 1 or more years of seniority shall receive 1 week's vacation. If an employee has worked 2 months or beyond the probationary period and then is ill for the next 10 months, is he entitled to 1 week's vacation pay? It is clear that the definition of continuous service for purposes of layoff and promotion may have significant implications in the administration of the vacation and holiday provisions. The parties may choose to define continuous service differently in handling these separate matters. (See Case 28 and Section J.)

Finally, as indicated in Section B, the parties may assign to certain employees or groups of employees, a seniority rating which is unrelated to actual length of service. Shop stewards, union officers, and committeemen are frequently accorded top seniority for the purposes of layoff. In return for this protection of union representatives, some companies have bargained the contractual right to establish a roster of key employees, who are retained at the time of a layoff regardless of their actual length of service.

The merger of two companies or the amalgamation of two or more plants of a company may also give rise to the assignment of service dates unrelated to actual service. The dovetailing of two seniority lists under these circumstances is worked out through collective bargaining, although the bargaining may be actually more between the two union groups than it is with the company.

In rare cases the operation of a disciplinary program may

affect seniority credit by providing for the subtraction of service credits as a penalty for misconduct.

So firmly established is the principle of seniority as a property right that courts have invalidated contract provisions which revise seniority credits without justification. They have also outlawed the creation of separate seniority lists which resulted in racial discrimination. Under the Wagner Act the Board ruled that an employer may not threaten his employees with loss of seniority because of their union activity.

The Selective Service Act provided that "veterans shall be restored to such position or to a position of like seniority, status and pay, unless the employer's circumstances have so changed as to make it impossible or unreasonable to do so." This meant that time spent in the service was added to the employee's seniority record when he was re-employed. At least one state (Rhode Island) went beyond the federal law in granting seniority benefits to veterans. It provided that a veteran employed by a company, even if he had never worked for that company before, was to be given a seniority rating which included his years in the armed services unless he signed a waiver agreement.

In the reading of cases under Sections D, E, and F, some consideration should be given to the broader social and economic questions raised by the emphasis on seniority in collective bargaining. It has been said that "by their seniority and security schemes, many unions are destroying opportunity and growth alike."[1] Does a study of seniority clauses suggest that length of service is applied rigidly by the parties to the exclusion of other criteria? To what extent are layoffs and promotions handled differently under collective bargaining than in the absence of union organization? Do seniority provisions affect adversely employee initiative and incentive, or do they free the employee from the fears of insecurity which interfere with efficiency? To what extent do seniority rights decrease mobility in the labor market? This problem was given special attention during the war years when it was essential to attract employees to defense industries. In 1942 a survey of men interviewed in forty United States Employment Service Offices revealed that less than one third of the men were willing to move to war jobs regardless of the attraction of better

[1] David McCord Wright (Editor), *The Impact of the Union* (New York, Harcourt, Brace & Co.), p. 277.

pay. Forty per cent of this number gave as the reason their desire to retain their seniority and other benefits related to length of service on their present jobs.[2] These findings have been confirmed in more recent studies.[3] If a decrease in over-all labor mobility because of seniority is assumed, is it seriously harmful to the economy? Does the decrease in labor turnover produce cost-savings for the individual employer and prompt him to exercise greater care in the selection of employees?

Seniority also gives rise to internal problems for the union in reconciling conflicting interests among different groups of employees with different lengths of service. When an employee presents a grievance claiming he has been laid off improperly while a junior employee has been retained, the Union's support of the senior employee may be considered unfair by the junior employee. The same conflicts arise in the case of promotion grievances. Any system for determining the relative rights of individuals is almost certain to be found unsatisfactory by some union members. Since the union is in some respects a political institution, it feels the pressures of these dissatisfied members. No seniority system has been devised which is considered wholly satisfactory by everyone. The cases in this Section and in Sections E and F are designed to illustrate the problems which arise in the administration of layoffs, transfers and promotions, and the efforts of some parties to perfect the measurement of relative rights of employees (members).

Case 25

ILLUSTRATIVE SENIORITY CLAUSE

The following articles of agreement appear in the contract negotiated between Republic Aviation Corporation and the International Association of Machinists, February 19, 1952:

"Article XVII (Seniority). Seniority shall be defined as an employee's continuous length of service with the Company since his date of hire, except that if there has been a break

[2] War Manpower Commission, Manpower Mobilization; *A Report on Progress and Problems* (Planning Division Memorandum). November 30, 1942, p. 5.

[3] Lloyd G. Reynolds and Joseph Shister, *Job Horizons: A Study of Job Satisfaction and Labor Mobility* (New York: Harper and Brothers, 1949).

in his continuous service with the Company then it shall be computed from the most recent rehire date. However, employees who were in the employ of the Company on February 15, 1949, and have since that date had no break in their continuous service, shall have their seniority adjusted to show their actual length of service with the Company irrespective of a break in continuous service prior to February 15, 1949. All time spent outside the employ of the Company, between the original date of hire and February 15, 1949 will be subtracted from the total length of service with the Company and the seniority date advanced by that extent.

"Any employee entering the Armed Services under the provisions of the Selective Training and Service Act, as amended, and the Universal Military and Service Act, as amended, will be given full credit for seniority for all time spent in the Armed Services, provided that such employee makes application for job restoration under the provisions of the above stated Government regulations, or other Government regulation.

"*Section 17.2.* A newly hired employee or one who is rehired after a break in continuous service shall not acquire any seniority until the expiration of a period of sixty (60) days service with the Company. Such employee shall be considered a probationary employee and, if continued in the employ of the Company after the expiration of such sixty (60) day period, the seniority shall be computed from the date of hire or re-hire. There shall be no responsibility on the part of the Company for the re-employment of probationary employees laid off or discharged during such period.

"*Section 17.3.* Seniority shall be by job classification. An employee's seniority may consist of two (2) parts as follows:

"*a*) The length of service on his most recent job classification, provided he has been classified on that job for not less than sixty (60) days.

"*b*) Where the employee has held jobs in two or more different job classifications, his total seniority with the Company will apply to that job classification which he held immediately preceding his most recent job classification in which he has seniority.

"*Section 17.4.* Loss of Seniority. An employee shall lose

his seniority upon the happening of any one of the following events:

"*a*) Resignation.

"*b*) Discharge for just cause.

"*c*) If, after a layoff, the employee is notified to report by mail or telegram, addressed to him at the last address filed by him with the Company, and fails within five (5) working days either to report for work or to deliver to the Company a reasonable excuse for failure to report.

"*d*) If the employee is laid off for a period of time exceeding twelve (12) consecutive months.

"*e*) If the employee is recalled to a job of like position, grade and pay and refuses such employment.

"*Section 17.5.* An employee who is transferred from a job classification covered by this Agreement to a job classification not covered by this Agreement shall continue to accrue seniority in the job classification previously held except where the transfer is to the following departments:

"Department 10—Tool Development
                11—Tool Design
                19—Factory Administration
                20—Production Analysis
                21—Planning
                22—Standards
                24—Plant Protection
                28—Purchasing
                32—Industrial Relations
                35—General Services
                51—Executive
                52—Public Relations and Advertising
                53—Financial and Accounting
                55—Military Contracts
                56—Field Service
                61—Engineering

"In no event shall an employee continue to accrue seniority in any classification above that of foreman.

"*Section 17.6.* For the purpose of this Article, the job classifications of Riveter, Grades 2, 3, and 4, and Assembler-Structure, Grades 1, 3, and 5 shall be separated as follows:

"*Original Classification*	*New Classification*
"Riveter	Riveter-Parts (includes all Riveters in Departments 01, 02, 03, 04, 05, 14 and those Riveters in Department 07 engaged in parts work as designated by the Company).
	Riveter-Assembly (includes all Riveters in Departments 08, 09, 16, 17, 41, 43 and those Riveters in Department 07 engaged in assembly work as designated by the Company).
"Assembler-Structure	Assembler-Structure-Parts (includes all Assemblers in Departments 01, 02, 03, 04, 05, 14 and those Assemblers in Department 07 engaged in parts work as designated by the Company).
	Assembler - Structure - Assembly (includes all Assemblers in Departments 08, 09, 16, 17, 41, 43 and those Assemblers in Department 07 engaged in assembly work as designated by the Company).

"The above-named job classifications shall be separate and distinct for the purposes of layoff and recall. The separation of the jobs as outlined herein does not result in the creation of any new or changed job and the provisions of Section 35.3 do not apply.

"*Section 17.7.* Procedure to be followed in the event of an indefinite layoff of employees:

"*a*) All probationary employees in the department affected will be terminated first, provided there are available employees remaining in the department who have seniority in those jobs which are vacated and who are willing to perform the work of the probationary employees to be released.

"*b*) Thereafter, layoffs shall be effected in accordance with the job classification seniority provided for herein and in inverse order to the seniority status of the employees within such job classification, in accordance with the following provisions:

"(1) An employee with less than one year of seniority with the Company shall not bump outside his current department;

"(2) An employee who is to be laid off shall be given opportunity to accept an assignment to an equal or lower rated job in which he had acquired seniority status, provided that his seniority status therein shall be greater than that of some other employee who may be working therein and further provided that (1) and (3) are complied with.

"(3) No employee will be allowed to make more than one (1) bump to a previously held job except in the case of an employee with more than five (5) years seniority, one additional bump to a previously held job is allowed.

"*Section 17.8.* An employee offered an available equal or lower-rated job shall before the end of the next work day inform his supervisor of acceptance of such job or else forfeit his rights to such job. Any employee may refuse a transfer to a lower-graded job in accordance with the above procedure and accept layoff in lieu thereof.

"*Section 17.9.* Procedure to be followed to increase the work force following an indefinite layoff.

"A. When there is an increase in the work force after an indefinite layoff, employees will be recalled in the inverse order of their layoff.

"*Section 17.10.* Employees who have grown old or disabled while in the service of the Company will be given preference on any available light work which they are capable of performing.

"*Section 17.11.* The parties shall have the right by mutual consent to alter the provisions of this Article during the term of this Agreement.

"ARTICLE XVIII

"*Changes in Job Status*

"*Section 18.1.* Change of an employee's work station: Employees who are moved laterally from one job to another, within the same classification and same labor grade shall not receive a reduction in hourly wage rate. Such changes may be made by the Company irrespective of the seniority of the employees affected.

"*Section 18.2.* Upgrading: When the Company upgrades an employee, such upgrading shall be made on the basis of seniority, i.e., the most senior employee in the next lower labor grade in the same classification in the Department shall be assigned to the open or newly-created job provided the employee can perform the work. The upgraded employee shall receive the minimum rate of the labor grade to which he is upgraded or five (5¢) cents higher than his previous rate, whichever rate is greater.

"*Section 18.3.* Downgrading:

"*a*) An upgraded employee who is found not qualified for the higher graded job shall be returned to the job he previously held at his former rate of pay or to the rate he would have received had he not been upgraded.

"*b*) Downgrading, in lieu of layoff shall be made upon the basis of seniority, i.e. the least senior employee in the classification affected shall be demoted to the job previously performed by him. In such instance the employee shall have seniority in the new job in accordance with the seniority provisions of this Agreement. Such employee shall be paid as follows:

"(1) The maximum wage rate of the labor grade to which he is reclassified provided that the employee's rate of pay for the higher graded job is equal to or higher than the maximum of the rate range for the labor grade to which the employee is reclassified;

"(2) No reduction in his hourly wage rate provided his hourly wage rate in the higher graded job is less than the maximum of the lower rated job to which he is reclassified.

"*Section 18.4.* Transfers to Jobs Outside the Bargaining Unit:

"Transfers to jobs outside the bargaining unit, may with the approval of the employee involved, be made at the option of the Company.

"*Section 18.5.* The parties shall have the right by mutual consent to alter the provisions of this Article during the term of this Agreement.

"ARTICLE XX

"*Information to Be Supplied to the Union*

"*Section 20.2.* The Company agrees to supply to the Union a list of those employees recalled after layoff at the time of such recall. The Company also agrees to advise the Union of those employees who are discharged or who quit the Company's employ at the time of termination. The Company will furnish the Union with a copy of the current seniority roster at three intervals during the year.

"ARTICLE XXIV

"*Seniority of Union Representatives*

"*Section 24.1.* Officers of the local Lodge, Chief Stewards, Senior Stewards and the five (5) officially designated Union Labor Relations Committeemen, together with the five (5) officially designated Job Evaluation Committeemen, shall have plant-wide top seniority in the Bargaining Unit for layoff purposes only, except as otherwise provided herein, during their respective terms of office.

"*Section 24.2.* Shop Stewards shall have top seniority over the employees over whom they have jurisdiction for layoff purposes only, during their respective terms of office.

"ARTICLE XXXIII

"Temporary Layoff

"*Section 33.1.* Temporary layoffs due to breakdown, shortage of materials, or causes of a like nature not to exceed ten (10) working days may be made by the Company irrespective of any provisions of this Agreement. In such cases, the Company will, in lieu of layoff whenever possible, reassign employees to other jobs during the period of such layoff.

"*Section 33.2.* An employee shall not be temporarily laid off under this Article more than once in any contract year until all other employees in the same classification in the department affected shall have been temporarily laid off once under this Article.

"*Section 33.3.* If there is a series of such temporary layoffs the Company will so far as it is practicable make an equal distribution of such lost time computed upon a contract years' basis.

Case 26

THE MEASUREMENT OF SENIORITY

The following is an excerpt from the October 23, 1952, agreement between the Hood Rubber Company (Division of the B. F. Goodrich Company) and Rubber Workers' Union, F.L.U. No. 21914, AFL:

"GENERAL INSTRUCTIONS

"A Seniority Rating Sheet shall be recorded for each employee on the Factory Payroll. This rating sheet is to be filed in the department in which an employee works within three months following the entrance of the employee into the department. Rerating of all employees in a department occurs every six months at regular rating periods established for that department. The only new rating sheets that will be made out for employees between regular rating periods will be for those employees who have entered the department since the last rating period.

"The Union Stewards may upon request to the department head, examine the rating sheets of all employees in their districts.

"Ratings on Factors I, II, and III are based upon strictly factual information taken respectively from the records of the Employment Office, Health Office, and Payroll Office, with the possible exception of Day Workers on Factor III who must be rated according to the judgment of supervision.

"The rating on Factor II—Attendance, shall record the number of periods of chargeable absence that have occurred during the six months immediately preceding the month in which the rating occurs. Every period of chargeable absence, regardless of cause or duration, shall be included in this record. Employees' absence from Saturday, Sunday or holiday work which the employee has agreed to perform will be treated like absence on a normally scheduled work day. Any period of absence for reasons other than the following shall be considered chargeable for the purpose of this factor:

"1. Jury duty or employee's presence in court under supoena as a witness.

"2. Federal or State Auxiliary Service such as National or State Guard, when prior approval of employee's absence has been given by supervision.

"3. Employee's Industrial Accident

"4. Death of employee's father, father-in-law, mother, mother-in-law, husband, wife, sister, sister-in-law, brother, brother-in-law, son, son-in-law, daughter, daughter-in-law, aunt, uncle, first cousin, or adopted children, but for a period not to exceed five (5) working days and on condition that the employee upon request of the Company shall furnish evidence satisfactory to the Company of such death and relationship.

"5. Employee's union activities authorized by the Business Agent, when prior approval of absence has been given by supervision.

"6. When employee is sent home by Company hospital.

"7. Employee's sickness supported by doctor's certificate.

"Ratings on Factors IV, V, and VI are based upon facts

and the judgment of supervision as shown by the questions listed under each factor.

"Supervision shall complete each rating sheet except for Factors I and II and total service record. Sheets will then be forwarded to the Employment Office for completion and returned to supervision. The total credit (seniority rating) of each employee will then be posted in the department where the rating applies."

SENIORITY RATING SHEET

Name ....Dept. ....No. ....
Present Job ....Date ....
Rated by ....(Foreman)..........Checked by .....(Supervisor).....
Approved by ....(Superintendent).....................
Approved by ....(Employment Department).................

I. LENGTH OF SERVICE
One point of credit allowed for each year of service.
Total Service........ Years........ Months........ Days........

Factor I Total Credit ....

II. ATTENDANCE

0–1 Absences	4
2–3 Absences	2
4–5 Absences	1

III. QUANTITY
Day Workers:

Above Average	4
Average	2

Bedaux Workers:

80 Point Hour and Over	4
70–79 Point Hour	2

IV. QUALITY
A. To what degree is the product of the employee up to the department's accepted standard of quality?
1. Meets standard requirements.
Yes 1
2. Not more than occassionally below standard requirements.
Yes 1
B. Workmanship
1. Properly cares for tools, equipment and materials.
Yes 1

Factor IV Total Credit ....

V. VERSATILITY, ADAPTABILITY, SKILL
1. Satisfactorily performs two major jobs
Yes 1
2. Satisfactorily performs three major jobs
Yes 1
3. Has capacity to learn another major job
Yes 1

Factor V Total Credit ....

VI. Co-operation

    1. Is this person always willing to carry out instructions and requirements of job?

Yes 1

    2. Does this person notify Supervision regarding conditions that reasonably require attention?

Yes 1

    3. Is this person one who does not offer excuses or alibis to avoid accepting his proper responsibilities?

Yes 1

Factor VI Total Credit   ....

Total Credit
(Seniority Rating)   ....

QUESTIONS

1. What is the difference between the measurement of seniority based upon the above rating sheet and that based solely on length of service? How significant is this difference for long service employees, such as those with 20 years of service?

2. What are the advantages of rating seniority, as defined in this contract, at stated intervals rather than on the occasions when decision on layoffs must be made?

3. Since the seniority rating of individuals is subject to grievance procedure in the contract, should a time limit be imposed for the filing of such a grievance? Why?

4. How can management assure a uniformity of rating among supervisors where discretion is exercised, as in Factors IV, V, and VI above? What can the Union do about this problem?

Case 27

CONTINUITY OF SERVICE

Union: United Electrical, Radio & Machine Workers of America

Company: General Electric Company

On March 11, 1949, the Union requested arbitration of the following grievance:

"The Union claims that the Company's failure to include in H. Kaspar's continuity of service record his period of employment from April 27, 1926 to January 4, 1944 and in Herman Hirschfeld's continuity of service record his period of employment from May 5, 1925 to November 28, 1942, was in violation of the National Agreement dated April 1, 1945, the National Agreement dated April 1, 1946, and said National Agreement as amended in 1947 and further amended in 1948; and the Union requests that the period of H. Kaspar's period of employment with the Company from April 27, 1926 to January 4, 1944 and Herman Hirschfeld's period of employment with the Company from May 5, 1925 to November 28, 1942 be included in their continuity of service record. Both are employees of the General Electric Company at its Schenectady, New York plant."

BACKGROUND

H. Kaspar was employed by the Company on April 27, 1926, and with the exception of two layoff periods in the 1930's, worked continuously until January 4, 1944. On that date the Company received an order from the Commanding Officer, Second Service Command, which directed that Kaspar "be removed from employment on or access to work under War Department and Navy Department contracts, and from anything relating to such work." Since all of the work being done at the plant fell into this restricted category, the Company found it necessary to remove Kaspar from the plant. The employee was told why this action was being taken and was also advised that he had certain appeal rights to the appropriate government agency. To provide him with an opportunity to process such an appeal, the Company gave him a 3 months' leave of absence without pay. The employee was told that if the directive remained in effect, his employment would be terminated.

Kaspar appealed to the Industrial Employment Review Board in Washington which sustained the original directive on February 8, 1944. Accordingly, on May 5, 1944, the Company denied Kaspar's request for an extension of his leave of absence. The record shows that in May, 1944, Kaspar cashed a check from the Company representing payment of his Pension Fund money. For the remainder of 1944 and during 1945, he worked as a toolmaker for another concern in Schenectady. Finally, on October 30, 1945, the Company received a letter from the Second Service Command stating that the Review Board had withdrawn all objections to Kaspar being employed on War and Navy Department contracts, except those classified as secret or top secret.

On November 26, 1945, Kaspar was again employed by General Electric Company. Five days prior to his employment, November 21, 1945, he signed a "Continuity of Service" card which stated:

"In accepting re-employment this day with the General Electric Company I have been notified that I do so as a new employee and that my continuous service record will therefore start from the date on which I report for work. I understand that any exception to or appeal from this decision and the reasons therefor must be made in writing to the Employment Office within thirty days from this date, otherwise the notification remains effective and final."

A re-engagement card, also signed by Kaspar, states that his continuous service record started from the date he reported for work, November 26, 1945. When the question of his prior service was raised by the employee and the Union, the Company submitted the facts to the General Electric Pension Board composed of company-designated members which decided that the circumstances did not justify a restoration of past service.

Herman Hirschfeld first worked for the General Electric Company in Germany in the early 1920's. As soon as he arrived in this country, he started to work as a toolmaker in the Schenectady plant, his hiring date being April 28, 1925. Except for two brief layoff periods in the 1930's, he was employed continuously from that date until November 28, 1942. On that date the Company received a letter from the Commanding Officer of the Second Service Command, the contents of which were the same as in the Kaspar case. Hirschfeld was told by a company representative that he was being removed from employment, and he was advised of his appeal rights. He was given a 3 months' leave of absence; but after government denial of two appeals, his leave of absence was not extended. The Company thereafter considered Hirschfeld in the status of an employee who had been discharged. On several occasions he refused to withdraw his money from the Pension Fund; but finally in the fall of 1944, he received a check from the Company and cashed it. While absent from General Electric Company, he worked at various jobs for other employers in the area. On October 30, 1945, the Second Service Command cleared Hirschfeld for all work except on contracts classified as secret or top secret. He was re-employed by the Company on November 29, 1945. Immediately prior to his re-employment he signed a continuity of service statement, described above in the Kaspar case, although he insists he protested having to sign it at the time; in addition, he signed a re-engagement card which stated that his continuous service would start on November 29, 1945. The Pension Board reviewed his case and found no basis for restoring prior service.

RELEVANT CONTRACT CLAUSES AND DOCUMENT REFERENCES:

I. *1942 Agreement*

"*Article XII* (Continuity of Service)

1. The continuity of service record of those re-employed after layoffs is at present reviewed. Regulations have been set up so that each re-engaged employee is notified as to his service record. The service record of any employee who has been out more than one year will be sent to the Committee on Eligibility and Allowances for review. It has been and is the intention of the Company to automatically restore service of an employee at the time he is rehired, if he is eligible."

The Continuity of Service clause was the same in the 1944 agreement.

II. *General Instruction,* effective July 1, 1941, Paragraph 10, (Unilateral Management Policy).

"Continuity of service is broken when an employee:
"(*a*) Leaves voluntarily or is discharged.
"(*b*) Absents himself from duty for 2 consecutive weeks or longer without satisfactory explanation.
"(*c*) Is not re-employed after a temporary layoff because of reduction in force. (See paragraphs 5 (*c*) and 5 (*d*).

"(*d*) Absent because of illness, fails to keep his department head informed monthly, or is absent for a continuous period of more than 1 year.

"If an employee, after breaking his continuity of service, shall be re-employed, he shall be considered a new employee."

Paragraphs 5 (*c*) and 5 (*d*) referred to under (*c*) above provide:

"(*c*) Continuity of service will be broken if an employee: (1) Is not re-employed within 1 year from date of layoff; (2) is notified within 1 year that he may return, but fails to return or to give satisfactory explanation within 2 weeks.

"(*d*) If an employee's absence exceeds 1 year, but does not exceed his length of service, the Manager will submit the case to the Committee with his recommendation and the Committee will determine whether continuity of service will be restored."

III. *1945 Agreement*

"*Article XIV* (Continuity of Service):

"The continuity of service record of those re-employed after layoffs will be reviewed at the time of re-employment and, in each case, the employee will be notified if his service is restored or broken.

"Continuity of service is maintained unless an employe:

"(*a*) Leaves voluntarily or is discharged.

"(*b*) Absents himself from duty for two consecutive weeks or longer without satisfactory explanation.

"(*c*) Absent because of illness, fails to keep his division head notified monthly, or is absent for a continuous period of more than one year.

"(*d*) Is not re-employed within one year from date of layoff for lack of work.

"(*e*) Is notified within a year he may return but fails to return or to give satisfactory explanation within two weeks.

"Under established rule, the service record of an employee who has been out for more than one year due to lack of work will be sent to the Pension Board for review if the time out does not exceed his length of service."

POSITION OF THE COMPANY

The Company raises the threshold question that the grievance is not even arbitrable for several reasons: (1) Hirschfeld's service was broken as of November 28, 1942, and the agreement then pending contained no arbitration provision. This precludes arbitration of any question concerning the break in Hirschfeld's service record. (2) Articles XII and XIV of the 1942 and 1944 agreements, respectively, apply only to continuity of service of employees re-employed after layoffs; these contracts are silent on the question of whether a service record may be broken and under what circumstances. Thus a determination to break the record is left solely to the Company's discretion. (3) Article XIV of the 1945 agreement covers continuity of service with reference to those re-employed after layoffs; Kaspar and Hirschfeld were not laid off. The same Article lists the reasons for breaking an employee's service, and none of them relates to the Kaspar-Hirschfeld cases, except Section (*a*).

Both Kaspar and Hirschfeld were, in effect, discharged and did not remain in a "state of suspension" as the Union suggests. The directives issued by the Service Command required immediate removal of these men from the plant and the termination of their employment. The directives would countenance no other action. It is of no significance that the Company when it took this action failed to say in specific terms: "You are discharged." The men must have understood this from the nature of the termination. Both men accepted their Pension Fund Money, secured other employment, and in so doing recognized the permanence of the termination.

The decision to discharge was a proper one, just as it would have been if the men were removed from employment pursuant to a jail sentence for the commission of some crime. In other cases, arbitration boards have held that a company may discharge an employee sentenced to jail on the grounds that he was to be absent from his work for an extended period and for an unjustifiable reason.

The action to break the service of these two men was consistent with the rules governing continuity of service. The General Instructions of 1941 under Section (*b*) provided that service was broken if an employee absented himself from duty for two consecutive weeks or longer without a satisfactory reason. These employees did not have a satisfactory reason.

Since the Company refused to restore the service of these two men in November, 1945, only the 1945 agreement is applicable in passing judgment on such refusal. This agreement for the first time distinguished between *breaking of service* and *restoration of service*. The first and third paragraphs of Article XIV indicate that review will be made only with respect to those reemployed after layoffs. Since the men had been discharged, there is no obligation for the Company to review the service record.

POSITION OF THE UNION

The two men cannot be considered as having been discharged by the Company. The only desire of the War Department was to remove them from work under Army and Navy contracts; removal from any and all employment was not directed. The Company never undertook to offer either man another job in the plant. It is important to note that neither Hirschfeld nor Kaspar was charged with the violation of company rules, or, for that matter, laws of the land. During the war, it was well known that the War and Navy Departments took action of a precautionary nature without finally establishing any real guilt of wrongdoing. In issuing directives of this type, these Departments did not desire to punish the employees so affected. Both the 1942 and the 1944 contracts outline the procedure to be followed in disciplinary cases. The 1944 agreement, which was effective when Kressner was finally dropped, says in Article XIX (7):

"*a*) Before any penalty is imposed upon any employee following warning notices, such employee shall be notified one week in advance during which time he might refer the matter to the Union representative, and if the Union so desires, the matter may be negotiated with Management . . . ."

The Company did not follow this procedure in either case, although the clauses were similar in 1942 and 1944. This fact is an admission that the action was not disciplinary in nature. The men themselves were never told, verbally or in writing, that they had been discharged. In the Union's opinion, their separation must be viewed as a forced leave or a state of suspension, neither of which would affect their continuity of service.

The Company places great stress on (*a*) the documents signed by the two men to the effect that they started as "new employees" in 1945, and (*b*) the withdrawal of Pension Funds. With respect to the first, the Union considers it a type of "yellow dog contract," signed in the case of Hirschfeld under protest because of the implied threat that employment would otherwise not be forthcoming. Such a company requirement is legally suspect and violates the contract. With respect to the second document, it will be observed that Hirschfeld refused to accept Pension Fund moneys at first. According to him, a company representative told him it would be more patriotic to withdraw it and invest it in War Bonds. He finally did so in October, 1944, almost two years after his alleged "discharge."

The Union argues that none of the bases for breaking continuity of service applies to the cases of these men. They are being deprived unfairly of many years of service, affecting their pension rights, vacation benefits, and their protection in the event of layoff.

QUESTIONS

1. Appraise the argument of the Company that when the contract is silent on the definition of the break of service, the Company has the sole discretion of making the determination. Is this a sound principle to be applied generally to the interpretation of collective bargaining agreements?

2. Did the parties have situations such as those involving Hirschfeld and Kaspar in mind when they negotiated the 1945 Agreement defining continuity of service? Is it possible for the parties to anticipate all the cases which subsequently arise?

3. What are the practical consequences in the plant of long-service employees being considered as new employees?

4. What was the status of Hirschfeld and Kaspar when they were separated at the direction of the Second Service Command? Were they discharged, suspended, laid off, on indefinite leave of absence?

5. Since the Second Service Command ordered their separation, did not the later clearance by the Second Service Command for all work except on contracts classified as secret or top secret create an obligation to return these men without loss of service rights?

6. The separation of employees by the Armed Services under circumstances similar to the case of these men is a cost of war? Who should bear this cost? The individuals? The Company? The government? What are the costs to General Electric Company of restoring service credits to these men?

7. What broad questions of employment policy does this type of case raise for General Electric Company and other companies with a large volume of defense contracts?

Case 28

EFFECT OF A LAYOFF ON CONTINUITY OF SERVICE

UNION: Industrial Union of Marine and Shipbuilding Workers of America, CIO

COMPANY: Wilmington Welding and Boiler Works

Article VII of the working agreement between the Wilmington Welding and Boiler Works and the Industrial Union of Marine and Shipbuilding Workers of America reads, in part, as follows:

"Every employee of the Company who has been in the continuous employment of the Company for one year commencing August 17, 1944, or for one year commencing with the date of his employment if he has been employed since August 17, 1944, shall receive one week's vacation with pay as hereinafter set forth.

"Every employee of the Company who may have been in the continuous employment of the Company for five years commencing August 17, 1944, or for five years commencing with the date of his employment if he has been employed since August 17, 1944, shall receive two weeks' vacation with pay as hereinafter set forth."

The present case concerns a shipfitter, Frank J. Foley. The personnel record indicates that he was hired on June 25, 1945, and continued to be employed without interruption until May 20, 1946, when he received a "clearout" due to a "reduction in force." Then on July 18, 1946, he was rehired.

The Company has refused to grant Foley a week's vacation on the ground that he has not been in "continuous employment" with

the Company for a sufficiently long period, that is, for one year.
The Union protests this position.

POSITION OF THE UNION

The Union contends that Foley had been in "continuous employment" with the Company for a long enough period to qualify him for one week's vacation with pay under Article VII of the contract. It argues that the contract between the parties provides for continued seniority in case of layoff up to one year after the date of layoff. Therefore, when a worker is given a "clearout" due to a reduction in force, he is still an employee of the Company since he continues to accumulate seniority. Provided this employee can otherwise qualify under the terms of the working agreement, he is entitled to vacation benefits as one in continuous employment.

The Union reasons further that if "continuous employment" means that an employee must be on the payroll all the time, i.e., that he must become ineligible whenever he is laid off because of lack of work, then a ruthless employer could so plan his layoff periods so as to make most employees ineligible for vacations with pay. In the case of Foley, except for the brief layoff period over which he had no control, his seniority rights and privileges continued throughout the period. The Union holds that Foley should be considered as having remained in continuous employment in meeting the spirit of the contract provision. To rule otherwise would mean that an employee could be required to work all but a few days each year without becoming eligible for a paid vacation.

POSITION OF THE COMPANY

The Company argues that Foley was severed from the payroll, and thus his continuous employment with the Company was broken. When the employee was rehired, he came in as a new employee. At other times when a worker is only temporarily laid off, he is so told and is instructed to return to work at a definite time. In such instances, his personnel records are not closed as they are when he is given a "clearout" due to a reduction in force.

The Company states that in denying Foley a vacation with pay, it is not seeking to deny vacations which workers have actually earned under the terms of the working agreement. Rather it believes that "continuous employment" means employment continuously and without break, except for properly granted leaves of absence or strictly temporary layoffs where the workers are told to report again for work at a definite time. The Company insists that continuous employment, in this sense, does not prevail in the case of Foley.

Finally, the Company contends that continuous employment and seniority are two separate and unrelated subjects and that it is not proper to relate one to the other. The Company concludes that, since Foley's record shows a complete severance of the employment relationship between himself and the Company, employment was not continuous as provided by Article VII; and Foley is not entitled to vacation consideration.

QUESTIONS

1. What are the possible meanings to the phrase "continuous employment?" Consider the following examples: (*a*) working every day, (*b*) working sometime during each payroll period, (*c*) name listed continuously on the payroll, whether working or not, (*d*) continuously available for work, and (*e*) name on the seniority roster.

2. Is the status of "continuous employment" to be determined finally by the Company on the grounds that it involves complex details of payroll administration?

3. What actions or events would you regard as breaking continuous service for the purposes of Article VII—sickness, layoff, quit, discharge for cause?

4. For the purposes of Article VII, is it appropriate to distinguish between layoffs with a fixed date of recall and layoffs with an indefinite date of recall?

5. How do you appraise the contention that continuous employment for purposes of vacations and for temporary layoff (seniority) should have the same meaning under the agreement? Is there any necessary relationship? Seniority rights for rehire may run typically for a year or two beyond the last date of layoff. Would you place vacation rights in essentially the same category? As a matter of union or management policy, should they extend as long as seniority rights after layoff?

Case 29

NEGOTIATION ON SUPERSENIORITY

UNION NEGOTIATORS: Kramer and Simpson

COMPANY NEGOTIATORS: Wittaker and Lawrence

KRAMER: "Let's discuss the union's proposal to add a

new section to the seniority Article. It's on page 5 of the proposals we gave to you. It says:

> 'Union officials shall be deemed to head the seniority list of their respective departments for the purposes of layoffs, demotion, promotion and transfer. This provision shall apply to employees who hold any of the following offices in the local union: President, Vice President, Recording Secretary, Financial Secretary, Treasurer, Steward, and Grievance Committeeman.'

"It's a standard clause, found in a lot of union contracts. Will the Company be willing to —"

WITTAKER: (interrupting) "I think we ought to discuss the union proposal in conjunction with the counterproposal we submitted on much the same subject."

KRAMER: "What's that?"

WITTAKER: "Look at page 8 of our proposed agreement. It's under the fourth paragraph.

> 'When management decides that the work force in any department is to be reduced for lack of work or for retooling, it shall have the right to post a list of employees who shall be placed at the head of the seniority list in their respective departments.

"By having this language, we'll be able to pick key men, fellows with a variety of skills. It will help keep operations efficient when there's a cutback."

KRAMER: "I don't mind discussing your proposal along with ours, but I think it's a waste of time. Why not be honest? You stuck in your request just for bargaining purposes. You're not serious about it, are you?"

WITTAKER: "Every bit as serious as you are about yours. You want the union leadership to be protected when there's a layoff. We want key personnel to be protected. Besides, why do you include all union officers for superseniority? I can see why uninterrupted service of the President and maybe some grievance committeemen is important, but not all the others too.

SIMPSON: "I don't agree. Only when all the union officers are on the job can our members be sure of full protection."

LAWRENCE: "How does the secretary or the treasurer of the Local help the members in the plant? They could still continue in the offices they hold while they're on layoff."

KRAMER: "Well, take Pete Morosky. He's the Treasurer, but he's also a steward in Department 60. And as a steward it's important to be in the department to handle grievances, even when the department is working with a small crew."

WITTAKER: "Then in his case he'd be covered by the steward's position. You wouldn't need 'treasurer' in the clause. There's another thing we don't like about your clause. Under your proposal you could increase the number of shop committeemen and stewards whenever you wanted to, and they'd all get superseniority. Pretty soon ability and actual length of service wouldn't mean a thing. Only status within the union would count.

KRAMER: "We wouldn't abuse the right. Obviously the members wouldn't vote for the creation of more offices and hurt their own job rights. Your own proposal for key people is every bit as indefinite. And so far as I'm concerned it's completely unnecessary. Chances are that the men with the greatest seniority will be those with the greatest skill and versatility."

WITTAKER: "That's not necessarily true. Some of our younger men have more all-round skills. We know who they are; and if I gave you their names, you'd have to agree that they were excellent and outstanding men."

KRAMER: "Then you'd agree to post a standing list of these so-called hot shots with an agreed-upon maximum number of names?"

WITTAKER: "I didn't say that. After all, the circumstances surrounding each situation vary. The crew we would consider necessary under one set of conditions might be quite different from the one needed in another situation. Decreases in work don't affect all product lines and departments equally. So it would be hard to freeze a list of key personnel."

SIMPSON: "But a moment ago you didn't like the idea of an indefinite list of union officers, yet you want to have an indefinite number on your 'X' list. There shouldn't be any more on your list than on ours. Furthermore, the union officers are specified for their term of office. So those on your list should remain fixed for the same period."

WITTAKER: "With no chance to make substitutions on the lists now and then?"

SIMPSON: "Well, substitutions could be made for vacancies created by quits, discharges, or transfers."

WITTAKER: "We can probably agree on how to limit the number of people on both lists. But the Company can't go along with a fixed list of exceptional employees entitled to superseniority. We wouldn't have enough flexibility. We ought to have the right to alter the 'X' list at our discretion at any time as long as it stays within a certain number."

KRAMER: "We'd be crazy to give you that right, and you know it. If we let you change the names on your 'X' list, it would give you a potential list much greater than any agreed-upon number. Take the case of a layoff. If the Company draws up the list at the time of the layoff, it can omit men who would ordinarily go on the 'X' list because it knows they'd be safe on their jobs with their actual length of service."

WITTAKER: "I don't follow you."

KRAMER: "Well, take Fred Taylor in the Automatic Screw Department for example. That guy is the handiest man in the department, and he's got 5 years' service. He's a man you would surely want to keep if things got slow. Now, if you draw up the list of key people at the time of the layoffs, you might tap a short-service employee instead of Fred if you saw that the layoff wouldn't go so far as to affect 5-year people. That way you'd get the equivalent of an extra man on the list. If there's to be a list, it will have to be fixed; and the Union has to have the right to challenge the names of anyone on the list.

LAWRENCE: "Wait a minute. The makeup of that list is to be the sole responsibility of management. After all, we don't try to tell you who can or can't be an officer of the Union. That's your undisputed right. So we've got the same right to pick the key men without any challenge from you people.

KRAMER: "Why should you worry about the Union's right to challenge? If really topnotch people are selected for the list, there's nothing to worry about. We'd never be able to sell the idea of such a list to our membership if we couldn't challenge the names through the grievance machinery. They'd be sure you'd discriminate in picking people."

LAWRENCE: "Obviously we wouldn't discriminate. We'd just want the best people."

KRAMER: "Try to tell the membership that. You might deliberately put nonunion men on the list. Of course, if you'd grant us the union shop this might not be a problem."

WITTAKER: We're not talking about the union shop. We're talking about superseniority."

LAWRENCE: "I think we've made clear the Company's position on the 'X' list. I'd like to go back to the union's proposal for superseniority for certain union officers. Your clause suggests superseniority for the 'purposes of layoff, demotion, promotion and transfer.' What are demotions and promotions in there for? I thought the Union wanted this clause to protect the union administration at the time of a layoff."

SIMPSON: "That's only part of it. By including 'promotions' in the clause, we want to give these officers a special benefit. It will strengthen their leadership position in the Union, and that's a good thing for the Company too."

LAWRENCE: "That's double talk so far as I'm concerned. If anything, I should think the granting of superseniority to union officers for any purpose beyond layoff would weaken their leadership position rather than strengthen it. Your members whose actual length of service was more than that of the officers would resent seeing them get all the gravy. We won't agree to superseniority which is so broad in it application."

KRAMER: "Of course, you overlook one thing. Our clause would promote membership interest in union elections. We'd have more candidates for office. That would keep officers on their toes."

WITTAKER: "Trouble is, most union officers think they're 'on their toes' when they succeed in keeping the Company in hot water all the time."

KRAMER: "Larry, you questioned only the inclusion of promotions and demotions. I assume you agree that the word 'transfer' is O.K."

LAWRENCE: "No, I don't."

KRAMER: "But what about a transfer in lieu of layoff which might actually be a demotion. In some cases that type of transfer might have the effect of removing an officer far from the area in which his constituents work. If the protection is adequate, superseniority must apply to transfers."

LAWRENCE: "Maybe there's some merit in your argument. We might be able to agree on superseniority for purposes of 'layoffs and transfers or demotions due to layoffs'—some language like that."

KRAMER: "Incidentally, I don't like that word 'superseniority'. I wish we could get into the habit of just saying 'heads the seniority list.'"

WITTAKER: "Call it anything you like. It's still superseniority."

LAWRENCE: "I'd like to ask you fellows another question. Assume there's a reduction in the forces of a department. What if the only jobs left are those which the steward can't possibly do without lengthy training? Is he to be kept at the time of layoff even under these circumstances?"

SIMPSON: "No, the Union wouldn't be that unrealistic. We'd agree that he would have to be able to do the remaining work."

KRAMER: "But in that case we would insist on the right to appoint another man as temporary steward who could perform the duties of a remaining job and who would then gain superseniority— I mean, head of the seniority list. Of course, the laid-off steward would still head the list for the purpose of recall to the first available job in the department which opens up."

WITTAKER: "Well, I think we've explored most of the issues in these two proposals. I suggest we break for lunch. It will give us a chance to think about these points. Let's start in again at 2:30 P.M. this afternoon."

QUESTIONS

1. On the basis of this discussion, draft contract language which you think would be most likely to be acceptable to both parties.

2. If you were a union negotiator, would you rather drop the demand for superseniority than to give the Company any form of "exceptional list?" From the point of view of management would you drop your proposal for an "exceptional list" rather than agree to some form of superseniority for union officers?

Section
E

LAYOFFS AND TRANSFERS

Two principal methods have been developed for the control of layoffs: (1) the equal division of work among employees, and (2) layoffs based upon seniority and related factors. In many cases both methods are combined. The labor agreement may prescribe first the layoff of all probationary and temporary employees, next a sharing of work among the remaining employees down to 32 or 36 hours per week, and then layoffs based on length of service if further curtailment is required.

EQUAL DIVISION OF WORK

In Section D it was noted that industries characterized by seasonal employment normally do not use the seniority principle exclusively. If layoffs were based on length of service in such industries, senior employees would enjoy relatively steady employment while junior employees would work only intermittently. The high mortality rate among companies in some industries has also prompted unions to avoid complete reliance on seniority. The sharing of work is accomplished either by reducing the number of hours worked by each employee in the slack period or by rotating the work force so that, for example, one third of the employees work a 40-hour week every third week. In either case, probationary and temporary employees are laid off before the remaining work is shared among regular employees. The reduction in the work week is used extensively in the needle trades. However, if it should be found that work is so slack that all regular employees are working a short workweek, even during the busy seasons, a reorganization of the work force takes place. In this process, some employees are laid off on the basis of length of service, and the remaining employees share the work at a higher average workweek. In the building construction industry, instead of controlling layoff, an informal system of rotation in hiring is observed through the union hiring halls to allocate available work opportunities. The rotation method is used primarily in those companies where continuous operations make it impracticable to schedule a short workweek.

Many unions have found strict observance of equal division of work unsatisfactory beyond a certain point. While employees are willing to share the available work down to 32 hours each week or to one 40-hour week in every 3 weeks, they are reluctant to share fewer hours. They express the view that under these circumstances they are sharing misery, not work. Moreover, the wages they receive for less than 32 hours per week might be less than they would receive from unemployment compensation, or the payment for hours worked would be so little more than compensation benefits that there is practically no inducement to work. Similarly, many companies have objected to extensive division of work. Some find it difficult to reorganize operations to permit equal division. Others complain that it prevents them from providing adequate service to customers.

Within recent years, some unions have tried to persuade employers to share the work on the basis of rotating rather than reducing the hours for regular employees in the workweek. By working 1 full week and then being on layoff for the next 2 weeks, an employee may be able to collect full unemployment compensation benefits. Although many companies, desirous of retaining their work force, have acceded to this request, some have resisted because under a merit rating system of unemployment compensation the employer's costs increase with the number of layoffs. This practice also raises, from the point of view of public policy, the question of whether unemployment compensation should be used to enable a firm to retain its work force during a period of work curtailment.

The sharing of work helps to preserve the union's numerical strength and to keep intact the company's labor supply at the time of curtailment, but if the reduction in take home pay for all employees is extensive or of long duration, disunity within the union may develop, and the company's production efficiency may be impaired. Senior employees will urge that layoffs of junior employees be made. If work opportunities exist in other plants in the area, even junior employees will prefer layoff, or they will quit.

Layoffs Based on Seniority

A decline in business may affect a single department of a plant or may involve the entire plant. The reduction may be temporary in character or may be permanent, as in the case of a secular decline in an industry or the elimination of a department. In writing the seniority provisions of a collective bargaining agreement, unions and managements usually differentiate among the types of layoff. The unit to which seniority is applied is often governed by the nature of the layoff. If the layoff is temporary, the seniority rights of an employee affected by the layoff are usually exercised only within the limits of his occupation or department. This prevents him from displacing or "bumping" workers in other occupations or departments who have less service with the company. On the other hand, if the layoff is to be permanent, greater security usually is afforded the senior employees affected by allowing them to "bump" junior employees elsewhere in the entire plant.

Because of the varying forms of layoffs, seniority provisions in the labor agreement are longer and more complex than most other provisions. Moreover, a high proportion of grievances relate to layoffs and the right of employees to "bump" in lieu of layoff. Some companies have developed special training programs for supervision to explain how layoffs and transfers are to be effected under the agreement. Westinghouse Corporation, for example, has prepared a film for supervisors on the application of seniority. Union educational directors devote considerable time to this subject in their workers' education programs.

The following discussion selects a particular seniority clause and describes its application in a layoff situation. The 1950 agreement between the Whitin Machine Works and the United Steelworkers of America provides the following:

"The word, 'seniority,' means the length of continuous service credited to an employee in accordance with this Article.

"For the purpose of administering the seniority provisions

of this Agreement, the departments of the bargaining unit are arranged in seniority zones as set forth in this Article.

"The continuous service record of an employee (other than a probationary employee) shall be computed from the date of his first hiring by the Company . . . .

"When an employee is transferred from one department to another he shall have all of his seniority credited to him in his new department and in his new zone, if any.

"Application of Seniority:

"Lay-offs and Recalls to Service:

"(*a*) Lay-offs for periods of one (1) week or less because of special circumstances or conditions of emergency shall be deemed temporary and shall not be subject to the provisions of this Article when compliance with said provisions would interfere with the efficient operation of any departments or of the plant.

"(*b*) In all other cases of lay-offs and of recalls to work, in connection with the decrease or increase of the working forces, length of continuous service with the Company shall govern provided the employee has the physical fitness and ability to perform the required work in a satisfactory manner.

"(*c*) Lay-offs shall be effected on a departmental and zone basis in accordance with this Agreement, and each employee's status will be determined in the department and zone in which he is employed at the time of such lay-off.

"An employee, about to be laid off, shall have the privilege of accepting a demotion in lieu of lay-off by displacing or 'bumping' in his department junior employees whose work said senior employee has the ability and physical fitness to perform. After exhausting his 'bumping' rights in his department said senior employee shall be privileged to 'bump' in his zone, one other employee having the most junior status in said zone and occupying a job which said senior employee has the ability and physical fitness to perform.

"An employee demoted in lieu of a lay-off to a job

classification not in his own department but in his zone, as aforesaid, shall have the right and shall be required to return to his original job classification, i.e., his job classification from which he was first demoted in lieu of lay-off, when such job classification again becomes available. Should such employee refuse re-transfer to such original job classification, his refusal shall be considered a voluntary quitting of his employment with the Company. This provision shall not be deemed to prevent the Company from offering, nor the employee from accepting, a job classification other than his said original job classification in his department if such original job classification is not then available and if such assignment will not prejudice the seniority rights of a senior employee.

"If a job opening or vacancy occurs in a zone and if there are no employees who have been laid off from such zone and who have any rights of recall to jobs in such zone, the Company will offer such vacant job to the most senior employee laid off from another zone, provided that such employee shall have the ability and physical fitness to perform the required work.

"A laid-off employee who demands to be recalled, on the basis of his seniority, to a job which, after such recall, he is found unable to perform satisfactorily, shall be again laid off as of the date of his original lay-off. Moreover, such employee shall thereafter have no recall rights except to the job from which he was first laid off, when such job again becomes open or available.

"*Seniority Zones*

Zone No. 1

410—Cutting-Off	442—Creels
413—Tin Shop	453—Freight House
432—Steel Fabricating	466—Carpenters
440—Box Making	466—Maintenance
441—Misc. Wood Work	466—Tenements
	466—Lumber

466—Village
466—Sheetmetal
466—Steel Fabricating
466—Outside Electrical
467—Plumbing
471—Yard
472—Garage

Zone No. 2

402—Machine Repair
411—Screw Machines
412—Punch Press or Bolt Job
414—Large Planers
415—Small Planers
423—General Machining
425—Jobbing Departments
426—Lathe and Grinder
428—Drilling
429—Spinning & Twister, Small Parts
431—Plating Department
436—Steel Rolls
450—Tin Cylinders
451—Roll and Brush Job
454—Tool Job
458—Millwrights
459—Oil Room
480—Laundry

Zone No. 3

408—Annealing Room
409—Blacksmith Shop
416—Milling Machine
417—Chuck Job
418—Automatic Chucking Machines
419—Card Cylinders

420—Gear Cutting
421—Card Rolls & Picker, Small
422—Card, Small Parts
424—Comber, Small Parts
427—Roving, Small Parts
430—Polishing
435—Flyer, Small Parts
437—Rings
438—Bolsters
439—Spindles
449—Schweiter Winders
452—Paint Job

Zone No. 4

406—Stock Room
407—International Material Transportation
433—Machine Division
443—Picking Erecting
444—Card Erecting
445—Comber Erecting
446—Drawing Job
447—Roving Erecting
448—Spinning Erecting
457—Power House
460—Sweepers
468—Pipe Department
469—Painting
470—Electrical Department

Zone No. 5 (Foundry Division)

403—Pattern Storage
404—Foundry
405—Cast Iron Room
482—Core Room

Zone No. 6　　　　　*Zone No. 7*

465—Bargaining Unit　489—Inspection Depart-
Employees in Pro-　ment
duction Depart-
ment

Each zone consists of a number of departments. The Union and the Company grouped these departments on the basis of the related skill requirements within the departments and the normal line of progression of employees from department to department.

For the purpose of illustration, assume that an excess inventory of small machine parts has developed. The Company decides to lay off a number of employees for 2 to 3 weeks. One of the departments affected in No. 412, Punch Press or Bolt Job, in Zone 2. This department is made up of 4 job classifications:

Setup Men—4 employees
Punch Press Hand, Class I—8 employees
Punch Press Hand, Class II—7 employees
Punch Press Operators—6 employees

The Company, after reviewing the probable needs in the department, decides to lay off one Punch Press Hand, Class I, two Punch Press Hands, Class II, and two Punch Press Operators. Because the lot size of parts to be produced during the period of curtailment is smaller, all of the setup men are needed to handle the required number of setups. The seniority of the employees involved is the following:

Setup Men
(1) Murphy—16 years
(2) Azarian—12 years
(3) Friedman—11 years
(4) Marshall—8 years

Punch Press Hand—I
(1) Smith—21 years
(2) Bentley—20 years
(3) Rodgers—18 years
(4) Fabreau—13 years
(5) Scalleter—11 years

(6) Brodin—10½ years
(7) Charett—10 years
(8) Trumbull—6 years

Punch Press Hand—II
(1) Timans—7 years
(2) Seymour—6½ years
(3) Downey—5½ years
(4) Sandhurst—5 years
(5) Billideau—4 years
(6) Franklin—3½ years
(7) Watson—2½ years

Punch Press Operators

(1) Hern—11 years
(2) Morgan—11 years
(3) Slater—7½ years
(4) Stapleton—3 years
(5) Trodja—2½ years
(6) Bender—2 years

The Company concludes that the Punch Press Hands—I are able to do the Class II work, and the Class II men are able to do the work of Punch Press Operators. The following moves are made under the terms of the agreement. Franklin, Watson, Stapleton, Trodja, and Bender are dropped from the department. Trumbull displaces Billideau through demotion in lieu of layoff; and Billideau, in turn, bumps Stapleton through demotion in lieu of layoff. These 7 actions (5 layoffs from the department and 2 transfers) reduce the complement of the various jobs in the amount desired.

However, this is only the first step in the procedure. Franklin, Watson, Stapleton, Trodja, and Bender are now each privileged to bump a junior employee in other departments of Zone 2, if they have the ability and physical fitness to perform the work. The jobs in the Laundry Department (No. 480) in Zone 2 are relatively unskilled and are occupied by employees with the least seniority in the zone. The five most junior men in the Laundry Department are:

(1) Sanderson—2½ years
(2) Rigoski—1½ years
(3) Ulman—1 year
(4) Falcetti—10 months
(5) Carmen—8 months

Franklin, Watson, Trodja, and Stapleton, exercising their option to bump, displace Rigoski, Ulman, Falcetti, and Carmen. Bender with only 2 years' service is junior to Sanderson; and since there is no other employee in the zone with less than 2 years' service doing work for which Bender has ability, he must be laid off.

In summary, the curtailment required in Department 412 results in the actual layoff of 1 man in that department (Bender) and 4 men from the Laundry Department. To accomplish this, 6 transfer actions were necessary. A total of 10 personnel actions were needed to lay off 5 men. The complexity of layoffs can be better understood if one adds to this illustration by assuming that simultaneous layoffs are being made in 10 or 12 of the 18 departments within Zone 2.

Why have the parties chosen this type of seniority arrangement? In their opinion, it is the most effective way of blending two primary considerations: (1) protection for the senior man, not only from layoff but from an excessive decrease in pay caused by demotion in lieu of layoff; and (2) maintenance of efficiency by restricting the bumping rights to jobs within the zone on which a senior employee has ability and physical fitness to do the work. Most unions and managements are in agreement on these objectives, and they realize that arbitrary rules may result in some hardship cases. For example, under the above illustration it is possible that a man in Department 412 may have actually worked in that department only 6 months, having been transferred to that department after 5 years' service in another zone. It is to be remembered that under this agreement when an employee transfers between zones, he carries his accumulated seniority with him. He will be retained, having a total of $5\frac{1}{2}$ years' service; while a man who has devoted his full 2 years of service to Department 412 is laid off (e.g., Bender). The Union is faced with the problem of trying to make Bender understand why he must give way to a man whose service in the department is less but whose total service with the Company is greater than his. Similarly, by limiting bumping on an intrazone basis, some hardships may result from the arbitrary definition of zones. In the above illustration, there are Punch Press operations in Department 409 (Blacksmith Shop) of Zone 3. But a senior Punch Press Hand in Department 412 of Zone 2 cannot bump a junior man in a similar job in Zone 3. The Union recognizes that some limitations must be imposed on the right of senior employees to bump indiscriminately throughout the plant if efficiency is to be maintained.

The President of a large International Union has made the following observations on these problems:

"It is very difficult to write a satisfactory seniority clause in a trade union agreement. As a matter of fact, even if the employers would agree to let us write our own seniority clause, I do not believe the Union itself could write a clause that would be satisfactory to all of our members. Some are in favor of seniority over the whole plant—when workers are laid off in their department to 'bump off' workers in other departments who have fewer years of service. Others contend that seniority should be on a departmental basis. I attended a meeting of one of the local unions recently and for about three hours I listened to a discussion whether it was right to 'bump' or not to 'bump.' For days afterward 'bump, bump, bump' rang in my ears."

Transfers by senior employees to avoid layoffs are usually allowed only when the employees are able to meet at least the minimum or normal standards of the job to which transfer is sought. The company makes the initial judgment in this matter, relying on evidence concerning the similarity of skills between the two jobs involved and the past related experience of the employee. Its decision is subject to the grievance procedure, and it is the exercise of this judgment which gives rise to most layoff grievances. In some cases, provision is made for a trial period on the job. This is particularly true when long-service employees (with more than 5 years of service, for example) are affected by a layoff. A few contracts provide a training period on a new job for senior employees whose jobs are eliminated permanently.

The recall of employees who are laid off is usually accomplished in the reverse order of the layoff. When business recovers, it may not require workers in exactly the same proportions among jobs as required when business declined. Accordingly, employees in different jobs may not necessarily be recalled in exactly the reverse order of their layoff or in exactly the reverse order of their transfer in lieu of layoff. Most agreements provide that no new employees may be hired while employees are on layoff status who are qualified to do the available work.

CONSIDERATION OF NONSERVICE FACTORS IN LAYOFFS

In some labor agreements, it is provided that only when other factors are relatively equal between two employees will length of continuous service decide which employee is to be laid off. The most common of these factors are general ability and skill, physical fitness, family status (single or married), and number of dependents. Less frequently are citizenship and place of residence considered. However, in recent years the use of these nonservice factors has declined. Managements and unions found that they were the source of frequent disputes. Nevertheless, they raise important questions of policy. To what extent should the family obligations of an employee weigh more heavily than length of service in determining whether or not he is to be laid off? Even though a senior employee is competent to do the available work, should he be laid off if there is a junior employee who is more competent to do the work?

Case 30

LAYOFF OR TERMINATION?

UNION: Textile Workers Union of America, CIO, Local 1007

COMPANY: Consolidated Textile Company, Inc., Windsor Print Works Division

BACKGROUND

In the course of wage conferences which followed a "wildcat strike" in November, 1950, the management told the Union that if certain wage rate increases were insisted upon it would be necessary to curtail operations as soon as possible. The parties negotiated a wage increase. Effective January 1, 1951, the first steps to curtail some operations were taken when the Company terminated nine printers, members of another bargaining unit. Its notice of December 30, 1950, states:

"In accordance with the terms of the Union contract between the Windsor Print Works Division of North Adams, Mass., and the Machine Printers Beneficial Association of the U.S., Providence, R.I., we are hereby giving notice under Section XIII that we are reducing our staff of Journeymen Printers and we are terminating your employment as of December 31, 1950 . . . ."

A decision to make more extensive terminations was deferred until late January. On February 2, 1951, the Company sent the following letter to 47 employees in the bargaining unit of Local 1007:

"Since we have curtailed operations we will have no further need of your service and therefore we are terminating your employment as of February 5, 1951 and removing your name from our payroll . . . . Under the terms of the Group Insurance you have a month in which to contact the local agent of the Aetna Life Insurance Company if you wish to retain the life insurance at your own expense."

None of the 47 employees had less than 30 days' service with the Company. Four of these employees were reinstated subsequently; the Company expressed a willingness to "restore their seniority, since they are now working." Immediately following the "terminations" of February 5, the Union made a protest to the Company.

POSITION OF THE UNION

The Union had no discussion with the Company prior to its unilateral action of February 5. It learned of the contemplated action for the first time through the February 2 letter. A general grievance was filed in behalf of these employees since the Union believed a basic contract clause was involved. Some of the people affected had as much as 5 to 9 years of service with the Company, while employees with only 2 to 3 years of service were kept on the payroll. If the Company's action is upheld, it means that all of these aggrieved employees will lose all past service credits and benefits accruing therefrom. The Company's willingness to isolate specific cases for special treatment, as in the case of the 4 employees, is no remedy. It would be discriminatory and violative of the contract.

Article VIII (Suspension-Discharge) of the contract sets forth the only basis for permanent separation and the loss of service rights. It also provides a procedure to validate the action of permanent separation.

"A) *Just Cause:* The right to discharge employees shall remain in the sole discretion of the Employer, except that no discharge shall be made without just cause—just cause to mean, among other things, inefficiency, insubordination or persistent or serious infraction of rules relating to the health or safety of other employees . . . ."

"B) *Procedure:* No employee shall be discharged without

first being suspended. The suspension shall become a discharge automatically, unless the Employer shall indicate otherwise, on the seventh regularly scheduled work day after the Employer has mailed to the Union and the employee involved a notice of the suspension or automatic discharge with the specific reasons therefor. Said notice shall be entitled "Suspension-Discharge Notice" and shall be mailed within two (2) regularly scheduled working days after the suspension . . . ." (There follows a statement of the grievance procedure which may be employed.)

The Company seeks to make a distinction between "terminations" and "discharges"; there is no such distinction, since only discharges have the contractual effect of destroying basic rights. Yet the Company did not follow the procedure outlined in Article VIII (B), nor can it show that any of the "causes" set forth in Article VIII (A) justified the action.

Article IX (Seniority) of the agreement allows temporary separation for reasons of curtailed operations, but there is definitely no loss of seniority involved; and the employer is obligated to call back laid-off employees in the order of their seniority before hiring new employees, provided they have the ability to perform the job. The Company has chosen to consider its action as other than a "layoff," and concludes falsely that by labeling it a termination it has no further obligation to the employees.

In summary, the Union makes the following demands:

"(1) Revocation of all termination notices.

"(2) Those jobs now occupied by new employees should be declared vacant and any terminated employee should be allowed to apply.

"(3) Before any new people are hired, terminated employees should be allowed to apply.

"(4) In any case where an employee was terminated who could and would apply for a job subsequently filled, he should receive retroactive pay from the time said job was filled."

POSITION OF THE COMPANY

The Company emphasizes the need for stabilizing its work force by reducing permanently the total staff. The following data were introduced to show the effect of the terminations:

Week Ending	Employees on Regular List	Employees Actually Working	Employees Laid-Off Sick, Etc.
12/23/50	495	474	21
12/30/50	495	465	30
1/ 6/51	495	384	111
1/13/51	496	341	155
1/20/51	485	385	100
1/27/51	474	403	71
2/ 3/51	413	358	55
2/17/51	408	388	20
3/17/51	407	383	24
4/ 7/51	408	386	22

It will be noted that after the terminations the regular list more closely conformed with the number needed. The regular list and the list of those actually working were more nearly equal after the week ending January 27, 1951.

In the Company's judgment, these people were neither *laid off* nor were they *discharged.* They were terminated for the just cause of curtailed operations. The Company gave them a termination notice to be fair to them. If they had been given any hope of re-employment, when the Company knew it would not need them in the future, their chances of securing other employment would have been harmed. Other companies are reluctant to hire people on "layoff" status, who might be recalled at any time. The current payroll indicates that the only new employees hired were in those jobs where the people terminated could not be used. Even if the action is construed as a discharge, the Company cites the phrase "among other things" in Article VIII (A) to show that the parties had other than disciplinary reasons in mind in defining "just cause." Under cross-examination the Company asserted that neither "terminated" nor "discharged" employees can claim any benefits under the agreement. It agreed that a "laid-off" employee does retain certain established rights.

QUESTIONS

1. How do you distinguish between a layoff, a suspension, a termination, and a discharge? In what way would these differences be reflected in the rights of employees under the agreement? What would be the differences in the personnel actions taken and in the records kept by the Company?

2. In what way do the rulings under unemployment compensation affect the status of employees under the agreement? If these employees received unemployment compensation, how would that fact affect your decision in this matter?

3. If discharge is the only basis for the loss of service rights under the agreement, as the Union contends, do employees retain rights of recall and re-employment indefinitely?

4. Is a large discrepancy between the number of employees on the regular list and the number of employees actually working of concern to the Company and the Union? What methods are available to the parties to prevent large discrepancies from developing?

5. Is the Union's demand for retroactivity practicable in the language in which it is stated under its point (4) above?

Case 31

A TEMPORARY OR A PERMANENT LAYOFF?

UNION: International Photographers of the Motion Picture Industries, International Alliance of Theatrical and Stage Employees, AFL

COMPANY: Walt Disney Productions

During the latter part of July, 1946, Walt Disney Productions found itself in difficult financial conditions and was obliged to undertake a drastic curtailment in its production schedule. A substantial number of layoffs were involved. A meeting was held in the company cafeteria where the circumstances were explained to the business agents of all the unions whose members were employed by the Company in order that these business agents and the members of their unions would fully understand the conditions which necessitated a reduction in staff.

On July 29, 1946, a memorandum was addressed by John Reedes, Vice-President and General Manager of the Company, to the cameramen. Each cameraman was notified that he would be included in the general layoff effective at the close of work, August 1, 1946. The memorandum stated that the Company took this action with reluctance and that the layoffs were dictated entirely by economic considerations. Nine cameramen were affected.

The Company had found it impossible to operate without further financial assistance and had applied for bank loans in order to work out its problems over a period of time. It was not known at the time of the layoffs just when a decision might be forthcoming on the bank loans. Consequently, no promise or commitment was made regarding recall or any future work.

Prior to this last day of work, August 1, 1946, all of the cameramen, excluding one man who was on vacation, were advised by their immediate superiors that the outlook was very "dark" and that they should not rely on the chances of obtaining future employment with the Company. They were advised to seek other jobs. The acceptance of other work would not prejudice their future employment opportunites with the Company, or the accumulation of benefits under the contract.

After August 1 most of the cameramen involved secured work in other studios. During the month of August, the Company gradually began to rehire its former employees. On August 8, 1946, Roy Hoar was offered and accepted re-employment. On August 20, Paul Martin was re-employed. On September 15, Leonard Pickley, who had been on vacation when the layoff occurred, was offered a job and returned to work.

On September 27, 1946, Herbert Aller, the business representative of the Union, addressed a letter to Bonar Dyar, Personnel Director of the Company, stating that a reasonable length of time had expired since the layoffs and that, therefore, he was requesting severance pay for the members of his Union under the terms of the contract. Section 11 of the collective bargaining agreement between the Company and Union reads as follows:

"Upon dismissal, employees with one year or over of continuous service will receive one week's severance pay; and employees with two years continuous service or more shall receive two weeks' severance pay to be computed at the highest rate of pay received by said employee during the twelve months prior to dismissal."

Negotiations and discussions regarding the severance-pay claim continued for more than 2 weeks, but no agreement was reached.

On October 15, 1946, two additional jobs became available; and re-employment was offered, in turn, to each of the remaining six cameramen according to their seniority. Messrs. Sharpe, Mann, Wilkins, and Nave refused the offer of re-employment on the grounds that the work was only temporary and they had already secured other employment of a more permanent or desirable nature. Messrs. Brandenburg and Gunderson accepted re-employment on October 15 when they were reached on the seniority list.

The Union submits that the laid-off cameramen are entitled to their severance pay. The Company opposed payment of this benefit.

POSITION OF THE UNION

The Union takes the position that under the terms of the severance-pay provisions of the contract, each cameraman became entitled to his severance pay immediately upon being laid off. The Union contends that there is nothing in the agreement which provides for the withholding of the severance pay pending a later determination of available re-employment, or which distinguishes between a permanent and a temporary layoff. According to the Union, severance pay had been paid on numerous occasions to cameramen during the war years; and in 1941 similar payments were made during a shutdown caused by a strike, in spite of the fact that it was commonly accepted that the plant would reopen and the men would be re-employed.

In the present case the Union points out that absolutely no commitments were made or could have been made regarding re-employment at the time of the layoff on August 1. Attention is called to the fact that the layoff notice received by the cameramen makes no mention of re-employment and that the advice given to the employees to secure other jobs naturally left them with no expectations of being re-employed by the Company at any predictable time in the future. The Union introduced the testimony of several of the cameramen involved to the effect that, when re-employment was offered and refused by some of the men on October 15, such re-employment was offered on a purely temporary basis. The Union argues that the refusal of these men to accept temporary work does not prejudice their rights to severance pay, since they should have received this pay before the offer of temporary re-employment was made.

The Union answers the Company's argument that it has an established practice of waiting 90 days after layoffs before making severance payments, with the statement that the terms of the contract contain no reference to any such practice, and that the decision in this case must be made on the terms of the contract.

The Union also answers the Company's contention regarding the accumulation of vacation rights and other benefits under the contract with the argument that these matters are separate and apart from the severance-pay provision and have nothing whatsoever to do with the application thereof.

In summary, the essence of the Union's claim is that, under the terms of the severance-pay provision, an employee who is laid off, dismissed, terminated, or discharged, becomes immediately entitled to the amount of severance pay for which he qualifies by length of service. The Union argues that this holds regardless of whether the employee is to be re-employed by the Company after 1 week, 2 months, or any other period of time.

POSITION OF THE COMPANY

The Company's position is that on August 1 it was forced by circumstances to put a general layoff into effect and that the circumstances surrounding this action were made very clear to all of the union business agents and the cameramen involved. It contends that there never was any question regarding the desire and intent of the Company to increase its production schedule as soon as its financial condition permitted and to re-employ as soon as possible all the men who were laid off.

The Company maintains that the cameramen involved were not discharged or dismissed but were laid off temporarily until such time as conditions permitted their re-employment. Furthermore, the Company insists that it has long had a policy of carrying employees who were laid off on the payroll for a period of 90 days, during which time such employees' seniority rights, vacation, sick leave, and other benefits were accumulated so that, if an employee returned to work, he suffered no loss of such benefits as a result of the layoff.

According to the Company's description of the practice, after the 90-day period has expired, the Company either makes a final discharge or termination of the employee and pays him everything to which he is entitled under the contract up to that date, or the Company notifies the employee that he is entitled to such things if he wants to claim them or that he can continue on a laid-off status for a longer period if there is a possibility of future employment.

The Company insists that everything it has done in connection with the reduction in force supports its contention that the layoff was, so far as the cameramen were concerned, of a temporary nature. It places a great deal of emphasis on the fact that re-employment was actually offered to each of the men involved and accepted by some of them. The Company states that under its practice, if the top men on the seniority list had accepted re-employment, leaving those on the bottom of the list unemployed after the 90-day period, then those cameramen who were not re-employed would have become entitled to their severance pay.

Thus, the essence of the Company's claim is that, when an employee is laid off with the possibility of future rehire, it is entitled to follow an allegedly established practice of waiting 90 days and then either paying severance pay to the employee or allowing him to exercise his option of taking such severance pay or waiting further for re-employment.

QUESTIONS

1. How could the question posed by this case be avoided in the future? Would you propose any contract language? Would you suggest any internal administrative rule which might be adopted by the Company?

2. Is it always possible to know at the time of a layoff whether it will be temporary or permanent? Who should bear the costs of this uncertainty?

3. If employees were told that they were laid-off permanently and were offered re-employment a week later, would they be entitled to severance pay under the contract provision?

4. What is the status of the alleged practice of the Company under the agreement?

Case 32

THE PRACTICABILITY OF STRICT SENIORITY IN LAYOFFS

UNION: Textile Workers Union of America, CIO

COMPANY: The Pantasote Company

The case involves the interpretation of the layoff provisions of the agreement. The contract provides that layoffs shall be in accordance with straight seniority "so far as is practicable."

In April of 1946, a lack of certain raw materials made it necessary for the Company to lay off 65 people out of a total employment of 205. If 12 so-called key people could have been retained without regard to seniority, 30 additional layoffs could have been avoided because these 12 men were embossing machine operators, mill men, and laboratory assistants, all of whom do preparatory work. A strict interpretation of the seniority provision would not have permitted these 12 men to continue in their jobs during this "slack" period, since the men did not have sufficient seniority ratings. However, to train other employees to do the work would have required 2 or 3 weeks. It was tentatively agreed between the parties that the 12 would be retained but that 12 senior employees would immediately be trained to replace them. The 12 incumbents, however, declined to work on this basis; and they and 18 others were laid off. The Union insisted that the Company would have to train senior employees for the job. The Company held that it could rightfully retain the key men without regard to seniority. The dispute was referred to arbitration under the agreement.

POSITION OF THE UNION

The Union contends that the seniority provision is one which needs to be rigidly interpreted and enforced. Seniority would soon cease to have much meaning if it could be disregarded as lightly as the Company seemingly desires. The "practicable" expression, according to the Union, has reference to a person like a boiler engineer or a fireman without whom the plant could not operate.

The Union argues that several provisions of the agreement evidence the Company's stated obligation to train employees for more than one job. In fact, the capacity to handle more than one job in this plant is expected. For example, Section 7 of the contract provides as follows:

"The parties recognize that in the operation of the plant the employees may be required to work on different jobs and are subject to transfer from one job to another as the exigencies of the business may require, subject to the provisions of the agreement and to the collective bargaining rights of the Union."

And in Section 16, it is stated: "Promotion shall be made on the basis of seniority and other necessary qualifications to perform the job."

The Union argues that, if the Company had been sincere in fulfilling its responsibilities and if it had been efficient in the conduct of its business, it would have given its qualified seniors training for these key or higher-paying jobs before the layoffs became necessary. The Company is in a position to plan promotions and transfers and should not wait for some emergency situation to arise. The present dilemma is felt to be a product of the Company's poor management. The Union insists that the principle of seniority is so important for the maintenance of harmony within its own ranks that only a strict interpretation should be allowable.

POSITION OF THE COMPANY

The Company maintains that the contract provision which stipulates that layoffs shall be in accordance with straight seniority "so far as practicable" contemplates the very type of situation here under consideration. The Company interprets "so far as practicable" to mean that there are situations where strict seniority should not be followed. A long layoff is not in prospect, and the Company feels that there is no good reason for wasting time and money in the training of senior employees for highly specialized jobs. It argues that the best way to resolve the issue would be to allow the 12 men to continue their jobs for this short "slack" period. The Company maintains that it would be foolhardy to penalize 30 people. It holds that a logical interpretation of "practicable" would allow the retention of any person out of seniority when a layoff is necessary if his work is such that his senior would require at least 2 weeks of special training.

QUESTIONS

1. Why do you suppose the 12 incumbents refused to work in accordance with the tentative agreement between the Company and the Union? What should the parties do under such circumstances? What methods are open to the union organization to secure approval of the agreement? Should union government provide that such an agreement be approved by the members directly affected?
2. What do you suppose the Union and management meant when the term "practicable" was included in the contract? Do you approve of such language in an agreement?
3. How do you appraise the rule proposed by the Company? Do you think the Union would accept such an administrative interpretation? Why?
4. How would you phrase the administrative interpretation of "practicable" that is suggested by the Union?
5. How do you appraise the contention of the Union that management should have prepared for the contingency by training senior employees more broadly in advance of such a situation?
6. Why is the Union willing to let 30 additional men be laid off rather than allow the 12 men to be retained out of seniority? What is the interest of the Union in this case?

Case 33

MANAGERIAL FLEXIBILITY IN MAKING LAYOFFS

UNION: International Association of Machinists, AFL

COMPANY: American Emery Wheel Works

On February 18, 1949, the Union filed the following grievance:

"We the Union feel that Mr. Koob is violating the seniority clause of the contract by transferring men into departments where there are men laid off. These transfers are on a wholesale scale at times."

The operations at the Company are divided into two general divisions: Preparatory and Finishing. The preparatory work is done in two departments on the first floor, one which is known as Preparatory and the other as the Kiln Department. Article VII (*Seniority*) provides that seniority shall be on a departmental basis. Recently, because of work curtailment, the Company was forced to lay off employees. Nine employees were laid off in the Preparatory Department and two employees in the Kiln Department. Mr. Koob, the foreman for both units, has been transferring the remaining kiln men to the Preparatory Department when the kiln work was slack; and although some of the jobs they have done involved sweeping and other menial tasks, it is admitted that they perform some operations which are recognized as belonging to the Preparatory Department. Approximately 800 hours of such transfer time are involved. Similar transfers have been made from Preparatory to Kiln, but to such a small degree as to constitute no offset.

POSITION OF THE UNION

The Union argues that the men in the Kiln Department are being favored in a manner which is violative of the contract. Since seniority is clearly on a departmental basis, the Company has no right to protect the men in one department from layoff by allowing them periodically to do work in another department where men are on layoff. Either the Kiln employees should be laid off themselves if no work is available for them in their own department or the Company should limit their transfer to those departments where no one is on layoff. The Union admits the latter alternative is not available, since every department has been affected by layoffs. If the Company is permitted to pursue its present policy, it could destroy the significance of seniority protection set forth in Article VII, Paragraph 2:

> "The parties hereto recognize and accept the principle of seniority in all cases of increase or decrease of the working force. Seniority shall be based upon length of service with the company on a departmental basis . . . .

The Union seeks a formulation of principle by the arbitrator; there is no claim for monetary remedies.

POSITION OF THE COMPANY

The Company defends its action on the basis of the nature of operations and the contract. This is a small concern, and at all times there is a need for transfer flexibility. The Union has recognized this in the past but takes exception at a time of layoff. In the Kiln Department, there are 9 employees. Four of these nine are not in question, since they operate the continuous kilns. The other 5 men are kiln packers who load and unload the large kilns. The Union agrees that a total of 5 employees are needed to load these kilns. Unfortunately the work on such kilns is spotty. From January 5, 1949, to April 15, 1949, when the grievance was submitted to arbitration only 7 kilns were fired, or an average of 2 per month in comparison with the normal average of 6 to 7 per month. Since the normal packing time is 3 days for the 5 men, this has meant only 21 days of work on the large kilns.

What would be the consequences of laying off these men between periods of kiln-packing? They would be off for a short period and then recalled to work for the next firing of a kiln. Under Article VII, Paragraph 9, they are required to report for work within 6 days of such recall notice or lose all seniority rights. The chances are that the period of layoff would be too brief to enable them to qualify for unemployment compensation. Thus, the periodicity of this operation would make the repetitive layoffs and recalls an unreasonable hardship for the men.

The Company asks that the consequences be viewed from another angle as well. If the men are laid off in the manner described above, some may seek employment elsewhere, thus creating a labor shortage when the next kiln is to be loaded. Subsequent operations would be delayed causing additional layoffs. If the men waited the full 6 days allowed by contract before responding to a recall notice, the same adverse effects upon operations could be expected.

The Company insists that its transfer policy is not only realistic, but it is allowed under the contract. Paragraph 5 of the Seniority Article states:

> "Each department shall transfer only employees having the lowest seniority except in special cases and then only after mutual agreement."

The Company has transferred only junior employees. There is nothing in the agreement which specifically withdraws or qualifies the right of the Company to transfer as it has.

QUESTIONS

1. Is there anything in the agreement which authorizes maangement to take this type of action? Is there anything in the agreement to preclude the Company from making the transfers it did?

2. Why do you suppose the Union in making its demand requested only the formulation of a principle by the arbitrator and did not request any monetary remedy?

3. From the Union's standpoint would the question of principle be less important if the number of transfer hours from Preparatory to Kiln were approximately equal to the number of transfer hours from Kiln to Preparatory?

4. To what extent should the parties give consideration to practicability and flexibility in administering the agreement? Can an arbitrator give the same consideration to these factors?

Case 34

PLANT-WIDE SENIORITY OF EMPLOYEES DISPLACED BY TECHNOLOGICAL CHANGES

UNION: United Automobile Workers, CIO

COMPANY: General Motors Corporation

Six separate grievances bearing on the same matter were presented at the Atlanta Chevrolet plant on September 30, 1941. The language of one of them may be considered as typical. It reads: "Request that I be placed on job in line with my seniority as to Paragraph 59 in the contract, also request I be reimbursed in pay difference due to my transfer."

On September 29, changes in operating methods resulted in the elimination of three jobs in the New-Car Conditioning Department, four jobs in the Inspection Department, and one job in the Repair Department.

The provisions of the agreement applicable to these changes were Paragraphs 59 and 63. Paragraph 59 reads in part:

"When changes in methods . . . would otherwise require the permanent laying off of employees, the seniority of the displaced employees shall become plant-wide and they shall be transferred out of the group in line with their seniority to work they are capable of doing, as comparable to the work they have been doing as may be available, at the rate for the job to which they have been transferred."

Paragraph 63 reads in part:

"The transferring of employees is the sole responsibility of the Management. In the advancement of employees to higher paid jobs when ability, merit and capacity are equal, employees with the longest seniority will be given preference."

Management took the following action in the above cases:

New-Car Conditioning Department. Three men have been inspectors in this department at $1.08 per hour. This department is a separate seniority group. When the three inspecting jobs were eliminated on September 29, management reasoned that, in compliance with Paragraph 59, their seniority was sufficient to let them remain in the same department as "tighteners" at $1.04 per hour. The junior tighteners then replaced or "bumped" the three youngest men in the department who were transferred out of the department to the Unloading Dock at $0.95 per hour. Three employees on the Unloading Dock were "bumped" and laid off.

The claimants remained on the tightener jobs until November 3, 1941, when two of the three men were transferred to the Inspection Department as assembly inspectors at $1.08 per hour. The third man remained on the tightener job until November 11, 1941, when he was offered a job as a road-tester in the Inspection Department at $1.08 per hour; but evidently he preferred to stay on the tightener job.

Inspection Department. Four men who had been employed as road testers at $1.06 per hour, when their jobs were eliminated, were transferred to the Unloading Dock at $0.95 per hour. On September 30, one day after the transfer, employee H was transferred to an assembly job at $1.10 per hour; on October 1, T was transferred to Assembly at $1.10. F went to the Assembly on October 16 at $1.10. Management reports that "he remained on this job for seven working days and was unable to 'carry the operation' so he was transferred back to the Unloading Dock." O was on the Unloading Dock until October 27, when he was transferred to a tightener job in New-Car Conditioning at $1.04.

Repair Department. S had been employed as a paint-touch-up man at $1.08 when his job was eliminated on September 29. He was transferred to the Unloading Dock at $0.95, and on October 6 to Assembly at $1.10.

THE ISSUE

What jobs are "available" to employees who become entitled to plant-wide seniority in accordance with the provisions of Paragraph 59 as a result of permanent discontinuance of their jobs?

POSITION OF THE UNION

The Union feels that "the real issue to be settled in this case is: When is a job available when an employee is entitled to plant-wide seniority"? It contends that an available job is "any comparable work that the employee is capable of doing, in line with his seniority."

The Union notes that all of the employees who filed the grievances in question "have more seniority than employees working in the following departments at a rate of $1.10 an hour on work they are capable of doing: Paint Department, etc. [five others]." It is contended by the Union that such jobs in these departments should have been assigned to the claimant employees on the ground that "any comparable job that the employee is capable of performing is available under Paragraph 59, if he has sufficient seniority to take the job."

With specific reference to the three inspectors in the New-Car Conditioning Department, the Union claims that, since their jobs had been discontinued, the men should have been transferred out of the group in line with their new plant-wide seniority on the basis of Paragraph 59. The Union contends that they were entitled to an assignment of work comparable to that which they had been doing rather than to demotion within the departmental seniority group. The Company had stated that they had sufficient seniority to remain "in the same occupational group."

POSITION OF THE COMPANY

Management contends that the employees whose jobs were eliminated by a change in method were properly transferred in accordance with Paragraphs 59 and 63 of the agreement. It is said that the three men, whose jobs were eliminated in the New-Car Conditioning Department, had sufficient seniority to remain in the same seniority group; and management maintains that they properly "replaced the three youngest men in the Department who were transferred out of the Department to available jobs on the Unloading Dock." The four eliminated jobs in the Inspection Department properly resulted, says management, in the transfer of the four men to the Unloading Dock "which was the only place where there were jobs available." The Unloading Dock had always been considered, states management, as a "clearing house" for hiring, laying off, and transferring employees.

Management does not interpret "as may be available," as contained in Paragraph 59, "to mean the right to bump an employee with less seniority, who has sufficient seniority to be working, even though it may be a job comparable to the work that he had been doing." In its statement of unadjusted grievances, management specifically contended "that a job is not available when another employee is working on the job" and further maintained that the plant-wide seniority of an employee whose job has been eliminated only gave a man a right to a job and did not entitle him to a job comparable to the work he had been doing until such jobs became vacant.

Supplementing their general position upon the issue, management and the Union offered the following comments upon their stand in specific cases:

Transfers of Three Inspectors in the New-Car Conditioning Department. Management contended that these three employees were not entitled to plant-wide seniority. In a previous decision, the Union replied, the umpire had interpreted that part of Paragraph 59 which reads : "When changes in methods, products, or policies would otherwise require the permanent laying-off of employees . . . ." It was held then by the umpire that this provision makes Paragraph 59 applicable "when job changes occur which would require the permanent laying-off of an employee unless his job classification is changed." Since these three claimants were inspectors in the New-Car Conditioning group, it is obvious, says the Union, that the changes in method required a change in job classification in order to prevent their permanent layoff. They were thus clearly entitled to plant-wide seniority under Paragraph 59. Management had erred, says the Union, in contending that the "bumping" had to be initially confined to the New-Car Conditioning Department with the employees displaced from the department "bumping" others on the Unloading Dock.

Management had contended that the three men had sufficient seniority to remain "in the same occupational group." (The Union replied by noting that the men actually were not retained in the same occupational group but in the same seniority group.) Management reasoned that the elimination of jobs in any seniority group, because of technological change, results in transfers, with its attendant bumping, within the seniority group wherever that is possible. The Union's counterargument held that, under such an approach, the status of such displaced employees would be entirely dependent upon the setups of the local seniority agreement—whether ratings were determined on an occupational, department, or plant basis. There is no evidence, the Union argued, of any understanding that the local seniority agreement in this plant is to be applied to determine the transfers of employees upon the elimination of their jobs for technological reasons. The Union went on:

"At any rate, however, Paragraph 59 applies on a national basis to all employees who are displaced by technological change and it cannot be modified by local agreements. Under Paragraph 59, displaced employees are those whose job classifications must be changed because of technological change and they are entitled to plant-wide seniority."

Transfers of Four Road Testers in the Inspection Department. These four men, upon the elimination of their $1.08 jobs, were transferred to the Unloading Dock at $0.95. Management's reason was that, under Paragraph 59, these jobs were as comparable to the work they were doing as was available. It interprets this paragraph as giving a displaced employee only a right to a job on the Unloading Dock or on some jobs where no more than one "bump" is required.

Transfer of Man Out of Repair Department. This man had worked on a paint-touch-up job. He was transferred to the Unloading Dock where he worked for about a day and was then transferred, at his own request, to a job that represented a promotion to him.

QUESTIONS

1. The company relies in part upon Paragraph 63 of the agreement which states: "The transferring of employees is the sole responsibility of management. In the advancement of employees . . . when ability, merit, and capacity are equal, employees with the longest seniority shall be given preference." Are the shifts resulting from the discontinuances of jobs because of technological or operating changes "transfers" with the meaning of Paragraph 63?

2. Assuming that the shifts involved in these cases are transfers within the meaning of Paragraph 63, does the phrase in Paragraph 63 stating that "the transferring of employees is the sole responsibility of Management" mean that the discretion of management is not limited by Paragraph 59?

3. Under the terms of Paragraph 59, which employees in the Inspection Department should be regarded as having acquired plant-wide seniority —the three inspectors who could "bump" within the departments or the three junior men who were transferred out of the department when they were bumped by the junior employees among the tighteners?

4. May an employee be regarded as threatened with "permanent layoff" by a technological change when he has seniority rights which would enable him to take the job of a junior employee in the same department? Is the answer to this question affected by whether or not the jobs within the department from which the employee might "bump" other workers pay less than the job destroyed by the technological change?

5. Is Paragraph 59 to be interpreted as an attempt to implement the principle that no employee shall suffer a wage reduction from technological change so long as there are jobs in the plant which are held by men junior in seniority and which the employee is capable of doing?

6. Does the seniority system embodied in the agreement between the Union and the Company contemplate that adjustments to changes in methods shall occur insofar as possible within seniority groups or within departments before men acquire plant-wide seniority?

7. Is the management correct in holding that "a job is not available when another employee is working on the job," even though the employee on the job has less seniority than the employee who would like to "bump" him? Would the management's interpretation of "available" be consistent with the purpose of Paragraph 59 of the agreement?

8. The Union in asking that Paragraph 59 be interpreted to confer plant-wide seniority upon employees displaced by technological change, even when these employees have seniority which enables them to "bump" other employees in the seniority group or department, is requesting that employees have greater seniority rights in cases of

displacement by technological change than in cases of displacement by ordinary falling off in business. Are there sound reasons, in your judgment, for the Union's seeking to establish such a distinction? For the Company's opposing it? Bear in mind that the seniority system establishes a distribution of rights among the workers—the more rights some workers have as a result of seniority, the fewer rights other workers have. Why give greater rights to the employees displaced by a technological change than to employees displaced by a decline in business?

Section

F

PROMOTIONS

The principle of promotion from within, widely accepted in American industry, is usually established in the terms of the collective bargaining agreement. Both unions and managements are widely agreed that every effort should be made to enable present employees to advance before new employees are hired from the outside. However, application of this principle involves numerous problems for the parties. What constitutes a promotion within the meaning of the agreement? What procedures will be followed in filling promotional vacancies or newly created positions? What standards shall be used in selecting an employee if there are a number of applicants competing for the job? These questions are of great importance to the union and the company. The union's desire to afford the present and long-service employees the greatest opportunities for advancement frequently may be at variance with the company's desire to retain flexibility and efficiency in its operations.

THE MEANING OF PROMOTION

A promotion normally constitutes an advancement to a higher paid job. Frequently, it is an upgrading, as in the case of a movement from a Class II to a Class I Electrician's job. However, for a number of reasons, an employee might consider a transfer to another job with no change in pay, or even a reduction in pay, as a promotion in the sense that it is more desirable to him than his present job. Among these reasons are the working conditions, convenience of hours of work, opportunity for training and advancement, and the desire for more congenial fellow employees. Some companies have tried to narrow the definition of promotion to jobs of higher pay on the ground that the "shopping around"

293

under a broad definition leads to frequent changes in positions and to inefficiency in the plant. Accordingly, a distinction in these circumstances is often made between promotions and the employee-requested transfer. Some agreements also differentiate between a temporary and a permanent job opening. If a job is vacant because the incumbent is ill or on a leave of absence, the employer often is free to fill the position as he wishes, irrespective of seniority or other considerations. However, if it is a permanent vacancy, his freedom is more circumscribed. Most agreements, in defining promotions, also specify that they refer only to advancement to jobs within the bargaining unit. Management reserves the exclusive right to select supervisors or nonbargaining unit personnel, although some agreements provide that employees within the unit will be "considered" before outside persons are hired for these jobs.

PROCEDURES IN MAKING PROMOTIONS

To insure equal opportunity among employees to apply for a vacancy, the agreement frequently requires that the job be posted for a specified period of time, usually one or two working days. If only those within the department in which the vacancy exists are eligible to apply, the posting is limited to that department. Employees interested in the promotion either append their signatures to the notice or apply in person to their foreman. When the posting period expires, no further applications are allowed. Some companies have refused to accept the posting arrangement. They argue that vacancies often are not known in advance and the delay of one or two days in filling the job on a permanent basis disrupts production. They also claim that posting encourages employees to bid for jobs for which they have little or no qualifications, and their inevitable rejection creates dissatisfaction. These companies prefer to fill the job directly in accordance with the criteria specified for making promotions. Others, however, accept posting as a protection from future claims by an employee that he would have applied had he known of the job opening.

STANDARDS FOR PROMOTION

The relative weight to be assigned to ability and to length of service is the most important subject of controversy between unions and managements in making promotions. The employer insists that ability should govern; and only when the ability of the employees being considered for promotion is relatively equal, should seniority be the deciding factor. Unions recognize that ability is a necessary consideration, but they usually try to give seniority as much or more weight. They argue that supervisory judgment concerning a man's ability may lead to favoritism and discrimination in promotions. The measure of ability of necessity involves discretion, while seniority is an objective standard.

This difference of emphasis may be minimized in a number of ways. First, the parties may limit promotions to positions within a department or a zone of related jobs on the assumption that all employees within the department or zone should have some familiarity with all the jobs in those units. Second, some companies and unions distinguish between groups of unskilled, semiskilled, and skilled jobs. Advancements within the group of unskilled jobs are made almost exclusively on the basis of seniority; within the semiskilled group, ability and seniority are given equal weight; and in advancement to or within the skilled group, ability is weighted more than length of service. Third, the development of a promotional ladder within a company insures that the employees on the rung immediately below the promotional vacancy are likely to have the greater skills and ability and will be the most qualified for promotion. Fourth, on-the-job training programs enable employees to prepare for promotion, and evidence of such training often eliminates disputes as to ability. Finally, a systematic employee-rating plan, based on clearly defined factors such as quality, quantity, attendance, and versatility (see Case 26, for example), reduces argument over ability when promotions are made.

The factor of ability is expressed in many different ways in the labor agreement. One of the most common clauses governing promotions provides that length of continuous service prevails only if the ability of those under consideration is relatively equal (see Case 39). Some agreements, however, specify that the senior employee shall be promoted if he is competent to do the work. Under this clause the comparative ability of applicants is not the foremost test. However, the phrase "competent to do the work" raises a number of questions. Must the senior employee be able to do the work without assistance as soon as he is promoted? Or is he to be allowed a reasonable time to meet standards? Is a man competent if he can perform only the minimum requirements of the job? How is competency to be proved if he has never before worked on the job? Is there to be a reasonable trial period to establish competency? A few agreements allow the employer to establish his own tests for competency. For example, the contract between the Cleveland Electric Illuminating Company and the Utility Workers Union of America, CIO, provides the following:

> "Selection for promotion to a vacant job within the bargaining unit will be made from available employees in the next lower job classification in the line of promotion in which the vacancy occurs on the basis of job qualifications and seniority. Seniority shall be given the preference, provided the senior employee in line of promotion has the necessary qualifications. In addition to considering the employee's record and past performance, the Company may require the employee satisfactorily to pass reasonable tests—oral, written, or practical—to determine his qualifications."

In an effort to discourage an employee from bidding on jobs for which he lacks competence, some agreements provide penalties if he is selected and proves to be incompetent. In rare cases, he will lose seniority. More frequently he will be transferred to the unskilled labor pool rather than to his former job, or he will be denied the right to bid on any other job for a specified period. Still another alternative is to subject him to disciplinary measures for incompetence.

The seniority versus ability argument in promotions cannot be resolved until several basic questions are answered satisfactorily. To what extent is there a high correlation between the ability of an employee and his length of service? Can ability measurements be devised which will remove suspicions of discrimination and favoritism? Does the emphasis on seniority as a standard for making promotions seriously harm efficiency of operations and the incentive of employees?[1] Accurate information is needed on these matters in a particular situation before the union and management can formulate an equitable promotion procedure.

---

[1] Dan H. Mater, "A Statistical Study of the Effect of Seniority upon Employee Efficiency," *Journal of Business of the University of Chicago*, April, 1941.

Case 35

WHAT IS A PROMOTION?

UNION: United Packinghouse Workers of America, CIO

COMPANY: Armour and Company

The contract between Armour and Company and the United Packinghouse Workers of America provides, in part, as follows:

"Seniority will operate on a departmental basis. Promotions, layoffs and re-employment will be based on length of continuous service, provided that the individual can perform the job to the satisfaction of the management, and provided further that this will not be used for the purpose of discrimination against any employee."

The present case raises the question: What is a "promotion"? The Company has been applying the above clause on the assumption that "promotions take place through advantageous movement at the same or to a higher rate of pay." This has led to the canvassing of men at the same or lower rates of pay when a job opens up. The Union challenges the Company's interpretation of "promotion" and its administration of the seniority clause. It claims that all men, regardless of rate of pay, should be canvassed when a job opens up.

The present grievance is raised specifically in the motive power department and reads as follows:

"On the 3:00 P.M. to 11:00 P.M. oiling job that is open at 87½ cents per hour, the management is not going to the head of the seniority list and contacting from the oldest man down. Only those men are contacted who are making this rate or less. We contend that all men in the department should be contacted so they can accept or reject this job, so they might exercise shift preference."

POSITION OF THE UNION

The Union considers that management is interpreting the word "promotion" too narrowly. Promotion means improvement.

Improvement can take place in other ways than in monetary income alone. A job on a more agreeable shift, an easier job, a cleaner job, a job with more chances of advancement, may all be a "promotion." A broad point of view should be applied, not one limited to dollars and cents. No single concept of a promotion should be applied.

The Union argues that its own interpretation of what constitutes a promotion need not necessarily be identical with management's view. The Union further holds that one employee might look at a promotion differently than another employee. Consequently, it is considered important that each man should have a chance to decide what he individually views as a promotion. In the Union's opinion, this should mean that *all* persons on the seniority list should be canvassed when a job opens up. Seniority gives a man the right to bid for the job he wants most, even though at a lower rate.

Finally, the Union contends that the Company did practice complete canvassing for some period between 1943 and 1946 and that the policy imposed no burden upon the Company. The Union requests that this practice become a permanent policy.

POSITION OF THE COMPANY

The Company maintains that the contract does not require complete canvassing. A promotion is viewed as the reassignment of a worker to a higher-rate job. The Company argues that this has been its practice for seventy-five years; and the contract does not, nor did it intend to, change it. Complete canvassing would create an impossible situation. The Company points out that it would have to canvass the entire seniority list every time it wanted to hire a common laborer. This procedure is felt to be so cumbersome, fruitless, and time-consuming as to be unworkable.

The Company admits that for a short time in 1943 it did canvass the gang; but this went beyond the contract, was improper, and was stopped. It was never taken advantage of by any single higher-paid man, and it never applied to all jobs in the gang but only to the ones involving some skill.

QUESTIONS

1. What group of employees should be canvassed under an agreement when considering a promotion?

2. What group should management consider in the case that there is no bargaining representative?
3. What elements do workers consider in determining whether or not a particular job classification would constitute a promotion?
4. What administrative rules would you suggest to minimize problems of "canvassing?" How do you appraise the device of posting job vacancies?

Case 36

MEANING OF SENIORITY IN PROMOTIONS

UNION: United Electrical, Radio and Machine Workers of America

COMPANY: Threadwell Tap and Die Company

The following statement of the issue was proposed by the Company:

"Did the Company violate the seniority provisions of the collective bargaining agreement of August 11, 1951, in refusing to transfer employee Emmet Larson or employee Robert Hunter to the position of operator of Sheffield Multi-ribbed Crush Grinder?"

The Union was reluctant to accept this narrow question. It wanted a general interpretation of the contract clauses applicable to the present cases. The Company agreed that the interpretation of the contract was more important than just the disposition of the Larson-Hunter cases. Accordingly, the scope of the issue was left to the arbitrator.

BACKGROUND

The Company is engaged in the manufacture of cutting tools, primarily taps and dies. One of the basic operations is thread grinding, which had been performed on a machine turned out by the parent company of Threadwell Tap and Die. On this machine only a single cutting point operation could be done, thus requiring many revolutions. Several years ago the Company brought in two new-type grinders known as the Sheffield which, because of multiple point grinding, could cut the thread in a single revolution. Only one man was needed to operate these two new machines.

Early in 1952, over a period of several weeks, two more of the Sheffields were introduced; and an operator had to be selected. The Company looked over its production staff and concluded that no qualified person was available to handle these machines. It finally assigned a Mr. Peabody to the job. Peabody had approximately 20 months' service in the plant on inspection and other grinding work. Two to three months before his selection, Peabody's own job had been moved out of the plant; and he had gone with his job to another plant on loan from Threadwell. However, he was still an employee of the Threadwell Company. His job in the other company was about to end, since others had been trained to replace him. Because his layoff was imminent, he was assigned to the Sheffield machines in late January, 1952.

On February 20, 1952, Emmet Larson (25 years' service) and Robert Hunter (23 years' service) filed grievances. Although there is some dissimilarity in the wording of these grievances, the complaint is the same in each. Both Larson and Hunter had applied for a transfer to the job on the multiribbed grinders without success. They believed themselves qualified because of seniority and experience on related jobs and entitled to the job under the agreement.

The contract provisions cited by the parties were the following:

"*Article IV (Seniority)*

"A. For the purposes of this contract, seniority wherever used hereafter, shall be defined as consisting of (1) continuous length of service with the Company and its predecessors, and (2) Skill, ability, and experience necessary to adequately perform the available work in line with the job requirements. The Company shall make the original determination of seniority as defined above, subject to the Union's right to protest under the grievance procedure that the employee not selected is capable of adequately performing the available work in line with the job requirements. Seniority shall govern in case of layoffs, rehires, transfers, and advancement within the bargaining unit except as hereafter provided.

"B. (1) Seniority in accordance with the provision of Article IV-A shall govern in case of transfers and advancements in the bargaining unit. Any employee who is transferred or advanced in accordance with this paragraph and who, after a 2 weeks break in period, fails to adequately perform the work in line with the job requirements shall be returned to his old job or at the option of the Company to a comparable job in line with his proper place on the seniority list . . . .

"C. The Company shall have the right to hire a new employee from the outside if he has the experience qualifying him to meet the job requirements at the time of hiring and if there is no available employee on the seniority list qualified to adequately meet such job requirements. Before hiring a new employee who does not have the experience qualifying him to meet job requirements at the time of hiring, the Company will carefully consider the laid off employees available whose seniority rights have not terminated and may select the one best able to fill the job and give him a 2 weeks break in period in which to qualify, and if he fails to adequately meet the job requirements at the end of such period he shall be returned to his appropriate place on the seniority list or at the discretion of the Company the break-in period in which he may qualify may be extended. If he still fails to adequately meet the job requirements he will be returned to his proper place on the seniority list and the Company may fill the job at its discretion but as much as possible within its discretion from employees having seniority rights . . . .

"K. The Company may make temporary transfers for a period not to exceed 4 weeks. In the event the Company transfers an employee to a job having a higher minimum rate than his personal rate, the employee during such period of transfer shall receive whichever rate is higher. If the Company transfers an employee to a job carrying a lower rate of pay than the employee's personal rate, the Company shall continue to pay the employee his personal rate while said employee is performing the duties of the lower paid job. The above shall apply to temporary transfers without complying with Article IV-A."

POSITION OF THE UNION

The Union argues that the phrase "skill, ability, and experience"in Article IV (A) is a standard of measurement and is not an absolute. As a result of careful negotiations the parties combined the two factors of (1) length of service, and (2) skill, ability, and experience. This was a compromise of the extreme positions taken by the parties in negotiations. Even in the testimony of company witnesses the latter phrase (2) is used as a measurement device, not as an absolute requirement. In this case the Union does not contend that either Larson or Hunter had absolute ability at the time they sought promotion, but it insists that their *relative ability* and clearly their relative "length of service" are greater than those of Peabody who was assigned to the job. Both Larson and Hunter have worked on many related jobs, and they have received good merit ratings. Unlike Peabody, these two men had done considerable thread grinding work; and there is every reason to believe that the breaking-in period would have been less for either of them. During negotiations the Company said it would follow the procedure of starting from the top of the seniority list and going down to fill vacancies. If this had been done, either Larson or Hunter would have been selected. Now the Company takes the tenuous position that if it cannot find anyone on the seniority list who has *absolute* ability *at the moment,* it is free to do what it wants. The Union agrees that the 2 weeks' period referred to in Article IV (B) is not a learning period; but if there is reason to believe that a man can qualify under seniority (as defined in Section A), he should have the 2 weeks to prove himself.

The Company has attempted to justify its action under Article IV (K) which allows temporary transfers for a period not to exceed 4 weeks. This is an arrogation of authority never intended by Section K. This clause was designed to give the Company the flexibility needed to handle emergencies. No emergency was involved here. The only reason for selecting Peabody was because his layoff was imminent. Moreover, this was obviously a permanent transfer. A ruling in support of the Company's position would wreck the entire seniority agreement. To illustrate: any time the Company wanted to lay off a senior man and keep a junior employee, it could first "temporarily transfer" the youngest man to a secure job, train him for 4 weeks, and then claim at the end of 4 weeks that he was the only person with absolute skill and ability to do the job. He would be kept while the senior man was laid off. The same injustice could (and in this case does) occur in making promotions. It is a distorted interpretation of Article IV (A, B, and K).

In summary, the Union states that the Company is expected to pick that senior employee with the ability adequately to do the work. Normally the Company will pick the employee it believes can do the work adequately at the end of a 2-week proving period. If no one can be expected to do the work within such a period, then seniority applies with the Company selecting the senior employee who best meets the job requirements.

POSITION OF THE COMPANY

It is clear from Section A that length of service is only *one* of *two* important factors used in defining seniority. And it follows that the factor of continuous service will not govern promotion unless the senior employee possesses the "skill, ability . . . to adequately perform the available work in line with job requirements." If the Company decides he does not, the only grievances the Union can raise is whether the aggrieved does, in fact, have the necessary skill and ability as defined. Section B (1) does not require that employees who are senior be given a 2-week break-in period on a new machine such as the Sheffield Grinder. Section B (1) is tied in directly with Section A. It means that only *if* a senior man is deemed to have the skill and ability under Section A, will he be given 2 weeks to demonstrate that he can do the job adequately. This 2 weeks' period is dependent upon the satisfaction of the basic requirements in Section A. The 2 weeks was incorporated to protect the employee who proved unable to do the job to which he sought transfer. The Company believes the union contention would require it to go down the seniority list, starting with the senior employees, giving each man a 2 weeks' trial.

The transfer of Peabody to the new machines was effected

304 • *COLLECTIVE BARGAINING*

initially as a temporary transfer under Article IV (K). When
Larson and Hunter presented a claim during the 4 weeks'
temporary transfer period, the Company applied the terms of
Sections A and B and concluded that neither had the skill and
ability needed. Even the Union admits that they only had related
experience and that they might not be fully qualified, even after
2 weeks on the job. It is significant that since no employee was
available with the necessary skill, the Company could have hired
a *new* employee to the job under Article IV (C).

QUESTIONS

1. Why does the Union insist that length of service be the most important criterion in promotions? Do you think there is any correlation
   between service and ability? Is service the only factor that can be
   measured objectively?

2. How should ability be applied as a standard of measurement? Which
   ability should govern: ability on the present job, ability presently
   possessed which is applicable to the new job, or potential ability to do
   the new job? Are all of these equally relevant in making promotions?
   Are they equally susceptible to measurement?

3. With which interpretation of the contract do you agree, the Company's
   or the Union's? Is the Company justified in bypassing the senior employee if no man is qualified to do the job at the moment? Since the
   Company could have hired a Sheffield operator from the outside, does
   this indicate that seniority is not governing if there is no presently
   employed qualified man?

4. Seniority is defined in Article IV (A) as consisting of (1) continuous
   length of service, and (2) skill, ability, and experience necessary to
   adequately perform the available work. How are these two elements
   to be weighted or combined in applying seniority? If no employee
   has the skill, ability, and experience necessary to adequately perform
   the available work, does length of service govern or is there no
   seniority as defined?

5. Could the Company have hired a new inexperienced employee and
   trained him for the Sheffield job? How long would a new employee
   have to demonstrate his qualifications for the job?

6. From the standpoint of sound human relations and union-management
   relations rather than that of contract terms, how do you appraise
   management's action?

Case 37

ARE MANAGEMENT'S DECISIONS ON PROMOTION FINAL?

UNION: International Union of Electrical, Radio and Machine Workers, CIO

COMPANY: The Chapman Valve Manufacturing Company

In late November, 1951, the Company was advised by Mr. Mulcare, a production expeditor, that he intended to leave the employ of the Company. The Production Planning Manager decided immediately to assign a replacement for Mulcare and also to add one more production expeditor. He was advised that posting of the vacancies would not be necessary if selections were made from present employees. Accordingly, on November 29, 1951, the Manager, following consultation with staff members, named James Morrison and William Edgren to the two openings. This, in turn, prompted the Company to post the job vacancy on Edgren's former job. The Union, noticing this posting, asked the Company for an explanation at a regular meeting held on November 30, 1951. When told of Edgren's new assignment, the Union protested that the Company was obligated to post the two original production expeditor vacancies for bid purposes. The Company acknowledged its error, since Article VI (Seniority), Section 7, provides:

"The Company will post all permanent job vacancies, within the bargaining unit, in their respective departments for twenty-four (24) hours with the following exceptions . . . ."

(There follows a list of the exceptions, no one of which covers the expeditor job.)

At the close of this meeting, therefore, the Industrial Relations Department told the Production Planning Supervision and the Personnel Department to proceed with the posting of the jobs. The posting was made at approximately 4 P.M. that day (November 30) and remained until the same hour on Monday, December 3, in accordance with the contract. Between 4:30 P.M and

5:00 P.M. on Monday, the Personnel Department sent to the Production Planning Department the names, seniority dates, and current job assignments of the 73 applicants who responded to the posting. The Production Planning Manager and members of his staff met promptly to consider the names. Late that afternoon, they selected Morrison and Edgren, the two pre-posting selections. On December 5, George DesRoches, one of the 73 applicants, filed a grievance claiming that Edgren's selection was a violation of the contract. Meanwhile, on Tuesday, December 4, Edgren started to work on the job.

A union-management grievance meeting was held on December 11, at which time the parties discussed the DesRoches grievance. There was no grievance on the Morrison appointment since he had once been a production expediter; he was on another job because of an earlier cutback so that this appointment restored Morrison to his former position.

The following facts relating to the service and work history of DesRoches and Edgren were agreed to, except as noted:

Edgren: Hired 12/18/29
  Positions:
    (1) Office Boy, Blueprint Machine Operator, Filing Blueprints, Filing Customers' Correspondence. The Union established that this breakdown was not in existence from 1929 to 1935, Edgren's period of incumbency on these jobs. This is a reconstruction of job duties originally performed under the heading of clerk.
    (2) Time Clerk (2/35—11/42)
    (3) Boring Mill Operator (11/42—12/51)
DesRoches: Hired 7/22/29
  Positions:
    (1) Helper (date of hire to 11/29)
    (2) Assembler (11/29—5/42)
    (3) Supervision (5/42—12/45)
    (4) Assembler (12/45—to date)
    (5) For the past two years DesRoches has been used as a substitute foreman during the absence of the assistant foreman; this practice was discontinued 6 months ago.

POSITION OF THE UNION

The clause governing assignments to job vacancies has undergone numerous changes, and the import of the present clause can be understood only if this background is stated. Prior to 1945 the contract provided:

"In all promotions or transfers to more desirable jobs the Company will not consider the factors of race, color, creed, national origin, sex, or any other factors than seniority and the ability to do the work."

Under this clause the Company felt it only had to *consider* the factors of seniority and ability, but its judgment was not challengeable by the Union. In the September 7, 1945, contract this provision was changed to read:

"In all promotions or transfers to more desirable jobs governed by this contract the principle of seniority shall be observed provided the senior employee has convinced the Company he has the necessary experience and ability to perform the job satisfactorily. It is agreed that the Company will not discriminate against any person or persons because of race, color, creed, national origin or sex."

At a later date the present contract clause was adopted (Article VI, Section 6):

"In all promotions or transfers to more desirable jobs governed by this contract, the principle of seniority shall be observed provided the Company is convinced that the senior employee has the necessary experience or related experience, and ability, to perform the job satisfactorily . . . ."

Since DesRoches is senior to Edgren, the only question is whether he possesses the "necessary experience or related experience and ability" for the production expeditor job. Neither man has ever performed this job, and only related experience and ability are involved. It is the Union's contention that DesRoches has these qualities and can do the job satifactorily. In recent years, he has worked on both small and later the large steel assembly and is thoroughly familiar with the expeditor duties which involve: (1) mental ability; (2) alertness; (3) blueprint reading; (4) knowledge of parts and equipment; (5) knowledge of metals; and (6) ability to get along with people. Because of his work as an assembler, he developed the related experience needed on the job. Even more important is the fact that as a supervisor from May, 1942, to December, 1945, he worked closely with the expeditors. A fellow employee—a stock selector—testifies that DesRoches knows the parts as well as he and certainly as well as Edgren. In fact, DesRoches trained new stock selectors; and he was considered pleasant to work with. These comments were corroborated by a fellow assembler as well.

In every respect DesRoches has developed the experience and ability needed for this job. As a senior employee, he is entitled to the assignment. It is suggested that the company representatives did not really bother to examine DesRoches' qualifications. Having once decided on Edgren without observing the procedural requirements of the contract, supervision went through the motions of considering the 73 applications; but the speed of their decision and the lack of full information about each candidate suggest that they had made up their minds on Edgren regardless of his junior status. The Production Planning Manager and his staff did not have before them the work histories of the 73 applicants. Yet this information is the only way to test "related experience."

POSITION OF THE COMPANY

The Company contends that it did give full consideration to DesRoches' qualifications and, having done so, reached the sincere conviction that he did not measure up to the requirements of the job. The staff group which reviewed the applications was familiar with the work of both DesRoches and Edgren. A careful examination of Article VI, Section 6, shows that the Company is given the right to reject an application by a senior employee if in its opinion he is not deemed satisfactory. It is argued further that no arbitrator has the power to make any decision based on his own convictions regarding the qualifications of either Edgren or DesRoches, since the contract clearly and specifically states that the judgment concerning an employee's ability to do a certain job is the prerogative of the Company and the Company only.

On the relative merits of the two men, the Company argues that DesRoches' capacity for working with people—a quality much desired in an expeditor's job—was limited. Moreover, Edgren has a superior clerical background, which is a requisite. Since the two men are separated by only 5 months in service dates, it cannot be argued that any injustice has been done to DesRoches.

QUESTIONS

1. Under Article VI, Section 6, can there be any challenge by the Union or by the arbitrator of the Company's judgment as to whether a senior employee can perform the job satisfactorily? Is the Company's decision absolute and final?

2. Does the history of the contract clauses help in determining the intent of the parties and in interpreting the present clause?

3. Under this clause is the Company required to make any showing of its examination of "necessary experience or related experience, and ability" of competing employees?

4. Do you attach any significance to the speed with which the selection was made after the bids were closed?

5. In a bidding system what are the dangers of making a temporary assignment to a job vacancy during the posting period?

6. What does the fact that 73 employees applied for two vacancies indicate concerning interest of employees in promotions and the problems which the parties have in developing acceptable standards of promotion? What does this tell you about employees' estimates of their own "necessary experience or related experience and ability"?

Case 38

DOES "REASONABLE CONSIDERATION OF SENIORITY" REQUIRE A TRIAL ON THE JOB?

UNION: United Automobile Workers of America, CIO

COMPANY: General Motors Corporation

John Harding held top seniority ranking in Occupational Group 11 of Department 1, consisting of 189 employees at the Southern California Division of General Motors. When a job in the Inspection Department became available, Sam Holt was chosen for transfer to it since management considered him the best man qualified to fill the vacancy. He held the fourth highest seniority in the same group.

The consideration required to be given to seniority by management in making transfers is stated in Clause 8 of the seniority section of the agreement as follows: "In transferring employees, seniority will be secondary to other qualifications but will be given reasonable consideration. Any claims of discrimination for union activity in connection with transfers may be taken up as grievances." The Union made it clear that no charge of union discrimination was being made in this case.

The Union objects to the transfer of Holt on the ground that he has less seniority than the claimant. Holt's seniority date was June 17, 1936, while that of Harding was June 3, 1936. Management stated that "Harding is one of our best men" but also insisted that Holt was better qualified for the inspection job because he was younger, better educated, and better adapted to inspection work, whereas "Harding likes to work with his hands." It was pointed out that both men had been "under observation" for transfer and that both were assigned to better jobs for which they were qualified.

On April 8, 1941, 2 months after he had filed the grievance, Harding was assigned to the emergency operators' occupational group and to a job which carried a rate of pay equivalent to the inspection job which is involved in this case. This assignment of Harding to a new job occurred 2 days before the consideration of his grievance at the third step of the grievance procedure.

It was recognized by both parties at the umpire hearing that the issue concerned only the basis of selection for transfer that had been used by the management in this case and specifically whether it gave reasonable consideration to seniority.

POSITION OF THE UNION

The Union's position is that "the man having the most seniority should be given a fair trial on the job involved, and the filling of a vacancy should not be left up to the judgment of the Foreman." Such a procedure is necessary, contends the Union, in order to provide the "reasonable consideration" to seniority that is required by Clause 8 of the seniority section. It is also claimed by the Union that the transfer in question should have been provided to Harding because a representative of management had promised him an inspection or a better job "if he would co-operate by not requesting a transfer into the service building."

POSITION OF THE COMPANY

The Company claims that John Harding merely was informed that he was under observation for a transfer. It is pointed out that he was transferred to a better job in April. The Union feels, however, that, since neither Holt nor Harding had worked on the inspection operation in question, Harding should have been assigned to it because he worked next to it for a long period of time and "by having more seniority would be better qualified to hold the job."

Management contends it chose the best man for the job. Reasonable consideration was given to seniority, it is contended, as is amply shown by selection for the job of the fourth man in order of seniority in the group of 189 men. Management states that it feels "reasonable consideration" was given to seniority since the selection for the job was made from the first ten of the group of 189. The selection was entirely proper, it is held, under the contract which states: "In transferring employees, seniority will be secondary to other qualifications, but will be given reasonable consideration."

In making this selection, management was governed, it states, by a realization that "inspection is intimately and inseparably associated with the quality phase of the production, and Supervision must select for the inspection jobs those employees they feel are qualified to do the work." By choosing the best-qualified employee holding fourth greatest seniority, management contends it conformed fully with the agreement.

QUESTIONS

1. How would you test whether management gave "reasonable consideration" to seniority in making transfers? Do you agree that the selection of any one of the 10 men with greatest seniority out of 189 indicates that "reasonable" consideration was being given to seniority?

2. How would giving a man a trial on the job help the management give reasonable consideration to seniority?

Case 39

THE "HEAD-AND-SHOULDERS" PRINCIPLE IN PROMOTION

UNION: United Automobile Workers of America, CIO

COMPANY: General Motors Corporation

On August 4, 1941, a reliefman vacancy occurred on the first shift of Occupational Group No. 20 at Plant No. 3 of the Chevrolet Gear and Axle Division of General Motors. This occupational group includes Spring Housing job and the King Pin Support job.

Employee T was selected to fill the vacancy. A grievance submitted by employee M claimed that, in accordance with Paragraph 63 of the national agreement, his seniority and previous experience entitled him to the reliefman's job.

Paragraph 63 of the agreement provides:

"The transferring of employees is the sole responsibility of the Management. In the advancement of employees to higher paid jobs when ability, merit and capacity are equal, employees with the longest seniority will be given preference. Any claims of personal prejudice or any claims of discrimination for union activity in connection with transfers may be taken up as grievances."

Management noted that the Spring Housing and the King Pin Support jobs had not been in regular production since 1938 and were operated at this time to supply service parts. Employees are used interchangeably between the two operations, and the reliefman is also required to be able to work on both types of work. The relief job in question was not in operation at the time of the discussion of the case in the earlier steps of the grievance procedure, but the Union "requested that M be placed in line for the job so that when work is resumed he will be made the reliefman."

The previous experience of T on this work included service as a reliefman on the King Pin Support job when it was in production as a separate job. He had had other service as a reliefman in this occupational group, but no significant experience as a reliefman on the Spring Housing job. Altogether T had had about 20 months' experience as a reliefman and had a seniority date of November 21, 1930.

The claimant in this case, employee M, had served as a reliefman on the Spring Housing job when it was in regular production, but apparently he had had no experience as a reliefman on the King Pin Support job. His experience as a reliefman totaled approximately 11 months, and he had a seniority date of March 12, 1924.

Neither T nor M had ever been classified as a reliefman, but they had held jobs which gave them a chance to work intermittently as reliefmen.

THE ISSUE

The relative weight to be given to ability, merit, capacity, and seniority under a clause requiring that employees with the longest seniority shall be given preference when ability, merit, and capacity are equal.

POSITION OF THE UNION

The Union recognized that the relief job in question required a considerable versatility to do various operations. The Union also recognized that only a few men have such all-around experience because the jobs were for past-model service rather than for current-model production. The Union contended, however, that M was not only better qualified for the job but had greater seniority than T. In its brief, the Union expressed its belief that, under Paragraph 63,

> "When a promotion is to be made, the Agreement implies that the employee with the longest seniority shall be the first considered and in the event he can do the job adequately, he is to be given the promotion without the personality comparisons usually made in promoting men."

POSITION OF THE COMPANY

Management held that T had better qualifications than M to fill the reliefman vacancy. Of the 16 machines included in the King Pin Support job, T was said to have set up 14 and to have operated all 16. Of the 17 operations on the Spring Housing job, T had set up 15 and had operated 16 of them. Management had weighted T's experience, which was said to provide him with better qualifications than M, who, it was claimed, had not set up any of the 16 machines in the King Pin Support job and had operated only 8 of them. Of the Spring Housing machines, management reported that M had setup experience on 10 and operating experience on 13 of them.

The selection of an employee for transfer to this vacancy had to take into account, states management, the necessity for interchanging employees between the two types of work. Therefore, it continued, the best-qualified candidate for the reliefman's job would be the one who was most familiar with the various jobs. T's longer and wider experience as a reliefman on both the King Pin Support job and later in Group No. 20 was considered to have given him superior claim to the job. The selection of T, management maintained, was a proper exercise of management's responsibility as outlined in Paragraph 63 of the national agreement.

DECISION OF THE IMPARTIAL UMPIRE

The umpire's ruling introduced the "head-and-shoulders" principle for interpreting Paragraph 63.

Paragraph 63 of the June 3, 1941, agreement provides, in part: "The transferring of employees is the sole responsibility of the management. In the advancement of employees to higher paid jobs when ability, merit and capacity are equal, employees with the longest seniority will be given preference."

There have been marked difficulties in the effort satisfactorily to apply this clause. It is difficult to define, let alone evaluate, such intangible factors as "merit and capacity." The Union certainly errs in its present arguments, however, that the clause specifies preference to the employee with the most seniority and gives him a right to promotion "in the event he can do the job adequately." Since such an interpretation would give importance to seniority irrespective of relative "ability and capacity," the approach of the local Union is obviously not in accordance with Paragraph 63 as written.

Under Paragraph 63 seniority becomes the determining factor in a selection for promotion only as between employees whose "ability, merit and capacity are equal." In order to attribute a reasonable meaning to the clause, it must be recognized that (1) the relative ability, merit, and capacity of individual employees cannot be precisely evaluated; (2) these factors in one employee's work will be differently rated by different supervisors because their appraisal involves personal judgment; (3) seniority is, however, a definite factor that can readily be measured; (4) in making a selection for certain promotions, under this clause, management may properly proceed by designating several men whose ability, merit, and capacity are considered by management to be equal. The seniority factor can then be applied in making the choice of the individual who is to be promoted.

In considering employees for promotion under Paragraph 63, it may be that an employee's record is so outstanding that he is "head and shoulders" above any other possible candidate. In such cases, he is entitled to promotion irrespective of seniority; and, if necessary, management should have no difficulty in pointing out his superior qualifications. Unless such an individual is available for promotion, Paragraph 63 can properly be effectuated by management's selection of several employees who are competent to fill the job and whose "ability, merit and capacity" are considered by management to be approximately equal. From the several candidates adjudged by management to be approximately equal in "ability, merit and capacity," it would then become possible to effectuate Paragraph 63 by selecting for promotion that individual in the group who has the greatest seniority.

Such a procedure follows Paragraph 63 in recognizing that qualifications of several employees are often approximately equal and in recognizing the compelling importance of seniority in such cases. The umpire must assume that the parties sought to give compelling importance to seniority as respects certain promotions or Paragraph 63 would have been written in different terms. It is emphasized that, under such a procedure, management retains the sole responsibility for designating the employees who are to be promoted.

How would such a procedure be applied to the facts of the present case? Management has made its choice as between T and M principally on the basis of the relative number of machines on the relief job that had been previously operated by each of these men. To be sure, this is a factor that is important because of the nature of the job. The relative ability of these men in operating such jobs is, however, a considerably different fact; and the mentioned experience has little to do with merit and capacity. It is the opinion of the umpire that the evidence does not show that T had the outstanding "ability, merit and capacity" for the job in question.

It is to be noted that the relief job is not now being operated. This provides an opportunity to apply the above-outlined procedure when it resumes operation. At that time the job should again be considered as a vacancy. If a review of the qualifications of the candidates for the job shows that one is "head and shoulders" above all others not only in experience but in ability, merit, and capacity, it is in conformance with Paragraph 63 for management to assign him to the job. If such an individual is not available, management may designate two or three employees who are competent to take the assignment and who are considered by management as being approximately equal in ability, merit, and capacity. The individual assigned to the vacancy should be the one in the group who holds the greatest seniority.

QUESTIONS

1. Does Paragraph 63 indicate whose judgment of "ability, merit and capacity" shall govern?

2. Suppose the Union and the management disagree as to the relative abilities of two rival candidates for promotion. Is this the kind of dispute on which the judgment of an outside neutral would be useful?

3. Is it part of the skill and special competence of management to appraise the capacities of workers and to decide which workers are best fitted for which places? Is this one of the duties for which managers are hired? Is it the purpose of Paragraph 63 to transfer this responsibility from management to the umpire?

4. The umpire's decision says: "The Umpire must assume that the parties sought to give compelling importance to seniority as respects certain promotions or Paragraph 63 would have been written in different terms." Reread Paragraph 63, and comment upon the above statement of the umpire. Is it reasonable to interpret Paragraph 63 as intended to give "compelling importance to seniority" when the paragraph states that employees with longest seniority will be given preference "when ability, merit and capacity are equal?" Is it more reasonable to interpret Paragraph 63 as intended to give "compelling importance" to ability, merit, and capacity?

5. Did the umpire interpret Paragraph 63, or did he rewrite the paragraph

and change the meaning of the agreement? Did he exceed his authority as an arbitrator?

6. If it is held that Paragraph 63 was intended to substitute the judgment of the umpire for the judgment of the management in cases where the "ability, merit and capacity" of candidates for promotion are in dispute, is the burden of proof upon the Union to show that its view of "ability, merit and capacity" is correct and that of the management wrong? Does the "head-and-shoulders" principle enunciated by the umpire change the locus of the burden of proof? Does it relieve the complainant from the necessity of making out a prima facie case? Does the opinion of the umpire indicate any view on this matter?

7. Is the principle enunciated by the umpire that the management may disregard seniority only when "an employee's record is so outstanding that he is 'head and shoulders' above any other possible candidate" consistent with the wording of Paragraph 63 stipulating that seniority will be given preference "when ability, merit and capacity are equal?"

8. The umpire implies at the opening of his decision that his interpretation of Paragraph 63 is necessary in order "to attribute a reasonable meaning to the clause." Do you agree?

9. If the Company believes that the umpire has abused his discretion in this case by altering the agreement instead of interpreting it, has it any remedy? How might a remedy be given the Union and the Company against abuse of discretion by the umpire?

Case 40

POTENTIAL ABILITY AS A TEST FOR PROMOTION

UNION: United Mine Workers, District 50

COMPANY: Lynn Gas and Electric Company

William Wynne was hired as a Mail Boy on August 13, 1945, when he was 15 years of age. On January 13, 1947, he was promoted to the job of Stockkeeper's Helper in the machine shop. On January 19, 1948, under the job posting clause of the 1947 agreement, he applied for and received a promotion to the job of Stockkeeper in the appliance stockroom. Here he came under the supervision of Mr. Edward Burdick. The Stockkeeper job carried a rate of $1.22 per hour.

Several months later on April 16, 1948, the Company posted notice of a vacancy on General Helper job in the workshop stockroom at a job rate of $1.20 per hour. On April 20, 1948, still another notice was posted of a vacancy in the Meterman's Helper job in the Electric Meter Department at a rate of $1.02. Wynne applied for both jobs, but in each case the Company passed over his application and chose an employee with less seniority.

On May 13, 1948, the Union requested a meeting concerning the status of Wynne. Such a meeting was held the next day at which time the Union's claim in behalf of Wynne was rejected by the Company. On May 24 the Company gave Wynne a written notice to the effect that his services as a Stockkeeper in the appliance stockroom were unsatisfactory, and he would be removed immediately from that position. It pointed out that the jobs previously held by Wynne (Mail Boy and Machine Shop Stockkeeper's Helper) were filled and concluded:

"Subject to your immediate acceptance we offer you a job of Laborer in the Gas Department with the provision that you perform satisfactorily the duties required of this classification during the usual probationary period."

Wynne took the Laborer job at the rate of $1.13 per hour, but a grievance in his behalf was filed. On June 2 the Union advised the Company of its desire to arbitrate the case under the contract. The question it wanted to have decided is the following:

"Did the Company violate the terms of the existing agreement in not giving William Wynne one of the posted jobs? If not, is Wynne entitled to the job of Stockkeeper's Helper?"

RELEVANT CONTRACT PROVISIONS

"*Article IX*

"*A. Seniority*

"Promotions, layoffs, and re-employment, shall be governed by departmental seniority, subject to determination by the Company of qualifications, fitness and ability . . . .

"The right of the Company is recognized to determine in good faith the number and qualifications of employees, to employ, promote, demote, transfer, or to discharge employees for cause.

"B. *Job Posting*

"Whenever a vacancy or a newly created position is to be filled, notice to that effect shall be posted at accessible places in the department affected, and shall remain posted for a period of seven (7) days, within which time applicants eligible and desiring to fill such position may apply in writing to the Company representatives designated in the notice.

"Regardless of seniority, the Company shall not be required to consider for such position employees who fail to apply in writing as set forth in this article. In the selecting of an employee to fill such position, the provisions of Article IX A relative to seniority shall be applied in the following order:

"First: To those employees within the department in the order of job classifications shown on a roster to be prepared and posted by the Company.

"Second: To the other employees within such department.

"Third: To the other employees of the Company.

"The provisions of this article relative to Job Posting shall not apply to the employment or filling the jobs of store clerks; laborers; nor to promotions to supervisory or other positions specified in Article I of this agreement . . . ."

POSITION OF THE COMPANY

Wynne is not qualified for promotion or transfer to either of the posted jobs, nor is he competent to retain the job of Stockkeeper in the appliance room. Moreover, there is no contractual obligation to transfer him back to his former job as a Stockkeeper's Helper in the machine shop.

Wynne's record as a Stockkeeper in the appliance stockroom shows that he was careless, unable to take care of the simplest tasks, required constant supervision, and showed no signs of improvement from January 19, 1948, to May 24, 1948. It is significant that even the Union admits Wynne was so nervous after being warned in the presence of a Shop Steward that he had to consult a doctor. In addition, the Union failed to produce Wynne or any of his fellow workmen in the stockroom as witnesses at the arbitration hearing.

In posting the jobs the Company is governed by the requirement of Article IX (B), but consideration must also be given to the maintenance of efficient and safe service. This is especially important in an industry involving the public interest. To illustrate, in the Electric Meter Department, jobs are graded up to first-class meterman; and each job becomes increasingly difficult and technical. To place a man on that promotional ladder who cannot comprehend simple assignments and who "shows symptoms of unexplained confusion and memory lapse" is unfair to the Company. There are no permanent "helpers" jobs, and the Company cannot be expected to carry a limited employee in departments where the higher rungs of the promotional ladder involve jobs requiring judgment and skill. The Company has no alternative except to transfer Wynne to the one vacancy which exists: a Laborer. It has done this to avoid the shock of discharge for incompetence.

POSITION OF THE UNION

The Union argues that Wynne as the senior qualified applicant should have received one of the jobs on which he bid. If he was qualified to handle a Stockkeeper's job at $1.22 per hour, surely he is qualified to perform either of the two lesser paid jobs for which he bid.

First, the charges of incompetence on his job as Stockkeeper appear to be greatly exaggerated. Wynne desired a transfer because he felt rightfully that Burdick, his foreman, was "riding" him. He was improperly trained, since Burdick assigned an inexperienced worker to break him in on the work. Burdick was an unsympathetic foreman who pounced on the most trivial mistakes.

Second, Wynne performed his duties as Mail Boy and Stockkeeper's Helper in the machine shop so commendably that the Company entrusted him with the promotion to the job of Stockkeeper. He was pursuing a course of study at Burdett College in an effort to improve himself, a fact ignored by the Company.

Third, and most important, the Union vigorously denies the

interpretation which the Company lends to Article IX-B by its theory of "promotability." In essence the Company is claiming the right to disregard the contractual requirements concerning job posting because in its judgment Wynne "is not promotable beyond the particular jobs posted." This is tantamount to saying that a person must be promotable to the highest position in order to receive a lower position, an untenable view in the light of contract provisions. The only way to determine a man's ability to do a certain job is to give him a chance to try the work. This is recognized by the contract clause providing for an original 6 months' probationary period for such a tryout. There have been many cases where employees were given the opportunity to try out on jobs and were returned to their former job or similar jobs when they failed to make the grade.

As a supplementary contention, the Union argues that at least Wynne should have been afforded the courtesy of returning to his former position. He sought a transfer within the 6 months' tryout period. It is a serious wrong to condemn him permanently to a job of Laborer on the tenuous grounds of nonpromotability.

QUESTIONS

1. Why do you suppose Wynne bid on two jobs which carried a lower rate of pay than he was currently receiving as Stockkeeper in the appliance stockroom? In submitting a bid was he requesting a promotion or a transfer?

2. Do "qualifications, fitness and ability" (as used in Article IX-A) refer only to the immediate position or also to higher rated jobs in a line of promotion?

3. Does the Company have the right to consider requirements of higher rated positions? Where there is a line of promotion, what difficulties are created for the Company by having people competent to do existing jobs but of doubtful ability to perform higher rated jobs on the promotional ladder?

4. Is it possible, and is it equitable, to judge the qualifications, fitness, and ability of an individual for positions several steps ahead in a promotional ladder? Are not these factors developed as a person makes each successive step in the ladder?

5. What would you consider to be the effects on Wynne of his being blocked midway in a promotional ladder by lack of qualifications, fitness and ability? Does a promotional ladder imply that all who put their feet on the lowest rung will ultimately reach the top?

Section

G

WORK SCHEDULES AND PREMIUM PAY

Fundamental interests of managements and unions are involved in the determination of work schedules. The hours of operations and the extent of work at premium rates are decisive for the costs of a management. The amount of leisure time and its distribution through the day and week are equally vital to working-men.

The managements of many enterprises desire a schedule of operations different from the regular workweek prevailing in the community, such as the current 8 hours per day, Monday through Friday. In some instances, technological and cost considerations are responsible for around-the-clock operations as in oil refineries, blast furnaces, and flat glass plants. The daily or weekly starting and stopping of these processes would be impracticable. Maintenance, heating, and protective services in most plants for these reasons require special schedules. In other cases the nature of the demand for the product creates the atypical schedule. Thus, utilities and railroads provide continuous service; the morning and evening rush hours in urban transit operations create unique scheduling problems; the hours of drugstores are a result of the peculiar role that institution plays in the American folkways. Managements will be interested in working schedules which permit flexibility of operations in response to changes in demand. For example, in recent years, department and retail stores have adopted the practice of remaining open one or two nights each week in the belief that these hours of service would increase sales volume.

These illustrations indicate that a distinction must be made between the hours of operation of a plant or a place of business and the schedule of hours worked by an individual employee.

The employee may work a fixed schedule each week, as in the straight 7:00 A.M. to 3:00 P.M. schedule, Monday through Friday. Or the employee may work a rotating schedule among different shifts. For example, one week he might work the 7:00 A.M. to 3:00 P.M. shift, the next week, the 3:00 P.M. to 11:00 P.M. shift, and the third week, the 11:00 P.M. to 7:00 A.M. shift, then repeat this rotation cycle. Another schedule pattern for individual employees, as distinguished from the hours of operation of the enterprise, is the staggered schedule. A simple staggered schedule which repeats itself every 14 days is 4 days on and 2 days off following by 6 days on and 2 days off.

The collective bargaining agreement will typically contain provisions relating to the following aspects of work schedules: (*a*) the schedule of operation of the plant, (*b*) the regular work schedule of employees, and (*c*) the hours of work and premium rates for work performed in addition to or outside a regular schedule.

SCHEDULE OF OPERATIONS OF THE PLANT

In many agreements the management clause lists the schedule of operation of the plant as one of the matters on which the management may exercise sole discretion. However, in the exercise of this discretion, management is frequently influenced by other provisions relating to the established schedule for employees and premium pay arrangements. For example, when a holiday occurs on a Tuesday the management might conclude that it would be better to close the plant on both Monday and Tuesday. Although it has the exclusive right to then schedule operations for Wednesday through Saturday to make up part of the lost production, its decision to do so will depend greatly on the effect of other provisions of the agreement. (See Cases 42 and 44.) In some agreements, the scheduled hours of operation are listed; and while management is allowed to change these hours, it may do so only after consultation with the union.

WORK SCHEDULE OF EMPLOYEES

A typical agreement provides the following:

"The regular work week shall commence on Monday except for engineers, firemen, and firemen's helpers, and

where the process requires otherwise, and shall consist of
five (5) eight (8) hour days. The regular work day shall
start at 7:00 A.M. and end at 3:00 P.M."

Even this relatively simple clause can give rise to a number of
problems in its application. Where the work schedule of the
employees is defined in this manner, can the management *require*
employees to work hours over and above the schedule? Some
unions have argued that an employee cannot be disciplined for
refusing to work or failing to report for work beyond 3:00 P.M.
or on Saturday, for example. (See Case 43.) If the employees
do work overtime, can the management require them to take off
some time during their regularly scheduled work period as an
offset? Normally this right is specifically denied the company in
the agreement. The definition of the employee's work schedule
also creates a firm expectation that work will be available to him
when he reports at the regular time on any one of the 5 scheduled
work days. The employee is usually protected from last-minute
changes in the company's operating schedule by *reporting pay*
provisions. The current agreement between the A. C. Lawrence
Leather Company and the International Fur and Leather Workers'
Union provides:

"If an employee reports for work without having been
notified the previous working day by his foreman not to report
to work, he shall be provided with a minimum of four hours'
work at his average earnings, provided he accepts suitable
work assigned to him in his own division, even though it
is not his usual work. If Management is unable to provide
at least four hours' work at average earnings, he will receive
four hours' pay at his average earnings.

"The above provision may be waived if there was no
opportunity to give the employee advance notice owing to
a catastrophe or an act of God, or a mechanical breakdown
beyond the control of the Company."

Many agreements also provide that a similar reporting pay
guarantee shall be given when an employee is called in for special work outside of his regularly scheduled hours of work.

The hours of work scheduled for individual employees may
also be affected by state laws. Some laws, for example, limit the

number of hours which can be worked in a given day or, as in the case of women, prevent their working during certain hours of the day.

HOURS OF WORK OUTSIDE A REGULAR SCHEDULE

Agreements normally specify that work performed by an individual outside or in addition to his regularly scheduled work week shall be compensated for at premium rates. The Fair Labor Standards Act requires that firms in interstate commerce pay time and one half for hours worked in excess of 40 hours per week. The Walsh-Healey Act, applicable to firms which have contracts on government work, goes further in requiring time and one half payment for hours worked in excess of 8 hours per day. Most labor agreements today reflect these overtime standards, even though they may not involve companies covered by the law. It is usually specified that there will be no pyramiding of daily and weekly overtime.

The typical labor contract, however, goes beyond the provisions of the law in arrangements for premium pay. The following refinements are fairly common:

a) In an effort to discourage work at less desirable work periods such as Sundays or holidays, unions have sought time and one half or double time payments for all work performed on those days. A distinction is usually made between premium payment for Saturdays and Sundays *as such* and for the sixth and seventh consecutive days worked. In industries with continuous operations, special arrangements are necessary because it is impossible to avoid operating at those times considered undesirable by the employees. Some agreements also specify that work performed in excess of 10 or 12 hours per day shall be paid at the rate of double time rather than time and one half.

b) It is frequently provided that days in the regularly scheduled work week will be considered as days worked for the purpose of computing weekly overtime, even though no work has been performed on those days. Among the reasons normally stated in the agreement are absence of an employee due to bona fide illness, occupational injury, jury duty, death in the immediate family, holiday observance, time lost due to layoff because of lack of work, official union business, or for any other reason the company finds justifiable.

c) Since the premium payments for overtime work may add considerably to an employee's take-home pay, agreements usually specify that overtime work will be distributed as equally as possible among the employees in their respective classifications or departments. This equal distribution is to be accomplished over a reasonable period of time.

In some instances the union seeks premium pay arrangements as a method for increasing gross wages rather than to discourage work at disagreeable times or to promote leisure time. It is clear that the administration of a given work schedule and premium pay provisions of the agreement will significantly influence costs. The same provisions may be made effective in a variety of ways. The cases which follow illustrate some of the problems in the negotiation and administration of these contract provisions.

Case 41

RIGHT TO RESCHEDULE

UNION: United Steelworkers of America, CIO

COMPANY: Worcester Pressed Steel Company

On June 23, 1949, in accordance with the arbitration provision of the contract, the Union filed the following demand for arbitration with the American Arbitration Association:

"Violation of Article XII, Section 2. The schedule established by the Company on March 3, 1949 is not proper and not reasonable. It is not proper because the principle intent is to eliminate the fifteen minute paid rest period and it is not reasonable because one proposal would provide for a lunch period different from one the employees have been accustomed to, and further it is different from the noon lunch periods in effect in New England Industry. The Union demands an eight-hour day, 7:00 A.M. to 3:00 P.M. with the rest and lunch periods as in effect prior to March 3, 1949."

In the arbitration hearing the Union clarified its position by making two general contentions: (1) the Company under the contract is obligated to schedule five, 8-hour days per week, and (2) the Company cannot revise the schedule in any way which will result in an improper reduction in pay.

BACKGROUND

The work schedule at the Company had been from 7:00 A.M. to 3:30 P.M. with a 15-minute rest period and also a lunch period from 12 Noon to 12:30 P.M. On February 24, 1949, the Company Superintendent prepared a tentative shop notice announcing new schedules to become effective on March 1. It provided that the first shift would work from 7:00 A.M. to 11:00 A.M. and again from 11:30 A.M. to 2:30 P.M., with a half-hour lunch period from 11:00 A.M. to 11:30 A.M. A similar schedule was shown for the second shift from 2:30 P.M. to 10:00 P.M. The Company, in a letter to the President of the local Union, explained that the postponements of shipments and the lack of new orders prompted a reduction in the workweek. It expressed the view that it would be better to reduce the hours than to lay off more employees, since the force had already been cut extensively. The letter stated in part:

"With recent changes in smoking rules and the addition of coke machines, we don't believe that it would work a real hardship to work for 4 or 4½ hours steady in the morning. Elimination of the rest period will decrease our overhead, and the savings will both lower our break-even point and permit us to quote somewhat lower prices to our customers. If the rest period is retained, its cost will go up in relation to our actual labor to a small degree, and reflect in our cost and a higher break-even point."

Between February 24 and March 1 there were several discussions between the Union and the Company. The Union said it would prefer an 8-hour day, 4-day week. This would give the men a chance to pick up work elsewhere on the fifth day so they could offset the drop in pay. The Company refused this suggestion on the ground that customers operating on a low inventory might want their orders in a hurry; it would be awkward to explain to them a full day's plant closure. The original schedule was not instituted, but on March 3 a slightly revised schedule was put into effect by the Company. It called for a first shift work day of: 7:30 A.M. to 11:30 A.M., lunch period to 12:00 Noon, and resumption of work 12:00 Noon to 3:00 P.M. The second shift had a similar distribution of hours from 3:00 P.M. to 10:30 P.M. This schedule of 7 hours per day eliminated the former 15-minute rest period with pay.

RELEVANT CONTRACT CLAUSES: (October 16, 1947, agreement as amended and extended by agreement of September 20, 1948.)

"*Article XII (Hours and Overtime)*:

"Section 1. This article provides the basis of calculating overtime, but makes no guarantee of hours or work to be provided per day or per week.

"Section 2. The regular work week shall consist of five (5) consecutive eight-hour days, beginning Monday and ending Friday, but the payroll week shall begin Monday at 12:01 A.M. and end at 12:00 midnight Sunday.

"The scheduled work week shall be determined from time to time, and shall consist of the daily and weekly hours to be worked. Any change in the scheduled work week affecting the whole plant, an entire department, or any other group of more than ten (10) employees, shall be discussed with the Grievance Committee three (3) days or more in advance. If no agreement is reached, the schedule may be put into effect, and if the Grievance Committee feels the schedule is not proper or not reasonable, the question shall be submitted in writing to the higher steps of the grievance procedure and to arbitration.

"Section 3. The daily hours of work shall be consecutive except for such rest periods or lunch periods as may be provided. Any shift working over four and one-half (4½) consecutive hours will be granted a fifteen (15) minutes rest period with pay. Any shift working four and one-half (4½) consecutive hours or less will not be granted a rest period."

The above clauses were carried over with few changes from the April 8, 1946, agreement. Prior to 1946 the reference to the rest periods or lunch periods was very general. The 1944 contract merely said that the daily hours of work would be consecutive, except for "such rest periods . . . as may be provided in accordance with the practice heretofore prevailing in the plant."

"*Article XIV* (*Wages*):

"Section 6. The wage schedule shall not be changed during the life of this agreement except by mutual agreement or in accordance with the provisions of Article XVIII.

"*Article III* (*Management*):

(There is a typical Management Rights clause with the following addendum:)
"The Company shall retain all functions of Management except as specifically modified by this contract."

The Company also cited Article XVI (*Matters Subject to Arbitration*) which, in part, states that the arbitrator must follow the agreement and "shall not add to nor subtract from any clause herein." Finally, Article XVII (*Changes or Amendments*) provides that the instant contract contains the complete agreement between the parties and no additions, waivers or deductions shall be made during its life except by the mutual consent in writing of the parties.

POSITION OF THE UNION

1. The Company had no right to schedule a work week of other than five eight-hour days from Monday through Friday unless agreement had been obtained from the Union.

Section 2 of Article XII, while it serves as a basis for computing overtime, also describes the precise schedule which is to remain during the life of the contract. That the detailed schedule is set forth in the overtime clause is an understandable convenience.

The second paragraph of Section 2 does not detract from the establishment of a 5-day week, 8 hours per day schedule. It was inserted to take care of two special problems: (1) the reasonableness of hours worked by the night shift employees in wartime who had transportation difficulties, and (2) the Company's right to require employees to work reasonable hours of overtime. While the Company is afforded considerable flexibility by this Section, it cannot unilaterally change Section 2 by scheduling a 5-day work week of less than 8 hours each day.

2. The Company had no right to reschedule out the paid rest period because to do so resulted in a cut in pay in violation of the agreement.

Before the new schedule went in the employees were given 40 hours' pay for 38¾ hours' work. Rest periods totaled 1¼ hours per week. Under Section 3 of Article XII a 15-minute paid rest period had been given each day. Now the men are paid 35 hours for 35 hours of work. Thus, there has been an obvious reduction in pay. The rest period practice is long-established, having begun in 1943. It has been mentioned in each labor agreement since that time. This allowance has been and must be considered an integral part of the wage structure. As evidence the Union cited a statement by the Company in its publication "The Presteel Press," July, 1948; it listed the rest period as the equivalent of 4 cents per hour. Moreover, in negotiations prior to the 1947 agreement, the Company offered to buy back the rest period for 3 cents per hour, but the Union refused.

There is nothing about the 7-hour day schedule which required elimination of the rest period. The Company admits it could have followed a 7:00 A.M. to 12:00 Noon and 12:30 P.M. to 2:30 P.M. schedule, thus continuing the rest period under Section 3. It chose to do otherwise for the deliberate purpose of saving money. Article XIV, Section 6, makes it clear that wage reductions are violative of the agreement. Conversely, if it was intended under Article XII, Section 3, to give the Company the right to change existing shifts for the purpose of eliminating the rest period, such right would have been expressly stated. Surely the Company recognized the permanence of this allowance when it proposed to buy it back in negotiations.

For the reasons stated, the Union asks the arbitrator to rule that the Company must return to its old schedule; at the very least the Company should be ordered to reschedule its hours so as to provide for a paid rest period, and the employees should be reimbursed for 1¼ hours' pay each week per employee since the new schedule was started.

POSITION OF THE COMPANY

The Company relies entirely upon the contract language. In its opinion many contract clauses justify its action. Section 2 of

Article XII is standard in nearly all labor contracts and has its origin in the desire to establish a basis for applying the Fair Labor Standards Act with reference to overtime compensation. Obviously such a clause cannot be construed as restricting management's right to operate a work week of less than 40 hours per week or 8 hours per day. Fortunately, however, the contract in this case dispels any doubt on this point, because Section 1 states that "this Article provides the basis of calculating overtime, but makes no guarantee of hours or work to be provided per day or per week."

The Company had sound reasons for revising the schedule. A reduction of orders, a condition common to many other companies in the area, necessitated a cutback in work. The Company felt a 1-day closing per week or the layoff of more people would be less desirable than the 5-day 7-hour-per-day arrangement. It is absurd to suggest or imply that the schedule change was based solely on the desire to eliminate the rest period. However, the Company admits freely that in altering the daily schedule, it considered it "advisable, prudent and proper" to do it in such a way as to drop the additional cost burden. This gesture was economically sound. It was also allowable under the contract. Section 3 of Article XII is unambiguous in defining the extent of the Company's obligation. As long as a shift works more than $4\frac{1}{2}$ consecutive hours, as it had prior to March 3, a rest period with pay had to be granted. But when the schedule was revised so that the shift worked less than $4\frac{1}{2}$ consecutive hours, such shift "will not be granted a rest period" under the specific terms of Section 3.

The Union's attempt to treat the rest period as a fixed obligation under any and all circumstances is denied vigorously by the Company. Article XIV, Section 6, refers only to "wage schedule"; and this term, by no stretch of the imagination, can be considered to include a paid rest period. Finally, the elimination of this allowance under the new schedule is consistent with the purpose of a rest period. It was put in as a result of normal fatigue arising from the long hours worked by employees during the war years. Now the consecutive stretches of work are lessened, and other privileges (smoking and coke machines) are extended, thus eliminating the need for this 15-minute period. Since the hours of continuous work have been shortened, the management is free to eliminate the rest period under the agreement.

QUESTIONS

1. Is the Union primarily challenging the right of management to re-schedule the daily hours of work, or is it more concerned with the reduction in pay for time worked, or with the elimination of the rest period resulting from the rescheduling?

2. How much weight would you attach to the fact that there has been a paid rest period for many years in this plant as compared to the weight you would attach to the specific language of Article XII, Section 3?

3. In what sense does the elimination of the paid rest period result in a reduction in wages? Is it equitable for the arbitrator to approve a rescheduling which results in the elimination of the rest period when the Union on a previous occasion could have bargained away the rest period for a three cents per hour general wage increase?

4. Discuss the powers of the arbitrator under Article XII, Section 2. What standards should he adopt in determining whether a work schedule is "proper" or "reasonable"?

Case 42

A CHANGE IN WEEK-END SCHEDULES

UNION: Amalgamated Association of Street, Electric Railway & Motor Coach Employees, AFL

COMPANY: Hudson County Bus Owners' Association

The Hudson County Bus Owners' Association comprises fifty-five bus owners. It acts as the employment agency for the owners. It trains the drivers, negotiates contracts, and performs other similar functions. In 1946 the Association entered into a collective bargaining agreement with the Amalgamated Association of Street, Electric Railway & Motor Coach Employees, which represents the drivers of the buses operated by the Association.

The drivers have been given a staggered day off each week so that every sixth week they have had a Saturday or a Sunday off. In the summer of 1946 the Association was able to charter their buses on week ends. They assigned as drivers of these buses the men whose day off fell on Saturday and Sunday. These men were then given another day off during the week.

The Union contends that, since the drivers were requested to work on their day off, they are entitled to overtime pay at the rate of double time for the Saturdays and Sundays they were required to work. The Company denies this claim and asserts that, since the drivers were given another day off, they are entitled to straight-time pay only.

POSITION OF THE COMPANY

The Association bases its case on Article XVII, Section 2, of the agreement which reads, in part, as follows: "Each employee shall be entitled to one day off in the work week." According to the Association, this provision merely obligates it to give each employee one day off in the work week; it does not obligate it to give a Saturday or Sunday off. Therefore, the Association argues that so long as a man does not work 7 days in a week, he is not entitled to overtime for working any of the 6 days.

The Association insists on its right to assign work schedules to its employees. This is held to be of particular importance in the transportation industry where the nature of the business is such as to require a maximum of flexibility in assigning men.

On the question of the rate at which overtime is paid, the Association points out that even if overtime were to be paid for Saturday and Sunday, the Union's demand for double time has no logical basis. Section 3, Article II, of the agreement provides that "overtime shall be paid for at the rate of time and one half."

POSITION OF THE COMPANY

The Union concedes the Association's right to assign work schedules to its employees. However, the Union argues that the issue in this case is not whether the Association has the right to make work schedules but whether, after having made the work assignments and following them for a substantial period of time, it can arbitrarily change the schedule of certain employees for the sole purpose of avoiding overtime payments.

The Union claims that the drivers have been working on a definite schedule which was made up by the Company. This schedule provided for a staggered day off each week so that every sixth week the men would get a Saturday or Sunday off. The Union maintains that both the Association and the drivers understood that certain days could be considered as days off, and the men could plan week-end trips. In the Union's opinion, it is not equitable for the Association to make out work schedules following certain principles and then assign the men another day off just to avoid the payment of overtime. It is inequitable to require a man to work on his week end off, particularly when it comes only once every 6 weeks, and then not pay him overtime for it. The Union holds that the inconvenience is so great as to warrant the payment of double time.

QUESTIONS

1. What is "charter work"? Would you expect such business to be profitable from the Company's point of view?
2. Is a previous work schedule a bar to a change in work schedule? What is the position of the Union on this question?
3. Is the Company obligated to assign work according to a definite schedule? Could it change its schedule of assignments daily? Why do you suppose the Company has followed a specific schedule practice?
4. Could the Company schedule "charter work" as a part of the regular schedule? Why do you suppose it has not done this?
5. Does the Union have a contract right for a day off on Sunday?
6. What contract provision would you suggest to prevent the reoccurence of this dispute? Draft an appropriate clause.

Case 43

OBLIGATION TO WORK OVERTIME

UNION: United Textile Workers of America, AFL

COMPANY: Connecticut River Mills, Inc.

ISSUE: Did the Company have the right to discharge an employee for not working Saturdays, and, if not, what compensation shall the former employee receive?

Myrtle Poland, a bobbin winder, was hired on March 12, 1946. She was discharged on April 19, 1946. Her discharge was over her refusal to work overtime on Saturday, April 20. It was testified that, whereas she worked 48 hours during the week ending March 23 (the first full week of her employment), she worked only 40 hours during the weeks ending March 30 and April 6; 48 hours during the week ending April 13; and 40 hours during the week ending April 20.

The plant had been operating on a 48-hour schedule ever since it was taken over by the present owners in September of

1944. Following Miss Poland's refusal to appear for work on several Saturdays previously, her foreman asked her on Friday, April 19, whether she would appear for work on the following day. When she replied that she would not, she was notified of her discharge. The 48-hour week had not only been in effect consistently for several years past but had received the approval of the vast majority of the employees through the medium of a poll conducted by management during the week ending April 20.

The contract between the parties in Article II, Section 1, reads as follows:

> "The eight (8) hour day and forty (40) hour week, commencing Monday at 12:01 A.M. and ending Friday (inclusive) shall be in effect without revision, during the term of this contract. Time and one-half shall be paid for all work done in excess of eight (8) hours in any day or forty (40) hours in any one week, and overtime paid for on a daily basis shall not be duplicated on a weekly basis."

POSITION OF THE UNION

The Union pointed out that the 8-hour day and the 40-hour week were fixed by contract, and the employee's obligation under the contract is met when he works 40 hours a week. No one under the contract can be required to work more than 40 hours per week against his will. Miss Poland worked at least 40 hours in each of the five weeks of work since the date of her employment. The action of the Company in discharging her because she refused to work more than the amount of time called for in the collective agreement was in violation of that agreement. The Union requests that she be compensated for her improper discharge.

The Union regards as irrelevant the facts that the 48-hour week had been worked by the plant for some time prior to Miss Poland's discharge and that a majority of the employees had consented to the 48-hour schedule through the medium of a poll conducted by the management. The work week is fixed by the contract; and while it places no barrier against an individual employee voluntarily working overtime, likewise it contains no requirement that any employee must work such overtime. The action of the employees in consistently consenting to work a longer schedule and in voting for such a schedule in no way alters the contract and does not impair any one's rights under the contract.

POSITION OF THE COMPANY

The Company argued that, regardless of the stated language of the contract, the workweek in the plant has been and (in deference to the wishes of the majority of the employees) continued to be 48 hours. The right to schedule hours of work is a prerogative of management. The purpose of Article II, Section 1, is to fix a basic workweek for the purpose of providing a basis for computing overtime payment. It does not mean that an employee can refuse to work a longer work schedule with impunity. Miss Poland was warned of her obligation to work the same number of hours as the rest of the employees; and when the warning was not heeded, she was discharged. The Company maintained that it could not operate on a 48-hour schedule if individual employees were to have the right to refuse to work that schedule. The organization would be disrupted by such intermittent attendance. Miss Poland's failure to work the 48-hour schedule was absenteeism of a type that justified discharge under the contract.

QUESTIONS

1. Is it the intent of the parties in Article II, Section 1, of the contract to define the conditions under which overtime will be paid, or do they intend the Article to go further and specify the length of the work week?

2. Article II, Section 1, meaningful unless management has the right to schedule longer hours of work than 8 per day and 40 hours per week? Does this right, in turn, imply the obligation of the Union and its members to work any scheduled work week? Does the work schedule have to be reasonable?

3. Would it make any difference in Miss Poland's case whether she had a reasonable excuse for failing to work on most Saturdays? What would you regard as reasonable excuses?

4. Does the poll of the employees have any bearing on this case? Does this vote constitute an implied "agreement" by employees to work overtime?

5. Does the fact that a 48-hour week has been scheduled for 2 years make any difference? Does the fact that Miss Poland accepted employment under these conditions make any difference?

Case 44

EFFECT OF RESCHEDULING ON PREMIUM PAY

UNION: Textile Workers Union of America, CIO

COMPANY: Kendall Mills, Thrift Plant

On December 10, 1951, the Company posted a notice which stated:

"Thrift Plant operations will cease, for Christmas Season shut down, at 11:00 P.M. Saturday, December 22, 1951. Operations will be resumed at 7:00 A.M. Wednesday, December 26, 1951. Monday, December 24, will not be a scheduled work day. Tuesday, December 25, Christmas Day, is a paid holiday."

A copy of this notice was sent to the local Union president, and there is no evidence that the proposed scheduling was protested by the Union prior to December 25. The plant was open for work on December 26, and employees worked through Saturday, December 29. For work on the latter day, they were paid at straight time rates. The Union filed a grievance on January 10, 1952, charging that the payment of straight time on Saturday constituted a contract violation.

The relevant contract clauses are contained in Section 7 (*Hours of Work and Overtime*) of the 1949 agreement:

"(*a*) Hours of Work. The normal work week shall be five (5) consecutive days of eight (8) consecutive hours each, Monday to Friday inclusive. For the purposes of this agreement, the work week shall begin at 11:00 P.M. Sunday, and end at 11:00 P.M. the following Sunday and the work day runs from 11:00 P.M. to 11:00 P.M.

"(*b*) Maintenance men, firemen, and watchmen may be staggered over seven (7) days, Monday through Sunday, eight (8) hours per day, provided a regularly scheduled work week is established.

"(*c*) It shall be the duty of each employee to report for work each day of the normal work week, unless excused under the provisions of this agreement. It shall also be their duty to so report on the sixth day of the work week if scheduled . . . .

"(*d*) Overtime Pay. The Company agrees to pay one and one-half times the regular rate of pay for time worked in excess of eight (8) hours in any one day and forty (40) hours in any work week, and for all time worked on the sixth day worked in any work week. Double the regular rate of pay shall be paid for all time worked on the seventh day worked in any work week.

"(*e*) Time lost from work for the following reasons shall be counted as time worked in computing the sixth and seventh days worked in any work week: [Six reasons are listed, two of which are pertinent to this case.]

"1. Employee told not to work or report for work on a scheduled work day.

"4. If any holiday named in the Agreement occurs or is celebrated on a day within the regular work week, and no work is performed on the holiday, that holiday is to be counted as a day worked."

Position of the Union

It is clear that Section 7(*a*) establishes the normal work-week as Monday through Friday. The employees have an obligation under Section 7(*c*) to work during the normal week as defined. The Company, in turn, has an obligation to pay overtime for work outside the normal workweek, Section 7(*d*). It is significant that the employees were told not to work on Monday, December 24, a scheduled work day; and accordingly this day must be counted as a day worked for the purpose of computing overtime under Section 7(*e*)(1). There is no disagreement that the holiday, December 25 is so counted under Section 7(*e*)(4). It follows, therefore, that Saturday, December 29, was the sixth day worked; and the overtime requirements apply. The Union agrees that when an employee has been out on his own volition, he should not receive overtime pay for the sixth day; but in this case the employees were willing to work on Monday, and work was available for them. Instead, the Company arbitrarily declared Monday as not being a scheduled work day, a right it is denied by the contractual definition of the workweek which means the scheduled workweek. If such a unilateral right were acknowledged by arbitration, the provisions of Section 7(a) would be rendered meaningless. By the simple expedient of posting a notice the Company could regularly work employees on Saturdays at straight time.

The phrase "regular work week" found in Section 7(e)(4) must mean the same as "normal work week" as defined in Section 7(a) or "regularly scheduled work week" in the case of the exceptions provided in Section 7(b). A contrary interpretation would allow the Company to "schedule out" the holiday and avoid premium payments contemplated by Section 7(d and e). If the Company wishes to revise the normal workweek to escape the overtime effect of holiday occasions such as this, it can negotiate with the Union. It cannot make the revision unilaterally.

POSITION OF THE COMPANY

It is very common in this and other plants in the area to have a 2-day shutdown when an official holiday falls on either a Tuesday or a Thursday. It is done not only in the interests of the employees, to give them a long holiday week end; but it is also more efficient for the Company. In posting its notice the Company indicated specifically that Monday, December 24, would not be a scheduled work day. Under the terms of the contract, straight time pay for Saturday was appropriate.

First, Saturday was not the sixth day *worked*, Section 7(d); counting the holiday as a day worked in accordance with Section 7(e) (4), Saturday was only the fifth day worked. It will be observed that Section 7 (d) speaks of the sixth day worked "in any work week;" it does not refer to a normal work week. Second, there is no understanding that an employee is to get premium pay for Saturday work whenever failure to work from Monday through Friday is for other than a personal reason. If this were the intent, there would be no purpose in listing the six reasons in Section 7(e).

The Company concedes that if the schedule is to be changed on a permanent basis, it must be negotiated with the Union; but it reserves the right to change the work week on occasion. The use of the word "normal" to describe a work week implies occasional resort to the "abnormal" or to exceptions the propriety of which can be determined by the rule of reason.

In the 1945 agreement it was provided that time lost because no work was available had to be counted as time worked in determining the sixth and seventh consecutive days worked. It provided further that when the "Company and the General Shop Chairman . . . mutually agree that the plant shall be closed on any day (other than a holiday) . . . such day shall not be counted as a day worked . . . ." This same clause appeared in the 1947 contract, but it was negotiated out at the Company's request in 1949. If this clause prevailed today the Company would have had to negotiate the closing on Monday, December 24.

The Union appears to be trying to gain through arbitration something it could not get through contract negotiation, a clause granting time and one half for all Saturday work, except where an employee is off during any of the five regular days at his own request. The arbitrator obviously should not support this attempt of the Union to expand the contract.

QUESTIONS

1. The Company's right to occasional rescheduling is not questioned. But does such a right relieve the Company from the premium payment obligations included in the contract?

2. Does the Company have the right to schedule a shortened work week during slack times? May it schedule such short work week Monday through Thursday? Wednesday through Saturday?

3. Are the overtime provisions for the sixth and seventh days worked intended to discourage week-end work as such or to assure premium rates for work in excess of 40 hours?

4. Discuss the meaning and intent of Section 7(e)(1) of the contract.

5. What significance do you attach to the fact that the Union did not protest the work schedule announced for Christmas week prior to returning to work on December 26?

6. If the Union had protested and the Company had offered to work on Monday or to operate a work schedule during Christmas week of Wednesday through Friday, what do you think would have been the reaction of the Union? Of the members of the Union?

Case 45

WHICH PREMIUM RATE SHALL APPLY?

UNION: United Automobile Workers of America, CIO

COMPANY: Ohio Steel Foundry Company

On March 17, Clarence Potter worked from 7:00 A.M. to 3:00 P.M. and on March 18 from 11:00 P.M. to 7:00 A.M. He was paid time and one half for the second 8 hours. The Union requests that Potter be paid double time for the hours after 11 hours, that is, for the last 5 hours of work on the second shift. The Company considers this request contrary to the provisions of the contract.

The contract provision pertinent to this issue is Article XI, Section F, which reads in part as follows:

"Time and one-half will be paid to all employees for all hours worked in excess of 8 hours in any one day. Double time will be paid to all employees for all hours worked in excess of 11 hours in any one day. A day shall consist of 24 consecutive hours from the time any employee begins the shift in which the work is performed."

POSITION OF THE UNION

The Union contends that, since the contract specifies that a day shall consist of 24 consecutive hours from the time the shift begins, then all of the 16 hours of work fell within a day. The Union holds that for the hours after the first 11, Potter should have received double time. The Union points out that the Company paid time and one half for all of the second 8 hours, thus recognizing that the second shift was hours over 8 in one day. The Union contends that double time should be paid for the hours over 11 in one day, particularly since the Company apparently relied upon this section of the contract in paying the time and one half.

POSITION OF THE COMPANY

The Company holds that the Union is misinterpreting the contract. It is argued that the intent of the parties in negotiating the contract was to protect employees from being worked more than 11 hours in a single stretch. The Company points out that Potter was swinging from one shift to another and that he had a full 8 hours of rest between the shift ending at 3:00 P.M. and the one starting at 11:00 P.M. In such a situation, the Company insists that the double-time provision is not applicable.

QUESTIONS

1. What is the purpose of the figure of 11 hours in Article XI, Section F, of the agreement?
2. What is meant by "swinging from one shift to another?" Under what circumstances does this scheduling problem arise? Illustrate by example.
3. What change in the contract would you suggest to validate explicitly the position of the Company? Draft such a revision in the agreement.
4. Was the clause cited by the Union intended to apply to this case?
5. When an arbitrator decides this case, what relation is he fulfilling to the collective bargaining process?

Section **GENERAL WAGE**

H **CHANGES**

The discussion of standards or criteria for general wage-rate changes in Chapter VI is to be regarded as an introduction to the cases in this section. Case 46, which follows, involves the comparison of a number of wage-reopening clauses in collective bargaining agreements. The demand for a general wage-rate change may be made in many situations during the life of an agreement, subject to the limitations expressed in a wage-reopening clause. The precise language of such a clause is decisive in indicating under what circumstances a wage change may be demanded, the form of the demand that can be entertained, and even the extent of any wage change.

Cases 47–49 provide an opportunity to apply the most frequently discussed standards for wage determination. These cases have been presented in considerable detail; they constitute a summary account of the evidence and the arguments presented by both sides. These cases depict the economic and industrial relations environment in which the controversy over the general wage level arose.

The "improvement factor" provision of the General Motors-United Automobile Workers, CIO, contract is presented in Case 50. The case raises a variety of basic questions concerning the relations between wage rates and productivity. Finally, in this Section, Case 51 involves the relations between a local union and the International Union in wage bargaining. It helps to focus attention on many of the fundamental questions involved in the public debates over industry-wide bargaining.

343

Case 46

WAGE-REOPENING CLAUSES

A number of different wage-reopening clauses have been summarized in this case. The following questions may facilitate an understanding of the differences among these various clauses as they may operate in practice.

1. What is meant by "wages" in the reopening clause? May a demand be made for "fringe benefits," such as vacations and holidays, in addition to a general wage-rate change? Does the term permit the making of demands for the rates of particular job classifications?

2. What happens in the event that the parties are unable to agree upon new "wage" provisions in bargaining growing out of the demands made under a reopening clause? Is the contract still in effect? Are the parties free to strike or engage in a lockout?

3. What provisions are made, if any, for the settlement of a dispute following an impasse in bargaining when a reopening clause has been invoked? Must the parties arbitrate their differences? Do the old provisions remain in effect?

4. Who may request a reopening of "wages?" Does the clause only permit demands by the Union for increases, or does it also allow the management to request decreases?

5. How often may a reopening provision be utilized in the course of a contract? Is there any limitation on the number of times or the dates on which "wages" may be subject to negotiations?

6. Are there any conditions which must be met before "wages" may be reopened? The cost of living may have had to be increased by a certain amount; there may have had to be changes in the rates paid by other firms in the industry; or "competitive conditions" in the industry must have altered. The reopening clause may be made conditional.

The foregoing questions illustrate the variety of ways in which the parties may shape a reopening clause of a contract to their special problems and relationships. The reader is urged to compare and contrast the implications of the clauses which follow in terms of the questions which have just been posed.

1. *Textile Workers Union of America, CIO, and Botany Worsted Mills, 1946*

"Wages may be revised twice a year upon the request of either party .by the giving of sixty days' written notice. Wage revisions shall be effective only on the 1st Monday of August or the 1st Monday of February following such notice.

"If the parties are unable to agree within fifteen days . . . either party may require arbitration thereof . . . ."

2. *United Electrical, Radio & Machine Workers of America, and Champion Aero Metal Products*

"At the option of the Union, this Agreement shall be re-opened on December 1st, 1946, for the purpose of negotiating an upward revision of the wages provided therein. In the event the parties are unable to agree as to the amount of the wage increase, the matter shall be arbitrated in the manner provided under the arbitration provisions of this Agreement . . . ."

3. *United Rubber, Cork, Linoleum & Plastic Workers of America, CIO, and Cords, Limited, Inc.*

"This agreement is the final settlement of all wage issues between the parties for the period hereof, provided, however, that if at the end of nine months from the date hereof there has been a general wage adjustment among the Company's competitors in the Company's industry, which adjustment brings the basic wage rates of the employees of said competitors to the level of or in excess of those agreed upon herein, the Company agrees to reconsider the wage structure provided for herein, within thirty days after a request therefor by the Union."

4. *International Longshoremen's & Warehousemen's Union, and Waterfront Employers Association*

"Semi-annually during the life of this contract, as of March 31 or September 30, the rates of pay and overtime rates shall, at the request of either party, be reviewed and if the parties cannot agree, shall, at the request of either party, be determined by the Impartial Chairman. The party desiring wage review shall give notice of such desire not less than thirty days prior to the semi-annual date on which wage review is requested."

5. *United Steelworkers of America, CIO, and Carnegie-Illinois Steel Corporation*

"The terms and conditions of this Agreement shall continue in effect until Midnight April 30, 1949, provided, however, that either party may, on April 1, 1948, give written notice to the other party of its desire to negotiate a general and uniform change in rates of pay. Within 5 days after the giving of such notice, the parties shall meet for the purpose of negotiating such issue. Failing agreement on such issue on or before April 30, 1948, this Agreement shall remain in effect until Midnight April 30, 1949."

6. *Insurance and Allied Workers' Organizing Committee, CIO, and John Hancock Mutual Life Insurance Company, August 2, 1951.*

"This contract shall be effective as of August 2, 1951, and all of the foregoing terms shall remain in full force and effect until and including June 30, 1953, provided, however, that either party may on one occasion on or after April 1, 1952 but not later than June 1, 1952, and on one occasion on or after October 1, 1952 but not later than December 1, 1952 request a review of compensation payable hereunder. Negotiations shall be entered into promptly by the parties when requested; and if no agreement is reached either party may elect within the aforesaid periods to terminate this contract by notice in writing mailed or delivered to the other party at least sixty days before the date set in such notice of termination and this contract shall terminate on such date."

7. *United Electrical, Radio and Machine Workers of America, Local 288, and Monsanto Chemical Company, Plastics Division, May 16, 1949.*

"This agreement shall become effective as of May 16, 1949, and shall remain in effect until May 1, 1951, subject however to the renegotiation of basic hourly wage rates only, as provided below. Should the Company or the Union desire to negotiate concerning a change in wage rates during the term of this agreement, notice to that effect shall be given to the other party on March 1, 1950. Negotiations pursuant to such wage adjustment shall not become effective earlier than May 1, 1950. Unless otherwise mutually agreed upon between the parties, the negotiation of wage rates as provided above shall be completed on or before May 1, 1950."

"This agreement shall automatically renew itself for periods of two years unless written notice of desired changes or termination is given by one party to the other at least sixty (60) days before the termination of any such period."

8. *The United Rubber, Cork, Linoleum and Plastic Workers of America, CIO, International Union and Local 45, and United States Rubber Company, Naugatuck Footwear Plant, August 3, 1951.*

"This agreement may be amended by mutual agreement between the parties. If either party proposes amendments to this agreement during the life thereof, negotiations on such proposals shall begin within thirty (30) days. If no settlement is reached, the provisions of this agreement shall continue in effect."

Case 47

COMPANY DEMAND FOR A GENERAL WAGE RATE REDUCTION

UNION: Textile Workers Union of America, CIO

COMPANY: Bates Manufacturing Company

BACKGROUND

The Bates Manufacturing Company, which operates five plants in Maine, is one of the largest textile employers in New England. In March, 1951, there were 6,751 production employees in these plants; a year later during the consideration of this case, employment had fallen to 4,843. These plants manufacture bedspreads, table cloths, drapery fabrics, broadcloths and poplin, fine cotton goods, soft-filled sheetings, and a variety of specialty products.

The postwar history of general wage rate increases is summarized in the accompanying table, which shows the minimum rate in the plant after each general increase. The agreement which expired on March 15, 1950, was extended for a full year. After the Korean outbreak in June, 1950, a voluntary reopening resulted in the 10 per cent increase of September 18, 1950. The

Date	Wage Adjustment Increase	Minimum Rate per Hour
Nov. 5, 1945....	$0.08	$0.65
Aug. 5, 1946....	0.08	0.73
Jan. 6, 1947..:.	0.10	0.83
Aug. 4, 1947....	0.05	0.88
Jan. 5, 1948....	10 per cent	0.97
Sept. 18, 1950....	10 per cent	1.065
Mar. 19, 1951....	6.5 per cent (approved by WSB)	1.135
Oct. 1, 1951....	0.01 cost-of-living escalator clause	1.145
Dec. 31, 1951....	0.02 cost-of-living escalator clause	1.165

peaceful negotiations between the parties over the agreement, which expired on March 15, 1951, resulted in a new agreement for a 7.5 per cent general increase, an escalator clause, and some improvements in fringe benefits. The Wage Stabilization Board modified the general increase to 6.5 per cent and reduced slightly the rate of escalation.

The present arbitration case arises from a provision of the 2-year supplemental agreement, signed March 27, 1951, which provided: "There shall be one reopening for general wage revision on March 15, 1952, subject to arbitration in accordance with the agreement." On January 12, 1952, the Company notified the Union of its demand for a wage reduction to be effective March 15, 1952. The Union took a strong stand against any wage reduction in negotiations. The following demands are presented by the Company to the three-man tripartite arbitration board for final and binding determination in accordance with the wage reopening provision of the contract:

"(*a*) A general wage reduction of $.30 per hour. The figure of $.30 per hour is the Company's estimate of the differential in wages and fringe benefits between its plants and southern textile plants.

"(*b*) Elimination of the cost of living escalator clause and of any obligation to pay the difference between the 7.5

per cent increase negotiated in March 1951 and the 6.5 per cent approved by the Wage Stabilization Board."

It is convenient to summarize the facts and arguments presented by the Company and the Union around certain topics or headings in order to present the contending positions in sharper relief.

1. *North-South, Differential, Wage Rates*

The Company argues that the differential in average hourly earnings between its plants and the average of all southern cotton and rayon textile employees is 21 cents per hour. The Company submits the following table from Bureau of Labor Statistics data showing average hourly earnings (including overtime payments and shift differentials) for "Broad Woven Fabrics, Cotton, Silk, and Synthetic Fibers" showing regional differences in earnings:

Year	North	South	Differential
1920	52.4 cents	42.0 cents	10.4 cents
1924	46.7	31.0	15.7
1928	39.4	27.3	12.1
1932	32.3	23.9	8.4
1936	41.8	34.6	7.2
1940	47.4	39.5	7.9
1944	72.7	60.9	11.8
1946	90.9	80.9	10.0
1948	119.7	107.7	12.4
1950	126.5	117.7	8.8
1951 Jan.	136.4	125.6	11.8
July	135.8	125.3	10.5
1952 Jan.	145.6	125.5	20.1

The straight time hourly earnings for March, 1952, for "Cotton Textiles" shows $1.38 for New England and $1.17 for the Southeast, a difference of 21 cents. The Company further points out that the differential with the South has substantially increased since the outbreak of war in Korea. In September, 1950, Bates along with other northern operators, increased rates 10 per cent; in March, 1951, 6.5 per cent was added to these higher rates, and 3 cents was later added by escalator clause increases. In the South most mills raised wage rates 8 cents or 8 per cent in September, 1950, and another 2 per cent (not pyramided, but based on pre-September, 1950, wages) in the spring of 1951.

The Union, on the other hand, contends that 11.5 cents per

hour is the present differential. In the Union's view: (*a*) any valid comparison should be made with southern union mills and not with nonunion mills; and (*b*) Bates is a manufacturer of fine cotton goods and rayons, and it is improper to include southern yarn mills and producers of coarser fabrics in any comparison. The Union submitted data for five union mills which showed differences in hourly earnings of 6 to 10 cents per hour with Bates. The minimum wage at southern union plants is $1.035 compared to the $1.165 at Bates. Average hourly earnings data issued by the state departments of labor for Virginia and North Carolina showed a difference of 8 and 13 cents from Bates earnings. The BLS survey of straight time hourly earnings for March, 1952, referred to by the Company, shows $1.39 for New England and $1.27 for the Southeast for "Combed Yarn or Fabric-Integrated Mills," a difference of 12 cents.

(Arbitrator's notes: Wage rates within the northern textile industry are relatively uniform. Southern earnings vary more widely between segments of the industry, by sub-areas, and between union and nonunion plants in the south. In short, the differential between Bates and the South is not a single figure for all products and for all grouping of firms. A further fact is relevant regarding the 1951 wage rate changes. Following the negotiations in the North, the union went on strike in a number of southern union firms to secure similar increases but was unsuccessful in achieving these demands. In many mills the union was defeated, and members returned to work in some cases without contracts.)

2. *North-South Differential, Fringe Benefits*

The Company estimates its differential in fringe benefits with the South to be 9 cents in accordance with the following calculations:

FRINGE BENEFIT	CENTS PER HOUR COST		
	Bates	South	Differential
Holidays with pay	3.7	0.1	3.6
Vacations with pay	4.9	2.8	2.1
Group insurance	3.0	1.0	2.0
Third shift premium	1.4	1.0	0.4
Severance pay	0.5	...	0.5
Social security payments	2.7	2.2	0.5
Totals	16.2	7.1	9.1

The Union objects to these estimates of the Company on a number of grounds. The data for the southern mills are BLS data for April, 1950, while the Bates data are current costs. Many southern mills have increased some fringe benefits since the spring of 1950. The southern estimates do not include the costs of maintaining southern mill villages. Some southern plants have severance-pay plans. The Company has again improperly compared its figures with an average of all southern mills rather than with union mills or with fine cotton mills alone.

3. *Textile Recession and the Financial Position of the Company*

The Company emphasizes that a textile recession started right after the March, 1951, negotiations. It was this recession which defeated the Union in its efforts, which had been successful since 1945, to keep pace in the South with the increases negotiated in New England. It had negotiated similar increases in southern union mills, and at nonunion mills the constant threat of organization had induced the nonunion mills to grant similar wage increases.

More than 80 per cent of the cotton spindles are in the South and less than 20 per cent in New England. Approximately 70 per cent of the cotton and rayon looms are in the South and only 20 per cent are in New England. While almost all northern mills are unionized, over 80 per cent of the southern mills are un organized. The recession immediately after the March, 1951, settlement in New England prevented the southern textile industry from following the northern wage leadership as it had done since the end of the second world war.

The extent of the recession on Bates operation is indicated by the following statistics:

Item	March, 1951	April, 1952	Per cent Decline
Production workers	6,751	4,843	28.0
Man-hours per week	273,520	176,160	35.6
Production weekly payroll	$361,090	$247,069	32.0
Spindle hours per day	6,616,000	3,800,000	41.8
Loom hours per day	157,726	100,446	36.3

The Company believes that Bates and the New England industry have suffered much more acutely in the recession than the South:

PERCENTAGE DECLINE IN YARDS PRODUCED, 1ST QUARTER, 1951, TO
4TH QUARTER, 1951

	Bates	Other New England	Other States (South)
Fine cotton goods	30.6	32.3	13.2
Rayon flat woven goods ...	95.8	40.4	16.7

The Company emphasizes that its profit position moved from a thoroughly satisfactory position in early 1951 gradually downward to a loss position at the time of the arbitration. Profits before taxes in March–May, 1951, were at the rate of $645,000 per 4-week period; while in March–April, 1952, there was a loss of $63,000 per 4-week period. Moreover, the common stock of the Company which sold at more than $18.00 a share in March, 1951, by the end of April, 1952, had declined to $9.00.

A substantial wage reduction by the elimination of the differential is not simply a need of the Company. Employees will also benefit by competitive costs. A relatively high hourly rate is not an advantage when work is not available. A wage reduction will restore the competitive position of the Company and expand employment and reduce the present short-time.

The Company also points out that the communities in which these plants are located are dependent primarily upon textile employment and payrolls. Further loss of textile business to the South will have most serious consequences for these communities. Once business is lost to the South, it is most difficult to regain. Some 2,000 employees have been laid off since March, 1951; and one third of the remaining employees are working less than 5 days a week.

The Union, on the other hand, emphasizes that Bates is not at a disadvantage wage-wise by comparison with its New England competitors. The Bates Company is basically in a sound financial position. Since 1945 the Company has spent $12.3 millions on new and modern equipment. The Company has conceded that its location does not put it at a serious competitive disadvantage with the South on materials costs. Since 1945 the Company has operated at high levels of capacity and has made "fabulous profits." The stockholders received in the period from 1946 through 1951 dividends of $124.13 per $100 share in 1945. Cash dividends totaled $10.6 millions. The Company's net worth at the beginning of

1952 was $33.4 millions compared to $9.4 millions at the start of 1946. All of these gains came out of profits. Companies which show the high profits of this one should be expected to carry through these short periods of inactivity. Losses are to be expected in depression periods if profits are to be expected in years of prosperity. Workers cannot be expected to underwrite and guarantee profits.

The Union contends that the level of cotton textile market activity has definitely begun to rise with increasing current orders and forward buying. Prices of textiles have recently risen slightly.

The Union believes the lag in southern wage adjustments is temporary and will be overcome as business improves.

The Union points out that a substantial part of the Bates business is on trade-mark or specialty items where costs are not the only factor in ability to secure business. Indeed, about 34 per cent of its total sales in 1951 were of products carrying the Bates name. These products are not subject to the same type of price competition as the remaining 66 per cent which was sold in the grey or finished state at market or government bid prices. The record of the Company in securing government bids, according to the Union, shows that the Company is competitive despite its testimony that on recent bids it has made a loss or just broken even.

A wage cut, in the view of the Union, is an obsolete and outdated economic philosophy. The crucial factors affecting the Company's future are nonwage in character, and a wage cut would not reverse the textile recession. Wage reductions would inject a new element of uncertainty which might only prolong the recession. Competition cannot and must not be conducted at the workers' expense. We are as a nation engaged in an international conflict to maintain the dignity of man. If our economic market forces challenge this dignity and our faith in constant progress, we must provide the underpinnings which will assure it. The workers should not be asked to bear the cost of competitive forces.

4. *Relation of Bates Wages to Other Wages*

The Union emphasizes that the general trend of wage rates in the economy is upwards. The Steelworkers have been granted a wage increase of 16 cents per hour. The Union points out that unlike other unions it is not now asking for a wage increase in 1952; it only seeks to prevent a wage cut. The Union believes that no one industry or group of industries can resist general trends for long. Many of the job classifications at Bates, such as maintenance and custodial jobs, are common to other industries. The Union believes that present wages are in line with those in other industries. Over the past decade the Union has fought to raise the textile industry from a very low wage industry to a medium wage industry, which exists at present. The Union resists a return to a low wage status. The present wages do not provide a high standard of living even in full employment. The rate is well below that estimated by the BLS for an "adequate but modest" budget for a city worker's family.

The Company points out that the industries currently securing wage increases are defense industries. For a year there has been a division in the economy between defense and related industries in which wages have moved ahead and soft goods industries where employees have not received comparable increases, or have taken wage cuts in a few instances. In any event the Company contends that its problems should be decided only on the basis of the cotton and rayon industry picture and not on the basis of industry generally.

(Arbitrator's notes: In the history of wage setting in the New England cotton textile industry, the Fall River and the New Bedford associations of employers have typically negotiated first; and the wage agreements agreed upon with the Union have typically been adopted by other New England firms. The Bates mills in Maine have been significant "independents," but they have likewise followed the New Bedford-Fall River pattern. At the time this arbitration proceeding was begun, there was also pending a request for discussion of wage levels by the companies in New Bedford and Fall River. The present case would be likely to have a significant effect upon negotiations and any arbitration at New Bedford and Fall River.)

5. *Other Considerations*

The Company points out that average hourly earnings increases plus fringe benefit improvements since 1945 have amounted to a total increase of 113 per cent in comparison to a 45 per cent rise in the cost of living over this period.

The Union points out that since the March, 1951, increase these has been no improvement in the real wage. The 3-cent increase was to offset increases in the cost of living. The cost of living can be expected to increase, rather than decrease.

The Union goes on to emphasize that it has co-operated with the management in increasing man-hour productivity. Fewer workers are now required to produce the same volume of output. Their past reward was loss of jobs for some and higher earnings for those who remained. The smaller work force, if the Company is to have its way, is to have its wages cut for all its efforts. "What price co-operation?" A wage cut would demoralize and outrage the employees and, in the Union's judgment, depress the Company's productive effectiveness.

QUESTIONS

1. The Union states that a wage rate reduction is an obsolete and out-dated economic philosophy. Do you agree? Examine carefully the impact of a wage reduction in this case. What would be the effect of a wage cut in Bates relative to all other New England textile firms? What would be the effect of a wage cut in all New England mills relative to the South? Is a New England cut likely to lead to a cut of all southern textile wage rates? What assurance can management give that a wage cut will narrow the differential with the South and that a northern cut will not be followed by a southern wage reduction in the textile industry? How would you appraise the impact of a wage cut on the price of cotton textile products?

2. The Union also states that the workers should not be asked to bear the cost of competitive forces. Since the decline in the cotton textile business which began after March, 1951, the workers at Bates have been bearing some of the effects of this decline in the form of un-employment and short time. The issue now is whether they should take a cut in wage rates in the hope that the burden of unemployment and short time would be reduced. How would you appraise the effect of a proposed wage cut here on unemployment and short time?

3. What do you understand by the "north-south" differential? What factors influence this differential? How would you expect labor cost differentials to vary in comparison to earnings? What additional factors affect labor costs? Why has the differential changed in the months prior to the arbitration? How has the northern cotton textile industry been able to survive with an adverse wage differential?

4. Why did nonunion southern cotton textile firms in the postwar period follow the wage leadership of the unionized northern mills? Why did they not do so in the spring of 1951? Can they be counted upon to do so in the future?

5. How do you appraise the argument that the Company should pay present wages even though it has just begun to lose money since it has had a prolonged period of satisfactory profits? The Union says that losses are to be expected in depression periods if profits are to be expected in years of prosperity. What does ability to pay mean? Does it refer to current profits? Profits over several years? Over the life of a firm? Would your position on the question of losses vary depending on whether you were considering a competitive industry like textiles or some more monopolistic industry? How frequently should wage rates be adjusted?

6. What assurances can the Company give that a wage cut will expand employment? Explain how the Company believes this expansion will take place. Would you advise the Union to propose a conditional reduction, wage rates would be restored when business of the Company had improved as measured by some index such as production or profits?

7. What are the prospects of this Company moving to the South? Would a company have to lose money for a substantial period before moving to the South? What interest have the employees or the Union in this matter?

8. Should these workers take a cut when other workers are receiving increases and the cost of living is rising?

9. How would you appraise the demand of the Company to eliminate the escalator clause? Is the issue a proper subject for arbitration under a wage reopening clause which permits consideration of general wage changes?

10. How would you appraise the effects of a wage reduction on worker morale and productivity? Would workers turn out more or less output? What are the contending arguments? Would it make any difference depending upon the way in which a reduction was explained?

11. The present case arises in a firm which has not been the wage leader in the northern textile industry in the past. Why do you suppose this is the case? Would this fact influence your decision?

Case 48

SHOULD WAGES FOLLOW A PREVIOUS PATTERN?

UNION: United Textile Workers of America, AFL

COMPANY: Hudson Worsted Company

The Union exercised its right under the contract to reopen the matter of wages 60 days prior to February, 1952. Since the parties were unable to reach an agreement, the issue of a wage adjustment was submitted to arbitration. The relevant contract clauses are as follows:

"Article VI (*Wages*), Section 7. Except as changes may be made by or pursuant to the provisions of this agreement, there shall be no changes in wage rates during the life of this agreement, but both parties reserve the right to take up the question of workloads and general wage adjustments, upward or downward, across the board, or in separate classification, twice a year, by giving notice, in writing, at least sixty (60) days prior to February 1 or August 1 of any contractual year. Upon receipt of such written notice, the parties shall immediately negotiate the request, and if they are unable to agree within thirty (30) days after February 1st or August 1st, as the case may be, the matter may be referred to arbitration by either party for final determination . . . .

"Article VI, Section 8. All wage revisions shall become effective on the first of February or the first of August."

BACKGROUND

Since the Union became the collective bargaining agent in 1945, the general wage increases put into effect have, for the most part, reflected the pattern of wage movements in the industry. Similarly, throughout this period, fringe benefits were granted which paralleled those generally made in the industry.

The history of the 1951 wage adjustment of $0.095 per hour is of significance to the present case. Under Article VI, Section 7, the Union wrote the Company on November 30, 1950, indicating its desire to reopen the wage question; it asked for a 10 per cent general wage increase and an increase in the minimum rate, pensions, and other fringe benefits. Subsequently, the American Woolen Company, an acknowledged pattern-setter in the industry, was struck by the Textile Workers Union of America, CIO, a rival union; and a settlement between those parties was not made until March 15, 1951. The wage negotiations with the present Company were postponed by mutual agreement until the American Woolen Company settlement was known. When the "leader's" pattern was set at 12 cents per hour retroactive to February 1, 1951, plus an escalator clause, this Union revised its demands to conform with the pattern. Still, uncertainty existed in the minds of the "followers" pending final action by the Wage Stabilization Board. It was not until August, 1951, that the Board acted on the American Woolen Company petition; it approved a general wage increase of $0.095 effective February 1, 1951, and an escalator formula of 1 cent per hour increase for each 1.18 points increase in the index. Immediately thereafter the subject parties resumed serious negotiations in the light of the industry pattern and the W.S.B. decision. The final agreement, reached November 13, 1951, provided for a retroactive $0.095 wage rate increase; the escalator clause and other economic benefits were not provided for in the settlement.

POSITION OF THE UNION

The Union is seeking a general increase of 3 cents per hour, which reflects the wage boost which thousands of textile workers secured under the operation of the escalator clauses adopted in the industry. The claim is based on the cost-of-living changes and the industry pattern. In view of the consistent adherence in the past to industry patterns, there is no reason why the employees of this Company should not also receive the 3 cents cost-of-living adjustment.

From February 1, 1951 (the effective date of the last increase), to February 1, 1952, the cost-of-living index increased by an amount which justifies the Union request. The Union finds no special circumstances in Hudson Worsted Company, such as inability to pay, which would warrant a disregard for the historical practice of observing the industry trend; on the contrary, if the arbitrator were to deny the adjustment, it would give this Company an undeserved competitive advantage and would undermine confidence in the machinery of arbitration.

The Company has argued that the November 13, 1951, agreement clearly omitted the escalator clause and that the Union is foreclosed now from seeking that increase which stems from the operation of such clauses throughout the industry. This argument has no validity. First, the Company never bargained constructively about the escalator principle in 1951 because it maintained that such a clause was not within the range of admissible demands under Article VI. Second, the Union informed the Company in November, 1951, that it would seek a wage increase in February, 1952, to reflect the cost of living. Third, the cost-of-living change and the industry pattern are proper criteria for the arbitrator to consider irrespective of the history of the 1951 wage negotiations.

POSITION OF THE COMPANY

It is apparent that the Union demand for 3 cents stems from the operation of escalator clauses in the industry. An award for the Union would be the exact equivalent of granting to the employees a wage increase based on provisions of other contracts in the industry, negotiated and executed prior to the November 13, 1951, agreement of the parties. The arbitrator is reminded that Article X, Section 2, provides that "No arbitrator shall have the power to add to or subtract from the terms of this agreement." The fact that the Union asked for an escalator clause in 1951 and subsequently accepted a $0.095 per hour increase retroactive to February 1, 1951, with no escalator clause means that the Union definitely bargained away its right for an adjustment which could stem only from the operation of an escalator clause.

The Company believes that the wage equities were satisfied *as of* the date of the November 13, 1951, settlement. There has been no *general wage adjustment* in the industry since that date. Further, the change in the index since November, 1951, would not justify the union demand. There has been only a 0.9 point change in the index, short of the 1.18 point change needed under the industry escalator formula to justify a 1 cent per hour increase.

The Company reminds the arbitrator that an award favoring the Union should in all fairness be accompanied by some method for providing relief to the Company in the event of a decline in the index; this is the privilege of other companies in the industry. But if this were done, the arbitrator would be adding to the contract in violation of Article X. This dilemma points up the difficulty of accepting the Union position under any cicumstance.

Finally the Company pointed to the depresed business conditions of the past year. As a commission wool combing company, its position is not as favorable as those combing firms owned or controlled by cloth-making concerns. It was recognition of this vulnerable position which prompted company representatives in the November, 1951, negotiations with the Union to avoid the fluctuations in labor costs which stem from an escalator clause. If wages go up automatically with the cost of living, the Company is not in a position to recover the loss; it has no inventory, and it is not able to get into its contracts with customers an adjusted price provision.

Business volume has fallen from 1.2 million pounds in August, 1950, to an average of less than a million pounds monthly during 1951 and to a further low of 0.6 million pounds in the first 4 months of 1952. This decline is reflected in employment: 1950—616 employees; 1951—540 employees; and 1952—448 employees. The Union's request comes at a time when additional cost burdens can only serve to aggravate an already depressed condition.

QUESTIONS

1. What are the merits of using February, 1951, as compared to November,1951, as a date from which to measure any change in the cost of living? Did the settlement in November, 1951, effective February 1, 1951, eliminate all claims based on living cost increases in the period February to November? What weight do you attach to the industry pattern in this case?

2. Must a firm remain a wage follower if it has been one in the past? Would the Union's interests in the industry as a whole suffer if it granted special consideration to particular firms?

3. What are the conditions which give rise to wage leadership? Are they to be explained in terms of economic, locational, or unionization factors? Compare the conditions in the textile industry with those of other industries in which wage leadership is practiced.

4. Is the Company consistent when it maintains that the Union bargained away its right to a cost-of-living adjustment at the same time that it claims that the introduction of an escalator clause was improper at the time of the wage reopening? Did the Union bargain away its right to seek a cost of living or any other kind of wage adjustment?

5. What is a wage reopening clause? Are there advantages to the parties in adopting such a clause?

6. If a wage increase is now granted, does the Company have any remedy if the cost of living drops and wages in other mills are adjusted accordingly?

7. Discuss the advantages and disadvantages to each of the parties of an escalator provision.

Case 49

THE APPEAL TO DIVERSE WAGE STANDARDS

UNION: Amalgamated Association of Street, Electric Railway and
Motor Coach Employees of America, AFL

COMPANY: Indianapolis Railways, Inc.

The arbitration proceedings arise over a demand of Division
1070, Amalgamated Association of Street, Electric Railway and
Motor Coach Employees of America, for a general wage rate increase of $0.30 an hour to be effective May 1, 1947. The request
of the Union was made under the following reopening provision
of the contract, entered into as of December 1, 1946, and
to continue until April 30, 1948:

"It is further agreed by the Company and the Association
that either party shall have the right to request changes in
the wages at any time from and after May 1, 1947, upon
giving the other party sixty (60) days' notice in writing, delivered by registered mail, and that such requested changes
shall be subject to arbitration in the same manner as provided
in Section 7 of this agreement."

THE PARTIES

Indianapolis Railways, Inc., was established as a reorganization of the Indianapolis Street Railway Company and took over the
transportation system from a receiver on June 1, 1932. Transit
operations in Indianapolis date from 1864.

The Company provides mass transportation by streetcar, trackless trolley, and bus, servicing a city with a population over 400,-
000. It operated 63.3 miles of track, 62 miles of trackless trolley,
and 143.5 miles of motor coach routes as of December 31, 1946.
On the same date, the Company operated 446 streetcars and motor
coaches and employed 1,606 employees. At the end of 1946, a
total of 1,432 employees were in job classifications covered by the
agreement with the Union, of whom 894 were operators. At the
time of the hearings, total employment amounted to 1,775, with
1,575 represented by the Union.

Indianapolis Railways, Inc., operates under a 99-year lease

the property of the Traction Terminal Corporation which consists of an office building, bus terminal, and parking lot.

Division 1070, Amalgamated Association of Street, Electric Railway and Motor Coach Employees of America, is the collective bargaining agency for operators and maintenance employees of the Company. The Union also represents in the same unit the employees engaged in operating the office building of the Traction Terminal Corporation. The current contract contains a list of all job classifications covered by the agreement. Division 1070 was organized in 1936.

POSITION OF THE UNION

The following major points are advanced by the Union in support of its request for a general wage-rate increase of $0.30 per hour.

1. The Union makes a number of comparisons with the rates for (one-man) operators in Indianapolis with those in effect on transit systems in other cities. The use of the rate for operators in intercity and intercompany comparisons is in accord with the long-established practices of collective bargaining in the transit industry. Such comparisons were also utilized in the wage stabilization program developed for this industry.[1]

a) The present rate of $1.20 per hour for operators in Indianoplis is compared with the rates in effect on all other properties in the country serving populations of 400,000 or more and under contract with this international union. There were 19 such companies with a weighted average rate in August, 1947, of $1.34 for those companies that had established 1947 rates. The Union contends there is a movement in these cities toward the rate of $1.50 per hour requested in this case.

b) The Union submits a list of transit companies in which the rate for operators in August, 1947, was $1.30 per hour or more by agreement with the international union. The list included 28 companies.

c) The Union also indicated the extent of wage-rate increases for the operator's rate from V-J Day to August, 1947, in these companies with rates in August, 1947, of $1.30 per hour or more under contract with the international union. The average increase

[1] *Policy Directive Regarding Wage Adjustments for Transit Company Employees,* issued by Economic Stabilization Director, April 14, 1944.

(unweighted) calculated from the data presented by the Union yields $0.361 per hour increase from V-J Day to August, 1947.

d) The Union compares the pattern of wage-rate changes for operators in the period since 1939 in Indianapolis Railways, Inc., with those in the Connecticut Company and the Connecticut Railway and Lighting Company. The Union selected these companies on the grounds that the population served, number of vehicles operated, number of employees, total revenue, revenue per mile, hours, and vacation provisions of the contracts are all comparable to the Indianapolis operations. In the case of Indianapolis Railways, Inc., the operator's rate rose from $0.70 on May 1, 1939, to a current rate of $1.20. During the same period, the rate in the Connecticut Company rose from $0.69 to $1.35.

2. The Union makes a number of comparisons with rates paid outside the transit industry in the Indianapolis area and with national averages for other industries.

a) The Union compares rates for a number of job classifications in the shops division (electrician, machinist, painter, etc.,) and the Terminal Building (janitor) with rates for job classifications it regards as comparable in industrial plants in the Indianapolis area. The Union cites rates in the General Motors Corporation, Marmon-Herrington Company, Inc., Chevrolet Commercial Body and United States Rubber Company to show that maintenance and custodial rates are $0.20 to $0.30 lower in Indianapolis Railways, Inc.

b) The Union also refers to the average hourly earnings reported by the Bureau of Labor Statistics for a number of industries —automobiles, iron and steel, machinery, printing, petroleum and coal, rubber products, and transportation equipment. The Union points out that the national averages for these industries range between $1.33 and $1.49 per hour compared to a weighted average of $1.179 for operators on Indianapolis Railways, Inc. (The average is less than $1.20, the top rate, because of lower rates for operators with less than 2 years' experience.) The Union emphasizes that the averages for these manufacturing industries include unskilled and semiskilled workers, while operators constitute a group of skilled workers. The Union stresses the skilled character of the work of the operator as a factor warranting comparison with highly skilled jobs in other industries rather than merely with average earnings for all employees in other industries.

3. The Union contends that these employees are entitled to share in the benefits of increasing productivity that normally takes place in the country as a whole. "I think it is an accepted axiom of American ideals, as well as the necessities of the American economy, that there be a gradual improvement in the real purchasing power of the American employee generally."

The Union points out that the real wage rate of operators for June 15, 1947, was only 7.1 per cent over that of May 15, 1939. (The hourly rate increased 71.4 per cent, but the cost of living rose 60.1 per cent in the same period.) The Union compares this 7.1 per cent rise in real wage rate with an increase of 26.7 per cent which would have taken place had the real wage increased cumulatively 3 per cent per annum over the period since 1939, a rate of increase which the Union regards as "normal." A rate of $1.42 or an increase of $0.22 would be necessary to provide these employees with the "normal" increase in real purchasing power.

The Union presents correlate estimates for the movement of real monthly earnings. Monthly earnings for operators in this case were reported to be $242.91 for June, 1947. This constituted only a 3.2 per cent increase in real monthly earnings over those of May, 1939. Weekly earnings in real terms in manufacturing as a whole are 32 per cent over May, 1939. The Union compares the 3.2 per cent rise in real monthly earnings with a rise of 26.7 per cent which would have yielded a 3 per cent per annum increase in real earnings since 1939, a rate of increase the Union regards as "normal."

4. The Union cites the cost of purchasing the Heller quantity-and-cost budget for a family of a man, wife, and two children as a basis for its wage demands. The Union estimates that the cost in June, 1947, of purchasing this budget in Indianapolis to be $3,210.05. The annual wage of operators, even after an hourly rate increase of $0.30, would amount to $3,156.00 calculated on a 40-hour week for 50 weeks a year (including 25 minutes per day for preparatory and turn-in time). This figure would not cover the $3,210.00 estimated cost of the Heller budget in Indianapolis in June, 1947.

The Union emphasizes the point that current weekly and monthly earnings contain substantial overtime payments. The Union estimates that actual hourly earnings would be reduced $0.173 if all work over 40 hours each week were eliminated, except preparatory and turn-in time. The Union believes that the earnings of the operators should be judged on the basis of the contract workweek of 40 hours.

5. The Union repeatedly urges that special weight be attached to the fact that during the 1930's the transit industry was depressed relative to other industries and as a consequence wage rates were kept below their appropriate level. The wartime prosperity of the industry could not be adequately reflected in wage rates because of the wage stabilization program. The Union contends that larger increases have recently been negotiated or arbitrated on other transit properties than in industry generally, reflecting recognition of these factors that retarded rates in this industry for many years.

6. The Union points out that a wage-rate increase is required to restore the real wage rate freely bargained between the parties at the conclusion of the wage stabilization program. On March 10, 1946, the wage rate was raised to $1.05 per hour (plus a $0.035 bonus) for operators by agreement. Between March, 1946, and June 15, 1947, the cost-of-living index for Indianapolis rose 21.5 per cent. Wage rates have risen only 10.6 per cent in the same period (when account is taken of the withdrawal of the bonus). An increase of "ten per cent or more" would be required merely to restore the real wage freely bargained between the parties at their first opportunity after the end of wage controls.

The Union points out, moreover, that in the immediate future the cost of living may be expected to rise further. The recent increases in the wholesale price index were introduced to support this conclusion.

7. The Union regards considerations of ability to pay advanced by the Company in these proceedings as irrelevant to a determination of the issue in dispute. The Union believes that an examination of the financial condition of the Company will refute the contention of the Company that it cannot afford an increase.

The Union cites the opinion of the Supreme Court in *Ames et al.* vs. *Union Pacific Railway Company*. It refers to a number of recent arbitration awards and opinions in cases in the transit industry to suport the view that wages should be fixed without particular attention to ability to pay. In the words of one recent arbitration opinion cited by the Union:

"Wage rates are fixed by objective standards, just as are the prices of materials and products. It is the duty of this Board to fix wage rates on the basis of those objective standards. Public Service Commissions and courts must determine for themselves what their duties are . . . ."[2]

The Union contends that if consideration is given in these proceedings to the higher costs of materials and new equipment, which are partly attributable to wage increases in other industries, the Company is in effect asking transit employees to "contribute" part of the wage increase granted to other workers.

8. The Union believes that the pending fare case before the Public Service Commission and the courts should be no bar to a wage-rate increase. The Union holds that it is the task of the duly constituted public body to set fares. The arbitration board is charged with the responsibility of determining a fair and equitable wage rate. "We do not feel that the employees of Indianapolis Railways should be called upon to subsidize the cost of transportation to the public in the form of the wage rates that are now being paid."

POSITION OF THE COMPANY

The Company advances the following major points in support of its position that no general wage-rate increase should be awarded in these proceedings.

1. The employees of Indianapolis Railways, Inc., can have no case for a wage-rate increase on the basis of increased living costs. The Company voluntarily agreed to two general wage-rate increases aggregating $0.27 an hour during 1946. One increase was for $0.15, effective March 10, and the other increase amounted to $0.12, effective December 1. (The second increase in rates was $0.15 per hour, while a bonus which amounted to $0.03 per hour was discontinued.)

During the period March 10, 1946, to June, 1947, the cost of living for Indianapolis increased 21.5 per cent, from an index of 130 to 158 (1935–39 equals 100), while the net increase in the operator's rate of $0.27 equals an increase of 29 per cent over the

---

[2] *In re Gary Railways, Inc. and Division 517 of the Amalgamated Association of Street, Electric Railway and Motor Coach Employees of America, Award of June 23, 1947.*

rates in effect prior to March 10, 1946 ($0.93 per hour including bonus).

If wage rates and the cost of living are compared for the period since January, 1941, the base date for the wage stabilization program, the employees are entitled to no increase. The operator's rate increased from $0.72 cents in January, 1941, to the current rate of $1.20, an increase of 66.7 per cent. The cost-of-living index for Indianapolis for June, 1947, was 54.9 per cent higher than in January, 1941. Moreover, except for a brief period in 1942, the real wage rate throughout the period 1941–47 was higher than in January, 1941. At the present time, it is higher than at any other time.

2. The Company emphasizes the date, April 6, 1944, as appropriate for a base from which to compare the rise in wage rates and living costs. On that date the Director of Economic Stabilization approved an operator's rate of $0.90 per hour on this property. The top stabilization authority found the $0.90 rate to be the maximum sound and tested rate at that time. Between April, 1944, and June, 1947, the cost-of-living index for Indianapolis rose 27 per cent. In the same period the operator's rate increased 33.3 per cent. If the bonus, equal to $0.04, be added to the operator's rate for April, 1944, the wage per hour increased 27.7 per cent. In either event, wage rates have risen more than the cost of living since the date of the decision of the Director of Economic Stabilization.

3. The Company points out that there is no basis for a wage-rate increase in that the weekly earnings of the operators have increased more than the cost of living. The operator's average weekly earnings in the 6-month period January 1 to June 30, 1947, was $55.96 compared to $32.85 in the 6-month period November 1, 1940, to April 30, 1941. In this comparison, weekly earnings have increased 13.5 per cent more than the cost of living in Indianapolis.

A similar comparison is made with the 6-month period September 1, 1945, to February 28, 1946, during which the 44-hour week was still effective. In that period the operator's average weekly earnings were $45.43, as compared with $55.96 for the period January 1 to June 30, 1947. In this comparison, likewise, the operator's weekly earnings have increased more than the cost of living in Indianapolis.

4. The Company contends that there are no grounds for a wage increase on the criterion of comparison of the $1.20 rate in effect for operators in Indianapolis with the rates in effect in other comparable cities. The Company points out that there are many cities with a population of 400,000 or more which do not have a rate even as high as $1.20.

The Company presents a wage comparison with the 9 cities in the north central section of the country with population of 400,000 or more which shows that between January, 1941, and August, 1947, the operator's rate in Indianapolis has increased $0.48, which is equal to or greater than the increase in 6 of the cities. Only Chicago, Detroit, and Cleveland, with $0.54, $0.56, and $0.49 increases respectively over January, 1941, exceed the increase in Indianapolis.

Moreover, the Company argues that, when two additional factors are taken into account, the intercity position of the Indianapolis operator's rate appears even more favorable:

a) The cost of living in Indianapolis is relatively lower than in other cities of comparable size in the North Central States. Living costs in Indianapolis rank eighth in a group of 9 cities. The relative position of Indianapolis has remained unchanged since 1942. The cost of a budget for a 4-person manual worker's family at maintenance levels in Indianapolis is estimated for June 15, 1947, to be $2,035.19 compared to $2,268.02 in Chicago. The difference in living costs should be considered in comparing rates between cities.

b) The fare structure of Indianapolis Railways, Inc., is relatively lower than other cities of comparable size. The present fare in Indianapolis is $0.10, or 3 tokens for $0.25. In Detroit and Chicago, for example, there are no tokens; and the fares are $0.20 and $0.09 respectively. The Company argues that these fare differences are significant in intercity comparisons of wage levels. (The problem of the level of fares in Indianapolis is discussed in detail below.)

The Company emphasizes, moreover, the unique aspects of Indianapolis. The question before the arbitration board is the rate in Indianapolis. Other rates can only be of limited relevance. "We cannot extend our business out of this state or this city . . . . When you begin to compare wage rates in different areas you must know all the facts as to what makes for a fair wage determination or a permissible wage determination."

The Company points to the fact that, at the present time, and continuously since 1938 except for two brief periods during the war, the average weekly earnings of its operators have exceeded the weekly earnings for the average of all manufacturing in the Indianapolis area and, further, that since 1938 employment in the Company's service has been regular and has shown a steady increase, while employment for all manufacturing in the Indianapolis area has been subject to severe fluctuations. It contends that such regularity and continuity of employment is an important factor to be taken into account in determining the wage rates to be paid by the Company.

The Company points out that the wage rates which it now pays in the Traction Terminal Building are greatly in excess of those paid by competitive office buildings in the city of Indianapolis and contends that the wage rates to be paid by this Company for those classifications should be determined with relation to those of its competitors.

5. The Company refers to the many special compensation provisions of its agreement with the Union. These provisions include premium time for a spread in excess of $11\frac{1}{2}$ hours per day, 8 hours' pay for runs having as much as 7 hours and less than 8 hours, 16 minutes' paid preparatory time, paid turn-in time, paid travel time, minimum pay time of 3 hours, etc.

6. The Company holds that "a dangerous imbalance already exists between that part of the Company's revenue which is required to pay its labor cost and what is left of its revenue for other requirements, and that imbalance would be aggravated by a further increase in labor costs." The Company compares the movement of operators' total payroll and gross revenue to show payrolls have increased substantially relative to revenue. It also compares the movement of operators' total payroll in dollars with car miles operated to show that, while units of transportation service have increased only 20 per cent since 1940, the dollar labor cost of said units of service has increased 180 per cent. The Company cites the fact that operating expenses have risen from 65.5 per cent of transportation gross revenue in 1936 to 70.5 per cent in 1945 and 84.7 per cent in 1946. (Revenue excludes money impounded in the fare proceedings in the courts.)

7. The Company is a public utility, and the fares it charges for transportation services are subject to public regulation. "So as a practical consideration this employer cannot even fix its prices to undertake to absorb the increased wage; it is between two millstones in that regard and is doing its best to keep from being ground to pieces itself." In the view of the Company, the fares prescribed by the Public Service Commission will not allow the Company to pay any further wage-rate increase and remain solvent. Since June 29, 1943, the Company has been in continuous dispute before the Public Service Commission and the courts concerning its fare structure.

The unions which represent the employees of the Company, including that involved in these proceedings, intervened in the fare proceedings to impress the commission that they have an interest in what the rates and the revenues of this utility are.

The principal features and events of the controversy over the fare structure are outlined in the following paragraphs. These developments indicate how slow and difficult it has been for the Company to secure any increase in fares despite substantial increases in operating costs.

a) From the organization of the Company on June 1, 1932, until September 15, 1945, the same fare structure was in effect as charged by the predecessor company. That structure consisted of a $0.07 cash fare on streetcars and trackless trolley cars, with a token fare of 0.06\frac{1}{4}$ (4 for $0.25), a charge of $0.02 for transferring from through-line to through-line and a $0.10 straight cash fare for motorbus lines.

b) As an outgrowth of proceedings that had been initiated in 1943, the Public Service Commission entered a temporary order, effective September 15, 1945, for a 90-day trial schedule consisting of a $0.10 cash fare, a token fare of 0.06\frac{7}{8}$ (8 for $0.55), and a transfer charge of $0.02 on all vehicles. This schedule was in effect until January 20, 1946.

c) The Commission on January 9, 1946, reduced the token fare in the trial rate schedule from 0.06\frac{7}{8}$ to 0.06\frac{1}{4}$. The Company objected to this action but agreed to a 90-day trial period on this reduced schedule. The Company states that revenue was reduced $90,000 per month from the trial schedule introduced on September 15, 1945, and $30,000 below the revenue derived from the rate schedule in effect from 1926.

d) Following the wage-rate increase of March 10, 1946, the Company petitioned the Commission for an emergency rate schedule of a $0.10 cash fare, an $0.08⅓ token fare, and a $0.02 transfer charge. After this petition had been denied by the Commission on June 27, 1946, the Marion Circuit Court on August 12, 1946, issued a temporary injunction enjoining enforcement of the order and prohibiting the Commission from interfering with the collection of the higher emergency fare schedule until final hearing and judgment. The court ordered, however, the difference between the $0.08⅓ and the $0.06¼ token fare impounded until final determination of the case. On April 17, 1947, the Supreme Court of Indiana affirmed the temporary injunction.[3] A sum of $1,382,172.18 was impounded while the temporary injunction was in effect. The Marion Circuit Court subsequently entered a permanent injunction against the Commission enjoining it from enforcing its June 27, 1946, order and from interfering with the $0.08⅓ token rate until the Commission fixes nonconfiscatory fares. The impounded funds were ordered turned over to the Company. The Commission has appealed this final injunction to the Supreme Court of Indiana.

e) Since November 30, 1945, the Company has been seeking from the Public Service Commission, under Clause No. 17782, a full investigation to determine "just and reasonable" fares. The Company has repeatedly presented to the Commission additional information as wage and other costs have changed. On July 1, 1947, the Commission entered a rate order providing for a $0.10 cash fare, an $0.08⅓ token fare, all transfers to be free, and required the Company to submit a schedule for a $0.05 school fare. The reduction in revenue from the present schedule the Company estimates to be $450,000 a year. The July 1, 1946, order is under review in an appeal now pending in the Circuit Court of Hancock County.

8. The Company estimates that each cent-per-hour wage increase would cost the Company approximately $37,800 a year. This estimate is derived from the fact that during the first half of 1947 the Company paid for 1,889,652 hours of work (exclusive of student operators). The demand of the Union for $.30 per hour would increase operating costs by more than $1,100,000. This estimate of the cost of the demand of the

[3] 72 N.E. 2nd 434.

Union is to be appraised in terms of the financial position of the Company.

a) Any examination of the financial position of the Company must take into consideration the fact that revenue for 1946 and 1947 will depend on whether the Company ultimately receives funds impounded by court order. Whether depreciation is figured in accordance with the books of the Company or in accordance with that approved by the Public Service Commission in its rate order of July 1, 1947, will also affect the measurement of the financial position of the Company.

At one extreme, if the impounded funds are not granted to the Company ultimately and depreciation is figured on the basis of the books of the Company, the first half of the year 1947 will show a loss of $521,222.13. At the other extreme, if the impounded funds are awarded to the Company and depreciation is calculated as ordered by the Commission, the first half of the year 1947 will show net income before taxes of $285,006.81, or $176,704.22 after taxes. If the fares as ordered by the Commission on July 1, 1947, were to have been in effect during the first half of 1947, the Company would have shown a loss of $53,655.92 using its depreciation methods, or a profit of $20,-052.73 after taxes if the depreciation methods approved by the Company were used. These figures in the view of the Company indicate no room for any wage adjustment.

b) The Company points out that gross revenue has been falling as a result of reduction in traffic. Through the first 7 months of 1947 total passengers carried were 66,350,904, compared with 69,515,068 for the same period of 1946—a decrease of 3,164,164. This reduction in volume may be expected to continue.

The Company stresses the unfavorable underlying conditions and long-term trends to which the transit industry is subject. It further points out that the prewar wage rates in the transit industry, to which the Union refers as unduly depressed, in reality reflected the economic impact of these conditions and trends. The Company contends that the industries with which the Union makes comparison are not subject to the special factors which have influenced the transit industry. It emphasizes that at the present time these unfavorable trends are becoming increasingly manifest, particularly in the form of declining traffic, increasing competition from the private automobile, and increasing operating costs over which the Company has little control.

c) The Company emphasizes that the cost of materials and new equipment has risen substantially. These increases further limit the capacity of the Company to pay any wage increase.

d) The Company stockholders have gone a total of nearly 11 years of its 15 years of existence without dividends. No dividend has been paid since March, 1946. A further wage increase would deny the stockholders all opportunity for a dividend.

9. The Company emphasizes its record of modernization of equipment and service in its statement that:

> "You are not dealing with an employer who is indifferent to its obligations to the public but one that has done and wants to do its best. You are not dealing with an employer that is indifferent to its employees, or believes in low wages . . . but you are dealing with an employer who wants to stay alive and well."

10. The Company rejects the contention of the Union that the Heller budget is applicable to this case. The Company points out that 1,282 out of 1,741 employees claim 2 or less dependents, compared to the 3 (family of 4) assumed in the Heller budget calculations.

11. The Company concludes that "if any wage increase is awarded it should be conditioned on obtaining approval from the (Public Service) Commission of a commensurate increase in the Company's rates (fares)." The Company points out that in a recent arbitration between the Amalgamated and the Oklahoma City Company a wage increase provided in the award was made conditional upon the granting of an increase in fares and that in recent contracts negotiated between the Amalgamated and the Portland, Oregon, and Chattanooga, Tennessee companies wage increases were similarly conditioned.

The Company calls attention to the fact that recent arbitration awards in some 8 cases in the transit industry, particularly at Kansas City, Missouri, and St. Louis, Missouri, expressly take into account the ability or inability of the employer to pay the wage increases contended for, referring to conditions similar to those under which this Company operates as reasons for refusing wage increases which might have been justified by other standards and rejecting union contentions that the financial condition of the employer should be wholly disregarded. These awards stress the fact that the transit industry is not only a public utility which is not at liberty to increase its charges at will and is subject to rate regulation by public authorities but also a public utility of a very special kind, which is subject to competition in various forms and to economic hazards with which other public utilities do not have to contend. They call attention to the long history of receiverships and reorganizations in the transit field with their resulting large losses to investors, the declining trends in traffic, the necessity for constant modernization of system and equipment, the necessity for attracting new capital for the purpose of carrying out such programs, and the necessity for providing in revenues for the retirement of property made obsolete thereby. And they call attention to the danger of resort to public subsidies or municipal ownership with their burdens upon the taxpayer.

ANALYSIS OF THE ARBITRATION BOARD

The question presented in these proceedings is a straight forward wage-rate issue—the extent of a general wage-rate increase, if any. The Company and the Union have each suggested different standards by which the arbitration board is invited to measure the appropriateness of the demand for a general increase. Moreover, the same standards have been applied quite differently by the two sides.

The Union pointed to higher rates in some companies and localities; the Company referred to lower rates in other situations. The Union cited the rise in living costs from the first post-war negotiations; the Company pointed to the comparative movements of wage rates and living costs from earlier dates. The Union held that the employees in question are entitled to the "normal" increase in productivity in American industry; the Company insisted it cannot afford any further wage-rate increase. As is normally the case in wage issues, the parties have appealed to conflicting standards or have applied a proposed criterion in conflicting ways.

The problem presented to the arbitration board is consequently that of appraising and balancing conflicting standards.

The task is to decide how much weight to give to one standard as compared to another. The case presents no serious dispute over facts; they have been carefully and clearly presented by the parties. The decision must consequently be a judgment of the relative significance to be assigned to each of the standards proposed by the parties. The arbitration board has not attempted to develop any criteria or standards of its own; it has applied only those proposed by the parties. There can be no simple formula nor system for determining the wage rate.

The principal standards proposed by the parties are briefly summarized below, including the wage rate which each standard or each interpretation of a standard would yield. The discussion is confined to the rate for operators in accordance with the collective bargaining practice in the industry and the explicit argument of both parties in these proceedings.

1. *Cost of Living.* Both parties compare the movement of the operator's rate and the cost-of-living index for Indianapolis. But the Company and the Union propose different base dates for this comparison. The Company proposes January, 1941, used in the Wage Stabilization Program, and April 6, 1944, the date on which a $0.90 rate was approved on this property by the Director of Economic Stabilization. The Union proposes to compare the movement of the operator's rate and living costs from the date of the first postwar wage-rate increase, March 10, 1946. The Union holds that the real wage rate established in these "free" collective bargaining negotiations should at least be maintained.

The increases in the operator's rate and living costs from selected dates are summarized in the accompanying table.

TABLE 1

	Operator's Rate*		Index of Living Costs, 1935–39 Equals 100
January, 1941	$0.72		102.0
April, 1944	0.90	(0.94)	124.4
March, 1946	1.05	(1.085)	130.0
June, 1946	1.20		158.0
Percentage increase:			
January, 1941–June, 1947	66.7%		54.9%
April, 1944–June, 1947	33.3	(27.7)	27.0
March, 1946–June, 1947	14.3	(10.6)	21.5

* The operator's rate and percentage changes in parentheses include the bonus in the operator's rate.

The choice of the base period is clearly decisive for the question whether any wage-rate increase is appropriate solely on the criterion of the cost of living. The base periods proposed by the Company yield no wage-rate increase under the cost-of-living standard, while the base period urged by the Union indicates an increase of $0.132. The strictest application of the cost-of-living standard, from the base dates proposed by the Company, would indicate a decrease in wage rates since they have risen more than living costs.

2. *Rate Levels in Other Transit Companies.* The Company and the Union both refer to the level of wage rates for operators on transit properties in other cities. Both parties are agreed, apparently, that size of population served is a decisive factor limiting comparisons since each side presented comparisons with properties serving cities with a population of 400,000 or more. The Union stressed rates on those properties organized by the Amalgamated. The Company presented rates on all properties in this population group, including those unorganized or under contract with other unions. The unweighted average of the operator's rate in the companies cited by the Company is $1.245 or $0.045 more than the current rate in effect in Indianapolis Railways, Inc. The Company also compared the level of rates in Indianapolis with the rates in effect on August 15, 1947, on 9 properties in other cities having a population of 400,000 or more in the north central part of the United States. The unweighted average rate was $1.256. The average of the operator's rates in the list of companies cited by the Union was $1.341, or $0.141 more than the rates currently in effect in Indianapolis. There is one further difference between these averages, aside from the question of contract with the Amalgamated. The Union's average only includes properties on which a rate "has been established for 1947," while that calculated from Company data includes all company rates in the size-of-city group as of August 15, 1947.

The parties in their previous collective bargaining have not regarded the rates in any other single city or the rates in any fairly carefully defined group of cities as decisive to wage-rate determination in Indianapolis.

3. *Rate Increase in Other Transit Companies.* The application of the standard rate increases in other transit companies

can yield divergent results, not only because different companies are included in the group used for comparative purposes but also because different periods are selected for the wage-rate changes. The Union reports that wage-rate increases have averaged (unweighted) $0.361 per hour between V-J Day and August 15, 1947, for a group of companies in which the rate equaled or exceeded $1.30 per hour on the later date. On this standard an increase of $0.09 is appropriate since Indianapolis rates have increased $0.27 since V-J Day.

The Company refers to the $0.48 per hour increase in the operator's rate on Indianapolis Railways, Inc., since January, 1941, compared to the increases granted in the same period on 9 properties in the North Central States serving cities of comparable size. The Indianapolis increases are exceeded only by Chicago, Detroit, and Cleveland ($0.54, $0.56, and $0.49 respectively).

4. *"Normal" Increase in Productivity.* The Union proposed that the "normal" increase in productivity in American industry, which the Union holds to be 3 per cent per year, be used as a standard in this case. The Union finds that since 1939 the real wage rate has risen 7.1 per cent, while an increase of 26.7 per cent would be appropriate on this standard. An increase of $0.22 per hour the Union seeks to justify on this basis. The Company rejects this standard.

5. *Ability to Pay and Fare Limitations.* The Company proposes as a significant standard the financial capacity of the property to stand any further wage-rate increase which in turn has been affected by the inability of the Company to secure higher fares. The Company believes that if any wage-rate increase is awarded in these proceedings, it should be conditioned on securing a commensurate increase in fares.

The Union, on the other hand, contends that the ability to pay a wage-rate increase, including the question of adequate fares, is an irrelevant standard to these proceedings.

The application of the ability-to-pay standard in this case presents more than the ordinary complications of interpreting financial statements and weighing conflicting estimates of the trend of business conditions. In the first place, certain funds derived from fares have been impounded by the courts, and while the Marion Circuit Court has ordered these funds returned to the Company the case is on appeal. In the second place, Indianapolis

Railways, Inc., has made every effort for many months to secure higher fares for its services in the face of mounting operating costs. Undoubtedly these factors materially affect the ability of the Company to pay the existing wage-rate structure, not to mention any increase in wage rates. The arbitration board, however, is in no position to predict the outcome of those court and commission proceedings.

The relation of wage setting to price or fare determination can logically be conceived in three possible forms: (*a*) wages could be fixed first and fare or price setting could assume these costs; (*b*) prices and fares could be fixed first and assumed as given for purposes of determining wages; and (*c*) both wages and prices could be set simultaneously. In public utilities, including the railroads, there appears to be a long tradition of separation of wage and rate setting. This does not mean that rates and prices are irrelevant to wage setting, but rather that wage rates have tended to be fixed with some general reference to financial capacity, and then these costs in turn have been taken into account by the rate- or fare-making body. Such has been the actual relation between collective bargaining or emergency boards determining wage rates and the Interstate Commerce Commission setting railroad rates and fares. The transit industry has tended to follow an analogous practice.

In addition to these five standards the parties have emphasized a number of other considerations which the board has taken into account. The Union has argued that the depressed condition of the industry in the 1930's and the stabilization program entitle these employees to special consideration. The Company has strongly urged that the board decide the case in the light of all the unique factors in Indianapolis.

QUESTIONS

1. Complete the arbitration award indicating your decision and the basis for your award.
2. Write a critical appraisal of the way each side applied the principal standards noted above—cost of living, comparable rates, productivity, and ability to pay. (See Chapter VI.)
3. What do you think of the suggestion that any wage increase be made conditional upon a fare increase?

Case 50

IMPROVEMENT FACTOR

The contract dated May 29, 1950, between the General Motors Corporation and the International Union, United Automobile, Aircraft and Agricultural Implement Workers, CIO, contained the following provision:

(Paragraph 101 *a*) "The annual improvement factor provided herein recognizes that a continuing improvement in the standard of living of employes depends upon technological progress, better tools, methods, processes and equipment, and a cooperative attitude on the part of all parties in such progress. It further recognizes the principle that to produce more with the same amount of human effort is a sound economic and social objective. Accordingly, all employes covered by this agreement shall receive an increase of 4 cents per hour, effective May 29, 1950, and an additional increase of 4 cents per hour annually on May 29, 1951, May 29, 1952, May 29, 1953 and May 29, 1954, which will be added to the base rate of each wage classification."

In any appraisal of this clause, it must be remembered that the contract also included, among other terms, a cost-of-living escalator, a contract duration of 5 years, a modified union shop, and a provision which empowers management to establish production standards subject to the grievance procedure but explicitly not subject to arbitration. The 1948 contract between these parties had provided for a 3-cent per hour improvement factor and for the cost-of-living escalation. The 1950 contract increased the improvement factor to 4 cents a year, added the modified union shop, increased the duration of the contract to 5 years, improved the medical and hospital insurance plan, and added a pension program.

QUESTIONS

1. Would you recommend that all other companies generally adopt this type of contract? What problems would this provision pose for firms in industries with marked price competition? Is the clause adaptable to small firms?

2. Why do you suppose some unions are opposed to this type of contract provision? Are they opposed to the policy of increasing wage rates faster than the rise in living costs? What effect would you expect a long-term agreement to have upon a union and the relations between the union and the rank and file of members?

3. Do you expect long-term agreements to spread in American industry? What advantages and problems do they pose for the parties?

4. What is the rationale, if any, for an improvement factor of 4 cents per year? Why not 3 cents or 7 cents?

5. Does this improvement factor seek to gear wage rates to increases in productivity in General Motors? Is the yearly increase in productivity in a company stable from year to year?

6. What would happen to the wage structure of the country if wage rates were closely geared to increases in productivity in each plant, or company or industry?

7. What do you understand by productivity of labor? What factors affect its movement over time? How do you relate the concept of productivity used in this contract to the "marginal productivity" concept of economists?

8 Under piecework or incentive methods of wage payments, earnings typically drift upwards as workers on these operations capture some of the gains of increased productivity. In this company there are few incentive or piece rates. What would you say about the relative merits of improvement factors in day rated and piecework industries?

9. What significance for increasing productivity is there to the contract provision which permits General Motors to set production standards for day work subject to grievance but not to arbitration? If the parties fail to agree on a standard, they are free to strike or lockout on the operation. Why did the parties develop this type of clause? What pressures does it put on each side for agreement? What conditions are requisite for such a clause to operate without considerable strife and many work stoppages?

10. Discuss the relative merits of sharing gains of productivity by declines in prices and increases in money wage rates.

11. Indicate some of the problems which the General Motors-UAW contract would pose for a wage stabilization program? Should such a program permit increases to go into effect which are provided for by such long-term contracts? What would be the effect of disapproval of these contract provisions? What effects do approval of these provisions have on wage rates in other industries? Can the gains of increased productivity be passed along to workers when a large proportion of gross national product is going to military end items?

BIBLIOGRAPHY

HARBISON, F. H. "The General Motors–United Auto Workers Agreement of 1950," *Journal of Political Economy,* October, 1950, pp. 397–411.

KERR, CLARK. "The Short Run Behavior of Physical Productivity and Average Hourly Earnings," *Review of Economics and Statistics,* November, 1949.

KENDRICK, J. W. "National Productivity and Its Long-Term Projection," *Studies in Income and Wealth,* Vol. XV. New York: National Bureau of Economic Research.

ROSS, A. M. "General Motors Wage Agreement of 1948," *Review of Economics and Statistics,* February, 1949.

FABRICANT, SOLOMON. "Of Productivity Statistics: An Admonition," *Review of Economics and Statistics,* November, 1949.

Case 51

WAGE SETTLEMENT AT THE LOCAL OR INTERNATIONAL UNION LEVEL

UNION: United Steelworkers of America, CIO

COMPANY: A Steel Fabricator

INDUSTRY BACKGROUND

The wage policy committee of the United Steelworkers of America, CIO, formulated a demand for $2.00 a day (25 cents per hour) wage increase on September 11, 1945, following V-J Day. The demand was presented to more than 1,100 companies in the basic steel, iron ore, and steel fabricating industries which had contracts with this Union. Negotiations were started with the steel producing subsidiaries of the United States Steel Corporation. This Company advised the Union on October 23, 1945, that the then existing price ceilings did not enable the Company to grant a wage rate increase.

Secretary of Labor Schwellenbach on November 3, 1945, requested the Union and steel producing subsidiaries of the United States Steel Corporation to resume negotiations. The Company stated that collective bargaining was "futile" until OPA granted a substantial price increase estimated at $7.00 a ton to compensate for past cost increases and gave adequate assurances that prices would be further increased to compensate for any wage rate increase negotiated with the Union.

The Union set January 14, 1946, as a strike deadline following a strike vote conducted under the War Labor Disputes Act which showed 411,401 to 83,839 in favor of a stoppage. On December 31, 1945, the President appointed a 3-man fact-finding board which requested the parties to resume negotiations.

The parties did resume negotiations on January 9, 1946, in New York. The Company offered 12½ cents, and the Union finally reduced its demand to 19½ cents. The Company then offered 15 cents. At this point the negotiations deadlocked.

At the request of the President, negotiations were moved to the White House on January 11, 1946; and the Union agreed at the request of the President to postpone the strike a week. On January 17 the President proposed to the parties a settlement at 18½ cents. The Union accepted, but the Company rejected the proposal; and on January 21, 1946, at 12:01 A.M. a nationwide steel strike was begun. A few smaller companies, such as Kaiser, accepted the proposal and were not covered by the strike.

The International Union called out on strike not only employees of the basic steel companies but also those working in steel fabricating plants under contract with the unions which were open for negotiations. More than 750,000 employees were on strike. Many of these fabricating companies are relatively small. They produce no steel; but they manufacture steel products from steel rods, shapes, sheets, or bars produced by the basic steel companies.

During the strike there were extended discussions between steel executives and government officials over the appropriate price increase. The OPA had first proposed $2.50 per ton increase, later $4.00 per ton was discussed; and finally Secretary of the Treasury Snyder negotiated a figure of $5.00 per ton, and the strike was settled on February 15, 1946, the day of the price announcement, at a figure of 18½ cents per hour increase. The price settlement was complex, since varying price amounts were ultimately to be allowed different types of steel products.

The basic steel settlement on February 15, 1946, was part of the process of determining a new general wage rate level for manufacturing industries immediately after World War II. On January 10, 1946, a fact-finding board had recommended a wage rate increase of 19½ cents in the General Motors-UAW dispute. Two days later a fact-finding board recommended 18 per cent, equivalent to 21 or 22 cents, in the oil industry based to some extent on an earlier settlement by Sinclair Refining Company at this figure. Ford Motor Company and Chrysler Corporation settled for 18 and 18½ cents per hour respectively on January 26, 1946. Radio Corporation of America settled with the Electrical Workers, CIO, for 17½ cents on January 28, 1946; and after a prolonged strike, General Motors settled for 18½ cents on February 9, 1946.[1]

The unions were pushing for substantial wage rate increases in this period on a variety of grounds. Wartime hours and take-home pay would be reduced, and an increase in wage rates was sought to compensate for this reduction. The unions had become restive under wage controls and had fought to eliminate the Little Steel formula. They held companies were able to pay these increases, and the carry-back and carry-forward provisions of the tax laws assured profitable operations in the transition to peace-time operations. The unions feared that if they did not immediately press for wage rate increases, unemployment would develop, and the opportunity would pass.

Management likewise had become restive with controls, and it was anxious to have all controls completely eliminated. Management felt that in view of the uncertainties of reconversion, these readjustments should be completed before substantial wage rate increases were granted. Productivity could not be immediately increased. It would take time before new machinery could be purchased, discipline and personnel standards re-established, and markets for peacetime products recaptured. If any wage-rate increases were to be allowed in this transition period, they should be fully reflected immediately in price adjustments under price controls.

The following case of a particular steel fabricator is presented in the context of developments outlined above in the basic steel industry and the economy generally.

THE CASE OF COMPANY Z

The Company employed 1,400 workers who had been organized by the Steelworkers Union since 1937. Relations between

[1] For a discussion of the factors affecting labor, business, and government views of the period, see John T. Dunlop, "The Decontrol of Wages and Prices" in *Labor in Postwar America* (Brooklyn: Remsen Press, 1949), pp. 3–24. Also see *Terminal Report of the President's Fact-Finding Board,* February 25, 1946.

management and the local Union were extremely good. There had been no work stoppages since the Union's inception. Like scores of other companies in the steel fabricating industry, Company Z was under a collective bargaining agreement with the International Union, which had been certified as the bargaining agency for all production and maintenance employees. The International Union acts in behalf of its local unions in collective bargaining contracts. An agreement between a local union and company representatives is not binding until it is approved and signed by officers of the International.

After the Union's initial request for reopening the contract in the fall of 1945, neither the Company nor the local Union wished, at that point, to bargain collectively. Both preferred to await the outcome of the negotiations between the Union and Big Steel. The Company did not want to make a settlement higher than that agreed to by the major producers, and the Union did not wish to prejudice its position in the major negotiations by making concessions to Company Z. These parties had followed the basic steel settlements in the past. The strike deadline of January 21, 1946, found Company Z unwilling to make any offers until the wage issue had been resolved with the major producers. The Company informed the local Union in conference that unless the OPA allowance on steel price increases was considerably higher than the $4.00 a ton that had been rumored, Company Z could not meet the 18½-cent figure.

The plant went on strike as a part of the national shutdown and remained closed for 8 weeks. Not a single incident occurred during the strike to disturb the harmonious relationship that had existed. Indeed the parties entered into an agreement concerning the conduct of the strike. The Company agreed not to operate, and the Union agreed to place no pickets. The Union agreed to furnish all men required for essential maintenance and protection of the plant and equipment.

Within a few days after the price figure of $5.00 per ton was allowed by OPA and the wage settlement in Big Steel on February 15, 1946, practically all of the remaining large steel producers had also settled. Many of the small fabricating companies, however, claimed inability to pay and sought to reach a wage settlement with the Union for amounts less than the 18½-cent pattern set in the basic steel industry.

Company Z, like many other small units, found it impossible to secure reliable information on the precise extent of the price increase granted by the OPA on each type of product. The local union officers were informed by the Company that resumption of operations would necessarily be delayed pending clarification of the pricing problem. Meanwhile the local union members were becoming increasingly restive; they felt themselves entitled to the 18½ cents agreed to by the basic steel industry and were anxious to return to work immediately. Constant pressure for action was exerted on the local union officers.

Negotiations with the Local Union

On the fourth day following the settlement in Big Steel, on February 19, 1946, Company Z informed the local Union that it was prepared to discuss the wage issue. The Company announced flatly that the 18½-cent figure was out of the question. It offered 12 cents per hour. Every member of the negotiation committee of the local Union was presented with an 8-page statement answering each of the wage increase contentions generally advanced by the International Union. This statement sought to differentiate Company Z from the general industry picture. The statement stated in part as follows:

"1. The steel industry is already saving $195,000,000 annually as a result of the elimination of overtime pay and the return to the 40 hour week. The case at Company Z is as follows: The company continues to pay a considerable amount each pay day in overtime. In order to prove this assertion, we list the amount of overtime paid in the year 1945. Total overtime paid: $248,000, or approximately $20,500 per month. Average overtime per pay period: $9,500. Average overtime per pay period before V-J Day: $10,100. Average overtime per pay period after V-J Day: $8,400.

"2. The great increase in profits has been due to the rise in manpower productivity and installation of government financed modern plants that are eliminating the high-cost mills. The case at Company Z is as follows: In recent years there has been no mechanical equipment installed which has decreased the manhours per ton in the manufacture of any products sold by the company. No installations were made that were financed or owned by the government.

"3. Since V-J Day, the take-home pay of steelworkers has been cut from 25% to 50% due to the shortened work week, downgrading and other factors. The case at Company Z is as follows: During the month of April, 1945, the average employee received $1.266 gross hourly earnings. In November, 1945, the average employee received $1.226 gross hourly earnings. These months represented comparable output and tonnage. These figures prove conclusively that Company Z's employees' take-home pay has not been cut 25% to 50% due to any set of factors.

"4. Even after taking into consideration a substantial wage increase, the operation of the steel industry would result in a substantial profit for 1946 which would be 45% more than in the best war years, and manufacturing concerns throughout the United States would make a profit of 7½ billion dollars after taxes in 1946. The case generally at Company Z is as follows: During the year 1944 after all charges, the company reported earnings of $325,000. This represented 3.3% of the company's net sales. The earnings for the year 1945 will be reported after all charges at $250,000 or 2.6% of our net sales. The management at Company Z obtained a price advantage granted by OPA after their careful analysis of Company Z's high cost of production. Our selling price has been in excess of the prices used generally by the steel industry. In 1944 this price benefit totaled $375,000. In 1945, $200,000. It is an indisputable fact that if this price advantage had not been granted, our earnings in 1944 and 1945 would have been reduced materially and it is of importance to note that the price relief granted for 1944 exceeded the net earnings of the Company and that in 1945 the price advantage total was within approximately $50,000 of the net profits indicated above. It is reported that the industry may be granted an increase in price of from $2.50 a ton to $4.00 a ton. An increase of these proportions will not improve the situation at Company Z except to a very slight degree. When new prices are established we will be forced to meet them and will no longer be the beneficiaries of a price advantage.

"5. The steel industry is assured of over $300,000,000 in tax refunds from the federal government. The situation at Company Z is that during 1944 and 1945 a total of $240,000 of income was subject to excess profit tax. If our profit in 1946 is $196,000 or less, we will be able to claim 85½% of the amount which has been subject to excess profits tax as a refund. However, that same amount of profit will be subject to the normal and sur-tax rate of 40% so that the company would receive a net benefit of $108,000. In order to claim a refund for all normal and excess profit tax, we would have to lose $680,000 in 1946 and $515,000 in 1947. If the management anticipated losses of this character, we would be wise in liquidating at once.

"6. Total cost to the company of an 18½¢ per hour wage increase to all employees including salaried is $420,000 per year. The 18½¢ per hour increase, if granted, would cost the company an amount even greater than the profit earned during the best war years.

"7. Because of the manpower shortage in the locality, there is little likelihood that for some time to come there would be even an attempt made to reduce the work week down to the 40 hour level. For this reason a continuation of premium pay is inevitable.

"8. The company had not been able to pay a dividend in the past 14 years. Under these circumstances, liquidation is more desirable than the possibility of placing the company's financial position in a more precarious condition through granting a wage increase of such large proportions."

At a mass meeting of the local membership, the proposal of the Company was explained in detail by the negotiating committee. Before a vote was taken, the International Union's district representative warned the meeting that an acceptance of the recommendation would not constitute a final agreement since only the officers of the International were vested with authority to approve an agreement. Nonetheless, the meeting voted almost unanimously to accept the Company's proposal and to return to work.

THE INTERNATIONAL UNION ENTERS THE NEGOTIATIONS

The International Union acted quickly and decisively. Approval of the agreement was denied and a continuation of the strike ordered. The public reaction was unfavorable. The International was accused of dictatorial methods and of unjust and undemocratic interference with local union affairs. Community groups exerted determined pressure on local union members to disregard the strike order. A constructive labor-management relationship was threatened, and the International Union faced a most difficult situation.

In good faith the local union members and officers had accepted the Company's declaration of inability to increase wage rates by more than 12¢ per hour. Confidence between union officers and members was likewise in a precarious state. Members grumbled. Did the negotiating committee do right to recommend acceptance of the compromise wage increase? If so, the continued loss of earnings was unnecessary. On the other hand, if the negotiating committee could have secured the full 18½-cent increase and yet did not, its ability and honesty were questionable. Rejection of the local union leadership or International Union loomed as a possibility.

If the International Union approved the local settlement of 12 cents, it would place those competitors of Company Z who had already agreed to the full wage increase at a serious competitive disadvantage. For the welfare of these companies and for industrial stability, the International Union could not allow preferential treatment unless it was decisively evident that Company Z could not pay the increase and survive. When the International Union ordered a continuation of the strike, it faced the possible loss of support from local union officers and certain denunciation from management officials. Under these conditions a continuation of strike action might result in a successful "back-to-work" movement with the possible loss of a local union.

The International Union had its staff experts examine the Company's statement made in reply to the Union's demand. The following appraisal of the Company's position was presented by the International Union representatives in meetings with local union and company officials:

"1. Steel price increases granted by OPA had been clarified and would average $5.00 per ton on all of the products of Company Z.

"2. Company Z's total maximum and expected production amounts to 13,000 tons per month, or 156,000 tons per year. An average increase of $5.00 per ton equals $780,000 in increased revenue per year.

Price relief granted by OPA in 1945 as stated in Company's report, $228,000 per year.

$780,000 minus $228,000 equals $552,000.

Cost of 18½¢ wage increase as stated in company's report, per year, $420,000.

$552,000 minus $420,000 equals $132,000 balance.

"3. This balance of $132,000 should provide for whatever increase there might be in material costs incident to the wage increase assumed by raw material suppliers.

"4. In 1945 excess profit taxes were $100,000, and normal income tax, $300,000. In 1946 the Company will pay no excess profit tax and its normal tax will be reduced by 5%, making a total tax savings well above the $100,000 mark.

"5. Cost incident to the loss of production during this strike should be somewhat below the $50,000 mark.

On the basis of the above facts, the International Union concluded Company Z could not only meet the 18½-cent per hour wage increase but could expect to operate in 1946 more profitably than in 1945.

Company officials continued to press for preferential wage treatment on the ground of a great fear of postwar competition. They argued that a wage differential would place them in a much stronger position to meet the competition and that broader profit margins during the boom period would insure a far greater degree of job security later. Company officials became convinced that the strike would be continued unless they met the 18½ cents per hour wage increase. They reluctantly agreed to the full amount, and the strike was terminated. Union officers agreed to do everything in their power to stimulate greater productive efficiency in the plant and, should the need be evident, to review the whole situation in a few months.

The International Union representatives then turned to the problems of restoring good faith between its local officers and fellow members and between the workers and the Company. Restoration of the mutual confidence which had existed previous to the strike was considered to be of paramount importance. Union officers initiated discussions with employees in which they reviewed and explained the controversies. They publicly credited the local officers with requesting assistance of the International organization in examining all facts pertaining to the compromise agreement. They absolved the Company of bad faith in the minds of the employees by making it clear that during the negotiations with the local Union, the Company had been unable to obtain official information on the extent or application of steel price increases. Not selfishness, but fear of the future, the Union concluded, motivated the Company's early refusal to grant the full wage demand. The firm, after the uncertainty of the war period, was honestly afraid that it could not stand on its own feet in peacetime.

QUESTIONS

1. Appraise the arrangement under which the agreement with a company is made with the International Union. Under what types of circumstances and in what industries would you expect this arrangement to develop? Why is it not universal in collective bargaining?

2. How much autonomy should a local union have? What supervision should it have? What obligation does the International Union have to competitive companies and to the employees of these other companies, also members of the Union?

3. Under what circumstances should a union make a concession from a general pattern settlement? Define these conditions carefully. When would you expect a concession to be made in the sequence of bargaining with different companies?

4. If wage concessions are made to high-cost producers, has management an incentive left to increase efficiency? Do wage concessions to high-cost producers amount to workers subsidizing a company?

5. What do you mean by industry-wide bargaining? Does it exist in the steel industry? What is the unit certified by the NLRB? In what units do negotiations actually take place?

6. How do you explain the fact that wage adjustments negotiated by one or two leading basic steel producers spread to so many other companies? Did the Union create this condition? What do cost-price relations have to do with wage leadership? What does the location of the plants of the principal producers have to do with wage leadership?

7. Why do firms like Company Z choose to follow the wage leadership of other companies?

8. In the 1946 strike the International Union struck fabricating plants as well as basic steel producers. In the 1949 and 1952 strikes, only the basic steel producers were struck. Why do you suppose the Union changed its policy?

WAGE STRUCTURE

Wage structure problems are one of the major focal points of all collective bargaining. The way in which wage structures are handled on a day-to-day basis may affect the labor cost and competitive position of a firm as decisively as general wage changes. A high proportion of all grievances concern these matters. The discussion of wage structure problems in this section is divided into three parts: methods of wage payment, establishment and administration of internal wage structures, and administration of incentive methods of payment.

METHODS OF WAGE PAYMENT

The choice of the method of wage payment—hourly rates, piece rates, or incentive rates—is one of the most important questions in a collective bargaining relationship. The choice among these methods will depend partly upon technological and economic factors. In a job shop, for example, where only a limited number of pieces of a certain product are produced at a time and where quality is more important than quantity, it is not always feasible to use an incentive method of payment. The importance of labor costs and the extent to which individual or group effort can in fact influence output or quality also affect the choice. The traditions of the bargaining organization and their experience with different methods of wage payment may also influence the method of payment. Some unions are strongly opposed to incentive systems, such as the United Automobile Workers, CIO, in assembly plants. This position reflects attitudes developed during the formative stages of the union. Union members often fear that incentive systems may result in rate cutting and unemployment. In other cases, such as in the clothing industry, there is a long tradition of satisfactory operation of incentive plans.[1]

The hourly rate method of payment may take two forms: a single rate or a range of rates to be paid to each employee in a job classification. Normally unions prefer the single hourly rate under the principle of equal pay for equal work. However, some companies have a rate range for each job with employees receiving a rate within the range on the basis of length of service or merit or a combination of both. In recent years, there has been a tendency toward automatic progression based on length of service, at least to the mid-point of the range. Thus, a punch press operator job might carry a range of $1.55 to $1.75. An employee starting at $1.55 might move automatically to $1.60 after 6 months' service and to $1.65 at the end of 1 year's service. Thereafter any further increase within the range is based on management's review of his ability at periodic intervals. Where individual merit determines in whole or in part the rate of an employee within the range, the union usually reserves the right to bring a grievance in behalf of an employee who has not received a merit increase. (See Case 52.)

A number of problems arise in the choice between the two alternative forms of hourly wage payment, the single rate and the rate range: Does the single rate prevent adequate acknowledgment of differences in ability among employees? Does the single rate minimize the complaints and dissatisfactions which may result from having a number of different rates paid within an established range? Is there a tendency over the long run under a rate range to have most of the employees concentrated near the maximum? If so, will there be discontent because of the employees' inability to receive further increases? Will such discontent result in union pressure to increase the maximums? How much spread in a rate range is necessary to give reasonable merit increases? What proportion of the rate range should provide for automatic progression, and what proportion should consist of merit increases? If the range is narrow and merit adjustments

---

[1] For an extended discussion of the choice of methods of wage payment in collective bargaining and union attitudes toward them, see Sumner H. Slichter, *Union Policies and Industrial Management* (Washington, D.C.: Brookings Institution, 1941), chaps. x and xi; and Van Dusen Kennedy, *Union Policy and Incentive Wage Methods* (New York: Columbia University Press, 1945), chap. iii.

amount to only a few cents each time, are the adjustments likely to be irritants rather than rewards?

Piecework or incentive systems have significant consequences for the collective bargaining relationship. Under piecework systems the union tends to concern itself with the amount and quality of output, since these factors directly affect the income of wage earners. The union may be led quite far into an interest in production problems. For example, if managerial inefficiency causes delay in the flow of materials, adversely affecting the ability of employees to produce, the union will be quick to complain or to demand some protection of earnings under these circumstances. Managerial organization will be influenced greatly by this method of wage payment. Specialized personnel will be required to do time study and rate setting and to direct attention to methods of production and to quality standards.

ESTABLISHMENT AND ADMINISTRATION OF INTERNAL WAGE STRUCTURES

One of the most significant impacts of collective bargaining has been to develop explicit wage scales under all methods of wage payment. In recent years, it has become the established practice to reduce to writing the rates paid for each job. The specification of the wage scale in the form of an exhibit or appendix is normally regarded as part of the collective bargaining agreement. Under piece-rate operations, enumeration of all of the piece rates for all the various operations may run into volumes. In most cases, wage scales cannot be changed during the term of the agreement, with certain exceptions to be noted. In some collective bargaining relationships, however, the parties seem to be satisfied with provisions which permit a change in rates for particular job classifications at any time. A wage scale that is fixed during the life of the contract has the advantage of permitting the company to estimate labor costs more reliably. It gives both sides a period of freedom from negotiations over wage rates.

When rates are fixed for a contract period, some provision must be made for the setting of rates on new job classifications and the revision of rates for existing jobs which have been altered, normally to a "substantial degree," as a consequence of technological change and changes in methods of production. In industries where there are frequent changes in job content, provisions of the agreement specify the procedures to be followed in the case of new or changed job classifications. (See Case 56.)

As a part of the development of explicit wage scales, written descriptions of the job operations are prepared. These are useful not only in ranking the jobs but also in determining whether or not a substantial change in job content has occurred which might justify a review of the rate.

In a collective bargaining relationship which encompasses a number of job classifications, an important range of problems concerns the ranking the wage rates of these various jobs. A strict craft-union relationship would be less concerned with these problems. The ordering of the rates in the wage structure is of major significance under industrial unionism. Both unions and managements in large establishments, in the absence of a systematic method of ordering job rates, have found themselves constantly confronted by individual claims of wage inequities. Frequently jobs were being paid rates which bore no relationship to the job content. Individuals on the same job were often receiving widely divergent personal rates. In recent years, many industries, partly under the impetus of the National War Labor Board and partly as a result of collective bargaining, introduced substantial revisions in intraplant wage structures.

This concern over internal wage structures is reflected in the growth of formal job evaluation plans. Excerpts from an illustrative evaluation plan are presented in Case 53. Job evaluation is the attempt to rate jobs on a formal basis and to measure the worth of a job in relationship to other jobs. The formal plan may be a product of collective bargaining, or it may be instituted initially by the company with the union reserving the right to challenge the evaluation of any job. Some unions set up their own Job Evaluation Committees whose responsibility is to participate with management in the development and administration of the plan. Some formal job evaluation plans have been criticized by unions for a number of reasons. First, it is claimed that the so-called skill factors, such as education and experience, are weighted too heavily in evaluating jobs. This has a tendency to undervalue the manual labor jobs. Second, the plans developed by industrial engineers and consultants are often too rigid. They are not applicable to the special needs of a particular plant. Moreover, many of them attempt to draw very fine lines between jobs. In the rating of jobs, one such plan has no less than 20 degrees for the skill factor alone, ranging from "extremely high skill, very high skill, high skill, moderately high skill," and so on down to "no skill."

A variety of forces play upon the internal wage structure of any plant. In most plants, some jobs are likely to be quite similar to those in plants in the same industry and even in other industries. It is also likely that there will be some unique jobs. (*a*) The rates for a job in one plant will be influenced by the relative supply and demand for this type of work in other plants. Labor market shortages, for instance, will affect rates. (*b*) The customary differentials in the plant will be important. Frequently they reflect social judgments of status within the work community. (*c*) The internal power alignments among departments and groups in the work establishment will affect relative rates.

Against the background of these forces, it will frequently prove difficult, if not impossible, to impose and to maintain a hierarchy of job rates based solely upon a formal and mechanistic job evaluation plan. However, a job evaluation plan may prove a useful guide to an orderly wage structure. It may serve to reduce the number of job classifications and rates. It may provide guideposts and bench marks for rate setting in collective bargaining discussions. But the internal wage structure of a plant ordinarily cannot long be fixed by slide rule or rote under collective bargaining.

ADMINISTRATION OF INCENTIVE METHODS OF PAYMENT

An incentive system of wage payment involves a special range of problems for collective bargaining. Among the important policy questions are the following:

a) Shall the union take any responsibility for the system of time study and rate setting? Most unions believe that some control over these matters must be secured through collective bargaining. To this extent, union participation is general. Normally the labor agreement will at least require that management keep the union informed of its time study procedure and its application to particular jobs. The master agreement between the Continental Can Company and the United Steelworkers of America, CIO, December 1, 1949, for example, provides that:

"Management will, before the establishment of an incentive rate for a new or changed job not previously paid on an incentive basis, explain to the Union Committee the necessity for, and the procedure to be followed, in establishing the incentive rate. Management will then develop the incentive rate in accordance with the Company's established industrial engineering practices and procedures."

In a few agreements, it is provided that the union may designate its own time-study expert to be present at the time study of any job. Normally, however, the rate is set by the company; and the union is furnished with copies of the standard. The standard includes a breakdown of the elements of the job under a company-prescribed method for doing the job, the timing assigned to each element, and the total time allowed for the job. For the most part the union's participation is limited to challenging the rate if it considers it to be unfairly established.

b) Most incentive systems provide for a minimum guarantee to which all workers shall be entitled, regardless of actual production. This guarantee is usually the base rate for the particular job classification, although some parties assign an hourly rate to the job which may be different from the base rate. A frequent issue is whether the guarantee is to be computed on an hourly, daily, or a weekly basis. The union will normally seek a guarantee for a shorter period, and the company for a longer period. Consider the following illustration of a daily guarantee. An employee on a job with a $1.25 base rate makes incentive earnings of $1.50 for each of five hours. During the remaining 3 hours, his incentive earnings drop to $1.10. Under a system of daily guarantee, he is entitled to $10.00 (8 hours time $1.25). He actually receives a total of $10.80 for the day. His incentive yield above base for the 5 hours is offset by the extent to which his earnings fall below base. On an hourly guarantee basis, he would receive $11.25 for the day, which includes a 15 cents per hour "makeup" for the 3 hours he earned below the guaranteed base rate.

c) What allowance should be made in an incentive system for the fatigue and personal needs of an employee? Most systems apply a flat percentage to all standards to cover these factors. The amount of the allowance, however, is frequently a source of dispute between management and unions.

d) Most incentive systems also indicate the rates to apply in a series of contingencies, such as a breakdown in the machinery, a run of inferior raw materials, and periods of setting up new styles or products in which production is experimental. The worker may be paid on the basis of his previous average hourly earnings or the base rate for his job. Similar arrangements are often made when an employee is transferred from incentive work to an hourly-rated job for the convenience of the company.

e) One of the most difficult problems under an incentive system is the revision of incentive standards when there has been a change in the method of operation. If only a small part of the job has been changed, should the entire job be restudied? Or should only those elements affected by the change be restudied?

f) What special arrangements, if any, should be made in the arbitration procedure for the review of grievances involving the standards or incentive system? Some agreements require that an industrial engineer be called in by the arbitrator on any disputes relating to time studies. Other agreements designate a separate arbitrator, at times an engineer, to resolve all such questions. Ordinarily, however, no distinction is made between this type of case and other cases in the grievance procedure.

One of the central problems of collective bargaining concerns the way in which the benefits of technical changes are to be shared. The administration of a rate structure, under an hourly or a piece-rate system of wage payment, compels attention to this fundamental question. Technical change normally produces some change in the nature of the work performed. A piecework system of wage payment ordinarily permits wage earners to capture immediately some of the benefits of technical change. When the method of wage payment is by the hour, the contest for the benefits of technical change must take other forms in which the union seeks a rise in the rate. The Union may seek an increase on the particular job or in effect use a number of minor technical changes as the basis for a general wage-rate increase.

Case 52

MERIT INCREASE WITHIN RATE RANGE

UNION: Chase Brass & Copper Workers' Union, CIO

COMPANY: Chase Brass & Copper Company, Inc.

On November 3, 1950, the Union filed the following grievance:

> "The Union feels that Robert Blanchard deserves top rating. This involves correctness in merit rating and will require an interpretation of Article IX, Sections C and F of the contract."

Robert Blanchard was hired in 1942, when he started an 8,000-hour apprenticeship training course as a toolmaker. He received his certificate in 1945 and from that date to 1949 worked as a journeyman toolmaker. Business reductions forced his layoff from the toolroom in 1949; and, exercising his bumping rights under the contract, he took a job in Department 15 as an inspector at the rate of 90 cents (plus a constant factor of 42 cents), 30 cents an hour less than his toolmaker rate. Further curtailment of operations necessitated his layoff for 3 months. In November, 1949, he was recalled to Department 15 as a Processed Material Inspector and continued at the 90-cent (plus constant) rate. At the end of 3 months, his rate was adjusted to 95 cents; and after an additional 5 months, he received a second merit increase, bringing his rate to $1.00.

It is important to note that during this time and, in fact, until mid–1950, there was no elected union representative in this department. A steward for the department was chosen in June, 1950. After observing the conditions in the department the steward filed a grievance to bring Blanchard's basic rate to the top of the range or $1.13 as of November 3, 1950. During the processing of the grievance the Company did raise his rate from $1.00 to $1.05 under the merit increase provisions of the agreement, but the Union believes that the resultant rate—now 8 cents below the top of his job classification range—is still unsatisfactory.

RELEVANT CONTRACT CLAUSES

"*Article IX* (*Wages and Other Economic Issues*)

"*Section C:* While the general wage level and standard rates and job rate ranges remain fixed by the above provision, changes in the rates of an individual employee, based on reclassification, promotion, demotion, merit increases, transfer, and other such changes of an individual employee's rate, shall not be prevented by such provision and may be brought up by the Union under the Grievance Procedure, including the step of arbitration, providing that no such grievance which would change the standard rate or rate ranges of a job shall be brought to arbitration unless such grievance is based on a change called for by the Job Evaluation Agreement.

.   .   .   .

"*Section F: Merit Rating:*

"2. Merit Rating shall be conducted by the Company, by departments, at regular six-month intervals. If unusual circumstances prevent the completion of a Merit Rating within such six-month interval, the steward of the department involved will be notified, in writing, of the reasons for the delay, and any merit increases called for shall take effect in the month originally due . . . .

"3. It is agreed that there should be correct understanding by all concerned regarding the principles, procedures and application of Merit Rating. The Union will maintain in each major plant a Merit Rating Committee, consisting of three stewards, to meet with the Management representatives in charge of Merit Rating, at the request of either party, for the purpose of discussing and resolving general problems connected with Merit Rating . . . ."

POSITION OF THE UNION

The Union emphasizes the superior qualifications of Blanchard when he went on the inspection job. As a trained journeyman toolmaker, he has a working knowledge of all the instruments which an inspector normally uses. Since he had to make tools as a journeyman toolmaker and be able to read blueprints, it follows that he would be able to inspect for any type of production with respect to the requirements of tolerance and quality. His work with the Chase Brass & Copper gave him a familiarity with many sections of the plant. Although his work is now in the automatic screw machine department as an inspector, he has also worked in Departments 11, 58, 115, 73, and 78, covering such operations as drill presses, hand screw machines, edging machines, and eyelet machines. The Union contends that even as of the time he was transferred to Department 15 he should have been given more than the 90 cents starting rate.

The evidence proves that it is not uncommon to start a man at a rate higher than the range minimum, consistent with the skill and knowledge he brings to the job. To illustrate this point, the Union cited two cases: (*a*) C. Yauman, a setup and operate man in Department 59, was transferred to Department 15 as a Processed Materials Inspector in 1949 at a starting rate of $1.10 or 20 cents above the minimum. In March, 1950, he was given a merit increase which brought him to the top of the range, $1.13; (*b*) J. Cassidy also was transferred and retained his base rate of $1.02 or 12 cents above the minimum. After 9 months Cassidy was raised to $1.07, and he was given the maximum rate after he had been on the job 17 months. The record shows that these men had no more experience than Blanchard; in fact, it is questionable whether they had as much training. Regardless of the reasons why they were started at such rates, the action establishes two significant facts: First, it is not essential for a man to start at the minimum; and, second, the higher a man starts above the minimum, the faster will he progress to the maximum rate under the applied merit system. Using the Company's records of progression for employees on this job in Department 15, the Union demonstrates that if Blanchard had started at $1.00 per hour (less than the rates given to Cassidy and Yauman), he would have reached the top of the range 1 month before the grievance was filed, or in October, 1950.

It would be entirely appropriate for the arbitrator to award an increase of 13 cents per hour as of the date of the grievance, minus the effect of the 5 cents per hour increase which he received in the interim. Since the Company erred in the starting rate, this is the only fair method for remedying the injustice to Blanchard.

POSITION OF THE COMPANY

The Company made a detailed analysis of the starting rates and the merit progression pattern of each employee on this job in Department 15. With respect to the first, it showed that many employees, including Blanchard, had started at the 90-cent rate (or its equivalent as the range minimum at the date of starting). Some others had started at 93 cents, one at 94 cents, and three at 95 cents. The employees who received this initial starting rate advantage of from 3 cents to 5 cents were credited with the inspection experience which they brought to the job. For example, one of the union witnesses was started at 93 cents because, according to his own testimony, he had approximately 20 years' work in inspection previously.

It is true that Cassidy and Yauman were started at $1.02 and $1.10, respectively, but they must be considered as special cases because of the circumstances involved. These two men did not enter the department through the normal channels. They were long-service employees (28 years and 30 years) who, in recent years, were operators in the screw department. In 1949 a drastic change in the organization of the automatic screw machines left the department with a surplus of nine operators. Since Cassidy and Yauman had reached the point where their efficiency was below normal, it was agreed by both parties that they could be laid off from the screw department out of their regular seniority, provided they were transferred to other jobs at their existing rates. Allowing them to start at the unusual high rates of $1.02 and $1.10 was a result of a special agreement and constitutes a clear exception. It is wrong to cite their starting rates as relevant to the case of Blanchard.

The pattern of merit progression in Department 15 also proves that there has been no discrimination against the aggrieved employee. Actually Blanchard's three-step adjustment was accomplished more rapidly than most adjustments in the department. Of those who have reached the range maximum (apart from Yauman and Cassidy), it is significant to note that it took Peters 28 months, Wyman 29 months, Smith and Bodle 34 months, and Sweatt 36 months to reach the top. Blanchard in a period of only 13 months is within 8 cents of the top, yet the Union seeks to place him at the maximum in even less than 13 months. Peters, with many years of inspection experience, had not even reached

Blanchard's present rate at the end of 13 months, even though he started at a rate above the range minimum. There is nothing unusual about the treatment of Blanchard. If anything, the rapid advancement sought by the Union would create an injustice for the other men. The Company recognizes that the toolmaker training is helpful to him in his inspection work, but it is not an adequate substitute for actual inspection experience which other people had.

In summary, the Company believes that its judgment should stand unless there is definitive proof that it is incorrect or discriminatory. It denies any desire to behave in an autocratic manner or on a unilateral basis. Under Article IX (F) (3) the Union has the complete right to discuss merit rating problems through its Merit Rating Committee. But when it comes to arbitration the Company believes that its merit rating decisions should stand unless proved wrong.

QUESTIONS

1. In your opinion is this essentially a merit rating case or is it a question of the rate at which a transferred employee should be started in Department 15? Can the question of the proper rate of a transferred employee be raised under the Merit Rating section of the contract?
2. What are the principles and procedures you would recommend to the parties in applying a merit rating program? What steps would you develop to prevent inequities from arising among the ratings of individual employees? How would you handle cases like Cassidy and Yauman?
3. Does the fact that there was no elected steward in Department 15 at the time of Blanchard's transfer influence your judgment of the case? Why?
4. What is the purpose of merit rating? Is it intended to reflect the increase in skills and experience which an employee acquires while on a job? Is it appropriate to use it as a substitute for seniority to protect an employee's earnings when he transfers to a lower-rated job in lieu of layoff?
5. Under a merit rating plan would you expect all employees to advance to the top of the rate range or only the exceptional employees? What would you expect with respect to the speed of advancement of employees?
6. If a merit rating system is to operate effectively, how objective must be the standards of measurement of merit? How do you explain the failure of the parties in this case to appeal to such standards?

Case 53

WAGE-RATE DIFFERENTIALS IN A DEPARTMENT

UNION: Textile Workers Union of America, CIO

COMPANY: Forstmann Woolen Company

Approximately 25 first-class cylinder fullers earning $0.84 per hour claim they are entitled to an increase. Comparison with the rates for certain other jobs in the wet finishing department, it is alleged, shows that this job classification is subjected to an inequity. The first-class cylinder fullers maintain that the skill and judgment required of them has not been given sufficient weight in slotting their jobs in relation to other jobs. The comparison made by the fullers is with the dryers, the teazling operators, the wet decaters, all of whom also receive $0.84 per hour, the washing operators who receive $0.79 per hour, and the examiners who receive $1.01 per hour.

The adjustment is requested under the provisions of Article III (B) of the contract between the Company and the Union, which reads in part:

"Nothing in this Article shall prevent either party hereto from requesting, at any time, an adjustment of individual rates of pay which, in its opinion, should fairly be made because of intraplant inequities or inequalities. Upon such request, which shall be submitted in writing, the rates of pay in such cases shall be negotiated and the parties shall in good faith endeavor to reach an agreement. If no agreement is reached within 15 days after receipt of such request, the dispute may be submitted to arbitration by either party thereto in accordance with Article VIII of this Agreement. A wage adjustment arrived at in accordance with this clause shall not be used by either party as a basis for claiming other inequities or inequalities."

POSITION OF THE UNION

The Union argues that the fuller's rate is too low and that the Company's job description does not sufficiently emphasize the elements of skill and judgment required on the job. It is held that the fullers are left more to their own judgment and experience than are any of the persons in comparable jobs, with the exception of the examiners. All the other work is tied much more closely to machine and automatic devices. It is also true that the fullers have a greater direct responsibility for the material they are handling. Mistakes on their part would lead directly to damage and rejection of goods, either by overshrinkage or undershrinkage. While their foreman works closely with them, harm can easily be done if the fullers are careless or incompetent. Finally, it is agreed that at least 4 months and probably 6 months of training are necessary for the job. On the basis of these factors, the Union argues that no inequity would be created by raising the fuller's rate. An inequity exists in maintaining the present rate.

POSITION OF THE COMPANY

The Company holds that the existing rate for first-class cylinder fulling operator is appropriate for the duties entailed in the job. The Company's job description reads:

"The Operator pushes a loaded truck to the machine and places the pieces in the machine by hand, making sure to equalize the length of the strings. He measures the length and width of pieces and fills out the Work Slips. He then adds soap solution as required and sets the machine for the proper Fulling operation. The Operator remeasures the pieces from time to time during the Fulling process, and occasionally resets the machine and rearranges the pieces. After the pieces have been processed, they are opened at the seam, and folded out by hand on to a receiving truck. The Operator records the final measurement on the Process Control Card and Work Slip. He cleans, oils and greases the machine whenever necessary. One man operates two machines."

In establishing a rate of $0.84 for this job, the Company holds that it has taken adequate cognizance of the skill and judgment factors involved, also of other factors important in valuing a job, namely, the amount of physical effort required, the responsibility for the work and for the safety of others, the nature of the physical working conditions, and the exposure to dangers of accident.

The Company further contends that it has achieved a delicate balance in the components of its wage structure. Any upward movement of rates in one job would cause a certain amount of dissatisfaction in related jobs. The history of the various job rates is cited as an important element indicating the long-established character of the existing wage relationships. The Company indicates that with slight qualification, the record shows that the fullers have had the same relative rate through a whole series of adjustments since January, 1931, as have the dryers, the teazling operators, and the wet decaters, ranging during this period of years from a low rate of $0.45 to the present rate of $0.84. Until September, 1941, the washing operators also had either the same relative rate or a rate only $0.02 per hour below the fullers, although they are now receiving $0.05 per hour less. The examiners, on the other hand, have always earned at least $0.15 and at some times as much as $0.20 more than the fullers.

QUESTIONS

1. From what circumstances may this grievance have arisen? How can the Union request an increase for some workers in a department and not for all workers?
2. How much weight should be given to the historical differentials that have prevailed within the department?
3. What are the merits and disadvantages from the point of view of both parties of a contract provision such as Article III (B) which permits the raising of a grievance on a particular job rate at any time during the contract year?
4. If the rate for a particular job is to be changed, how can the dangers of creating dissatisfaction among other workers be minimized?

Case 54

JOB EVALUATION METHODS

One of the most widely used guides to job evaluation is the Manual prepared by the National Metal Trades Association for use by its member companies. According to this method, each job is broken down into its component parts; and points are assigned according to the degree to which each factor is present. The total number of points thus assigned determines the Labor Grade for the job. All jobs in the same Labor Grade should make approximately equal demands on the workers performing them. One wage or rate range applies for all jobs in any given Labor Grade.

A few illustrative excerpts from the Manual are presented here. First is a table of the points assigned to eleven factors and the distribution of total point values over the twelve Labor Grades. Then follows the definition and description of four of the factors, one from each major group.

In addition a typical occupational rating sheet is presented. It shows the basis for rating a particular job under the National Metal Trades Association plan.

POINTS ASSIGNED TO FACTORS AND KEY TO LABOR GRADES

Factors	1st Degree	2nd Degree	3rd Degree	4th Degree	5th Degree
Skill:					
1. Education	14	28	42	56	70
2. Experience	22	44	66	88	110
3. Initiative and Ingenuity	14	28	42	56	70
Effort:					
4. Physical Demand	10	20	30	40	50
5. Mental or Visual Demand .	5	10	15	20	25
Responsibility:					
6. Equipment or Process	5	10	15	20	25
7. Material or Product	5	10	15	20	25
8. Safety of Others	5	10	15	20	25
9. Work of Others	5	10	15	20	25
Job Conditions:					
10. Working Conditions	10	20	30	40	50
11. Unavoidable Hazards	5	10	15	20	25

Score Range	Men's Grades	Women's Grades
−139	..	25
140–161	..	24
162–183	10	23
184–205	9	22
206–227	8	21
228–249	7	..
250–271	6	..
272–293	5	..
294–315	4	..
316–337	3	..
338–359	2	..
360–381	1	..

INITIATIVE AND INGENUITY

Initiative and ingenuity appraise the independent action, exercise of judgment, the making of decisions or the amount of planning which the job requires. This factor also appraises the degree of complexity of the work.

1st Degree

Requires the ability to understand and follow simple instructions and the use of simple equipment where the employe is told exactly what to do.

2nd Degree

Requires the ability to work from detailed instructions and the making of minor decisions involving the use of some judgment.

3rd Degree

Requires the ability to plan and perform a sequence of operations, where standard or recognized operation methods are available and the making of general decisions as to quality, tolerances, operation and set-up sequence.

4th Degree

Requires the ability to plan and perform unusual and difficult work where only general operation methods are available and the making of decisions involving the use of considerable ingenuity, initiative and judgment.

5th Degree

Requires outstanding ability to work independently toward general results, devise new methods, meet new conditions necessitating a high degree of ingenuity, initiative and judgment on very involved and complex jobs.

PHYSICAL DEMAND

This factor appraises the amount and continuity of physical effort required. Consider the effort expended handling material (the weight and frequency of handling), operating a machine or handling tools, and the periods of unoccupied time.

1st Degree

Light work requiring little physical effort.

2nd Degree

Light physical effort working regularly with light weight material or occasionally with average weight material. Operate machine tools where machine time exceeds the handling time.

3rd Degree

Sustained physical effort, requiring continuity of effort working with light or average weight material. Usually short cycle work requiring continuous activity. Or the operation of several machines where the handling time is equivalent to the total machine time.

4th Degree

Considerable physical effort, working with average or heavy weight material. Or continuous strain of a difficult work position.

5th Degree

Continuous physical exertion working with heavy weight material. Hard work with constant physical strain or intermittent severe strain.

RESPONSIBILITY FOR WORK OF OTHERS

This factor appraises the responsibility which goes with the job for assisting, instructing or directing the work of others. It is not intended to appraise supervisory responsibility for results.

1st Degree

Responsible only for own work.

2nd Degree
Responsible for instructing and directing one or two helpers 50% or more of the time.

3rd Degree
Responsible for instructing, directing or setting up for a small group of employees usually in the same occupation, up to 10 persons.

4th Degree
Responsible for instructing, directing and maintaining the flow of work in a group of employees up to 25 persons.

5th Degree
Responsible for instructing, directing and maintaining the flow of work in a group of over 25 persons.

Occ. Code No. 69
Dept. _____

OCCUPATIONAL RATING—SUBSTANTIATING DATA
(PLANT AND OPERATING OCCUPATIONS)

Job Name   STOCK SELECTOR _____Class _____

FACTORS	DEGREE	POINTS	BASIS OF RATING
Education	2	28	Able to read and write, add and subtract. Assist in keeping stock records, making inventories. Accuracy in checking, counting, weighing. Equivalent to 2 years high school.
Experience	2	44	3 to 12 months experience in stock room to become familiar with products, records, forms and location of bins.
Initiative and Ingenuity	2	28	Follow detailed instructions. Some judgment required in counting out, filling requisitions, storing or piling stock, taking inventories, accumulating orders, delivering material, to manufacturing departments.
Physical Demand	3	30	Sustained physical effort. Lift and carry boxes and cartons. Occasional heavy lifting, as items may vary considerably in weight.
Mental or Visual Demand	2	10	Frequent mental or visual attention in counting out, filling requisitions and storing material or parts.
Responsibility for Equipment or Process	1	5	Little damage to equipment involved (hand truck).
Responsibility for Material or Product	3	15	Careless handling or incorrect issuing may result in losses up to $250.
Responsibility for Safety of Others	2	10	May injure another employee when handling product, or when using hand truck. Only reasonable care to own work necessary.
Responsibility for Work of Others	1	5	None.
Working Conditions	2	20	Good working conditions. Might be slightly dirty.
Unavoidable Hazards	3	15	May crush hand or foot when handling material. Some possibility of hernia.
Total		210	
Labor Grade:	8		

UNAVOIDABLE HAZARDS

This factor appraises the hazards, both accident and health, connected with or surrounding the job, even though all safety devices have been installed. Consider the material being handled, the machines or tools used, the work position, the possibility of accident, even though none has occurred.

1st Degree
Accident or health hazards negligible.

2nd Degree
Accidents improbable, outside of minor injuries, such as abrasions, cuts or bruises. Health hazards negligible.

3rd Degree
Exposure to lost-time accidents, such as crushed hand or foot, loss of fingers, eye injury from flying particles. Some exposure to occupational disease, not incapacitating in nature.

4th Degree
Exposure to health hazards or incapacitating accident, such as loss of arm or leg.

5th Degree
Exposure to accidents or occupational disease which may result in total disability or death.

Case 55

THE EVALUATION OF A JOB

UNION: International Association of Machinists, AFL

COMPANY: Schick, Inc.

A job entitled "Returned Materials Checker" was evaluated by the Company and placed in Labor Grade 8 with 218 points under the National Metal Trades Association job evaluation plan in effect. (See Case 54.) The Union immediately protested the evaluation, arguing that the job belonged in Labor Grade 7. The ratings on three factors were challenged by the Union:

FACTOR	PRESENT		UNION PROPOSAL	
	Degree	Points	Degree	Points
(4) Physical demand	2	20	3	30
(9) Responsibility for work of others	1	5	3	15
(11) Unavoidable hazards	1	5	3	15

These changes proposed by the Union would yield a total of 238 points, placing the job in Labor Grade 7.

The job description of "Returned Material Checker" is as follows:

"Opens Service Station returned packages of parts and checks for return authorization. Counts material and compares quantities to authorization, noting discrepancies. Segregates returned and rejected material as listed, sends returned material to proper department for inspection and disposes of rejected material as directed. Opens returned shavers, separates shavers from accessories and sends shavers to proper department for inspection. Inspects Farrington boxes for obvious defects and returns to stock. Checks returned cord sets, tests for opens and shorts and sends to stock. Checks returned Shaverests for functional operation and broken parts, disassembles and reassembles from good parts and sub-assembles and sends to stock. Inspects returned Lube Kits, reassembles good components and sends to stock. Prepares necessary inter-departmental transfers and keeps simple records."

POSITION OF THE PARTIES

Physical Demand. The Union states that this employee has a considerable amount of heavy lifting to do; he handles shavers in quantity. Moreover, there is exertion in the use of tools. For comparison, the Union cites the job of Packer which is assigned a third degree for this factor.

The Company feels that a third degree is unwarranted. The Packer is usually standing and the rating basis for that job so specifies. The Returned Material Checker is seated at least 75 per cent of the time. The Company also observes that the two Repairman-Salvage jobs, which are comparable to the Checker job in Physical Demand, have a second degree for this factor.

Responsibility for the Work of Others. The Union emphasizes that this man works alone on the job. He must be sure that no thefts occur and that defective parts are destroyed so they will not be used again.

The Company relies heavily on the NMTA Manual to support the 1st degree rating. This degree specifies that a man is "responsible only for his own work." The descriptive language for the second and third degrees could never apply to the Checker job.

Unavoidable Hazards. The Union states that occupational diseases are very possible, since the returned shavers are used and may have hair and sediment in them. It would be easy to contract a skin disease.

The Company countered by saying that there are 41 service stations in the country. They take the faulty shavers and examine them carefully. Thousands are handled, and not once has an occupational disease occurred. In any event, the man on this job is provided with rubber gloves; but significantly he seldom uses them.

In addition to the comments on the specific factors, the parties offered evidence on the relationship between this job and other jobs on whose evaluations the parties are in agreement. The Company argued that this job consists of unpacking and simple inspection. Although the man inspects, he does not put final approval on the product. The job is no more difficult than other inspection or packing jobs which are now in Labor Grades 8 or 9. For example, the jobs of Pre-Packer and Parts Inspector are in Labor Grade 9, while the Product-Inspector and Packer-Shipper jobs are in Labor Grade 8. The foreman testified that the Product Inspector's job is more difficult than the Checker job.

The Union concludes that the job should be compared with Repairman-Salvage rather than inspection jobs. In fact, originally this was a salvage job in Labor Grade 6. The Union admits that some changes have taken place, but they do not warrant a reduction in the evaluation by two Labor Grades.

QUESTIONS

1. Explain the grievance and the position of the parties in terms of the Job Evaluation Plan outlined in Case No. 54.

2. What standards are used to classify the Physical Demand factor within the five degrees? How consistently would you expect any one individual to classify a factor of a job from one week to the next? Would you expect all management representatives to make the same ratings? What considerations account for the difference in the degrees assigned to a factor by representatives of the union and management?

3. Why did not the Company in this case when the Union argued that three factors had been underrated, urge that other factors had been overrated? Would such bargaining strategy be in keeping with the spirit of job evaluation? Would it be sound policy?

4. How do you appraise job evaluation as a system of establishing internal wage structure? What are its principal advantages and major limitations?

Case 56

MAY THE COMPANY UNILATERALLY ESTABLISH A NEW JOB RATE?

UNION: United Steelworkers of America, CIO

COMPANY: Carnegie-Illinois Steel Corporation

The Company transferred the manufacture of a part of a steel product from one mill to another. The Company set a new incentive rate on the operation in the new mill. Both Union and Company recognize that the operation in question, the rolling of a section, which was previously handled in one mill becomes a *different* job when transferred to a different mill. The Union contends that the setting of the new incentive rate under such conditions should be done by negotiating a mutual agreement between the parties and not by unilateral action of the Company. The sole question in this case is the right of the Company to establish rates under these circumstances without union agreement.

Section 11 of the agreement on rate establishment and adjustment reads in part:

"It is recognized that changing conditions and circumstances may from time to time require adjustment of wage rates or modification of wage rate plans because of alleged inequalities, development of new manufacturing processes, changes in the content of jobs, or improvements brought about by the Company in the interest of improved methods and product. Under such circumstances the following procedure shall apply:

"1. When a bona fide new job or position is to be established:

"*a*) Management will develop an appropriate rate by the regular procedure in effect in the Company.

"*b*) Such procedure having been conformed to, the rate proposals so developed will be explained to the grievance committee with the objective of obtaining their agreement to the installation of the proposed rate, or, to the installation of the proposed rate for an agreed upon period which will serve as a trial period. Management may thereupon establish the rate and it may subsequently be subject to adjustment as provided in Paragraph *c* below.

"*c*) Grievances may be alleged by either the employees or Management concerning such rates as follows: In the event there has been no agreement as to the rate to be installed, it shall be considered as if a grievance had been filed in writing on behalf of all employees covered by such rate as of the date of the installation of the rate and the employee commencing to work.

. . . .

"If the grievance filed hereunder cannot be satisfactorily adjusted by mutual agreement, the question as to the equity of such rates in relation to the plant rate structure or such Company rate structure as may result from Paragraph 2 hereunder and the requirements of the job or position as established by sound industrial engineering may be appealed to an impartial umpire . . . ."

POSITION OF THE UNION

The Union argues that nothing in the agreement allows the Company to install a rate or classify a section when the product to be rolled is transferred to another mill. The Union agrees that the contract gives the Company the right to install new rates on their products. However, there is no provision in the agreement applying to the setting of rates on old established products that are removed to another mill for rolling. Since the Company did not have such authority under the agreement, the setting of new incentive rates on such old and established products should be by negotiation between the management and the Union. The Union insists that there should be mutual agreement reached on the new rate prior to its being installed. This demand is held to be thoroughly in accord with the principles of collective bargaining.

The Union holds that the Company's unilateral establishment of rates had, in this instance, adversely affected the workers in a double manner.

a) The workers in the mill on which the section was being rolled lose work which was yielding satisfactory earnings.

b) The workers in the mill to which the rolling of the section was transferred get a rate for the work which is inadequate. The Company revaluates the job and sets a rate yielding a lower average of earnings. The Union estimates that the drop in earnings tends to average some 15 to 20 per cent. Inasmuch as the rolling of the section in the new mill requires great effort and sacrifice on the part of the workers in developing the rolling into a smooth and efficient process, it is the judgment of the Union that the Company should give at least average pay. Since the section to be rolled is usually transferred to a faster mill the result is that the workers produce more tonnage but have lower earnings because the rate is set too low.

The Union contends that in order to protect itself against such an adverse condition, it is privileged under the agreement to negotiate the new rates to be set on the section in the new mill. Particularly, a union committeeman should be present with the industrial engineer who is making the study through which the new rate is to be set. The Union insists that a rate so negotiated and established would be satisfactory to both parties. Either the rate should be set by such mutual agreement, or else the section should be continued on an average-earnings basis.

POSITION OF THE COMPANY

The Company holds that in the operation of its plant, it must often make changes in the productive process, the removal of a section for rolling from one plant to another is a case in point. The new mill in which the section is to be rolled may have a different incentive system, a different capacity, a faster or slower rate of production, and a tonnage capacity per turn (shift) entirely unrelated to the capacity per turn of the mill from which the section was removed. The standard which may have been proper in the mill from which the section came may have no application to the mill to which the section is moved.

The Company argues that the rolling of the new section in the new mill under the conditions indicated constitutes a new job. Under the agreement the Company insists that it has the unquestioned right to institute an appropriate rate for this new job, and the Union correspondingly has the right to test the equity of the rate by resorting to the grievance procedure. The contract is held to make no requirements that the Company negotiate a rate with the Union prior to its establishment. The Company maintains it has a right under the agreement initially to classify a section or set the rate.

It is further argued by the Company that the procedure it follows in setting the rate is in complete conformity with the requirements of the agreement. After the rate is developed by the industrial engineering department, it is discussed between the foreman and the grievance committeeman. The latter, in turn, discusses it with the workers. Opportunity is given to the Union to express its idea as to whether the rate is right or wrong. Under the agreement, management has the right to install the rate which it deems to be appropriate. The Union is privileged to protest the rate through the grievance procedure and arbitration.

The Company points out that it has for many years followed the practice of classifying or standardizing new or previously unrated products under existing plans in the mills. The Union recognized this practice in innumerable instances by resorting to the grievance procedure to protest the equity of the rates established by the Company, without questioning the right of the Company initially to establish such rates. The Union seeks to establish by indirection a principle which it was unable to establish through direct negotiation.

QUESTIONS

1. Does the transfer of operations involved in this case fall under any one of the following headings mentioned in Section 11: "development of new manufacturing processes," or "changes in the content of jobs," or "improvements . . . in the interest of improved methods and product?" If so, which one?

2. In your view should the contract be written in sufficient detail to include the case of a transfer of work between departments? Is there any logic to distinguish the case of transfer of work from a genuinely new operation?

3. What should happen in the Union's view if the parties cannot agree upon a new rate as a result of bargaining? State carefully the Union's position.

4. Why should the Union be opposed to the Company setting a rate on a part of the work transferred between mills? What would be the effects on earnings if the piecework system had many loose rates and the Company could frequently transfer work?

5. Does step 1 (*b*) in Section 11 require the Company to bargain with the Union before placing a rate into effect?

6. What protection does the Union enjoy under Section 11? What rights of management are guaranteed?

Case 57

WHAT CONSTITUTES A CHANGE OF OPERATION?

UNION: International Fur and Leather Workers Union of the United States and Canada

COMPANY: A. C. Lawrence Leather Company

BACKGROUND

During the early years of World War II, the Company undertook the processing of Army re-tan leather. At that time the job of wrapping and tying was studied, and a standard was set; this old standard is identified as No. 27A. The payment under the 27A Standard was based upon the sizing in the Crust Department; once the footage was noted in that department, the size designation was retained through the entire process up to and including the wrapping and tying of the leather into bundles. The size classes developed in the original standard were: Extreme, Large, Very Large, and Extra Large. The measuring machine dial was marked off into segments; for example, the range of $14\frac{3}{4}$ to $17\frac{3}{4}$ embraced the "Extreme," the range average being $16\frac{1}{4}$. The extremes would then be segregated as a size class and would be processed completely without losing their identity as extremes. The same applied to the other three size-classes. The size groups were not mixed. The Company discontinued the processing of Army re-tan in the latter part of 1945.

Late in 1950 or early in 1951 the operation was resumed because this leather was needed in the production of Army shoes. Because the Company believed that a change in the operation (within the meaning of the contract) had occurred, the job was studied by the Standards Department; and a new standard was developed, identified as Standard 34B. This standard was applied for the first time on May 23, 1951, and gave rise to an immediate grievance. Although the alleged changes were not limited to one feature, the important change is in the basis of payment. Under the new methods, as the skins are processed they lose their identity as extremes, large, etc. When the finished skins reach the operation just before wrapping and tying, they go through a measuring machine; and the footage is tabulated. Instead of reaching the wrap and tie job as an "Extreme" lot or a "Large" lot, the skins arrive in mixed lots as to their area classification. The only sorting which has taken place to segregate the skins is by grades of leather. Thus the new standard is based upon the finished measurement. Other alleged changes are: (*a*) Improvement in the quality of the paper and the rope used in wrapping and tying; (*b*) removal of certain elements in the old job, such as positioning of paper, and the addition of other elements, such as walking; (*c*) changed alignment in the room; (*d*) separation of right and left skins in the wrapping.

The relevant contract provisions are in Article V (Standards):

"*Section 1.* The Standards System shall be continued on the present basis. It is understood that the employees will perform the work as set up by the Management at time of study, unless there has been an authorized change of operation. No operation shall be re-timed unless there is a change in said operation.

"*Section 2.* Notice of timing, or of re-timing of an operation shall be given to the Union twenty-four (24) hours in advance."

In addition, the Company refers to Article X (Management), which gives to the management the exclusive right to determine ". . . the schedules of production and methods, processes and means of production . . . provided this will not be used for the purpose of discrimination against any employee, or to avoid any of the provisions of this contract."

POSITION OF THE UNION

The Union analyzes the contract clauses. With respect to the last sentence of Section 1, it argues that the retiming of a job is forbidden *unless* there is a change in the operation. Before the Company can initiate any retiming, it must first be able to prove that there has been a real change. If a question then arises whether the change is real or imaginary, that issue must be processed through the grievance machinery, including arbitration, before the restudy can be made. A company representative has said that if a restudy were made and there had been no changes in the operation, it is probable that the net result would be the same as the previous study. The Union contends that if this were the case, the specific restrictions mentioned in Article V, Section 1, would have been entirely unnecessary. The same company spokesman also alluded to those changes which are not easily detected but which, in composite form, might well justify a restudy. Such an approach suggests a company belief that it does not have to prove the change of operation before making a restudy; the Standards Department does not have to determine whether there is a change in operation prior to the restudy. In essence, therefore, the proof of change is to be found only in the new time study itself. Such a theory is obviously untenable under the terms of this contract.

The one-sidedness of the Company's approach is highlighted by its admission that if the Union claimed a change of operation and asked for restudy and if the Company contested such a claim, the question of whether a restudy was warranted would have to be processed through the grievance machinery before restudy could be made. It is readily seen that the Company's interpretation would deprive employees of any protection afforded them by Section 1. The Company could restudy any job at will and then claim that it was justified because the new standard differed from the old standard. The Union cited several observations made by an arbitrator in another dispute involving the parties:

> "Once the standard is determined, many companies use an incentive system to provide a means of compensating an employee for above-average effort and skill. In other words, it provides 'an incentive for greater production.' As a guarantee against abuses, most union contracts provide that standards are not to be changed unless there is a significant change in method . . . . Sheer length of time in working on an operation where the method has not been changed and which contains a high proportion of manual elements often results in the operator exceeding the $33\frac{1}{3}$ task."

The Union also analyzes the nature of the "change" in operation contemplated by Section 1. The "change" should be significant. It should not be construed so broadly as to allow the Company to create some little change that does not reflect in the method of operation or, more importantly, in the amount of effort that a worker has to put into that operation. Any other interpretation would enable the Company to deprive a worker of extra earnings and force him to do the extra work for nothing. In the specific case of the Wrapping and Tying of Army Re-tans, the Union concludes that there is absolutely no evidence of change. Even the Company admits that "to all outward" appearances the operation is the same now as it was under the 1943 standard. The size of the skins per bundle is no different; the method of tying and wrapping is the same, and the effort is unchanged. Even though the leather is measured now in its finished state instead of in crust, this has no effect whatsoever on the work performed by the operators. It is only a revision in the record keeping. The only tangible item offered by the Company was an improvement in the type of rope used. This must be dismissed as insignificant, because even the time study did not consider it important enough to be counted as one of the elements in the job. If the Company felt the difference in the quality of the rope constituted a "change" under Section 1, why did it not restudy all of the bundling operations in the plant?

POSITION OF THE COMPANY

The Company is confident that a change has occurred in the operation. First, the basic change is from crust measurement, with segregation of the four size categories, to finished measurement. Since finished footage is the only criterion available, it was essential to develop a standard based on the new measurement. Second, the quality of the rope has improved to the extent of affecting the operation. In World War II (when the original standard was set), it was difficult to secure good rope, with the result that any strain caused the rope to break, and much reknotting was required. With the better rope, it is easier to make a knot which will hold. Third, under the old standard the operator was required to adjust and fold the ends of the bundle under as necessary. This is not necessary now and is not done. Moreover, the new standard provides for a two-roll bundle and a one-roll bundle; the old standard had provision only for the two-roll bundle. Other changes are the omission of the requirement that the bundle be tied very tightly and the addition of the requirement that the piling on the skid be done in crisscross fashion. The Union has not successfully denied these changes. The Company emphasizes that the question involved is not the *degree* of change but whether or not there was a change; *any change is sufficient under the contract.* It was made clear from the evidence that the old 27A Standard could not be applied under the new measurement system. To force its application would require the Company to revert to its former process; and this, in turn, would negate the Company's rights as set forth in Article X of the agreement.

Given the proof of change, it follows that under Section 1 of Article V the Company is permitted to retime the job. In a prior case involving this clause an arbitrator said:

"Article V allows a restudy when there is a change in an operation. In his opinion the only realistic approach is one which allows an examination of change in any or all of the elements of a related operation which might have a bearing on the operation in question."

Changed operations must be restudied in the interests of both the management and the employees. Failure to do so could create intraplant inequities and distort the entire standards system.

The Company claims that the Union's interpretation of Section 1 and Section 2 is invalid. There is no stated requirement that mutual consent of the parties must precede a job restudy. Moreover, the past practice of the parties has always acknowledged the Company's right to proceed with a timing or retiming when it felt there was a change of operation. The Union has the full right to bring a grievance once the action is taken. To make the restudy wait upon the processing of a grievance, possibly through arbitration, would destroy the standards system. Such a system can operate successfully only if there is an avenue for immediate adjustment to changing conditions.

QUESTIONS

1. Describe carefully what have been the changes between the work steps as performed during World War II and 1951 in wrapping and tying Army re-tan. Does this change constitute a "change in operation" within the meaning of Article V, Section 1?

2. What is an "operation" under Article V, Section 1? Is it the entire job of wrapping and tying? Is it only that portion of the total job which is directly affected by the change?

3. Evaluate the Union argument that the question of whether or not a change has occurred must be decided before the Company may re-time the operation.

4. If a Company re-times an operation and finds that the time required in the elements of the operation has been significantly reduced from the initial timing, is this a valid argument that there has been a change in the operation? Is it presumptive that there has been such a change?
5. Does the contract language require that a change in operation result from explicit and conscious actions of management? Is a change in the quality of raw material purchased a change in operation? Is a change which results from increased skill and experience of workers a change in operation within the meaning of the contract?

Case 58

EFFECT OF PRIOR EARNINGS ON NEW INCENTIVE RATES

UNION: Amalgamated Clothing Workers, CIO

COMPANY: Atlantic Parachute Corporation

BACKGROUND

With the outbreak of the Korean conflict, the Atlantic Parachute Corporation, a wholly-owned subsidiary of Textron, Inc., decided to devote its facilities to the manufacture of parachutes, as it had done in part in World War II. The government is the primary customer. In 1950 the first contract was with the Air Force; and because of the uncertainty as to costs, this contract included a "redetermination clause" to allow recovery by one or the other in the event the cost estimates in the contract bid were too high or too low. This first contract with the government also included a cost item to cover the training of inexperienced operators. A 28′ parachute was being made in late 1950 and in 1951, and in the Company's judgment the piece rates were set somewhat loosely.

As Korean hostilities continued and as the demand for parachutes was sustained, the government looked upon the Company as more than a temporary, "one-shot" enterprise. Its relatively permanent status was established in 1952. At the same time the 2 years' experience prompted the government to change to competitive bidding and fixed price contracts.

In the spring of 1952 the Company received an order for a 64′ cargo parachute which it had not made before. The manufacture was started on the sixth floor, and no piece rates were set for the first 2 weeks on the cross-seam and main-seam stitchers' operations. Time studies were made, and rates established. The Company contends that these rates were accepted by the sixth floor stitchers. However, the long-range plans called for the gradual transfer of the 64′ parachute production to the third floor where the contract on 28′ parachutes was running out. On June 19, 1952, some of the stitchers were transferred from the 28′ chutes to the 64′ chutes on the third floor. Almost immediately the rates were protested by the girls. The Company made further time studies to determine the validity of the rates.

The parties agreed that for the first week of the changeover the employees would receive 85 per cent of their earnings. But at the end of the week the problem persisted. With Company re-timing of the job, the rate on *cross-seam* stitching was increased from $1.25 to $1.456 per chute. The girls protested that they still could not make out and asked that the ripping element be removed from their assignment. Another study was made; and the rate was revised to $1.52 per chute, including the ripping out of bad pieces of cloth. The girls were still dissatisfied with this solution; and after a meeting of the parties, the Company offered to give them a ripper at the piece rate of $1.456. On the *main-seam stitching* the rate had been set at $1.38 per chute. A similar protest was made, and after 5 weeks the Company adjusted this rate to $1.51. But in both cases, there was an inability to agree on the appropriate rates for the 64′ chute.

The parachutes, regardless of size, are made of nylon fabric. This fabric goes to the cutting department where it is cut into sections. The pieces then go to the stitching room where two operations are performed: (*a*) *cross-seaming*—sewing the small sections into a larger panel on a 2-needle machine; (*b*) *main-seaming*—where the panels are joined to make one complete canopy. The issue involves the rates for these two operations. While these processes are the same for all types of chutes, it is agreed that there is a difference in the cloth used, handling involved, and method of sewing.

RELEVANT CONTRACT CLAUSES:

"*Article XIII* (*Production Tasks*)
"The Company has developed and will maintain properly trained time study personnel in order that production tasks shall be established by scientific methods. These tasks will be established at a level which will permit earnings substan-

tially above the guaranteed minimum wages. The time elements for which the task is developed not only can but will be permanently guaranteed as long as the method, process, materials or equipment remain unchanged. In the event that changes in any of these items occur, the Company will have new studies made covering the new conditions and new tasks will be established which will provide the same opportunity for earnings as existed before the change in conditions took place.

"In the event that after a reasonable period of trial by a normally skilled operator, the new tasks do not appear to provide the same opportunity for earnings as existed before the change in conditions took place, these new tasks shall be reviewed by a qualified representative to be appointed by the Union in collaboration with a qualified representative to be appointed by the Company. If the representatives of the parties are unable to agree as to whether or not the new tasks provide the same opportunity for earnings as existed before the change in conditions took place, the matter shall be referred to arbitration in the manner provided in Article XIII and Article XVII hereof, provided that in any such arbitration the impartial arbitrator shall use the services of a qualified and competent industrial engineer . . . .

"*Article XVII* (*Arbitration*)

". . . the arbitrator or arbitrators shall not have the power . . . to arbitrate away, in whole or in part, any provision of this agreement nor shall he have the power to add to, delete from, or modify any of the provisions of this agreement . . . ."

Position of the Union

The piece rates established for the 64' chute are not adequate to maintain the earnings which existed on the 28' chute. The contract specifies that after a "reasonable period of trial," it is expected that the new piece rates (tasks) will yield the same opportunity for earnings as existed before. The records of earnings show that as of the time immediately prior to the arbitration hearings (5 months after work on the 64' chute started), the girls still had not been able to achieve the level of prior earnings. The

Union will go along with a couple of weeks as constituting a "reasonable period of trial," but it cannot allow employees to suffer a serious loss of earnings over a protracted period. It must be remembered that the loss is through no fault of the cross-seam or main-seam stitchers. The Company has not contended that poor employee effort is involved. Rather, the Company has argued that it takes a long time to develop proficiency when the girls are switched from one type of chute to another. However, under Article XIII it is not intended that earnings suffer for such an indefinite learning period. The concept of a 1-week guarantee is ridiculous, given the Company's own admission concerning the length of the so-called learning period. In any event, the Union doubts whether the girls can ever achieve the prior earnings. It is convinced that they are now operating at peak efficiency, yet their average earnings are still well below the prior level.

Several of the employees testified at some length concerning the reasons why they were finding it difficult to make out under the new rates: *Cross-Seam:* more yardage and more panels; extensive handling on the 64' chutes; more frequent changing of bobbins; more stitching. *Main Seam:* more handling; fabric is heavier; frequent repositioning of the material as panels are added; more stitching; greater fatigue.

The Union does not believe that this is a matter which requires an engineer under Article XIII. Rather, the problem relates to the question of whether the facts show that the same opportunity for earnings was demonstrated after a reasonable period. The Union recommends that a system of graduated payment be negotiated or that the arbitrator recommend such a system. This is the only way to protect earnings during a long learning period.

The Union asks that a rate increase be awarded for the two jobs which will yield the earnings on the 28' chute for the social security quarter preceding June 19, 1952. Adjustment should be made retroactive to the date when the girls first started work on the 64' chutes.

POSITION OF THE COMPANY

First, the same engineering principles were used in setting these rates as had been used in the past. The time study staff reviewed the rates on at least two occasions. Second, the earnings trend on the 28' chute shows that the stitchers involved took almost a year to reach maximum efficiency. Sewing steadily on the 28' chute, the cross-seam stitchers increased earnings per hour from $0.963 in the 1st quarter of 1951 to $1.562 in the 2nd quarter of 1952; the main-seam stitchers' earnings increased from $0.970 to $1.70 in the same period. The record shows that from 1950 to April 6, 1951, the two operations received increases in the piece rate per 28' chute; and the Company suggests that these rate adjustments were based more on expediency than on sound engineering principles. But the "loosening" of rates was not alone responsible for the earnings increase, as evidenced by the upward trend from April 6, 1951, to the spring of 1952. Third, other earnings data prove that when cross-seam and main-seam stitchers change from one type of chute to another, their earnings suffer until acquired efficiency on the new chute allows earnings to approximate former levels.

The Company argues that this is the reason why earnings on the 64' chute have not yet reached the prior level. It is not because the rates themselves are at fault. Each week from July 19, 1952, to the weeks immediately prior to the arbitration hearing (October 11, 1952), the earnings of the stitchers have improved. This trend is likely to continue, especially if one remembers that during the summer months the heat and humidity prevent the nylon fabric from running smoothly through the sewing machines. Inevitably earnings are less in this period. The Company stated that whenever operators are changed from one type of product to another, the operator accepts the assignment, even though earnings are affected, provided the rates are set properly. In this case the Union does not appear to question the engineering soundness of the rates. Rather, it is basing its case on the simple, but contractually invalid, claim that because the stitchers are not making as much on the 64' chute as they did on the 28' chute there must be something wrong with the rates. In the light of the foregoing facts, this reasoning is unsound.

The Company emphasizes that the contract does not grant any guarantee of past earnings. Voluntarily the Company has granted a 5 working days' guarantee at the time of a changeover. However to extend such a guarantee over a longer period would destroy any incentive. The arbitrator would be adding to the terms of the contract if he ruled a guarantee of earnings. The arbitrator is also reminded that under Article XIII he must use the services of a qualified engineer in a case of this type.

QUESTIONS

1. Refer to the language of the contract which provides that "new tasks will be established which will provide the same opportunity for earnings as existed before the change in conditions took place." What does this contract language mean? How would you measure the earnings which "existed before" the change? What period would you use?

2. How would you determine what is "a reasonable period of trial by a normally skilled operator?" Should it be a uniform period among operations, or should it vary with each new operation? Should the arbitrator establish in this case what is a reasonable period?

3. What purpose would a competent industrial engineer serve in this case? Must the arbitrator use the services of an industrial engineer?

4. If from 6 months to a year is needed before a normally skilled operator can become proficient on a new operation, is there the "same opportunity for earnings as existed before the change," even though the incentive rates were set on sound engineering principles? If the employees took 6 months to reach a plateau of earnings on the 28′ chute, can they be required to take a similar period on the 64′ chute before the piece rates set for the 64′ chute are questioned through the grievance machinery? How is your answer influenced by the frequency of changes in the style or size of parachutes which affect the operations?

5. Discuss the policy of rate setting established in Article XIII, Paragraph 1. Is it practicable to establish production tasks by scientific methods and at the same time insure that in the event of changes new rates will be established which will provide the same opportunity for earnings as existed before? Is it ever possible under this contract to reduce out-of-line or loose rates?

Case 59

EXTRA COMPENSATION FOR OPERATING "OLD" MACHINES

UNION: American Federation of Hosiery Workers, AFL

COMPANY: Lincoln Hosiery Company

In the hosiery industry a National Labor Agreement in negotiated jointly by companies affiliated with the Full Fashioned Hosiery Manufacturers of America, Inc., and representatives of the American Federation of Hosiery Workers. The agreement aims at establishing uniform piece rates and working conditions for all member firms. It further provides for the appointment of an impartial chairman to settle controversies arising under the existing agreement.

The present case is concerned with the adjustment of a piece rate to compensate for operating an "old" machine. The Brentmore mill of the Lincoln Hosiery Company operates what is termed by the Union "old" 39-gauge legging machines. The Union requests the payment of 5 cents extra per dozen to operators of these machines to compensate for the added effort and risk and the decreased production that accompanies knitting on these machines. The Company maintains that production secured from the machines is not comparatively low, and therefore no extra compensation is in order. Production records show that the average weekly output, over a period of 7 recent weeks, was about 53 dozen per week.

As early as October 28, 1929, the joint negotiating committee considered the principle that extras should be paid on old equipment. At that time the minutes of that committee disclosed that such an extra was discussed in connection with the principle of uniform rates. The committee recognized "that difficulties may arise [difficulties in achieving uniformity of rates] in view of possible conditions on old equipment. In such cases, no deviation from the principle shall be inaugurated without investigations and approval of the impartial chairman."

In the present case, the decision of the chairman must serve to define the conditions under which extra payments should be made to operators on old equipment.

POSITION OF THE UNION

The Union contends that operation of the Company's "old" 39-gauge legging machines requires added effort and skill for which increased compensation should be awarded. The machines are said to be of an extremely low-speed type, which means that production is decreased through no fault of the employees. The low production of the old machines is not due to any lack of efficiency on the part of the operators, rather to the antiquated character of the equipment. The Union argues that it is unjust that those who work on subnormal equipment should be further penalized by having, in addition to the added effort involved, a low production which no amount of skill or effort can overcome.

POSITION OF THE COMPANY

The Company opposes the Union's demand for 5 cents extra and questions the standards suggested by the Union for determination of the appropriateness of an extra compensation. First, the Company argues that the age of a machine is not in itself a sufficient factor in determining whether or not an extra should be paid. If production and earnings are adequate, then payment of extras would mean a deviation from the principle of uniformity established under the national labor agreement. Or if low production and earnings can be traced to the inefficiency of the operator rather than of the machines, then no extra compensation is in order.

It is the Company's position that the necessity for securing an adequate income on old machines should be stressed rather than the necessity of securing a certain dozen pairs of production. Thus, earnings rather than production is regarded as the criterion for determination of the appropriateness of extra compensation. The Company holds that this distinction is essential because of the variations that occur in specifications in the stockings. It is conceivable that an average production of a loosely knit stocking may not result in average earnings to the knitter.

In the present case, the Company cites figures to indicate that employees on the old machines do earn the average weekly income. The average full-time production of these machines is 53 dozen a week, while the average earnings for a full-time week approximate $29. This condition is said to prevail generally on all machines at this plant. Thus, inadequate earnings do not result from the nature of the "old" equipment.

QUESTIONS

1. What is the purpose of a uniform piece rate in the hosiery industry? What does this tend to equalize among firms? Earnings of wage earners? Labor costs?
2. What would be the effect of a 5-cent "extra" on older equipment?
3. Who should bear the costs of the lower productivity of older equip-

ment? Should men be expected to work harder? Should they receive lower earnings? Should rates be higher or lower?

4. Under a piece-rate system, does the Union have an interest in the age and condition of equipment? What action may the Union take when it believes that equipment is not being properly maintained or is obsolete?

5. Under what circumstances would you recommend a differential in piece rates for older and less-productive equipment? Should the piece rate be higher or lower than on more modern equipment? What is the case for each position?

Case 60

LOSS OF EARNINGS DUE TO PRESENCE OF NUMEROUS INEXPERIENCED WORKERS

UNION: United Automobile Workers of America, CIO

COMPANY: General Motors Corporation

THE GRIEVANCE

"We demand to be paid at $1.10 per hour as we always made it. Because we have a group of new men we cannot maintain production. We are working and pushed all day long and getting paid less money. Until such a time as production is maintained, we demand to be paid our regular rate."

BACKGROUND

The export department of the Chevrolet plant was shut down on July 29, 1941, for what management states was a change of model. Production was resumed on August 4, but it was found necessary to increase the number of men in the department because of expanded production requirements. The additional manpower required was obtained from other piece-work departments that were not working at that time. The price for the 1942 model remained the same as for the 1941 model, i.e., $1.10 per hour for 100 per cent efficiency. The regular men in the department were called in, but, because of the augmented force, they were unable to obtain 100 per cent efficiency and were paid at a rate lower than the full-efficiency rate.

When the increased production in the export department made evident the need for additional men, management states that, following a discussion with two shop committeemen, it agreed that the guaranteed rate customarily applicable to the starting up of the truck line would be paid to the regular workers in the export department after the first day of operation following the shutdown. In any event, a meeting was held between management and the shop committee on August 6, at which time management made clear what it felt was the agreement it had made in this matter, viz., to pay the regular guaranteed rate of $0.95 per hour to the new men in the export department "until they were able to carry the job," but to pay the $1.05 per hour starting-up rate of the truck line to the regular men in that department, after the first day of operation.

Because of the presence of the new men, the regular earnings for the export department for the week ending August 9, fell considerably below $1.10 per hour. However, these earnings were made up to $0.95 per hour for the first day of operation, and to $1.05 per hour for the remainder of the week. On August 12 and thereafter, this department attained 100 per cent efficiency and was paid the earned-rate of $1.10 per hour.

POSITION OF THE UNION

The Union claims that the loss in production was not the fault of the regular men in this department and that, in the absence of any regular model change-over, no guaranteed rate should apply. In place of the guaranteed rate that was paid to these men, the Union maintains they should have received their regular earned rate for the job.

In the absence of a change in the model, the Union claims management had no right to apply the guaranteed rate of pay, especially since the loss of production was caused by the presence of additional men who had little or no experience in the operation of the department. The Union feels that it is unfair to have a number of new workers placed with a group of regular workers and thereby cause a loss in earnings to the regular workers in the department. The Union contends that the guaranteed rate of pay of $0.95 per hour, contained in the local wage agreement, was not intended to apply in an instance of this nature and that management's attempt to apply it here was a violation of that agreement. The Union therefore requests that the regular export department operators be reimbursed to the extent of their full $1.10-per-hour earnings "until such time as production was maintained."

POSITION OF THE COMPANY

Management maintains that it acted well within the terms of the local wage agreement when it paid as it did for the start-up of the export department. Management points out that notice of this addition to the regular starting rate was communicated to the operators through several committeemen and later through the entire shop committee.

The extension of the guaranteed rate, says management, rather than being a violation, represents greater liberality than required by the agreement. Management holds that these employees have no regular earned rate but rather are governed by the production on a group piecework basis which is subject to a guaranteed rate, if group earnings fall below the guarantee (except for breakdown or material shortage when regular earnings are maintained).

The local wage agreement clearly provides a guaranteed rate, which, by past practice, has been paid upon the starting up of a department after a model change-over, after an inventory period, and during certain other occurrences when earnings fell below such guaranteed rate. The only exceptions noted to the application of the guaranteed rate have been when breakdown or material shortages occur. In such cases the regular 100 per cent efficiency rate has been paid.

The Company argues: "If the guaranteed rate is not applicable in this instance, it is difficult to conceive of any circumstances to which it would apply."

QUESTIONS

1. Does management appear to have violated the local wage agreement?
2. Should the local wage agreement be changed so that regular earnings are paid in a case of this kind?
3. If, as the Union implies, the inflow of new workers which brought down the group earnings was caused by poor management planning, should management be made to pay for such inefficiency, or should the employees simply accept it as one of the routine occurrences of industrial life?
4. Would the problem have arisen under a piece-rate system as distinguished from a group-incentive system? Should workers under a group-earnings plan have any right to say who shall be employed in the group?

VACATIONS AND
HOLIDAYS

Vacations and holidays with pay are perhaps the two most common supplemental pay practices to be found in collective bargaining agreements, at least in industrial plants. These forms of compensation, which had been established for executives and office personnel for many years, were generally extended in the past decade to industrial workers. Vacations and holidays were marks of social status. Both are designed to provide leisure from work without loss in pay. The historical quest of working men for more leisure took the form of vacations and holidays with pay in recent years more frequently than the traditional reduction in the regular workweek.

The rapid expansion in these contract provisions reflected the growth of collective bargaining in industrial plants. The wartime stabilization programs permitted the extension of relatively standard vacation and holiday pay plans to parties which previously had no such benefits. The ceilings on wage compensation tended to shift contract settlements toward these so-called "fringe benefits." Vacations and holidays with pay were of real interest to workers who genuinely desired more leisure in an era of high employment. The government in its employment practices for its own employees for many years has had these pay practices. For all these reasons, vacations and holidays with pay have become very general in American industry.

In industries with markedly seasonal and casual employment patterns, these practices have not ordinarily prevailed. In some of these cases, however, such as the garment industry, vacation and holiday plans have been developed through an association of employers; a percentage of each payroll is paid into a central fund administered by the association, or jointly with the union, from which these benefits are paid in accordance with the extent of the employee's attachment to the industry.

VACATION PROVISIONS

While 25 per cent of the workers under collective bargaining agreements in 1940 were covered by vacation provisions, by 1952 almost 95 per cent were under a vacation plan.[1] In this same period, there was a trend toward longer vacations. Only a few isolated vacation plans provided for more than 2 weeks vacation at the end of World War II. In 1952 almost half the plans provided for a maximum of 3 weeks vacation for the most senior employees; and a few plans, particularly in the oil refining industry, specified a maximum of 4 weeks vacation with pay.

An examination of vacation provisions of agreements will illustrate two points made in the introductory chapters of Part I. First, while vacations with pay are a relatively simple idea, the parties have very great latitude to shape and mold a vacation plan to their special needs. A law providing for vacations with pay, as in some countries, would have to be relatively standardized. Collective bargaining has produced almost infinite variations and shadings in vacation plans to meet the special needs or interests of the parties. Second, vacation provisions underscore the fact that detailed administration of a contract may decisively determine both costs and benefits. Similar contract provisions may be made operative in a variety of ways.

The following constitute some of the more important features of vacation plans usually specified in agreements.

a) *Eligibility* to vacation pay may be defined and restricted in a variety of ways. Length of service is the most frequent limitation on eligibility. Employees with various service records, such as 1, 5, 15, and 25 years are eligible for various rates of vacation pay. Eligibility may be limited by the test of continuous service. A variety of events, such as discharge, retirement, sickness, voluntary quit, military service, layoff, or strike may be variously treated as interrupting continuous service and affecting vacation rights. Eligibility for vacation benefits may be further defined and restricted by a provision specifying that an employee must actually have worked a specified minimum time during the year. One third of

[1] Dena Wolk and James Nix, "Paid Vacation Provisions in Collective Agreements, 1952," *Monthly Labor Review,* August, 1952, pp. 162–67.

the contracts have such provisions. Thus, to be eligible for a vacation with pay, employees may be required to be on the payroll a full year before the start or before the end of the vacation season and to have worked in a given percentage of payroll periods.

b) *Vacation pay* may be computed in a variety of ways. In the most common method, vacation pay is calculated by multiplying hours of vacation pay by a rate of pay. The hours may be the actual hours of work during a period prior to the start of the vacation season, the scheduled hours of work of the plant, or some arbitrarily bargained figure. The rate of vacation pay may be the average hourly earnings over some base period, including the effects of overtime, or straight-time hourly earnings, or even the base rate on piece-rate occupations. Vacation pay may be computed in another way as a specified percentage of annual earnings, occasionally with a minimum. Thus, 2 or 4 per cent of annual earnings after 1 or 5 years of service would be a common application of this method of vacation payment. The percentage-of-earnings vacation pay plan has the advantage of resolving at the same time many difficult questions of eligibility.

c) *Vacation plans* typically make provision for a variety of lesser matters. The time of the year during which employees may be entitled to take their vacation may be specified. The order in which various employees may be granted preference in their choice of vacation dates must be determined for any vacation during which the plant is not shut down. The status of holidays with pay that occur during a vacation period must be clarified. Are employees to receive both benefits? The contract frequently may provide for payment of vacation benefits in lieu of vacation where an employee may be required to continue work during the vacation season.

Each relationship must face most of the problems outlined above in contract negotiations or in the administration of the vacation plan. There are certain to be many other questions which are peculiar to the particular relationship. Two illustrative contract provisions are as follows:

1. *International Union of Operating Engineers, Local 647 and Cities Service Gas Company, Oklahoma City, February 15, 1952*

"Vacations shall be on a yearly basis. Employees having one year's continuous service shall be eligible for a vacation of one week with pay. Employees having two or more years of continuous service shall become eligible for a vacation of two weeks with pay. Employees having fifteen or more years' continuous service shall be eligible for a vacation of three weeks with pay.

"Vacations must be taken within the year in which they fall due, otherwise the right to take same will be forfeited. The Company vacation period shall be from March 1st to November 30th each year.

"Vacation pay will be computed on the basis of the employees' respective regular rates of pay at the time said vacation is taken; provided, however, the computation of vacation pay for any employee who is on a combination classification, involving more than one rate of pay, shall be based upon the weighted average of the rates of pay received by said employees during the twelve months' period preceding said vacation. The Company and the employees will cooperate in working out vacation schedules in any calendar year. Where two or more employees in the same Station or Division request the same vacation periods and the Company finds such a schedule will be impractical in view of operations, the employee with the longest service shall have preference in the choice of vacation dates, and the employee with less service shall be required to request another date for his vacation, provided, however, vacations may be taken only at such times as the Company is in a position to furnish qualified relief."

2. *International Association of Machinists, Lodge No. 147 of District No. 64 and Whittet-Higgins Company, November 12, 1951*

"1. On or before May 1, 1952, the Company will determine the date for, and the length of, the vacation period (not less than one week), and will post notices accordingly.

"2. Employees in the employ of the Company on June 30, 1952 and employees who have been laid off or granted leave of absence due to personal illness or disability prior to June 30, 1952, but who still retain seniority rights under Article VII, will be paid vacation allowance based on a percentage of their gross earnings with the Company for the twelve months ending June 30, 1952, as follows:

"Six months but less than one year..........1 per cent
"One year but less than five years..........2 per cent
"Five years but less than ten years..........4 per cent
"Ten year or more.....................6 per cent

"3. For the purposes of this Article an employee's seniority will be determined as of June 30, 1952."

HOLIDAY PROVISIONS

Before holidays with pay became customary, collective bargaining agreements and industrial practice specified certain named (unpaid) holidays for operating purposes. On these unpaid holidays the company sought to shut down its operations. This was not practicable in continuous process operations. Managements also had to operate on holidays in case of emergencies or great demand. Employees who were requested to work on these holidays, and did so, received a premium rate of time and a half or double their regular rate. This rate was paid in consideration for their working on a day like Christmas or Thanksgiving when other employees were off duty.

In the past decade, holidays with pay have become very general in American industry. They are now only slightly less common than vacations with pay. In 1950 approximately 75 per cent of workers under collective bargaining agreements received some holidays with pay.[2] The number of holidays with pay varied widely, from as low as one to as high as twelve or more. At least half the agreements, however, specified six holidays with pay.

The most frequently occurring holidays, as might be expected, are: Thanksgiving, Christmas, Labor Day, the Fourth of July, and New Year's Day. Other holidays with pay mentioned in agreements include: Memorial Day, Jefferson Davis Day, Washington's Birthday, Yom Kippur, Easter Sunday, Mardi Gras Day, Bunker Hill Day, Franklin D. Roosevelt's Birthday, and in a few cases even the birthday of the individual employee. There is considerable adaptation to regional and religious interests. Employees usually receive their regular rate of pay for the designated

[2] Irving Rubenstein and Rose Theodore, "Holiday Provisions in Union Agreements, 1950," *Monthly Labor Review,* January, 1951, pp. 24–27.

holidays with pay. In the case of piece workers, this may be the average daily earnings for a designated period, base rates for a day, or the minimum daily guarantee.

Employees may be requested to work on paid holidays. There is considerable variation in collective bargaining agreements over the total compensation such employees should receive when they do work on such holidays. Contracts vary from time and a half to triple time. Time and a half means that an employee receives only an extra half-time compared to what he would have received had he not worked. Double time means that he receives his holiday pay and his regular compensation. Contracts with double time and a half or triple time provide a premium rate for working over and above holiday pay.

Experience with the administration of a contract clause may reveal problems which become the subject of subsequent contract negotiations. Holiday with pay provisions, despite their relative simplicity, are no exception. Some companies found that employees tended to take off without pay just before or just after a holiday, particularly when the holiday fell on a Thursday or a Tuesday under a normal workweek. The desire for an extended week end is understandable, but many companies have sought to remedy this abuse of holiday pay by a provision requiring, as a condition of holiday pay, attendance immediately before and immediately after a paid holiday if these days are scheduled days of work in an employee's workweek.

An illustrative contract provision is as follows:

United Mine Workers of America, District No. 50, Local No. 13061, and Hercules Powder Company, Hopewell, Va., Plants, November 3, 1952

"(*a*) The pay policy as outlined herewith shall apply only to the following holidays, each of which shall be observed on the day of legal recognition: New Year's Day, Memorial Day, July 4th, Labor Day, Thanksgiving, Christmas.

"(*b*) For all hours worked on a holiday, double time shall be paid.

"(c) Whenever an employee is excused from work on a holiday occurring on a day which would otherwise be one of his scheduled days of work, he shall receive eight hours of straight time pay for such holiday not worked, provided that no employee will be eligible for this pay if

"(1) he is in unexcused absence on the holiday or on the scheduled work day next preceding or next succeeding the holiday, or if

"(2) he works part of the holiday, in which event he shall receive double time for all hours worked on the holiday and straight time pay for the number of hours by which the hours worked are less than eight.

"(*d*) Only the holiday hours actually worked shall be counted for weekly overtime purposes.

"(*e*) Premium pay for hours worked on a holiday shall be in addition to weekly overtime or overtime for any day.

"(*f*) A holiday not worked shall not be considered a day of work for the purpose of determining the seventh day.

"(*g*) A holiday not worked for which straight time pay is allowable under this plan shall be considered a work day for the purpose of computing wages due under the Company benefit plans.

"(*h*) A holiday which occurs during an employee's vacation period shall not be deemed a day of his vacation if it is a holiday to which he is normally entitled.

"(*i*) The Company shall be the sole judge as to whether or not work shall be scheduled on a holiday."

Case 61

IS VACATION PAY A REWARD FOR PAST SERVICE OR PREPARATION FOR FUTURE SERVICE?

UNION: United Packinghouse Workers of America, CIO

COMPANY: Armour and Company

Two employees, Dominick Panek and Gus Skoglund, would have received 2 weeks' vacation with pay, each, in 1945, had they not died. Panek had taken 1 week vacation with pay before his death. The Union is presenting a grievance requesting that the latter's wife be paid for the second week's vacation. Skoglund, on the other hand, had taken no vacation; and the grievance requests that a check for 2 weeks' vacation pay be given his wife.

The grievances read as follows:

"Dominick Panek began working for Armour and Company in 1936. On May 1, 1945, Dominick Panek took one week of vacation. On May 7, he returned to work and worked one week, and then became sick and went home. On June 8, 1945, Dominick Panek died. Some time later his wife applied for the one week's vacation pay that he still had coming, but the Company refused to give her the vacation check. It is our contention that Dominick Panek had one week's vacation still coming and therefore this money should be given his wife.

"The committee requests that the two weeks' vacation pay due Gus Skoglund, formerly of the Sausage Department, be given his wife. It is our contention that Gus Skoglund had qualified for his vacation under the vacation clause and therefore this check should be made available for his wife."

POSITION OF THE UNION

The Union contends that the two employees in this case had fulfilled their service requirements. One man had already taken part of his vacation, and the other one had requested his vacation but had no chance to take it since he dropped dead on the job. The checks for the men were already made out but had not yet been picked up. The Union argues that in the past the Company has paid "fringe issues" to the estates of deceased employees and in at least one case paid vacation benefits to the wife of a deceased employee. This is considered as establishing a precedent in favor of the payment of vacation pay to the heirs of the deceased.

The Union holds that the men had earned their vacation pay and thus accumulated a right which should not be taken from them. Death should not fortuitously enrich the Company and deprive the survivors of the deceased of their just compensation. The Union calls particular attention to Clause 35 of the contract, which provides for 2 weeks' vacation with pay for male employees with over 5 years of service, and to Clause 44, which reads as follows: "Employees who have earned vacations under this vacation plan, but who may become sick, laid off by management, or injured prior to the date selected for their vacation, may, upon request to the management, receive their vacation pay." It is the contention of the Union that deceased employees fall in the above category of employees who are specially protected in their vacation rights since death, like sickness, injury, and lay off, is involuntary in nature.

POSITION OF THE COMPANY

The Company argues that it has never had a practice of paying vacation money to the heirs of deceased employees and that the Union has no right to present these grievances. The Union represents live people, not dead people. Dead persons are not employees, thus are not in the bargaining unit, and thus are not subject to representation by the Union. Vacations are not earned; rather they are granted. They look forward, not backward. They are not a reward for past service; they are a preparation, through rest, for future service. Dead men cannot take vacations.

The Company cites Section 47 of the contract which lays down the general principle that "Employees entitled to vacation will not be allowed to take money in lieu thereof." While this is qualified by Section 44 (quoted above) which permits vacation pay, in lieu of vacations, to certain groups of people, the Company insists that dead people are not included. Further, the Company points out that employees who quit are not entitled to vacation pay; and these men quit, albeit involuntarily.

QUESTIONS

1. The Company contends that a vacation is a preparation for future service, while the Union holds a vacation is a reward for past service. How do you appraise these contending positions?
2. Is there any basis in the sections of the contracts quoted on which to choose between the two positions?
3. Should such problems be treated in the contract? Should such problems be handled in company rules?
4. Is vacation pay to be regarded as part of the wage? Is it a deferred wage payment? If the employees had died without receiving their pay checks for their last week's work, would the Company be obligated to make them payable to the deceased's heirs?
5. Apply the theory you develop in this case regarding vacations (question 1 above) to the situation in which an employee is laid off for

lack of work after the first 3 months of service in a year and not re-employed during the year. Should vacation pay be prorated? Why or why not?

Case 62

EFFECT OF A STRIKE ON VACATION ELIGIBILITY

UNION: United Packinghouse Workers of America, CIO

COMPANY: Armour and Company

The contract between Armour and Company and the United Packinghouse Workers provides that employees absent for specific reasons, including illness, for over 60 working days lose certain vacation rights. Two men, Mayfield and Lloyd, were absent 62 and 64 days, respectively, if the 10 days of strike in January and February, 1946, are counted as working days; and thus they lose their rights. They were absent only 52 and 54 days if the 10 days of strike are not considered working days; and thus they retain their rights. The Company insists that the first interpretation is correct. The Union holds that the second is the correct interpretation.

POSITION OF THE COMPANY

The Company argues that, while very few people reported for work during the 10-day strike period, the plant was open; and the Company stood ready to put anyone to work. Thus, these 10 days were working days and should be counted as such. The Company considers only the following as nonworking days, namely, Sundays, holidays, and "dark days." "Dark days" are defined as days when the Company says no work is available. The Company does not consider strike days as "dark days" since the Company stands ready to offer work on these days; so far as the Company was concerned, there was no shutdown.

POSITION OF THE UNION

The Union holds that the strike was legal and authorized on a nationwide scale. It points out that such strikes, which embody mass organization and result in complete or almost complete withdrawal of the labor force, are an accepted phase of our national life and part of the recognized tactics of national unions.

The whole industry was on strike, and thus the men could not work. Consequently, the Union argues that days on strike are not working days but rather are legal "dark days." Any other interpretation would have the effect of using strikes as a means of impairing the rights of employment.

QUESTIONS

1. What are the possible definitions of "working days" that could be applied to this case?
2. What is the basis for the distinction between "dark days" and a strike? What did the Company mean when it stated that so far as it was concerned there was no shutdown?
3. Would it make any difference in your decision whether the two employees were sick during the 10-day strike period?
4. How should this type of problem be handled in a collective bargaining relationship? Can it be anticipated?

Case 63

WORK PRIOR TO AND AFTER A HOLIDAY

During the 1947 negotiations General Motors and the United Automobile Workers, CIO, bargained a provision for payment for specified holidays with certain eligibility requirements. Among these rules was the following:

"3. The employe must have worked the last scheduled workday prior to and the next scheduled workday after such holiday within the employe's scheduled workweek."

In negotiations between the Union and the Ford Motor Company, the identical clause was inserted in that agreement.

The following year grievances arose under both contracts as to the meaning and application of eligibility rule, number 3. In each case, the question was appealed to an impartial umpire for interpretation. The two umpires apparently made different rulings as to the meaning of the contract language. The two cases are summarized below, including the analysis of the two impartial umpires.

CASE A

UNION: United Automobile Workers, CIO

COMPANY: General Motors Corporation

The six employees who are the subject of the grievance were employed on the 3:30 P.M. to midnight shift in the Nickel Plating Plant which was scheduled to work the full 8 hours on New Year's Eve. The dispute arose when these employees, after being denied permission to leave the plant before the end of their shift on New Year's Eve, nonetheless left shortly after their lunch period on that night. They had worked from 4.5 to 5.2 hours of the shift. Management denied them pay for the New Year's holiday because they had failed to work the entire scheduled workday prior to the holiday and thus failed to meet one of the eligibility requirements for holiday pay.

In seeking pay for the holiday for these employees, the Union maintained that an employee need only work *on* the day before the holiday in order to establish eligibility rather than *all* of the scheduled hours of that day.

The impartial umpire held that the sole issue presented is whether an employee who quits early on a day before a holiday, although denied permission to do so, removes himself from eligibility for holiday pay under the terms of the agreement. There is no concern in this case with an employee who refuses to work overtime on the day preceding the holiday; nor with an employee who reports for work late; nor with an employee who is sent home early for lack of materials; nor with an employee who becomes ill during the day. These and numerous other possible problems concerning eligibility for holiday pay will have to be considered in the light of their own fact situations, in the event that the parties themselves cannot resolve them.

When interpreting contract language that is susceptible to alternative meanings, that interpretation which best effectuates the purpose of the disputed clause should be chosen. Manifestly, the purpose of Paragraph (7) 3 is to discourage the absenteeism that occurs on the days immediately before and after a holiday. The Union's contention that Eligibility Rule 3 should be read as if the word "on" were inserted between the words "worked" and "the last scheduled day . . . ," if adopted, would nullify this purpose to a greater or lesser degree, depending upon the length of time actually worked on the day preceding the holiday. For if the purpose of the eligibility rule is to discourage absenteeism, then by the same token it is to encourage normal plant operations. Employees who absent themselves without being excused after half a day's work are in the category of partial absentees. Their absence can hardly be deemed an encouragement of normal plant operations. To construe the clause as urged by the Union would be to blunt its purpose.

Conceivably, in the case of employees failing to work only a small portion of the day preceding or following a holiday, the "de minimis" doctrine might be invoked; and the argument made that the purpose of Eligibility Rule 3 had been substantially accomplished. But the complainants have no standing under these doctrines, even if they should be found valid. They absented themselves without permission for nearly half of the pre-holiday shift.

The argument that employees who leave the plant without permission on the day preceeding a holiday can be disciplined for violating shop rules but may not be deprived of holiday pay is also without merit. In order to receive holiday pay an employe must qualify under the prescribed eligibility rules. Whether he fails to qualify because he violated shop rules or because of other reasons is immaterial. In either case, he has not met the conditions precedent to the granting of holiday pay.

The impartial umpire denied the grievance.

CASE B

UNION: United Automobile Workers, CIO

COMPANY: Ford Motor Company

The submission in this case was in the form of an agreed-upon question calling for the interpretation of the contract provision.

The case relates to partial absence on the day preceding or the day following the holiday. The question concerns the eligibility of an employee who worked only part of either or both of those days. The Company argues that the purpose of the third basic condition of eligibility is to deter absenteeism which is likely to occur immediately before or after a holiday, especially when pay for the holiday is anticipated. The Company holds that any exception for excuses would create a very difficult administrative problem and that the purpose of the condition requires the disqualification for any absence for any reason. The purpose and the language of the contract apply to partial as well as total absence before or after a holiday.

The Company does not believe the issue is whether the absence can be justified. It is whether partial absence for whatever reason is a disqualification. In other words, the question is whether the third basic condition requires that the employee must have worked the *whole* of the scheduled working day or that he must have worked *on* that day.

The Company construes the phrase "scheduled working day" to mean, not the hours regularly scheduled in advance, but rather the hours which the employee is asked to work on the particular day. Thus, if an employee who has reported for a regular day's work is sent home, either immediately or after a few hours, because of a sudden machine breakdown, the Company regards him as having worked the day. Likewise, if an employee is directed at his regular quitting time to work overtime and refuses, the Company regards him as not having worked the scheduled day, even though he put in his regularly scheduled hours. Again, if an employee reports for work late or leaves early, the Company argues that he does not satisfy the requirement of working the scheduled day. The Company, however, holds that if an employee's tardiness does not exceed one hour and is excused by his foreman, it does not disqualify him from holiday pay.

In the view of the impartial umpire, it can hardly be said that the language of the third condition is wholly conclusive on this question. Either view requires the interpretation of one or more words in the text. The answer must depend upon good judgment as to which is the fairer reading. In the impartial umpire's judgment the fairer reading is that work *on* the day rather than for the whole day is required. The purpose of the provision doubtlessly is to discourage the absenteeism which the holiday induces. But that purpose is substantially accomplished if the employee is required to work on the day, whether the whole or a part. His presence for any part of the day removes the possibility of extension of the holiday for a full day and permits it only for some hours. Moreover, lateness on the day preceding the holiday can hardly have any connection with the temptation for a more extended holiday.

The award of the impartial umpire is that if an employee works any part of the scheduled day involved, he satisfies the third basic condition; absence for part of the day for whatever reason is not a disqualification for the holiday pay; but the absence, whether by late arrival or early quitting, is a ground for such disciplinary measures as are appropriate for similar partial absence in a nonholiday week.

QUESTIONS

1. How do you evaluate the two different approaches to the problem presented by these cases? One approach would deny eligibility to holiday pay, while the other would grant eligibility and discipline for early leaving or tardiness of return to work. Do these approaches come to the same thing?

2. Does it make any difference that one case was a particular grievance and the other a general stipulation?

3. How do you appraise the concept of "scheduled working day" advanced by the Ford Motor Company? If an employee refuses to work overtime after his regular working hours has he failed to work the last scheduled workday prior to or after a holiday within the meaning of the contract?

4. What are the consequences of different interpretations of the same contract clauses in a community like Detroit? In your judgment should there be some way of securing uniform interpretation?

Case 64

ELIGIBILITY FOR HOLIDAY PAY UNDER EXCEPTIONAL CIRCUMSTANCES

UNION: United Furniture Workers of America, CIO

COMPANY: Steinway & Sons

The present case concerns a union claim that 18 employees were denied holiday pay for Washington's Birthday, 1947, in violation of the contract between the parties. The pertinent section of the contract (Article XV) provides in part:

"The following shall be holidays . . . . for which employees shall be paid, without working, at the employee's then regular hourly rate for 8 hours; Thanksgiving Day, 1945 and 1946; Christmas Day, 1945 and 1946; New

Year's Day, 1946 and 1947; Washington's Birthday, 1946 and 1947; Independence Day, 1946 and 1947; Election Day 1946; provided that the employee works his regular shift on the regular work days immediately preceding and following the holiday, unless prevented from working because within 2 months immediately preceding the holiday date, he was either bona fide ill or laid off."

On Friday, February 21, 1947, the regular workday immediately preceding the holiday in question, a snow storm of blizzard proportions struck the New York metropolitan area, in which the Company's plant and the residences of the employees involved are situated. Normal means of transportation to the plant were disrupted, and many employees were unable to get to work on that day. The Union is of the view that this failure to appear at work on the day prior to the holiday should not make the employees ineligible for holiday benefits. The Company holds that the agreement clearly spells out the conditions of eligibility for holiday payment. The 18 employees involved in this case cannot meet these requirements and hence are ineligible.

POSITION OF THE UNION

The Union contends that the failure of the 18 employees involved to report for work on February 21, 1947, was due to conditions beyond their control. The extremely bad weather conditions adversely affected the health of many of them; yet all of these employees made reasonable efforts to get to work but were unsuccessful. Since the failure of these employees to work was not intentional or willful, the Union argues that they should not be penalized by a denial of holiday benefits due them under the contract. The Union further claims that it was not intended by the parties that the conditions precedent in the contract, entitling employees to holiday benefits, were to be applicable to a situation or to circumstances present in this case.

POSITION OF THE COMPANY

The Company concedes that the failure of the 18 employees to report for work on the day preceding the holiday was not willful nor intentional and was attributable to the adverse weather conditions prevailing that day. The Company, however, contends that the contract between the parties specifically sets forth the conditions under which employees shall receive the holiday benefits, and that unless these conditions are met, irrespective of the reason, or unless the employees fall within the stated exceptions, they are not entitled to the holiday benefits. The Company further claims that even though the circumstances present in this case are unusual, it was the intention of the parties to avoid the acceptance of excuses that led them to put in the restrictions in the holiday provision. The Company frankly concedes that if any of the employees involved were genuinely ill on the preceding day, they fall within one of the stated exceptions and would be entitled to the holiday pay. However, the Company insists that to extend the contract provision to include a further exception of "special circumstances," as is requested by the Union, would be contrary to the intentions of the parties and is beyond the authority of the arbitrator.

QUESTIONS

1. What standards can be applied to this type of a case?
2. What is the function of the arbitration process in these circumstances?
3. What is the purpose of the limitations on holiday pay included in Article XV of the contract?
4. How would you appraise the relationship between these parties on the basis of the arguments advanced above?

Case 65

RIGHT OF "DISCHARGED" EMPLOYEES TO HOLIDAY PAY

UNION: United Textile Workers of America, AFL

COMPANY: Hudson Mohair Company

Before July 4 and before September 1 (Labor Day) of the year 1947 a layoff was made at the Hudson Mohair Company. The Company refused to make holiday payment to those who were laid off before or at the time of these holidays. It was the Union's contention that there was nothing in Article III of the contract to disqualify an employee who was laid off and that the Company's refusal to pay holiday pay was a violation of the contract. Article III provided in part:

"The Company agrees that all employees coming under the terms of this contract who have been in the employment of the employer for six (6) months shall be paid eight (8) hours pay at the employee's straight time rate for the following six (6) holidays: January 1, May 30, July 4, Labor Day, Thanksgiving and Christmas Day."

The first layoff took place on June 6, 1947, when the plant was closed for 5 weeks; everyone was returned on July 13, 1947. Late in July, a notice was posted:

"This shop will close indefinitely July 31, 1947. The management is very sorry the following men are to be discharged:"

There followed a listing of all peak force employees.

The plant was reopened September 8, 1947, when the normal force employees were returned to work. After September 8, some of the peak force employees listed on the "discharge" notice were called back to work.

POSITION OF THE COMPANY

1. Those who were specifically listed on the July 31, 1947, notice were entitled to nothing for the Labor Day holiday. The notice stated clearly that the men were discharged, and Article IX of the agreement specified that ". . . all such cases of discharge shall be taken up within five (5) working days from the date of such discharge or the employee waives his rights herein." No grievances were raised by the Union, yet "everybody knows what it means to be discharged." The Company argued that it was immaterial what its reasons were for discharging the peak force employees, just as it was immaterial what it did with respect to unemployment compensation for these men. In summary, these men had no rights; and if any or all of them were rehired, they were to be considered as new employees.

2. Article III used the term "employees" and later "in the employment of." An employee was a person who was working; a person whose work had ceased and who might never work again for the Company was not entitled to the benefits of the provision. One thing only attached under the contract to an employee at the

time of layoff, viz., the right to be recalled when work was available. All other rights under law or under the contract ceased and were inoperative during the layoff period. The fact that these men were not specifically excluded by the provision was a ridiculous theory for the Union to advance. They were entitled to nothing unless the contract specifically *included* them.

3. The original grievance was dated September 25, 1947, almost 3 months after the first layoff including the July 4 holiday. Evidently the Union recognized no equities in its claim until a very late date.

POSITION OF THE UNION

1. The Union insisted that the action accompanying the July 31, 1947, notice took the form of a "layoff," not a "discharge," regardless of the language used by the Company. The Company was quite right in saying that most people knew what a "discharge" was, and it was for precisely that reason that no grievances were brought. The men themselves merely considered it a formal notice of layoff prompted by the closing of the plant.

2. A man who was laid off was still considered an employee of the Company. He preserved rights during the period of the layoff. It is true that an extreme situation might develop if a layoff were to continue for several years, but the contract duration was only 1 year. Furthermore, the clause in question specified an eligibility requirement which each of the aggrieved employees had satisfied.

3. The Company's theory with reference to holiday payments was too narrow. In addition to restoring the losses which were incurred with plant closure on holidays, the payments were intended as a premium to the employees.

QUESTIONS

1. Examine the eligibility of various groups of "employees" for holiday pay: sick employees, occupational injuries, leaves of absence, military leave, temporary layoffs with fixed dates of return to work, employees discharged for cause, employees laid off with no date of return specified.
2. Does the Company's use of the word "discharge" in the notice make the difference between a discharge and a layoff? What is the difference in the meaning of a discharge and a layoff?

3. What do you think should be the eligibility of seasonal employees, temporary employees, or part-time employees to holidays with pay? What contract language would you suggest to make your position clear?

4. The Union may be concerned with the possibility of a company instituting temporary severances from the payroll before holidays to avoid holiday pay. How would you handle this problem?

Case 66

COMPUTATION OF VACATION PAY

UNION: Textile Workers Union of America, CIO

COMPANY: American Felt Company

ISSUE

"Under the terms of the contract of June 20, 1950 and the supplement thereto negotiated in May 1951 should the cost-of-living adjustments be included in computing vacation pay of employees at the Franklin Plant of the Company?"

BACKGROUND

Section VII (*a*) (*Vacations*) of the 1950 contract provides:

"Any employee in the employ of the Employer on June 1 of each year during the term of this contract and having a length of continuous service with the Employer of less than one year, but more than three months . . . shall during each calendar year while this contract is in force, *receive 2% of the amount of his regular earnings from the date of his most recent employment by the Employer to June 1, it being understood that his regular earnings for each week shall be computed at his regular hourly rate of pay for the number of hours worked that week up to but not in excess of forty (40) hours . . .*" (Italics added.)

Subsection (*b*) applies to those with 1 year or more but less than 5 years' service who are to "receive one week's vacation with pay at the employee's regular rate for forty (40) hours." Subsection (*c*) provides for a prorated vacation for 1–5 year persons, allowing 1 additional day for each year of service over 1 year, such extra day to be "with pay at the employee's regular hourly rate for eight

(8) hours." Subsection (*d*) provides 2 weeks' vacation with pay "at the employee's regular hourly rate of pay for forty (40) hours for each of the two weeks." The phrase "regular earnings" appears also in subsection (*f*), but the same definition of regular earnings as appears in subsection (*a*) is repeated.

Another section referred to by both parties is Section VI (*Holidays*). This clause lists 7 holidays and states:

"An employee who works some part of the week in which such holiday occurs or some part of the previous or following week shall receive his *regular rate* of pay for such holiday whether worked or not . . . . Employees who work on such holidays shall receive one and one-half times their *regular rate* of pay for the hours worked (which shall be in addition to the holiday pay provided for)."
(Italics added.)

Section V (*Wages*) contains two relevant clauses:

"*Subsection* (*b*): Workers employed on the second shift shall be paid their *regular rate of pay* plus four cents (4¢) per hour premium, and workers on the third shift shall be paid their *regular rate of pay* plus 7¢ per hour premium."

"*Subsection* (*e*): Any employee who is required by the Employer to report for work and is then sent home or refused work shall receive not less than four hours' pay for first and second shifts and eight hours for the third shift *at his regular hourly rate* . . . ."
(Italics added.)

In May, 1951, the parties entered into a supplemental agreement which added an escalator arrangement as a new subsection (*f*) to Section V. For the most part, the terms were similar to other cost-of-living clauses. However, Paragraphs 2 and 4 of this subsection are relevant:

"(2). The Cost-of-Living Adjustment shall be treated as an add-on in cents per hour for each hour worked . . . .

"(4). The amount of any Cost-of-Living Adjustment in effect at the time shall be included in computing overtime premium, holiday payments, and reporting pay."

The instant grievance arose when the Company excluded the cost-of-living adjustments of 3 cents per hour then in effect when computing the vacation payments under Section VII in 1952.

POSITION OF THE UNION

The Union argues that the specific words "cost-of-living adjustments shall be treated as an add-on in cents per hour" mean that it should be included in vacation pay. The only reason the "add-on" approach was used instead of incorporating the adjustments in the base rates was to avoid increases in excess of wage stabilization regulations which would result from the latter method. It is clear from the repeated use of the phrase "regular earnings" in the Vacation Section, particularly subsections (a) and (f), that employees were expected to receive no less for the vacation period than they would have received if working. Moreover, it is standard practice to make this inclusion under the many escalator clauses now in effect in American industry.

The Union rejects the reasons offered by the Company in denying this claim. First, the Company emphasizes the phrase "add-on in cents per hour *for each hour worked*," arguing that vacation pay hours are not hours worked. This is not a tenable theory. In many bankruptcy cases the courts have held that vacation pay due employees is to be given priority as part of wages earned. Similarly, vacation pay of a prior year has been included by arbitrators in the computation of total earnings from which the pay for the current year's vacation is derived. Therefore, vacation hours must be treated as hours worked. Second, the Company stresses Paragraph 4 of the new Section V, subsection (f), on the basis that the inclusion of cost of living in some computations, among which vacation pay is not listed, is significant. The Union denies this for several reasons: (1) Those items listed—overtime premium, holiday payments, and reporting pay—might have been in doubt; and this is the only reason they were given special reference. There could be no doubt insofar as vacation pay is concerned in view of the use of the phrase "regular earnings" in Section VII. (2) Paragraph 4 does not specifically exclude vacations (3) The Union points out that Paragraph 4 was not the subject of discussion or real negotiations. After agreeing on the basic principles of cost of living and other matters in the supplement, the Company attorney offered to draft the agreement; and it was then sent to the Union. Paragraph 4 was evidently written in by the Company, and therefore it cannot be said that there was any intent or true meeting of minds on the exclusion of cost-of-living adjustments from vacation computation.

POSITION OF THE COMPANY

The Company argument was summarized in a letter it sent to the Union on July 16, 1952:

> "The agreement does not provide that the cost-of-living adjustment shall be included in the regular hourly rate, but 'shall be treated as an add-on in cents per hour for each hour *worked.*' As the vacation hours are not hours worked, they are, of course, not entitled to the addition of the add-on. This fact is further emphasized by the provision in Paragraph 4 of the Cost-of-Living Adjustment provision, to the effect that the cost-of-living adjustment 'shall be included in computing overtime premium, holiday payments and reporting pay.' There is no corresponding provision that the cost-of-living adjustment shall be included in computing vacation pay. The computation made by the Company is, therefore, in entire accord with the contract."

The logic of this conclusion is strengthened by an analysis of other contract provisions, some of which have been quoted above. Section VI (*Holidays*), for example, shows that the phrases "not worked" as opposed to hours "worked" have a practical meaning to the parties. The Union's reliance on the term "regular earnings" in Section VII (*Vacations*) is useless, since regular earnings are defined by reference to the "regular hourly rate," just as that term is used in holiday pay, down time, and overtime. When the term "regular hourly rate" is used, it can be defined by subsection (*c*) of Section XX (*Miscellaneous*) which provides:

> "A schedule of hourly rates of pay currently in effect is annexed hereto and made a part hereof and designated Schedule C."

These were rates which did not include shift differentials and incentive earnings, and obviously they did not include any cost-of-living adjustments.

The Arbitration Board is reminded that it is not to decide whether it was good or bad to exclude these adjustments from vacation pay. It is to decide only whether the contract as written calls for their inclusion.

QUESTIONS

1. How much significance do you attach to the fact that Section V, subsection (f) (4) makes no reference to vacation pay? Is the cost-of-living adjustment part of the regular rate for purposes of computing vacation pay? Holiday pay?

2. What is the basis for determining vacation pay in the ordinary case? Should vacation pay entitle a worker to what he would have received had he worked? Have the parties adopted this view in Section VII (a)? Consider the cases of workers who work short time and overtime. How is vacation pay computed for incentive workers?

3. Does Section VII (a) provide for vacation pay on the basis of 2 per cent of an employee's regular earnings?

4. Does it make any difference in interpreting an agreement which party drafted the contract language in dispute? Would it make any difference in your judgment if the Union stated it had accepted the Company's language in the belief that the cost-of-living add-on applied to all supplemental compensation?

5. Assume there are 200 employees in this plant. What would be the approximate additional cost to the Company of including the 3 cents cost-of-living adjustment in vacation pay? Why do you suppose the Company refused the request of the Union?

HEALTH, WELFARE, AND
PENSION BENEFITS

In the last decade, there has been an enormous expansion in health, welfare, and pension plans in the American economy. Hospital expense protection, for instance, covered 86 million people at the end of 1951 compared to only 15 million 10 years earlier. Protection against the cost of surgical care expanded from 7 million in 1941 to 65 million at the end of 1951.[1] These figures represent all types of coverage: Blue Cross and Blue Shield and plans sponsored by medical societies, group insurance protection, and individual insurance policies; they include plans developed under collective bargaining as well as those initiated by business, nonprofit agencies, and government. Group life and disability insurance and plans for partial compensation for loss of earnings from sickness and accidents have also grown by leaps and bounds. The expansion in private pension plans is indicated by the following figures: 400 plans in 1929, 1,500 plans in 1942, and more than 10,000 plans in 1950.

A number of factors have contributed to the rapid growth in health and welfare plans. They were first introduced on any scale by companies during World War I and the 1920's as part of a welfare program designed to improve morale and to attach the loyalty of the individual employee to the company. The advances in medical science have helped to create a demand for health and welfare programs. Surveys of depressed conditions in the thirties and the disparity of health conditions among regions have helped to highlight health problems. World War II showed the poor health standards of a surprisingly large proportion of

[1] The Health Insurance Council, *Accident and Health Coverage in the United States, as of December 31, 1951,* (New York: The Health Insurance Council, 1952), p. 16.

men called for induction into the armed services. Military service conditioned people to higher standards of medical care than they had been accustomed to in private life. The postwar inflation increased the costs of medical care and stimulated interest in other ways of meeting these costs. The wage stabilization programs of World War II and the Korean period encouraged welfare plans to a degree as limitations on wage rate increases turned the attention of the parties in collective bargaining to this form of fringe benefits. The recession of 1949 affected the bargaining strategy of many unions. Since the cost of living showed little increase or a decline, unions tended to press for welfare plans instead of general wage-rate increases. Indeed, in many durable goods manufacturing industries the 1949 "round" was a health, welfare, and pension round.

Additional factors have been operative to stimulate plans for retirement. The population is getting older. In 1820 one half of the population was under 17 years of age; today the median age is 30.[2] Persons 65 years and older increased from 1 million in 1870 to 9 million in 1940 and 11.6 million in 1950; the estimate for 1960 is 15 or 16 million. Life expectancy at birth has risen from 49.2 years in 1900 to 67.2 years in 1948. Life expectancy at age 45 increased from 24.8 (69.8) to 28.0 (73.0) in the same period, and life expectancy at age 65 increased from 11.9 years (76.9) to 13.4 years (78.4).[3] It is little wonder that retirement problems have attracted widespread attention and that geriatrics has become a common term. These basic facts of age composition contributed to the introduction of social security (OASI) in 1935. Contrary to many fears expressed by private insurance companies at the time, social security has increased the interest in all types of private pension plans. The delay in increasing benefits under social security—a retired man and wife received benefits of $39 a month at the end of 1946—with rising prices of the war and postwar period greatly accelerated interest in private pension plans designed to supplement social security benefits.[4] The decisions of the NLRB and the courts holding that companies were

[2] Henry S. Shryock, "The Changing Age Profile of the Population," *The Aged and Society* (Industrial Relations Research Association, December, 1950), pp. 2–23.

[3] The life expectancy at 65 was 12.4 for males and 14.4 for females.

[4] See "Old-Age and Survivors Insurance" *A Report to the Senate Committee on Finance from the Advisory Council on Social Security,* 80th Cong. 2nd sess., Document 149 (Washington, D.C., 1948).

obligated to bargain collectively with unions over pension plans also stimulated the growth of retirement plans as unions were fortified in making them a demand in collective bargaining negotiations.

HEALTH AND WELFARE PLANS

There are very great differences in the health and welfare plans developed in collective bargaining. Indeed, this flexibility in collective bargaining is one of its major advantages as compared to a government program. Health and welfare plans differ according to the level and types of benefits, the eligibility of various types of employees, the responsibility for administration of the plan, and whether or not employees contribute to the support of the plan. The contract provisions on health and welfare plans are frequently a supplemental agreement, since they run many pages and may have a different expiration date from the main agreement between the parties.

A brief outline of one particular agreement will suggest the wide range of possible variations among health and welfare plans. The plan in effect between Local 807 of the Teamsters and various trucking industry employes in New York City has been summarized as follows:[5]

"Types and Amount of Benefits

"Life Insurance: $1,000.

"Accidental Death and Dismemberment: Death $1,000; dismemberment loss of both hands or both feet, or sight of both eyes, or of one foot or hand and sight of one eye, $1,000; loss of one foot or hand or sight of one eye, $500.

"Weekly Accident and Sickness: $25 weekly, up to 13 weeks for each disability; benefits begin on first day in case of accident, on eighth day for sickness.

"Hospitalization (employee and dependents): Semiprivate accommodations in member hospital for 21 days per disability, plus 50 per cent discount for 180 additional days, benefits outside New York area include cash allowance of $6 per day toward board and room for 21 days and $3 for

[5] See *Digest of Selected Health, Insurance, Welfare and Retirement Plans under Collective Bargaining* (Washington, D.C.: Bureau of Labor Statistics, July, 1950), p. 48.

an additional 180 days; additional allowance of $7.25 for out-patient service. With certain exceptions, maternity benefits are limited to $80.

"*Surgical:* According to schedule of allowances for specified operations, $150 maximum.

"*Source and Methods of Financing*

"Program is financed entirely by the employer, who pays into the Welfare Fund of New York City Trucking Industry an amount necessary to provide the stipulated benefits, currently $6 per month per employee covered. From this fund premiums are paid to a commercial insurance company for the following benefits: Life insurance, accidental death and dismemberment, accident and sickness, and surgical. Hospitalization coverage is purchased through Blue Cross.

"*Administration*

"The program is administered by a board of trustees consisting of 3 employer members, 3 union members, and an impartial chairman."

The parties may choose not only varying levels of health and welfare benefits, but they may elect to spend a given total cost in a variety of ways. They may be relatively more interested, for instance, in group life insurance, or they may have a higher preference for hospitalization; they may include or exclude dependent coverage and maternity benefits; they may elect a longer or shorter waiting period under nonoccupational accident and sickness provisions. They may choose to extend benefits to retired employees, taking reduced benefits or coverage in other directions. Moreover, the cost of a given program of benefits will vary with the particular employees covered by the plan. The age of the group, the proportion of women, and the racial composition of those covered are among the factors influencing the cost of a given schedule of benefits or the benefits which can be secured with a given cost since these factors influence the incidence of sickness. The schedule of hospital fees and doctor fees in the locality will also no doubt be considered by the parties since they influence the relation of costs to benefits.

It is apparent that bargaining on a health and welfare program can be conducted on either a "cost" or a "benefit" basis. The parties may agree on a particular schedule of benefits and then provide for the financing of these benefit standards; or in the alternative, they can agree upon the cost of a program in cents per hour, and then provide for the specific benefits which the sum will purchase. In actual practice, some parties bargain on a cost basis and have approximate benefits in mind; and in other cases, they bargain on a benefit basis and have approximate costs in mind.

In the New York Teamsters plan outlined above the entire cost is borne by the employers. There are many health and welfare plans in which the covered individual employees contribute part of the cost, particularly for hospitalization and surgical items, through payroll deductions. The shares of the individual employees and the company vary widely among contributory plans. For instance, in the New York photoengraving industry, employer and employee each contribute one dollar a week to a jointly administered health and welfare fund. The Ford Motor Company and the United Automobile Workers, CIO, have the following arrangement:

> "For life insurance, accidental death and dismemberment, and weekly accident and sickness benefits each employee who elects coverage pays toward premium cost from $1.72 to $3.44 per month, according to wage brackets; Company pays remainder. Employees pay total cost of hospitalization and surgical benefits. Hospitalization benefits are purchased from Blue Cross, surgical benefits from Blue Shield, all other benefits from a commercial insurance company."[6]

It is argued that when employees pay part of the cost of a health and welfare program they will be more interested in reducing preventable illness and will have a greater interest in the administration of a plan. On the other hand, it is contended that a health and welfare plan should be borne entirely by a company as a legitimate normal business expense; these costs for workers are held to be akin to the cost of providing for maintenance and depreciation of plant and machinery. In recent years the larger

[6] *Ibid.*, pp. 21–22.

number of health and welfare plans have been financed entirely by employers.

A health and welfare plan may be administered entirely by the management, in conjunction with insurance carriers if policies have been purchased from them; by a joint management-union committee, with or without an impartial chairman; or by the union alone. The Taft-Hartley law (Section 302) sought to preclude the creation of new plans administered solely by the union. The Ford Motor Company plan, referred to above, is administered by the respective carriers: the commercial insurance carriers, Blue Cross, or Blue Shield. The New York Teamster plan is a case of joint administration with an impartial chairman. The Amalgamated Clothing Workers Union and the International Ladies' Garment Workers Union are illustrative of unions which have primary responsibility for the administration of health and welfare programs financed by employer contributions in accordance with a "payroll tax." In some instances in which the employer is solely responsible for the administration of the plan, there may be provision for limited arbitration of questions of fact such as eligibility of employees under the agreement. In most cases, however, the decision of the carrier is final on all claims for payment of benefits.

PENSION PLANS

A pension plan is ordinarily a more complex matter for bargaining than a health and welfare plan. A pension plan involves commitments, morally if not legally, which extend over the indefinite future. Many questions arise in considering a pension program for employees, some of whom may have already retired, others soon to do so, and others just entering employment, some of whom have years of service ahead of them. It may be helpful to start the discussion of these problems by a brief summary of a particular pension plan, that negotiated between the Bethlehem Steel Company and the United Steelworkers of America, CIO.[7]

"Types and Amount of Benefits
"Age and Service: Any employee with at least 15 years of continous service at age 65 or over shall be entitled to receive a pension. The amount shall be one per cent of

[7] *Ibid.,* pp. 7–8.

average monthly compensation for services during the 120 months prior to retirement multiplied by the number of years of continuous service, *reduced by* (1) primary social security benefits and other public pensions, except for military service (2) other pensions to which company contributes, decreased by the amount 'attributable to the contributions which . . . pensioner shall have made . . . ,' and (3) discharge liquidation or dismissal allowances (at the discretion of the Pension Board), and if so deducted the provision in (2) shall apply. *Provided,* however, that a pension granted after March 1, 1950 to an employee having at least 25 years of continuous service, shall not be less than $1200 per year (including primary social security benefits and other payments listed above). For an employee with 15 or more years of service at age 65 amount will not be less than the part of $100 which his years of continuous service bear to 25. Present age pensioners will have their annuities increased · in accordance with new minima effective upon any increase in primary social security benefits.

"*Permanent and Total Disability:* An employee with at least 15 years of continuous service at any age is entitled to receive an amount not less than $600 per year *or* one per cent of average monthly compensation (over 120 months preceding retirement) multiplied by his years of continuous service. Upon reaching age 65, the minimum guarantee for old age retirement becomes effective.

"*Source and Methods of Financing*

"Plan is financed entirely by Employer, who contributes into trust fund for any year during agreement an amount which, together with moneys paid in previous years, shall not be less than an amount which on a sound actuarial basis shall be estimated to be sufficient to pay the pensions granted during the year and such previous years.

"*Administration*

"Administration of the plan is in charge of a General Pension Board of five or more officers or employees of the Bethlehem Steel Corporation, appointed by the Board of Directors of the Corporation.

"A provision is made for the establishment of a joint union-management committee of 10 members (equal representation) on insurance and pensions. The committee is to be furnished annually a report regarding operation of the pension plan insofar as it affects the employees, and also a copy of the annual report of the General Pension Board. Periodically during the existing agreement additional information is to be furnished the committee which will enable it to be properly informed concerning operation of the plan insofar as it affects the employees.

"Any differences between the Company and the Union regarding (1) continuous service (2) age of applicant (3) average monthly compensation and (4) cause of permanent and total disability are to be taken up as a grievance in accordance with provisions of the existing agreement. Differences of opinion between the physician appointed by the Company and the one appointed by the Union as to whether an employee is permanently and totally disabled will be settled by a third physician selected by these two."

There are a number of technical questions involved in the formulation of a pension plan that ordinarily involve the participation of tax experts and actuarial assistance. However, the basic questions of policy involved in a pension program, particularly when developed under collective bargaining, can be rather simply outlined.

a) One of the first questions is whether the plan is to be jointly contributory or whether the employer will bear the full cost. A contributory plan is said to increase the interest of workers in planning their retirement and to permit larger pension benefits with a given contribution by employers. A plan financed entirely by the employer is said to be cheaper to the parties since there is no income tax paid on employer contributions to a pension plan as there is on wages paid to employees which is in turn deducted as a contribution to a pension fund. In other words, to make a given contribution to a pension fund will cost a worker more than a company by the income tax the worker pays on the amount of the contribution. As in the case of health and welfare plans, the argument is made that pension costs are a cost of maintaining a work force and should be borne exclusively by the company.

The Bethlehem plan outlined above, as in the substantial majority of recent plans, provides that costs are incurred by the company.

b) The existence of a government administered social security program (OASI) raises the question whether private pension benefits are to be wholly in addition to social security benefits or whether such social security payments are to be offset against benefit levels prescribed in private plans. Most of the private pension plans adopted in the 1949 "round," such as the Bethlehem plan, provided that private pension benefits be reduced by the amount of the primary social security benefits. This type of provision not only affects the current estimates of pension costs; but should social security benefit levels be increased, the cost of private pension benefits would be reduced. The extent of the cost reduction to the company would depend on the extent to which the higher social security benefits were financed by a higher payroll tax on the employee, the company, or out of general government revenues.

c) A significant feature of a pension plan, and one which substantially affects costs, is whether employees who leave a company before retirement receive any of the contributions which the company has made toward a pension. This is the issue of vesting.[8] A pension plan is said to provide for vesting when an employee carries his accumulated pension rights with him on moving to another employer or receives cash or an annuity payable on retirement equal to the amount of the past contribution of the employer. Where there are no vesting rights, the cost of a pension per man-hour worked is reduced by the turnover of employees before retirement. The greater the number of man-hours worked to each retirement, the lower the average cost of pensions in the absence of vesting for those who do retire eligible to receive pensions. Only a very few pension plans in industry provide for vesting rights; pension costs would be sharply increased to provide for vesting rights.

d) When a pension plan is introduced, it is customary for pension rights to be created for present employees, and occasionally for those who have already retired. But no accumulation has been made in the past for these employees, and there arises the problem of "funding past service credits." A liability is created by promising

[8] Evan K. Rowe and Thomas H. Paine, "Pension Plans Under Collective Bargaining," *Monthly Labor Review*, March, 1953, pp. 237–45.

pension rights to existing employees. Thus, there will be no reserves accumulated for a pension of an employee who retires immediately after a plan is introduced. There will be opportunity for a small accumulation in the case of an old employee who retires 5 years after a plan is introduced. No problem of past service credits arises in the case of new employees for proper reserves will be presumably built up over the period of their employment. The adoption of a pension plan immediately creates a very large liability for a company in the form of these past service credits. It is customary to fund this obligation over a period, such as 30 years. A portion of the total past service credits, in addition to the contribution for current employees, is placed into reserves each year. Companies normally elect some variation in the amounts placed in reserve each year, depending upon their profits and tax liabilities.

e) Most pension plans make some provision for long-service employees who become permanently and totally disabled before the age of retirement. The Bethlehem plan outlined above contains this feature.

The way in which the parties to collective bargaining handle these major problems will substantially determine the type of pension plan developed. The cost of the pension program will depend on these factors and such other considerations as the level of benefits proposed, the age composition, sex, life expectancy, and work experience of the work force. The interest earnings on reserves are a most significant element in estimating pension costs.

Many of the larger corporations embarking on a pension program have set up a pension fund of their own with trustees to determine the investment of current pension contributions and the funding of past service credits. Many smaller companies have elected to purchase policies for individual workers from insurance companies calling for the payment of a designated monthly sum after age 65 or some other age of retirement.

The growth of private pension plans raises issues of public policy beyond the questions which confront the parties in collective bargaining. Private pension plans must probably be confined to a small minority of the work force. Private plans cannot readily provide coverage to more than 11 million self-employed and to the many millions more who work in small establishments where turnover of firms is rapid or where the future is too uncertain to embark on the commitments required of a pension plan.

Private pension plans, without vesting rights, restrict the mobility of the work force. They are in part designed by companies to do just that. A worker with accumulated pension rights will be deterred from leaving a company. Mobility is also restricted in that companies with pension plans have a further reluctance to hire older workers (age 45–50), since they become eligible for pensions without the longer period of accumulating reserves involved in hiring a younger worker (age 25–30).

The extension of private pension plans tends to encourage retirement at age 65 or earlier. In 1950, 45.0 per cent of the males and 9.5 per cent of the females over 65 were in the labor force. It is to be recalled that 11.6 million of the population are over 65, and the estimate for 1960 is 15 or 16 million. There is serious doubt that the country can afford any marked shrinkage in the labor force and the associated decline in national product. An appraisal of retirement policies must also recognize that there have been notable advances in medicine affecting diseases of the aged. More progress can be expected. Some pension plans developed under collective bargaining now provide that an individual worker may elect to remain at work to age 68 if he can perform satisfactorily the work assigned, but he may continue after that age only on the consent of the company. The policies of management affecting retirement may be expected to be the subject of increased consideration in collective bargaining.

Cases 67–70

ISSUES IN PENSION NEGOTIATIONS

CASE 67. CONTRIBUTORY VERSUS NONCONTRIBUTORY PENSIONS

The question whether employees should share the costs of providing pensions was one of the most important issues between the companies in the basic steel industry and the United Steelworkers, CIO, in 1949. The President appointed a fact-finding board to hear the dispute and to make recommendations. The arguments presented on behalf of the industry and union positions are summarized:

A. *Arguments for contributory pensions:*

1. Joint contributory programs, based upon common consent, are likely to be more firmly established and are less likely to be discontinued because of changing interests or economic conditions. Stability is of great importance in plans for assuring security, especially in old age programs.

2. Contributory private insurance programs provide more secure protection to the individual since by contributing he, as an individual, becomes a party to a virtual contract.

3. With different contributions by workers of different rates of pay and lengths of service, differential benefits are justified. Such differential benefits are an important factor in preserving incentive and satisfying the quite natural sense of equity of each individual.

4. Joint contributions to a pension program justify the principle of vesting protection in the individual worker so that after a period of time the annuity purchased by the joint contributions becomes inalienably assigned to the individual, regardless of future health or employment.

5. Joint contributions assure a condition of mutual responsibility for the development, maintenance, and administration of a benefit plan. Regardless of the indirect effects of benefit costs upon wages, profits, or prices, the fact that both parties are making an immediate, measureable, and individual contribution has a very real effect upon the operation of the plan.

6. With private or public benefit programs financed by joint contributions, there is greater likelihood of an extension of such programs to areas other than old age and survivors insurance, including permanent and total disability insurance and temporary disability and health insurance.

7. Total pensions could be more substantial. At the same time, employee contributions would offer protection against imprudent demands in the future.

8. Noncontributory plans tend to discourage the hiring of older people.

9. Employee contributions are necessary to discourage absenteeism, malingering, and other abuses among participants in the plan.

10. Contributions are necessary to prevent adjustments in employee earnings in the event of possible ups and downs of business activity.

B. *Arguments for noncontributory pensions:*

1. The companies already accept the principle of non-contributory pensions in providing pensions for their executives. The fact that they do not contribute has not reduced their effectiveness as executives.
2. The employer should bear the full cost and recoup the expense in the price of the product just as he does with respect to depreciation of equipment.
3. The return to the employer in terms of greater workforce stability and employee efficiency justifies his bearing the full cost.
4. Under a noncontributory plan, all the workers will be covered since no worker will be tempted to remain out of the plan in order not to forego any part of his currently spendable income.
5. Since employer contributions are part of costs and not taxable, the net cost to the employer of providing a pension is much less than the cost to employees whose contributions are part of taxable income. At 1949 tax rates, a net contribution of 62 cents by an employer could buy the same type of pension that would cost an employee $1.20.
6. Financial stability will be promoted because costs can be better integrated into the labor cost structure. Flat cents-per-hour charges become part of the wage structure.
7. A contributory plan would have to include death and withdrawal benefits, thus increasing the cost of pensions. Of an employee's contributions, only two thirds would be applied toward strict retirement income, the rest being used for the refund benefit.

QUESTIONS

1. The contributory principle of the OASI has never been seriously questioned. Should the principles guiding the erection of a public insurance program differ from those guiding private plans? In what way?

2. One of management's arguments against noncontributory plans is that pension costs assume the nature of fixed costs which are inflexible over the cycle. Examine this argument. Does the method of financing affect the validity of this argument? . . . whether by production royalties, cents per man-hour worked, flat annual contribution per employee, fixed costs-variable benefits, or variable costs-fixed benefits. Under what conditions do pension costs become integrated into the wage structure? What if a pension is granted in lieu of a wage rate increase of an equivalent cost to the company?

3. How would the total costs of the two types of plans compare? What would be the effect on costs under each plan of employee turnover, death before retirement, pension administration?

CASE 68. FUNDING

A second pension issue which has led to a major industrial dispute in recent years is that of funding. In 1950, the United Automobile Workers, CIO, conducted a 100-day strike against the Chrysler Corporation in order to enforce its demand that an agreed upon pension be funded for past and future service credits of all employees. The positions of the parties were as follows:

1. The Company agreed to establish a pension plan which would guarantee the difference between social security payments and $100 a month. Unilateral administration of the plan would be retained by the Company, and the method of financing was to be at its sole discretion. Its offer "to pay pensions (had) behind it the highest credit a company can have, plenty of assets good earnings." In other words, the costs of retirement would be met as they arose out of current earnings or in any other manner the Company saw fit.

2. The Union demanded an actuarially and financially "sound" trust fund which would guarantee the payment of pen- sions. Specified and fixed payments per man-hour worked by the Company would maintain the fund. The Company proposal was rejected because an unfunded plan risks the loss of pension rights either through economic vicissitudes or renegotiation. Fur- thermore, the Company refuses to specify how much it would set aside to meet pension payments. The plan advanced by the Com- pany was estimated by the Union to cost only 3 cents an hour at present. Since the Union was demanding 10 cents worth of pen- sion and social insurance benefits *or* a 10 cents wage increase, the Company's proposal was deemed inadequate.

3. During the long strike, the Company moved through three distinct stages or positions before it finally agreed to a funded plan. The successive positions of the Company were:

1. An offer to fund pensions of workers as they retired but not to provide for past or future service credits before retirement.
2. An offer to fund pensions of workers as they retired with a 30 million dollar bank deposit. This deposit would not be in the form of a trust fund nor would it suffice to cover past service. However, interest payments would be made on past credits.
3. Finally, the Company accepted the principle of funding all service credits of all employees but retained unilateral administration of the trust fund. However, eligibility requirements were to be jointly determined.

QUESTIONS

1. Is funding of past and future service credits indispensable to the "soundness" of a pension plan as a general rule? Why would the Union hold out for a trust fund rather than be satisfied with a bank deposit of $30 million? Would your position on the wisdom of funding be the same for a private plan as for a government plan for its employees or for any other perpetual institution?

2. Are the long-run costs of a funded plan different from those of a pay-as-you-go plan? Which type of plan serves to postpone the cost impact of retirements?

3. How would the age of a firm affect the cost of funding? Discuss in terms of the likely age distribution of its employees and its need for working capital.

4. Under what conditions would a purchased annuity program be preferable to a trust fund?

5. Would an employer be responsible for pension payments to retired employees for life regardless of whether or not he remains in business or terminates the plan? Would the presence or absence of a trust fund have any effect on this obligation if, in fact, the obligation does exist? What happens to an employer-financed trust fund if he goes out of business?

6. The Company charged that the Union wanted a trust fund in order that it might exercise control over it and spend it for purposes other than pensions. Is this charge consistent with the nature of a trust fund? How might the Union accomplish this purpose?

Case 69. Compulsory Retirement

All pension plans prescribe a minimum age at which retirement is possible. Some specify a maximum age at which an employee must retire. For the most part, compulsory retirement is a feature of unilaterally established pension programs, while negotiated plans usually permit a flexibility in the application of retirement provisions. Unions generally prefer to govern retirement by the provisions of the collective bargaining agreement under which discharge must be for just cause (e.g., inability to do the work because of age) and is subject to the grievance procedure. Flexibility would allow a worker to remain at his job as long as he is able to perform its duties or as long as he desires.

The pros and cons of compulsory retirement were debated before the 1949 Steel Panel by the Steelworkers Union and the Inland Steel Company, which required retirement at age 65. A summary of the Company's arguments and the Union's rebuttal follows:

1. *Company:* The company's retirement plan and the establishment of annuity and pension benefits in connection therewith, is predicated upon the existence of a fixed retirement age. This is the general rule in industrial retirement plans throughout the United States. *Union:* The fact that this plan is predicated on a compulsory retirement age is no justification of the requirement. Its presence as a general rule in industrial annuity plans merely indicates that (a), the thinking of insurance companies had dominated the retirement field; and (b) opinion in industry always lags behind facts.

2. *Company:* The fixed retirement age gives the employee advance notice as to the length of his possible service with the Company and enables him to plan accordingly. *Union:* It also disregards the possibility that pressing financial need may require the postponement of retirement. In the absence of adequate pensions, compulsory retirement constitutes and invitation to tighten one's belt and accept a much lower standard of living.

3. *Company: a.* The fixed retirement age prevents grievances that otherwise would multiply as the question of
each employee's employability arose.

     b. The fixed retirement age prevents accusa-
tions of favoritism directed against supervision and
management in cases where one employee is retained
in service and another is retired.

Union: While these doubtlessly characterize some unilaterally operated plans, they do not apply to a plan
operated under the terms of a collective bargaining
agreement. One does not avoid unpleasantness in some
cases by being violently harsh in all cases.

4. *Company: a.* A fixed retirement age gives an incentive
to younger men.

     b. A fixed retirement age and retirement there-
under results in general improvement of the average
productivity of the workforce.

Union: Death also creates similar opportunities, but no
one advocates it as a method of providing incentives
to young workers. These arguments assume that every
retirement creates new opportunities for promotion.
While this is true in some cases, it is extremely difficult
to find a direct connection between the process of retirement and promotion especially in a dynamic industry such as steel. In fact, employers achieve pension
plan economies because the retirement process does
not result in promotions all along the line.

5. *Company:* It is unfair and destructive of employee
morale to discriminate between types of jobs of employees in retiring such employees from service. (E.g.,
retire clerical workers at 70, but warehousemen at 65.)

Union: This will disappear as an argument under conditions in which a proper pension is payable. Old men will
be glad to retire from jobs they cannot effectively fill
if they have the means to do so.

6. *Company:* The experience of this company has shown,
according to management, that the compulsory retirement rule has increased the efficiency of its workforce
to an extent which justifies the cost of the pension program.

Union: There is no evidence supporting compulsory retirement as a cause of increased efficiency. Bethlehem Steel, which does not have a compulsory retirement, cannot be shown to be less efficient than Inland.

QUESTIONS

1. One of the arguments advanced for pensions is that they permit the retirement of superannuated employees who otherwise could not have been "turned out." Is this purpose defeated by a flexible retirement age? Would the type of plan in effect influence the decision of workers to retire?

2. If postponement of retirement beyond 65 is permitted, should the employer continue to fund future service credits?

3. Are there pension cost advantages to be gained by the employer in accepting a flexible retirement age provision? Would these accrue if he continues to fund current service credits beyond the normal retirement age of 65?

4. Should an employee receive his pension at the normal retirement age regardless of whether he retires or continues to work? If not, what if he retires and accepts employment in another firm? Would he then be eligible to collect his private pension or his OASI benefits (assuming he is 65)?

5. If retirement is deferred, should the worker, when he does retire, receive only the benefits which he would have received had he retired at the normal retirement age? Should he receive, upon retirement, a larger pension since his life expectancy has been reduced by the number of years worked past 65? If not, should the fund's savings be credited to the employer toward the payment of service credits of other employees? Would this be consistent with the view of pensions as deferred wages?

6. Can compulsory retirement be justified as an antideflationary measure? How would it affect Personal or Disposable Income?

7. Would workers tend to have differing views about compulsory retirement in periods of depression and full employment? Depending on whether or not they are employed? Or whether they are young or old?

8. Under what conditions does compulsory retirement mean a net gain or loss in real national income?

CASE 70. COMPANY VERSUS INDUSTRY PENSIONS

Collective bargaining in part of the full-fashioned hosiery industry is conducted by the American Federation of Hosiery Workers, AFL, and an association of producers, the Full-Fashioned

Hosiery Manufacturers of America, Inc. In 1950 both parties exercised their rights under the contract and reopened the wage clause. The Association demanded that a substantial wage reduction be made; while the Union demanded, among other things, the immediate institution of a pension program financed by the employers. Failure of the parties to agree on either issue led to the submission of the entire dispute to arbitration.

Characteristics and Problems of the Industry. The Association represents 21 employers who operate 25 mills and employ 9,500 employees. These employers operate about 14 per cent of the total knitting machines in the industry and do so at the highest wage rates in the industry. Seventy-five per cent of the industry's machines are in nonunion shops, mostly in the South, which pay lower wages than the unionized sector. The remaining 11 per cent are in firms not members of the Association but organized by the Federation. The industry is sharply competitive, and the disappearance of the seller's market in 1949 placed the northern mills at a distinct disadvantage. While northern mills accounted for 58.3 per cent of the total machines in the industry in 1949, they produced only 47.5 per cent of the total output of full-fashioned hose. The seriousness of competition is increased by the continued growth of the southern sector of the industry and the faster rate of new machinery introduction in the South.

Moreover, there is considerable turnover of firms in the industry, and profits and net worth fluctuate widely. Some mills expand their personnel, while others contract theirs at the same time. Employees of the hosiery industry frequently move from one mill to another, either by choice or necessity.

These characteristics raise some thorny problems in the establishment of a pension program. Can workers feel secure that they will ever receive a pension if the life and financial health of a firm are uncertain? Does not the common necessity of changing one's place of employment jeopardize the worker's ability ever to qualify, by his length of service, for a pension? Since there are wide variations in turnover rates and age distribution among firms, would not pension programs on a company basis create cost differentials which could have serious implications for the ability of some producers to compete successfully?

Award. The arbitration Tribunal ruled that a pension program be established which would cover all the employees of the association members and which would be financed by contributions by the employers to a single pension trust fund. "The pension claims of long-service employees [will] run against the assets of a Pension Fund, which can be used only to pay pensions, and are not dependent upon the future ability of the employer to pay pensions." In addition, downward wage rate adjustments were ordered as were the elimination of "extras" on particular operations and the correction of several important "out-of-line" rates.

QUESTIONS

1. Does the wide adoption of pension programs throughout industry generally provide a justification for establishing one in the organized hosiery industry?

2. Keeping in mind the characteristics of this industry (small firms, rapid turnover of firms, small capital requirements, and product market competition), would an association or industry type of plan be advisable for any other similarly organized industry? Would you advise an industry-wide program for the steel industry?

3. One of the frequently advanced arguments against pensions (particularly in the absence of vesting rights) is that they become bars to labor mobility. What are the implications for mobility of an industry pension plan?

4. How would the costs and pension security under an industry plan compare with those under multiple individual programs on a firm basis?

5. Given sharply competitive conditions and variable production volume, what kind of a plan is advisable, one with fixed benefits and variable costs, or variable benefits and fixed costs? Would the question of complete funding be an important issue in setting up an industry pension program in hosiery?

Case 71

UNION REQUEST FOR A COPY OF A GROUP INSURANCE POLICY

UNION: Textile Workers Union of America, CIO

COMPANY: New Bedford Cotton Manufacturers' Association

Under Article III of the agreement between the parties, the member mills agree to procure and maintain in force an insurance policy providing certain benefits for their employees. Following a general outline of the benefits to be provided, these statements appear:

> "It is understood that the member mills will not operate this insurance benefit plan themselves, but will obtain a policy from a reputable and established insurance company, which will administer the benefits described above. These benefits will be subject to such conditions and limitations as standard practice in the insurance business prescribes. New employees shall become eligible for these benefits after such period of time following their employment as prescribed in ordinary group policies of this type."

The Union contends that it has been refused a copy of the policy issued to the mills and requests that the Association be required to furnish a copy. The Association holds that nothing in the agreement requires it to furnish a copy of the policy. The issue has been submitted to an arbitrator for a decision.

POSITION OF THE UNION

The Union argues that as bargaining agent for employees of the Association, it has a right to know the details of any policy which affects its members. It holds that it would be at a disadvantage in negotiation or discussion of questions arising under Article III if it were kept in ignorance of matters affecting the benefits available to employees. In the opinion of the Union, a reasonable interpretation of Article III, as a part of a collective bargaining agreement, would seem to indicate that the Union should be fully informed on such matters, particularly in view of the references to "standard" and "ordinary" practices.

Further, the Union holds that in the absence of a copy of the policy, disagreements will arise as to coverage. In fact, the mere refusal by the Company to furnish a copy of the policy is said to create an atmosphere of suspicion among the employees "that there is something wrong." The Union insists that the certificate and bulletins furnished to employees give only limited information. It is held that additional conditions with respect to the receipt of benefits are included in the master policy, and the Union and the employees are less than fully informed when they are not made aware of these additional conditions.

POSITION OF THE COMPANY

The Association argues that there is nothing in the wording of Article III which requires that a copy of the master agreement between the mills and the insurance companies be furnished to the Union. It holds that each employee is provided with a booklet and with certificates in which the details of the plan are fully set forth. The terms of the master policy relating to such conditions would serve merely to confirm this fact. However, the Association maintains that such data in the master policy as relate to costs and rates, to the financial arrangements between the mills and the insurance companies, are confidential matters. The Association argues that disclosure of such information might prove detrimental to the interests of its members, and, further, that nothing in the agreement can be interpreted so as to require such data to be submitted to the Union.

QUESTIONS

1. For what purpose does the Union desire a copy of the policy issued to the mills?
2. What use could the Union make of the information contained in such a policy?
3. When the Association says that disclosure might prove detrimental to the interests of its members, what specifically do you suppose it means?
4. What principles should govern questions which are not covered in the agreement? Does the absence of an affirmative right to the policy in the contract create a presumption against the Union's demand?
5. How do you appraise the position of the Association? Does it have a right to withhold the information? Is it wise in so doing?

Case 72

IS THE DEMAND FOR A HEALTH AND WELFARE FUND A DEMAND FOR WAGES?

UNION: Hotel and Restaurant Employees' International Alliance and Bartenders' International League of America, AFL

COMPANY: United Restaurant and Liquor Dealers of Manhattan, Inc.

On December 21, 1945, the Association and the Union entered into a 5-year collective bargaining agreement. Paragraph 20 of said agreement provides in part as follows:

"Reopening Provision

"This contract shall continue in existence for 5 years from date of formal agreement, but wages and working conditions set forth in paragraphs 6, 7, 8 and 9 may be the subject of negotiations each year upon 30 days' notice by either party prior to the annual termination date."

Paragraph 6 of the agreement establishes the number of hours to be included in the workday and the regular workweek. Paragraph 7 of the agreement establishes a minimum weekly salary, provides for overtime at the rate of time and a half, and fixes the minimum rate to be paid to extra bartenders. It also provides that wages shall be paid in cash at the end of each week's employment. Paragraph 8 of the agreement establishes a vacation schedule. Paragraph 9 refers to holiday pay.

Pursuant to the provisions of Paragraph 20, and within the period therein allowed, the Union reopened the agreement. Included in the demands made by the Union was a request for the creation of a health and welfare fund for the benefit of its members to be financed by contribution by members of the Association equal to 5 per cent of their respective payrolls. Agreement was reached by the parties on all of the demands raised by the Union with the exception of the demand for a health and welfare fund. The parties agree to submit this demand to an arbitrator for his decision.

POSITION OF THE UNION

The Union argues that the language of Paragraph 20 is ambiguous and that it was the intent of the parties, in framing the clause, to include in the annual discussions all "bread-and-butter" matters. It states that in executing a 5-year agreement, the parties intended only to fix, for that period, the union shop and the unlimited right of the employer to discharge any bartender. Therefore, it contends that any matters relating to compensation, including its demand for a health and welfare fund, may properly be raised by the Union, as a matter of right, in the annual negotiations.

The union counsel, who participated in the negotiations leading to the agreement of December 21, 1945, stated that the original contract presented by the Association to the Union did not contain the reference to Paragraphs 6, 7, 8, and 9 in the reopening clause but only stated that wages and working conditions might be reopened each year. This clause was accepted by the Union in the course of the negotiations. When oral agreement had been reached on all of the issues, counsel for the Association drafted the final agreement and inserted the reference to Paragraphs 6, 7, 8, and 9 in Paragraph 20 and submitted the same to counsel for the Union. The union counsel made some minor changes in this draft and redrew the agreement but made no change in Paragraph 20, which now included the reference to Paragraphs 6, 7, 8, and 9. The agreement as thus drawn was signed by the parties. The Union insists that no discussion was had during the negotiations of any limitation on its right to reopen annually all so-called "bread-and-butter" clauses. It argues that the insertion of the reference to Paragraphs 6, 7, 8, and 9 was not intended to alter the basic agreement between the parties that wages and working conditions might be renegotiated each year.

Lastly, the Union points out that counsel for both sides in the negotiations were members of the New York Regional War Labor Board; and the term "wages," as used in the agreement, was used in the sense in which it was interpreted during the war by the NWLB and the Director of Economic Stabilization, to include payments by an employer to a health and welfare fund.

POSITION OF THE COMPANY

The Association contends that the reopening clause is not ambiguous but is specific and precise; that it does not permit the raising in the annual negotiations, as a matter of right, of the issue of a health and welfare fund; that such a demand does not come within the scope of any of the subjects dealt with in Paragraphs 6, 7, 8, and 9 of the principal agreement, which are the only subjects expressly specified for annual renegotiation. It also argues that contributions to a welfare fund are not wages since they are not paid to the workers, and that they are not considered wages under the provisions of the Internal Revenue Code, the Fair Labor Standards Act, or the regulations of the Director of Economic Stabilization in effect during the war.

The Association is of the opinion that the addition of the words of limitation in Paragraph 20 at the conclusion of the negotiations between the parties indicated their intent to limit the subjects of renegotiation. It holds that the interpretation of counsel for the Union finds no support in the language of the agreement or the history of the negotiations. It further points out that Paragraphs 6, 7, 8, and 9 do not include all of the "bread-and-butter" clauses in the agreement. Thus, Paragraph 13 requires the employer to supply all bartenders one warm meal a day; and Paragraph 14 requires the employer to furnish and launder uniforms, coats, and aprons at its expense. Finally, the Association points to the language of the supplemental agreement of January 23, 1947, wherein the parties referred to the fact that only Paragraphs 6, 7, 8, and 9 might be reopened. It concludes by stating that the stability of the relationship between the parties requires that the Union's request be denied and that any other determination would destroy the integrity of the collective bargaining agreement.

QUESTIONS

1. To what extent is the history of negotiations to be used as a basis for deciding a case in the face of explicit contract language? Does it make any difference whether the specific point was dismissed in the negotiations?
2. What is the issue in arbitration? Is it the demand for a pension on its merits or the arbitrability of the demand for a health and welfare plan?
3. Would a strike for a health and welfare fund under the circumstances of this case constitute a contract violation?
4. As a matter of union policy, is there any way in which the Union could reinstate its demand if the arbitrator decided against the Union?

SPECIAL PROBLEMS

OF CONTRACT

INTERPRETATION

Some problems arise during the term of an agreement on questions on which the agreement appears to be entirely silent. These cases are instructive since the arguments of the parties tend to go to the fundamental nature of the collective bargaining relationship and to the nature of the agreement. Consider, for example, a demand of a union for compensation for a year to make up the difference between previous wages and military pay for employees entering the armed service. The contract contains no such provision, and at the outset assume that the company never had such a practice. The union simply files a grievance growing out of a large number of inductions to the armed forces. Is the issue the proper subject of a grievance? May it be arbitrated? Does the company have to bargain with the union on the question under the law? Does it have to agree to such a demand? Is the union free to strike on the question under the usual no-strike clause?

In approaching this case, two extreme positions may be taken.[1] (1) Some spokesmen for management look upon an agreement as a means by which the union and the employees secure specified and limited rights from management which at the outset had absolute prerogatives. "The powers which management does not surrender by contract, it is asserted management necessarily retains and may exercise unilaterally." Under this view the management unilaterally could institute the pay for employees entering the

[1] Archibald Cox and John T. Dunlop, "The Duty to Bargain Collectively during the Term of an Existing Agreement," *Harvard Law Review*, May, 1950, pp. 1097–1133. Also see Douglass V. Brown, "Management Rights and the Collective Agreement," *Proceedings of the First Annual Meeting of Industrial Relations Research Association* (1948), pp. 145–55.

armed services but the union may not raise the question. (2) At the other extreme is the view that the obligation of the statute to bargain collectively requires the company to negotiate in good faith at any time on any issue "in respect to rates of pay, wages, hours of employment, or other conditions of employment" not expressly covered by the agreement. Under this view the management would be required to bargain on the military pay question, but it would not necessarily have to agree to any such compensation. It would, however, presumably be an unfair labor practice for the management unilaterally to place such compensation into effect without approval of the bargaining representative.

The NLRB has apparently adopted the second of these views requiring the company to bargain during the term of the agreement on the issue raised.[2]

Neither of the two positions outlined above is in keeping with the practices of collective bargaining as developed by the parties in most cases. The basic difficulty with the second view is that it tends to break down the distinction between contract negotiation and contract administration. If carried to a logical extreme, the parties could at any time raise any issue not explicitly covered by the agreement. Managements could not be reasonably certain of labor costs for a specified period. The parties could be in continual negotiations. In fact, because of the uncertainty created by the NLRB rulings, some parties have adopted a waiver clause to prevent reopening issues or raising new issues during the term of the agreement. The following clause from the May 29, 1950, contract between General Motors Corporation and the UAW-CIO is illustrative:

"The parties acknowledge that during the negotiations which resulted in this agreement, each had the unlimited right and opportunity to make demands and proposals with respect to any subject or matter not removed by law from the area of collective bargaining, and that the understandings and agreements arrived at by the parties after the exercise of that right and opportunity are set forth in this agreement. Therefore, the Corporation and the Union, for the life of this agreement, each voluntarily and unqualifiedly waives the

[2] See Allied Mills, Inc., 82 NLRB 854 (1949); Tide Water Associated Oil Co., 85 NLRB 1096 (1949); Jacobs Manufacturing, 94 NLRB 1096 (1951).

right, and each agrees that the other shall not be obligated, to bargain collectively with respect to any subject or matter referred to, or covered in this agreement, or with respect to any subject or matter not specifically referred to or covered in this agreement, even though such subject or matter may not have been within the knowledge or contemplation of either or both of the parties at the time that they negotiated or signed this agreement."

The existence of such contract clauses is a measure of the degree of unreality of the rulings of the NLRB and a measure of the ordinary intent of the parties in signing an agreement.

The difficulties with the first view outlined above, the position that all rights not explicitly relinquished by the contract reside in management, can be explored most directly by a slight change in the initial illustration. Although there may have been no contract provision on the type of military pay, the company may have had an unbroken practice for a decade to make such payments. Can the company now unilaterally abolish the practice simply because there is nothing in the agreement? The first view of the agreement would sanction such action. If this view were to become general, agreements would become almost infinitely detailed as unions would seek to reduce to writing all practices which they wished to protect from unilateral action by management.

If the two positions outlined above both constitute an unsatisfactory answer to questions or issues not covered by the agreement, what view is to be adopted? The reader is encouraged to formulate his own conclusions in a generalized form.

In any concern with issues not expressly covered by the agreement, as well as in instances of a specific contract provision, the practice or custom of the parties is likely to be widely discussed. What is a practice? How many events have to take place before a custom becomes established? Does it make any difference if responsible management is ignorant of the custom? What is the status of the great many customs and practices that exist in a plant when an agreement is signed? What happens to those clearly in conflict with the agreement? What happens to those on which the contract is silent? May either party change these practices? These questions are not readily answered, but they may be more clearly understood in the context of the particular cases.

The problems of contract interpretation posed by such practices and customs may be expected to be particularly acute under a master agreement where divergent conditions may have developed or may have been inherited at different plants. Some of the problems created by uniform contract language and divergent practices are illustrated in Case 76.

Case 73

SUBCONTRACTING

The issue of subcontracting has a long history in collective bargaining. The problem arose first in the garment trades where unionized employers sometimes contracted out work to non-union shops with lower wage scales. This practice tended to transfer employment opportunities to nonunion conditions and created within the union an interest in regulating subcontracting through collective bargaining. Subcontracting is now subject to extensive regulation through collective bargaining in the garment industry today.

In recent years the issue of subcontracting has become more significant in the division of maintenance and construction work between the direct employees of a company and those working for a construction contractor. Most companies tend to contract out major new construction work; a few companies may contract out normal maintenance operations. The regular employees of companies have come to have an increasing concern with such subcontracting. They are interested in the employment opportunities, and they frequently resent the hiring of outside workers at the higher construction scales. A number of contracts contain provisions specifying conditions under which work may be contracted. Managements have a major interest in this matter since the extent of subcontracting affects the ability of a company to provide steady employment. Subcontracting makes it unnecessary to hire temporary employees. Most managements are anxious to guard the flexibility of operations which subcontracting may afford.

The following case illustrates the problems for the parties involved in subcontracting.

UNION: United Packinghouse Workers, CIO

COMPANY: National Sugar Refining Company

The present grievance concerns the propriety of the Company's subcontracting to an outside firm a $9,000 job for the improvement of bulk storage facilities. The job involved the erection of two hoppers and conveyors designed to move raw sugar across a ceiling and into Warehouse No. 3.

POSITION OF THE UNION

The Union contends that the Company violated the agreement between the parties by hiring outside contractors to do the construction work on the warehouse instead of assigning the work to regular employees of the Company who have by this action of the Company been deprived of work opportunities and earnings. The contract provisions held to be violated are as follows:

> "*Paragraph 1.* The Company hereby recognizes the United Sugar Refinery Workers' Local Union . . . as the sole and exclusive representative of its employees at the Long Island City Refinery for the purposes of collective bargaining relative to wages, rates of pay, hours of employment and other conditions of employment.
>
> "*Paragraph 2.* This Agreement shall apply to the regular employees of the Company . . . . The word 'employee' as used in this Agreement shall refer to said regular employees of the Company at its Long Island City Refinery other than those expressly excepted and to no others. Any such employee who has performed work, as an employee of the Company, on 30 calendar days, shall be considered as a regular employee . . . ."

The Union argues that there is a precedent for its grievance dating back to 1946 when it objected to outside contractors doing construction work on a warehouse, and the contractors were removed. At the same time, it stated that it had no objection to outside contractors erecting the outside shell of a new building, but that once the shell is erected, the installation of equipment and all inside work is under its jurisdiction.

POSITION OF THE COMPANY

The Company contends that it is its practice to permit its own employees to perform installation and construction work unless business expediency dictates otherwise. The Company pointed out that, for many years in the past, it has been engaging outside contractors to perform construction work. Since 1947 outside contractors have performed from 10 to 44 per cent of annual improvements and construction ranging from $640,000 to $1,300,000 per year.

In this instance, the Company let the work to an outside contractor because its own employees were completely occupied with other work. Earlier in the year the Company had recalled to work all mechanics who were in layoff status and, in addition, increased its force of mechanics by nearly 30 employees. During the month when the new conveyor and hoppers were being installed, the mechanical staff of the Company, in addition to its regular maintenance work, performed nearly 12,000 hours of work on other new installations and improvements in the refinery and worked either 5 or 6 days each week. It would not have been feasible to implement its staff still further, since its supervisors could not have directed the increased work force efficiently. Furthermore, nothing in the contract provisions referred to by the Union states that only union members or regular employees may perform work on refinery premises. There is no basis for the distinction between the erection of a shell of a building and the installation of equipment. Nothing in the contract prevents it from hiring outside contractors; and in the absence of such a contractual commitment, the hiring of an outside contractor to fabricate and install new equipment is a management prerogative.

The following arguments, apart from the National Sugar Refining Company case, are frequently advanced by the parties in cases involving the subcontracting issue.

UNION ARGUMENTS

1. An unlimited right to contract out would permit managements to use this device to break unions. By contracting out major operations freely, a company could undermine the position of the union and escape its responsibilities under the contract.

2. Companies can use the device to take jobs out of the bargaining unit. For instance, a steel company could engage a con-

tractor to operate the blast furnace so that the persons employed in that operation would be employees of the contractor rather than of the steel company. Thus, these workers may be removed from the protection of the agreement by unilateral company action.

3. Contractors may be engaged to do work which could be done by employees who have been laid off. This applies most commonly to construction, repair, and maintenance work which is often contracted out without any regard for the welfare or needs of a company's own employees.

4. At times employees of contractors are assigned to work side by side with the company's employees under different wage rates and conditions of employment. Such a practice is unfair and inequitable and gives rise to a great deal of resentment.

COMPANY ARGUMENTS

1. Restriction of this right could reverse long-standing practices of contracting out certain processes and operations to firms with specialized equipment and craftsmen. To force a firm to reverse this custom would be uneconomic, since many firms do not have a sufficient volume of such operations to justify investing in and operating these processes.

2. An alteration of present practices of subcontracting construction work would lead to labor discord, since it would mean the invasion of the jurisdiction of one strong union by another strong union in search of new members and more dues.

3. Small firms have neither the diversified shops and tools nor the men and range of skills necessary to many types of construction and repair work. To compel them to do all such work with "in-plant" forces would saddle them with burdens of employees and equipment which they are not able to carry.

4. Even for large firms, however, there are jobs which come up only intermittently and require special and expensive equipment and skills. To retain the maximum amount of equipment and personnel which might be necessary to undertake occasional big jobs would constitute an uneconomic drain on a company's resources and create serious shortages of skilled tradesmen and equipment in the construction industry.

5. A periodic expansion of the work force to meet temporary needs would create problems of administering pension rights, social insurance rights, seniority rights, and other employment

benefits which are designed for permanent employees. Furthermore, the maintenance of a company's good merit rating for unemployment insurance becomes impossible if it undertakes the casual hiring and laying off of forces for construction.

6. A firm must be free to act swiftly to meet emergency repair problems or to construct large new facilities without having every decision to employ an outside contractor subject to review and possible reversal in arbitration.

QUESTIONS

1. Do you think the right to subcontract is implied in the ordinary management clause?
2. Is there any satisfactory way of defining the type of work which may be contracted out? A few possible bases for definition are the distinctions between (1) major processes and those incidental to the manufacture of a product, (2) new construction and maintenance and repair, (3) outside and inside construction, (4) construction and installation, (5) regular and periodic or irregular work, and (6) a dollar volume limitation.
3. Analyze the approach to subcontracting which seeks to redefine an "employee" in the bargaining unit to include all those at work on the premises except where waived by local agreement.
4. In the *National Sugar Refining Company* case does the past practice of the Company create any right for the Union to seek to limit subcontracting in this instance? Was there any practice?

Case 74

IS A SEVERANCE PAY DEMAND ARBITRABLE?

UNION: Textile Workers Union of America, CIO

COMPANY: Textron, Incorporated—Esmond Mills

The issue in this case is whether or not under the agreement between the parties the employees of the Esmond Mills are entitled to severance pay.

On January 1, 1948, the Esmond Mills and the Union entered into a collective agreement, effective until March 15, 1950. In May, 1948, Textron Incorporated purchased the Esmond Mills, closed the plant, and proceeded to liquidate the machinery and equipment. The employees of the Company were terminated. It was acknowledged that Textron assumed the obligations resident in Esmond's agreement with the Union.

490 · *COLLECTIVE BARGAINING*

The Union requested severance pay for the employees. Forty-six per cent of the 1,100 employees involved have had 10 or more years of service, some as much as 30 years; 28 per cent from 5 to 10 years of service; 12.6 per cent from 3 to 5 years of service; and 12.8 per cent less than 3 years of service.

The closing of the mill came as a surprise to the employees and to the Union. The laid-off employees found an employment market in which textile mill jobs were scarce. After long training in the textile industry, the employees found it difficult to transfer their skills to other industries. They felt that they had built up an equity in their jobs and the abrupt termination of employment entitled them to severance pay.

POSITION OF THE UNION

The Union presented a long and detailed justification for its demand for severance pay. Considered solely in the light of the human problem involved, there is ample justification for some measure of compensation of these employees for the loss of their power to market their labor resulting from the abrupt closing of the plant in which many of them have spent such a large portion of their lives. The closing of the plant apparently was decided upon with little or no regard for the human beings involved. The new owner appears to have regarded the plant solely as a physical asset to be disposed of as it pleased, without limitation or inhibition. Likewise, the prior owners callously disposed of their property without making provision for the men and women who helped to make its growth and development a living fact.

In short, if the arbitrator has the power he should award the terminated employees severance compensation in some amount to assist them in their readjustment until they find other employment. But the central question is whether a third party has the power under the existing contract to make such an award.

The Union argues that such power exists. It bases this argument on Article VI of the contract which is entitled, "No Strike or Lockouts—Arbitration" and which contains in part the following language:

"Any dispute, difference, disagreement or controversy of any nature or character, whether or not a grievance, between the Union and the Employer which has not been satisfactorily adjusted within fifteen (15) working days after the initiation of conferences may be referred by either party to arbitration . . . ."

It also cites the preamble to the contract which reads:

"WHEREAS, it is the intent and purpose of the parties hereto to promote and improve the industrial and economic relations between the Employer, its employees and the Union, to establish a basic understanding relative to rates of pay, hours of work and other conditions of employment, and to provide means for the amicable adjustment of any and all disputes and grievances . . . ."

In addition, the Union points to the absence of a so-called "Management Prerogative Clause" from this agreement.

The Union contends that the phrase "any dispute, difference, disagreement or controversy" is language without limit and clearly conveys the intention of the parties that not only matters concerning specified provisions of the agreement as written can be arbitrated but also any other matters encompassed by the parties' relationship which might be brought up by them during the contract's life. There are no words, expressed or implied, denoting exception, inclusion, or limitation as to what constitutes any "dispute, difference, disagreement or controversy." This broad clause, while unusual in labor contracts the Union reasoned, was nonetheless drawn in this instance by parties well versed in the contents of such agreements. By virtue of their previous experience, they realized the impossibility of foreseeing all the problems which might arise under a contract; and they purposely used the phrase, "any dispute, difference, disagreement or controversy of any nature or character, whether or not a grievance . . . ." to allow for the arbitration of disputes the nature of which they did not anticipate when the agreement was signed. There is nothing in this language that reflects an intention to limit the arbitrator's jurisdiction in any way, the Union argues. If the parties had intended such a limitation, they had ample opportunity to express it in specific language. They would have written language to limit the arbitration provision to matters arising out of the application or interpretation of the agreement, such as most contracts contain.

In short, the Union argues that the parties signed a blank check in the sense that they left open to the possibility of arbitration any matter coming within the scope of the relationship of the parties. The Union denies the applicability to this case of the decision by Professor Douglass V. Brown in a case involving the same Union and the Naushon Mill in New Bedford. It points out that while the contract involved in that case made any dispute, difference, disagreement, or controversy arbitrable, it also contained a sentence which read, "It is understood and agreed that questions involving changes in the terms and provisions of this agreement shall not be subject to the foregoing grievance procedure or to arbitration thereunder." The contract at hand does not contain such language.

POSITION OF THE COMPANY

The Company maintains that the agreement between the parties dated January 1, 1948, covers in detail wage adjustments, piecework adjustments, hours of work, overtime, holiday pay, vacations, leaves of absence, layoffs, seniority, insurance benefits, and all matters normally covered in a collective bargaining agreement. The contract was the outgrowth of negotiations of demands; and in any event, no reference to it was included in the agreement. When the contract was entered into, the Union's demand for a general wage increase was not settled by agreement but was submitted to arbitration. The written submission to arbitration stated that "all the requests of the Union have been negotiated and agreed upon, and it is understood all of the provisions in the new contract except the matter of a general wage increase have been settled." The Company argues that the Union's request for severance pay for the employees is therefore outside the scope of the contract and not an arbitrable issue. While admitting that the language of the arbitration clause is broad, the Company maintains that it is the intent and purpose of the clause to permit arbitration only of matters arising under the contract and not to permit either party to raise and arbitrate issues not under the contract. To hold otherwise, it is argued, would destroy the validity of collective bargaining agreements and lead to chaos and strife.

OPINION OF THE ARBITRATOR

Despite my conviction that on equitable grounds there is much merit to the Union's request for severance pay, I am compelled as an arbitrator to give careful consideration to the parties' rights under their collective agreements. Granted the broad nature of the arbitration clause in this agreement, one must nevertheless consider whether the parties intended to permit a third party, through the medium of the arbitration clause, to drastically alter the basic nature of their contractual commitments. I cannot believe this to be the case. The substantive contract issues are contained in the parties' agreement which was drawn for a specific period. It could hardly be deemed an agreement if there could be constant additions to its basic terms by virtue of new demands carried to arbitration during its life. One of the basic purposes of a collective agreement is to furnish stability to the parties' relationship by defining the limits of their rights and obligations. This end is hardly served by a holding that additions to the structure of their relationship of an unknown and unforeseen character can constantly be carried to arbitration during the agreement's existence.

The parties in this case bargained over a contract, reached an agreement on its salient features, and determined that it was to govern their relationship for a fixed period. All of the important elements involved in their relationship were discussed, considered, and negotiated. On certain ones the parties reached common understandings and reduced them to writing. With respect to others, demands were made by one side and rejected by the other. Provisions covering such subjects were omitted from the contract. The agreement as finally written was an embodiment of all of the major elements in the parties' commitments. It defined the limits of their respective obligations. By reasonable implication, major categories of obligations not included in the agreement were not intended to be covered by it.

In this case, the above conclusion is reinforced by the fact that when the parties submitted the wage question to arbitration they acknowledged that "all the requests of the Union have been negotiated and agreed upon, and it is understood all of the provisions in the new contract except the matter of a general wage increase have been settled." In the light of this fact, the arbitrator cannot add to the parties' agreement an obligation to pay severance pay without fundamentally altering the understanding they had themselves reached. If he did so, he would not be effectuating the terms of the parties' agreement; he would be extending those terms to a field usually written into a contract by direct collective bargaining. It is not a reasonable conclusion from the instrument as drawn that such an extension of the agreement by arbitration to an area usually the subject of direct negotiations was contemplated by the parties.

QUESTIONS

1. In your opinion, did the parties intend that an issue such as this severance pay issue be submitted to arbitration? Carefully develop the reasons for your conclusion.

2. If the parties had intended to submit such an issue to arbitration, how could they have drafted Article VI any more clearly to make this evident?

3. If the issue is not arbitrable, does the Union have the right under the contract to strike for severance pay? What is the relative scope of the arbitration clause and the no-strike provision of the agreement?

4. Does the Company have an obligation to bargain over the severance pay demand under Section 8 (a) 5 of the Taft Hartley law? What does any such obligation mean?

5. In your judgment, how should the personal and community problems of readjustment presented by this case be handled? What costs should be borne by the owners, the workers, and the community?

6. What is the relation between severance pay and unemployment compensation?

7. Would you distinguish between the problems which can be raised through the grievance procedure and those which may be arbitrated?

Case 75

THE SCOPE OF THE NO-STRIKE CLAUSE: HOT CARGO

UNION: American Communications Association, CIO

COMPANY: Western Union Telegraph Company

FACTS OF THE CASE

The Union is the collective bargaining representative of the employees in the landlines and cable division of the Company. It is also the representative of employees of two other cable companies. After a failure to negotiate a new contract for the cable employees of the three companies, a strike was called for January 1.

In the ordinary course of operations, cablegrams to and from foreign points pass through the hands of the Western Union landlines employees. On January 3, the Union adopted a resolution declaring all traffic going to or coming from the struck companies to be "hot traffic" and directed landlines employees not to handle it. Although the order was ignored by many employees, "hot traffic" was blocked to an extent sufficient to cause the Company great concern. When the Company imposed discipline on employees refusing to handle "hot traffic" the Union requested that the issue of whether employees had the right to refuse to handle struck traffic be submitted to the impartial arbitrator as provided by the contract.

At the arbitration hearings both the Union and Company charged the other with the violation of Section 31 of the contract which reads:

> "Since the Company's business is one of serving the public and it is the mutual desire of both the Company and the Union to provide uninterrupted and continuous service, to promote industrial peace and to provide for stable labor relations, the Company agrees that there shall be no lockouts and the Union agrees that there shall be no strikes or other stoppages of work during the life of this contract."

Both parties agreed to waive the question of whether technically there had been a lockout or work stoppage and agreed to limit the issue to be decided to whether the employees had the right to refuse to handle struck traffic.

THE ARGUMENTS OF THE PARTIES

The Union argued that its refusal to handle "hot traffic" did not constitute a violation of Section 31. The language of this provision must not be interpreted literally because the practice in question is a tradition in the industry so deeply rooted and so universally accepted that it must be deemed a practice of the trade. Therefore the practice is as much a part of Section 31 as if it had been explicitly stated.

Precedents were cited by the Union in support of its position. Some cable contracts explicitly exempt employees from handling such traffic. Prior to this dispute, no company had ever insisted that its employees handle "hot traffic" against their will. Finally, there were several instances in the past when Western Union employees refused to handle "hot traffic" and were not disciplined for their refusals.

The Company claims that practices obtaining in other cable companies have no application to landlines companies. Regarding the past instances cited by the Union, the Company asserted that, in each instance, its failure to take disciplinary action was due either to the fact that the struck traffic was insignificant in amount or to the fact that the strike was settled before the Company regarded the situation as critical. Further, it contended that it has never recognized that its employees had the right to refuse to handle any part of its business. Finally, it argued that the refusal to handle traffic to or from struck companies other than the cable division of Western Union was an unfair labor practice under the Labor Management Relations Act.

ARBITRATOR'S DECISION

The arbitrator, viewing the history of the cable and telegraph industry as a whole, ruled that it is the practice in that industry for workers not to handle struck traffic. Therefore, he concluded that "the language of Section 31 must be read in the light of this practice and that it does not prohibit the Union from directing employees not to handle 'hot traffic' or the employees from following such directions." Since the arbitrator conceived of his function as one of determining the rights of the parties under their contract, no attempt was made to determine the extent to which the Company might be entitled to relief on application to the National Labor Relations Board.

Therefore, the Company was ordered to reinstate the suspended employees with back pay for time lost and to eliminate from the service records of these employees any reference to the suspensions. Since some employees, because of their unwillingness to handle struck traffic, might not be occupied full time, the Company was authorized, at its discretion, to make a proportionate deduction from the salary of any such employee.

THE COMPANY APPEAL

Dissatisfied by the arbitrator's decision, the Company went to the civil courts and moved that the award of the arbitrator be vacated. The Company contended that the arbitrator had exceeded his powers as set forth under Section 6(a) of the agreement. While he is given power to rule upon any dispute as to the "application or interpretation" of the contract, he "shall not have the authority to alter or modify any of the express provisions of the contract."

QUESTIONS

1. Do you agree with the Company charge that the arbitrator exceeded his authority under the contract?
2. Discuss the role of custom in the interpretation of a collective bargaining agreement. Should an agreement be interpreted literally without regard for tradition? What if there is disagreement between the parties as to whether a practice is a custom?
3. On what grounds does a civil court accept jurisdiction over an appeal from an arbitrator's decision? Should it accept jurisdiction over any appeal from arbitration?
4. Discuss the purpose of a "no strike and no lockout" provision of an agreement. Does such a clause require union members to cross the picket line established by a second union? Are all strikes under all contracts a violation of the contract during the term of the agreement?
5. Consider the conflict in jurisdiction over this case before an arbitrator and the National Labor Relations Board. Should the employer file an unfair labor practice against the Union? What is the function and the authority of each? What does a decision from each mean? What happens if they appear to make "conflicting" rulings?

Case 76

LOCAL WORKING CONDITIONS

The negotiation of a single contract which governs a number of plants of a single company raises a number of special problems. Similar problems arise with the multifirm agreement. A variety of customs or practices develop in these plants that are not readily reduced to writing or standardized. Some of the plants are older than others, and customs may be deeply rooted in both the local management and workers. Some plants may have been purchased from other companies and retain practices from the earlier management. Different types of equipment and operating problems may confront the parties in some localities. The Union will wish to retain the more favorable practices, and the management may not wish to disturb deeply-rooted local arrangements. It would require many pages of contract language to specify these practices. In this situation, some parties negotiate a "local working conditions" clause which specifies that local arrangements more favorable than the terms of the company-wide agreement shall not be changed.

A number of difficult problems arise in the administration of such contract provisions. It is not always clear what is a "local working condition." There may be little difficulty if the condition is set forth in a local agreement, or an exchange of letters. There may be difficulties, however, if there is only an oral agreement or a clearly established custom. In some cases, it may be difficult to establish a practice because of conflicting evidence or because events occur infrequently. Difficulties arise when there is a possible conflict between the explicit terms of the master agreement and an alleged local working condition. An illustrative case will help to clarify the problem.

UNION: Federation of Glass, Ceramic, and Silica Sand Workers of America, CIO

COMPANY: Pittsburgh Plate Glass Company

A grievance developed from layoffs of 9 employees between January and March, 1950, at the Creighton plant of the Company. Specifically, the Union charged that the Company had violated the agreement by not applying the "10-5 rule" of Section 5(i) to a layoff which was due not to the installation of new machinery or technological change but to a reduction in work arising from a prolonged strike in the automobile industry. No more than 2 weeks' work were lost by the laid-off employees. Section 5(i) provides as follows:

"Should any department in a factory be partially or permanently discontinued due to the installation of new machinery or technological changes, then such employees who have been affected shall be given opportunity for transfer to bottom of the promotion schedule in another department in the same plant providing they are qualified and meet the following conditions: (1) Any employee having five (5) years or more seniority in that department or plant can displace any employee with less than three (3) years plant seniority, or (2) any employee having ten (10) years or more seniority in that department or plant can displace any employee with less than five (5) years plant seniority.

"Exceptional conditions can be brought up for discussion between the Industrial Relations Committee and the Plant Management."

POSITION OF THE UNION

The Industrial Relations Committee, the grievance committee of the Union in the plant, holds that the Company had developed the practice and local understanding of applying Section 5(*i*) automatically to any reduction in force which it could not regard as temporary in a week or 10 days. Since this practice has been established, it is binding under Section 9 of the agreement:

"Provisions and rules set forth in Sections 5, 6, 7 and 8 shall be followed in each factory in substantially the same manner as now exists. Should any Plant Management or the Industrial Relations Committee in any plant desire to modify present practices with respect to these rules and regulations, but fail to agree upon such modification, the rules under Sections 5, 6, 7, and 8 shall automatically control."

The Union contends, moreover, that in the case of the employees which precipitated this grievance, the employment office of the Company was in the process of automatically applying Section 5(*i*) when the plant director of labor relations stopped this action.

POSITION OF THE COMPANY

The Company view is that Section 5(*i*) is limited by its expressed language to layoffs ". . . due to the installation of new machinery or technological changes." The Company has taken up, on an individual basis, cases under the "exceptional conditions" clause of Section 5(*i*), but in its view such action cannot prejudice the explicit language of the agreement, particularly where the parties do not agree. The Union sought in contract negotiations to eliminate the limitation on Section 5(*i*) to new machinery and technological changes but without success. The Company holds that no practice has been developed to apply Section 5(*i*) at this works to ordinary reductions in force.

In particular, the Company points out that a special wartime agreement was in effect from 1942 to 1946. No relevant layoff cases arose in 1946, 1947, and 1948, on account of rising employment. Two cases arose in March, 1949. The Company reports that differences between the parties over the meaning of Section 5(i) resulted in a series of meetings in view of the imminence of a force reduction. No agreement was reached; and on April 21, 1950, Mr. F. L. Stout, Jr., advised Mr. Leon Bouchat, President of Local 12, that it was Company policy "to treat each case on its individual merits." The Company reports that in the period of these negotiations it did permit the exercise of Section 5(i) in three cases. The Company states this was done while negotiations were in process and while a satisfactory solution was anticipated. The Company further reports that in November, 1949, a layoff occurred in the Wareroom and four girls with more than 5 years' seniority were offered the right to "bump" in accordance with Section 5(i); but the girls took a layoff instead on account of physical conditions of the work.

QUESTIONS

1. How would you define a "present practice" under Section 9 of the agreement? How many events make a practice?

2. May management make a series of decisions more desirable to the Union than required by the agreement and then revert to the explicit requirements of the contract?

3. Consider the following case: a foreman granted a worker permission to leave work half an hour early one day to tend to personal business. On another occasion when the request was made again the foreman denied the request, and the worker took the time off anyway. His defense against the discipline of a day's suspension was that the company had established a past practice. What would be your judgment if such a practice of time off for personal reasons had become extensive? How could management check abuses?

4. What does the last sentence of Section 9 mean? Does this language nullify the first sentence of the Section?

5. What standards would you develop to resolve conflicts between the explicit language of the contract in Sections 5–8 and the past practice provision in Section 9. Which takes precedence? Does it make any difference how clearly the past practice is established or how directly applicable the contract provision may be?

Cases 77–79

THE USE OF COMPANY BULLETIN BOARDS

CASE 77

Early in July, 1944, the officers of the Textile Workers Union, Local 140, submitted to the manager of one of the mills of a large woolen company the following notice:

Textile Workers Union

on

The Air

T.W.U.A.
CIO
on the
air!

Emil Rieve

President TWUA

on Program "Labor Speaks"

Help Bring This Important Message to Our Members and the General Public

1. Copy this leaflet and distribute
2. Post on bulletin boards
3. Take an ad in your local newspaper

This notice was submitted in accordance with Article X of the agreement between the Company and the Textile Workers Union, dated February 22, 1943. This article reads as follows:

"The employer will provide an adequate number of bulletin boards for the convenience of the union in posting official union notices, which shall be submitted to the mill manager before posting."

The manager declined to permit the posting of the notice on the ground that it was not an "official" union notice within the meaning of Article X.

Both sides agreed that a notice to be "official" within the meaning of the contract must come from the proper officers of the Union. It was agreed here that the notice had fulfilled this condition.

The Company held, however, that in order for a notice to be an "official" notice under the contract, it must be one that pertains to matters that would be of concern to the Union in its relationship with the Company, and in particular, with the relationship between the parties under the agreement as expressed in the preamble.

The Union claimed that the sole test of whether or not a notice is "official" within the meaning of Article X is whether or not it comes from the proper officials of the Union. The content of the notice has nothing to do with determining its "official" character, the Union claimed. The purpose of Article X, according to this view, is to prevent unathorized individuals from posting notices in the name of the Union.

Case 78

Local 390 of the Textile Workers Union of America complained that the Branch River Wool Combing Company denied it the use of the bulletin board for union announcements which included a notice suggesting that the members tune in to radio broadcasts pertaining to the CIO program. The Company also forbade the posting of notices from the Textile Workers Union international office.

The Union based its claim on Article XVIII of the contract providing that: "The union shall have the use of department Bulletin Board in the mill for the purpose of posting union notices."

Accordingly, any notice, the Union stated, that it desires to post is a union notice; and the Company should not deprive the Union of this right granted under the contract.

The Company contended that this clause was intended only to be used for union notices in the strict sense, notices limited to union meetings or other announcements confined to Local 390. It was not intended, the Company claimed, for use in posting notices involving controversial matters such as partisan politics, religious questions, or general questions not directly connected with production and personnel problems of the mill.

Testimony revealed that Union and Company had not discussed their respective intentions concerning the use of the bulletin board, and that there was no specific agreement as to the meaning of the term "union notices."

The Union urged that union activities at present included active participation in political matters as well as strictly economic matters affecting the local membership.

It is emphasized that in a great many contracts the posting of notices is accompanied by limitation wherein the Company reserves the right to approve notices before they can be posted. In this contract, however, no such condition was stipulated.

The term "union" was held to include the international union and the CIO, since the TWUA, CIO, was a party to the contract.

CASE 79

During July, 1946, the Retail, Wholesale and Department Store Employees of America, Local 13, was conducting a strike at the Atlas Dry Goods Company in Columbus, Ohio. In an effort to bolster the strength of the small unit at this store, the Union sent out a call for aid on the picket line to other units of the Local. One of these requests was received by the unit at the Schwab-Karnow Company in Columbus. The local bargaining committee then posted a notice on the bulletin board provided by the Company, calling for volunteers to serve on the Atlas Company picket line. The notice which originated at the local union office read: "Atlas Co. Employees Need Your Help. The Picket Line at Atlas needs support from other units. 10 Schwab-Karnow members are asked to volunteer for picket duty. Report to your local committee. Check in at the union office tomorrow morning at 9 o'clock."

The notice was read by most of the employees, and subsequently ten employees were absent from work the next day while they participated in the picketing of the competitor company. The Schwab-Karnow Company protested to the Union on the same day and itself removed the notice in question.

The Union claimed that it had the right under the contract to post such a notice and demanded that the Company restore the notice to the bulletin board. The Company, after reiterating an old complaint about absenteeism and asserting that every available employee was needed on the job at this time, refused to replace the notice. The Union brought the matter to a grievance.

The Union argued that the contract permitted it to post this notice. It referred to Article XI, Section 1, of the agreement which reads: "The Union shall have the right to post Union notices on the bulletin board which carry the imprint of Local 13 of the U.R.W.D.S.E.A. and are official union notices."

The Union claimed that all requirements of the contract with respect to this notice had been met.

The Company argued its case on the basis of two points in the contract. First, it cited Article X, "Management," which reads:

"The Management of the Company, including but not limited to the establishment of rules not in conflict with this agreement, *the direction of the working forces* (emphasis by the Company), the right to hire, promote, suspend or discharge for cause, the right to relieve employees from duty because of lack of work or for other just reasons, and to transfer employees from one department to another, is vested exclusively in the Company. This authority will not be used for purposes of discrimination against any employee."

The Company called special attention to its exclusive right to direct the working forces. In addition, the Company claimed that Section 3 of Article XI expressly forbade this action by the Union. The section reads:

"The Union agrees that during the term of this agreement there shall be no strikes, slow-ups, stoppage of work, *or any other form of Union interference with the business or employees of the Company* (emphasis by the Company) and the Company agrees that there shall be no lock-outs, nor shall there be any discrimination because of Union membership."

The Company maintained that the posting of this notice constituted a "form of union interference" in violation of the contract. The Union countered with the statement that Section 3 had not been intended to cover legitimate strike activity at the plant of another company and asserted that at times they were forced to place the exigencies of union strategy before concern for the company's welfare.

QUESTIONS

1. What distinguishes "official" notices from other notices?

2. Is any notice an "official" notice which is issued by the officers of the Union in their capacity as officers?

3. Must an "official" notice pertain to matters which concern the Union in its relations with the Company? Must it pertain to union business of some kind?

4. Is there a difference between an "official" notice and a "union notice?"

5. What is meant by the phrase: "The union shall have the use of the Department Bulletin Board . . . ?" Does this give use of the bulletin board to any member of the Union?

6. In the case of the Schwab-Karnow Company was the notice posted a "union notice?" Did the agreement between the Company and the Union give the Union the right to post *any* notice pertaining to the affairs or business of the Union regardless of the content of the notice? Might the Union post a notice asking all employees to strike in violation of the agreement?

7. Did the contents of the Union notice in the Schwab-Karnow Company case violate the Union's obligations under its agreement with the Company? Was the notice an "interference" with the business or the employees of the Company? If the Union might ask for ten pickets, might it ask for fifty? Might it ask *all* employees of the Company to absent themselves for picket duty? Would the Union be within its rights if it asked only a "reasonable" number of employees to be absent for picket duty?

8. Assume that the contents of the notice posted by the Union in the Schwab-Karnow case were a violation of the Union's obligation under the agreement. What would be the proper procedure for the Company to pursue? Was the Company within its rights in removing the notice?

INDEX

INDEX

A

Ability to pay, 95–99, 351–53, 377–78, 381–91
Absenteeism, 113
Agreement, the, 60–68, 69–84
Agriculture
  declining importance, 3–5
  influence on industrial workers, 9
American Federation of Labor, 12, 24, 90
Arbitration, 40, 81–84, 159–60, 443–47, 494–97
Assessments, 216–19

B

Bakke, E. Wight, 51
Bargaining unit, 23–26, 167–72
Break-even chart, 98
Brown, Douglass V., 482
Brown, Emily C., 33
Bulletin boards, 501–5
Business agent, 48

C

Call-in pay, 29
Checkoff, 20, 181–86, 194–97
Clark, John Maurice, 13, 33, 102
Closed shop, 11, 20, 22, 77, 182, 187–88
Coleman, John R., 68
Collective bargaining
  consultative process, 51
  different meanings, 53, 69
  elections, 21–22
  emergence, 8–9, 13
  extent, 12–13
  functions, 26–30
  influence of environment, 74–78
  obligation to bargain, 26, 67–68, 482–85
  process, 53–68
  public policy, 14–33, 67–68
Communication in organizations, 40–42, 79
Company rules, 112, 117–19, 126–30
Comparable wages, 86–90, 353–54
Congress of Industrial Organization, 12, 25
Cook, Anne P., 68
Corporation organization, 35–45
Cost of living, 94–95, 356–60, 375–76
Courts, 11–12, 138–43
Cox, Archibald, 18, 33, 482

D

Decision-making process, 37–40
Demands in negotiations, 54–57, 61
Demerit system, 119–21
Depression periods, 8
Dewhurst, J. F., 13
Discharge, 107–44, 152–57, 219–23, 272–76
Discipline
  management, 107–44, 157–61, 162–67, 177–79
  union, 186, 219–28
Dues, 185, 214–19

E

Emergency disputes, 23, 197–214
Emerson, Ralph Waldo, 9
Employment, high level, 16–17
Equal division of work, 262–64
Exceptional list, 254–61

F

Fabricant, Solomon, 92, 381
Featherbedding, 20, 22
Federal Mediation and Conciliation Service, 20, 22
Financial reports, 22
Flexner, Jean A., 180
Foremen, 43–44, 146, 172–79
Fraser, Russell, 79
Friedrich, C. J., 51

G

Gall, John C., 201
Gardiner, Glenn, 84
Gordon, R. A., 52
Grievance procedure, 29, 43–44, 48–49, 78–81
Group insurance, 476–78

H

Harbison, F. H., 68, 381
Hardman, J. B. S., 52
Health and welfare plans, 457–81
Herberg, Will, 52
Holidays with pay, 433–56
Hours of work, 6
Human relations, 34–35, 78–79, 108

509

This book has been set on the Linotype in 12 point Garamond leaded 1 point. Chapter numbers and chapter titles are in 18 point Futura Medium. The size of the type page is 25 x 45 picas.